RUNNING

Microsoft®
Outlook® 2000

Alan Neibauer

PUBLISHED BY
Microsoft Press
A Division of Microsoft Corporation
One Microsoft Way
Redmond, Washington 98052-6399

Library of Congress Cataloging-in-Publication Data
Neibauer, Alan R.
    Running Microsoft Outlook 2000 / Alan Neibauer
        p. cm.
    Includes index.
    ISBN 1-57231-939-9
    1. Microsoft Outlook.   2. Time management--Computer programs.
    3. Personal information management--Computer programs. I. Title.
    HD69.T54N443   1999
    005.369--dc21   98-31910
                                             CIP

Printed and bound in the United States of America.

1 2 3 4 5 6 7 8 9   QMQM   4 3 2 1 0 9

Distributed in Canada by ITP Nelson, a division of Thomson Canada Limited.

A CIP catalogue record for this book is available from the British Library.

Microsoft Press books are available through booksellers and distributors worldwide. For further information about international editions, contact your local Microsoft Corporation office or contact Microsoft
Press International directly at fax (425) 936-7329. Visit our Web site at mspress.microsoft.com.

Acquisitions Editor: Christey Bahn
Project Editor: Sandra Haynes
Manuscript and Technical Editing: Labrecque Publishing

To Barbara
Always in my heart

Chapters at a Glance

Table of Contents

Acknowledgments

There are many people who deserve my thanks and appreciation for making this book a reality. My thanks to Sandra Haynes, who served as project editor, coordinating everyone's efforts and keeping the entire process on track, and to Lisa Labrecque, who served admirably as project manager.

I wish to thank Curtis Philips, technical editor, for his attention to details. It wasn't easy keeping track of the various changes as Outlook 2000 went through its growing pains. Yet Curtis was somehow able to keep on top of everything.

I thank Lisa Auer, who acted as copy editor. The copy editor is often the last defense against typos, confusing grammar, and other glitches that squeak past everyone else in the process, and Lisa didn't miss a thing. My appreciation to desktop publisher Rick Altman, for his work in creating the attractive pages that you will soon be reading. I also want to thank William Teel for cleaning up and processing the screen art, and for standing in for other duties when it was needed. Thanks also to Erin Milnes, proofreader, for double-checking everyone's work. She made sure the pages you read are free from errors and caught a few glitches that got past the rest of us.

My thanks to Kim Fryer, acquisitions editor, who brought me on board, to Claire Horne, my agent, for knocking on the right doors and calling the right numbers, and to Lucinda Rowley, senior editorial manager.

Last, but never least, my undying love and appreciation to the remarkable woman I am blessed to call my wife, Barbara. We met 35 years ago, married three years later, and yet she still amazes and surprises me, and keeps me laughing, proving that while our bodies may grow old, true love never ages.

Alan Neibauer

Introduction

Microsoft Outlook 2000 seems to have been created for one overriding goal—to make your life easier. Here is a program that combines powerful communications tools, for both the Internet and your network, with the organizational tools you need to manage the details of both your professional and your personal life.

In this book, you'll learn how to use this wonderful program. If you are new to Outlook, you'll learn every phase of the program in easy-to-follow instructions. Before you know it, you'll be mastering Outlook's communications and record-keeping tools. If you have used earlier versions of Outlook, you'll quickly learn the powerful new features in Outlook 2000.

Parts I and II of the book walk you through the basic features of the Outlook environment and explore how to manage communications by using the e-mail, fax, and address book features as well as remote work options. You'll also learn how to use Outlook Express as an alternate e-mail system and how to share ideas and information with newsgroups.

Parts III and IV take an in-depth look at how to schedule people, appointments, tasks, events, and so on, and show you how to create your contact list and keep it up-to-date. You'll learn to take full advantage of the Journal folder and the Notes folder. And you'll learn how to conduct and participate in online NetMeetings using the latest voice and video technology.

Part V provides all the details about folders and folder items—how to work with them and how to manage their contents efficiently. Part VI gets into more advanced work with forms, which you use constantly in Outlook to record, display, and relay information.

Outlook and Windows

Microsoft Outlook is a well-tuned application for Microsoft Windows. It takes full advantage of the Windows interface for sharing information between programs, as well as for using Windows printers, fonts, and other resources. The program runs equally well under Windows 98 and Windows 95. Some features of Microsoft Outlook require Internet Explorer 5, which comes with Microsoft Office 2000.

If you have Windows 98, however, it may be set to open objects by clicking once rather than double-clicking. In Windows 95, for example, you would have to double-click to open a folder shown in the My Computer window or Windows Explorer. Windows 98 gives you the option to open items in the same way or with a single-click. To avoid confusion, instructions in this book use the term *open* rather than double-click or single-click. So if an instruction says to "open the Outlook icon on your desktop," it means to double-click in Windows 95, and either double-click or single-click in Windows 98, depending on how you've chosen to set up your desktop.

Folders and Folder Items

In Outlook, folders (which are similar to the folders you find in the My Computer window and in Windows Explorer) contain all the various bits of information you create and work with on a day-to-day basis. Each Outlook folder contains its own particular type of folder item, as does any folder you add. You'll learn to create, store, view, and revise the following types of information in Outlook's built-in folders:

- Electronic mail (e-mail) messages

- Appointments and meetings

- Contacts (names, addresses, phone and fax numbers, and other personal information)

- Task lists (to-do lists)

- Journal entries (records of your activities in Outlook and in Microsoft Office applications as you perform them)

- Notes

- Disk folders on a disk connected to your computer (a shortcut for the My Computer window)

- Discussions (postings and replies in public folders)

You'll also learn to add new folders for items that don't quite fit into Outlook's standard folders, and you'll learn how to set folder properties. To help you find and view items in folders, Outlook provides view options. You can modify these views and create your own.

Forms

All folder items are based on Outlook forms. Just about everything you'll do in Outlook, such as reading and composing messages, creating notes, and recording appointments, will use Outlook forms. Outlook supplies the standard built-in forms, but you can also create your own forms or modify existing ones (including the standard built-in forms) by using Outlook's form design tools. Custom forms can enhance your ability to manage your work efficiently.

Outlook and Servers

You can use Outlook as a stand-alone program, or as a "client" for an e-mail server. This means that you use Outlook to manage your own schedule and to communicate over the Internet through an e-mail provider. You can also use Outlook to work with information and communications systems that are stored and passed through a server or over a peer-to-peer network set up as a post office.

It's likely that a majority of people who use Outlook will be connected to a server that runs with Microsoft Exchange Server. Because of the intimate connection Outlook has with Microsoft Exchange Server, in this book you'll see several illustrations of dialog boxes that show "Exchange" in their title bars. If you're on an e-mail system that doesn't use Microsoft Exchange Server, you'll see "Windows Messaging Service" in the title bars instead of "Exchange." Also note that in some cases, certain features of Outlook are available only on systems that use Microsoft Exchange Server.

If you are not connected to a server, don't get confused between Microsoft Exchange Server, and the program Microsoft Exchange that you may see on your Windows menu when you click the Start button on the taskbar and point to Programs. While the two programs offer communications capabilities, they are quite different. The program Microsoft Exchange, a precursor to Windows Messaging, is a communications tool for non-networked systems to communicate via a modem and fax. Microsoft Exchange Server, on the other hand, is a network communications program designed to run on Windows NT and Windows 2000. If you are not connected to a network, features designed for Exchange Server will not be available to you.

Outlook, Outlook, and Outlook

Microsoft Outlook 2000 offers you three installation options: Corporate/Workgroup, Internet Only, and No E-mail.

The Outlook features described in this book are provided by the Corporate/Workgroup installation. This includes using Outlook as an e-mail client over Microsoft Exchange Server or through a peer-to-peer network. The fax capabilities described use Microsoft Fax on a client computer running Windows 95 or Windows 98.

The Internet Only installation provides communications only through a dial-up Internet service provider. This installation provides its own fax capabilities. If you are using this installation, some of the dialog boxes and menus you see will be different than those shown in this book.

The No E-mail installation option provides Outlook's record-keeping and time-management tools but no communication capabilities.

You are now ready to begin learning Outlook 2000. While this book is organized in a logical manner, you don't necessarily have to read the chapters in numeric order. I suggest starting with Part I, however, to learn the basics of Outlook, how to set up profiles, and how to customize it for your tastes. You can then go directly to chapters that have the information you need for a particular job. If you need to record an appointment, for example, you can go directly to Part III. You can then go back to Part II when you're ready to use Outlook's communications features.

If you have any questions about Outlook 2000, or want to share your thoughts about it, you can reach me at alann@att.net.

PART I

Getting Started

CHAPTER 1

Preparing for Outlook

Before you can use Microsoft Outlook, you must first choose an installation option for the type of e-mail you plan to use and then set up a *profile* that tells Outlook how to connect to your e-mail server, your network, or the Internet. You can set up your profile before you start Outlook for the first time. Since you're probably anxious to start using Outlook, however, let's create the profile from within Outlook after choosing an e-mail service option.

Starting Outlook

Depending on how you install Outlook on your computer, some setup options will appear the first time you run the program. So before looking at these options, make sure you know how to start—and exit—the program. To start Outlook, take one of the following actions:

? SEE ALSO

For detailed information about logging on to your network, see Chapter 2, "Discovering Outlook."

- Open the Outlook icon on your desktop, if it's present.
- Click the Start button on the Windows taskbar, point to Programs, and then click Microsoft Outlook.
- Click the Outlook button on the Microsoft Office shortcut bar.

Exiting Outlook

You can exit Outlook and log off any services you were connected to, or you can just exit Outlook. To exit Outlook and log off at the same time, choose the Exit And Log Off command from the File menu. You can exit Outlook without logging off in all the usual Windows ways:

- Choose the Exit command from the File menu.
- Choose the Close command from the Outlook icon in the upper left corner (or press Alt+F4).
- Click the Close button on the title bar.
- Double-click the Outlook icon.

Choosing an E-mail Service Option

You can use Outlook as a stand-alone program or as a *client* for an e-mail server. This means that you use Outlook to manage your schedule and to communicate over the Internet through an e-mail provider. You can also use Outlook to communicate through a network server, such as Windows NT and Windows 2000 with Microsoft Exchange Server, or a peer-to-peer network using Windows 95 or Windows 98. Because each method of communication requires different resources, Outlook offers three setup options: Corporate Or Workgroup, Internet Only, and No E-mail.

If you already have e-mail set up on your computer when you start Outlook for the first time, you'll see the E-mail Upgrade Options Wizard asking if you want to import your existing messages and addresses into Outlook. Depending on your setup, the options might include

Microsoft Exchange, Outlook Express, and None Of The Above. If you select Microsoft Exchange from the list, Outlook will begin using the Corporate Or Workgroup installation option. If you select Outlook Express, Outlook will begin with the Internet Only option. To select which option you want to use manually, choose None Of The Above and then click the Next button.

If you selected None Of The Above or if the E-mail Upgrade Options Wizard did not appear, you'll be given the options shown in Figure 1-1.

NOTE

> The E-mail Service Options Wizard might not appear if you are upgrading over a previous installation of Outlook.

Choose the Internet Only installation if you are not connected to a network and communicate only through a dial-up Internet Service Provider (ISP). This installation also provides its own fax capabilities. If you are using this installation, some of the dialog boxes and menus you see will be different from those shown in this book.

Choose the Corporate Or Workgroup installation if you are connected to a network. This includes using Outlook as an e-mail client with Microsoft Exchange Server or a Microsoft Windows–based peer-to-peer network, as well as using a dial-up account provided by an ISP. You can also use Outlook to send and receive faxes, but only by using special fax software available in Windows 95 or as an option in Windows 98.

The No E-mail installation option provides Outlook's record-keeping and time-management tools but no communication capabilities.

FIGURE 1-1.
The E-mail Service Options Wizard.

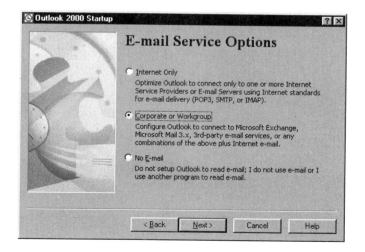

If you are not connected to a server, don't get confused between Microsoft Exchange Server and the Microsoft Exchange program that you might see on your Programs menu, especially in Windows 95. While both offer communications capabilities, they are quite different. The program Microsoft Exchange, a precursor to Windows Messaging, is primarily an e-mail client, and its capabilities are matched and greatly enhanced by Outlook. Microsoft Exchange Server, on the other hand, is a network messaging platform designed to run on Windows NT and Windows 2000.

The Outlook features primarily described in this book are those provided by the Corporate Or Workgroup installation. This book focuses on using Outlook with Microsoft Exchange Server but also covers using Outlook on a peer-to-peer network and on the Internet only. If you are not connected to a network, the Exchange Server and peer-to-peer network features described here will not be available to you.

Changing Your E-mail Service Options

If your e-mail configuration changes, you can select another service option from within Outlook. Start Outlook, choose Options from the Tools menu, and then click the Mail Services tab of the dialog box that appears. Click the button labeled Reconfigure Mail Support to redisplay the options shown in Figure 1-1, on the previous page. Choose your e-mail service option and click Next. The Windows Installer might need to access your Office installation disks, and then you will need to restart Outlook for the change to take effect.

Developing Your Profile

Your profile tells Outlook who you are and how you want to use the program to communicate. If Outlook was set up for you by your network administrator, or some other techno-guru, your profile has probably been created for you. After you choose an e-mail service option, Outlook will probably start using this existing profile and Internet account information.

If you do not already have a profile, you'll have the chance to create one after choosing the e-mail service option. You can use a single profile to get mail over your Exchange Server network, through a Windows-based peer-to-peer network, and through your ISP.

Profiles are only needed when you are using Outlook on a network. *If you use Outlook to communicate just over the Internet, see "Using Internet Mail Only," on page 18.*

The process for selecting an e-mail service option and creating a profile using the Inbox Setup Wizard is as follows:

1 In the E-Mail Service Options Wizard, choose Corporate Or Workgroup, and then click Next.

2 The first page of the Inbox Setup Wizard, shown in Figure 1-2, lets you select the services you want to include in the new profile. Select the check boxes for the services you want to include; click to clear the check boxes for services you do not need. (If you really know what you're doing, you can select the Manually Configure Information Services check box and then select the individual services and set them up the way you want. This book won't tell you all the things you need to know to take this path. You're better off letting the wizard supply the list and then selecting and omitting the services you want for each profile.)

To use Outlook on a Windows-based peer-to-peer network, you'll need Microsoft Mail installed on the computers. *For more information about setting up a peer-to-peer postoffice and configuring the profile, see "Using Outlook on a Peer-to-Peer Network," on page 13.*

3 Click Next.

4 Type a descriptive name for the new profile in the Profile Name box.

FIGURE 1-2.
The Inbox Setup Wizard.

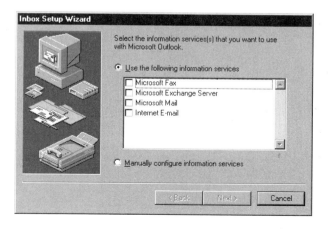

5 Click Next.

6 From this point on, the wizard displays only those pages that apply to the services you selected in step 2. Fill in the information on each page and click the Next button until you get to the last page. You'll learn some of the specifics for typical services in "Setting Up Services," below. If you don't know the information you need, check with your service administrator—you can later modify the profile to include the proper settings.

7 If a dialog box appears asking for the name of the personal address book, you can usually accept the default setting and click Next. You only need to change the setting if you want to use a personal address book that you have already created with a previous version of Outlook or another program.

8 Click Finish on the last page to close the wizard and start Outlook.

Setting Up Services

To set up a service using the Inbox Setup Wizard, you need to enter or select information in the wizard pages that appear. Much of the information requested is rather straightforward, but it pays to be prepared. Let's look at some of the specific information you'll need to know.

 NOTE

> If you are using the Internet Only setup, you have to create one or more mail accounts. The process is the same as setting up mail accounts in Outlook Express. *See "Using Internet Mail Only," on page 18.*

Setting Up for Internet E-mail

If Internet e-mail was one of the services you chose to add to your profile, you'll see a dialog box similar to the one shown in Figure 1-3. (You might have to click a button labeled Set Up Account to open the dialog box.) In addition to entering your own e-mail address on the General tab of the dialog box, you'll need to know these items to complete the entries on the Servers tab:

- Outgoing mail server name, sometimes referred to as the SMTP (Simple Mail Transfer Protocol)

- Incoming mail server name, sometimes called the POP (Post Office Protocol)

FIGURE 1-3.

The Servers tab of the Mail Account Properties dialog box.

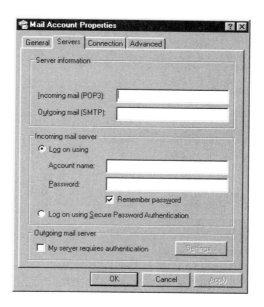

- Your mail server logon name, which is usually (but not always) the first part of your e-mail address

- Your mail server password, which might be different from your ISP logon password

Check with your ISP if you don't know any of this information.

NOTE

In the Internet Only installation, you can also use an IMAP (Internet Message Access Protocol) mail server. Check with your ISP for additional information about setting up this type of server.

SEE ALSO

For detailed information about setting up a fax profile and sending and receiving faxes with Outlook, see Chapter 6, "Sending and Receiving Faxes."

If you want to use the newsreader feature of Outlook, you'll also need the news server name. You'll learn more about setting up a news server in Chapter 8, "Communicating with Newsgroups."

Setting Up for Microsoft Exchange Server

If you connect to a Microsoft Windows NT server, your profile has probably been set up for you to communicate through Microsoft Exchange Server. If you need to add Microsoft Exchange Server to your profile, you'll see a series of dialog boxes for you to complete—click Next after each. In the first dialog box, for example, enter the name of your server and your mailbox name.

In the next box, you'll be asked if you travel with the computer. Choose Yes if you want to be able to read and compose mail offline, when you're not connected to the network. If you're not using a lap-top, or if you don't take it with you when traveling, choose No. You can always configure the profile to work remotely later on.

When you select Next again, you'll be asked to enter the path of your personal address book. You can usually accept the default name given. This is an address book you can use to store e-mail addresses of users not on the network.

Finally, you'll be asked if you want to run Outlook each time you start your computer.

To later modify your Exchange Server settings, open the Mail icon in the Control Panel to display your profile services, select the Microsoft Exchange Server service from the list, and click the Properties button. (You'll learn more about modifying a profile later on.) You'll see the dialog box shown in Figure 1-4. Click Check Name if you want Windows to confirm you've used the correct mailbox name. You can also choose to connect to the Exchange Server automatically or when prompted and set the number of seconds to wait for connection.

Setting the Delivery Point

When you use Outlook with Microsoft Exchange Server, you can have your messages and other information stored primarily on the server or on your own computer. While most network gurus recommend storing information on the server, you really have a choice.

FIGURE 1-4.
Exchange Server profile properties.

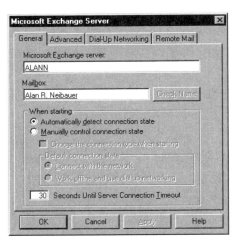

Your decision really doesn't matter if you are *always* connected to the server. However, if you do choose to store your data on the server, you should still create special folders, called offline folders, on your own computer for those times when the network goes down and you want to continue working. You'll learn how to do this in Chapter 9, "Using Outlook Remotely and Offline."

If you are mobile with a laptop computer, you do have to make a decision. If you use your laptop primarily when connected to the Exchange Server network—either directly or by remote dial-in—you can also store messages on the server and use offline folders to work with your data when you're away from the network. But if you use your computer primarily offline, or if you sometimes connect to a peer-to-peer network, it's probably best to store your information on the laptop itself. For this you'll use personal folders.

Use the Delivery tab of the Properties dialog box for your profile to set the location to which your mail and network messages will be delivered. To display the Properties dialog box for your profile, from the Mail dialog box, select the profile containing the service you want to set up, and then click Properties. The Properties dialog box lists all of the services in the profile, as shown in Figure 1-5, on the next page. Next click the Delivery tab and configure it as explained in the following sections.

Storing Information on the Server

If you choose to store your data primarily on the Microsoft Exchange Server, you'll need to set up the Offline Folders service so you'll be able to access your information when you're not connected, such as when you are in another location with your laptop or when the server is down. You then need to synchronize the offline folders with the server while you are still online. This transfers your most up-to-date information from the server to the offline folders, which you can then access when you're not connected to the server. You'll learn how to set up and synchronize folders for working offline in Chapter 9, "Using Outlook Remotely and Offline."

To use the Offline Folders feature, you have to make sure your Exchange mailbox is set up as the delivery point. This means that any mail sent to you goes into your mailbox on the server. Here's how to set up your Exchange mailbox as the delivery point:

1 Click the Delivery tab of the Properties dialog box.

2 Open the Deliver New Mail To The Following Location list and choose the item labeled Mailbox followed by your mailbox name.

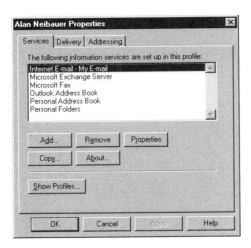

All of your incoming mail and other Outlook information will be stored
in folders on the server.

Storing Information Locally

If you want to store your information on your own computer, you'll
have to add the Personal Folders service to your profile, and then
choose personal folders as the delivery point for new messages.

First check to see if the Personal Folders service already exists. Open
the Properties box for the profile and see if Personal Folders is
included in the list of services. If not, follow these steps to create
personal folders.

Personal folders are stored on your hard disk in one file with the .pst extension.

1 On the Services tab of the Properties dialog box for the profile,
click Add to display the Add Service To Profile dialog box.

2 Select Personal Folders.

3 Click OK.

4 In the dialog box that appears, select the location for the new or
existing folder.

5 In the File Name box, type the name for the new folder, or select
an existing file.

6 Click Open to display the dialog box shown in Figure 1-6.

FIGURE 1-6.
The Create Microsoft
Personal Folders dialog
box.

7 Type a name for your personal folders in the Name box as you want it to appear in Outlook.

8 Choose an encryption setting.

9 Enter an optional password.

10 Type the same password again for verification.

11 Select the Save This Password In Your Password List check box if you don't want to be prompted for the password when you use the folder.

12 Click OK.

Now that your profile contains the Personal Folders service, you can designate this as the delivery point. This means that mail from the Exchange Server will be sent to your personal folders inbox even when you are connected to the network. Click the Delivery tab of the Properties dialog box for the profile, and choose Personal Folders from the Deliver New Mail To The Following Location list.

Using Outlook on a Peer-to-Peer Network

In addition to using Outlook with Microsoft Exchange Server and for Internet e-mail, you can use Outlook to send and receive mail over a peer-to-peer network running on Windows 95 or Windows 98.

If the Microsoft Mail option was available in the Inbox Setup Wizard, the Windows workgroup postoffice has already been set up on your network. Other wizard pages will ask you to select the postoffice folder for your workgroup and your mailbox name and to enter your mailbox password. Check with your workgroup administrator for this information.

With Windows, anyone can easily set up and use a network. Each computer needs a properly configured network interface card (NIC), the computers must be connected with the proper cables, and the network protocols must be installed using the Network option in the Control Panel.

If you're administering the network yourself, you must perform the following tasks to set up a peer-to-peer postoffice once the network components are in place:

1 Create a Windows workgroup postoffice.

2 Share the postoffice folders.

3 Add users to the postoffice.

4 Set up the Outlook profile to "talk" to the postoffice.

The following sections describe how to perform these tasks, assuming that your network hardware and protocols are already installed and that the network has been set to allow file sharing. If you need help with this, check the documentation that comes with the network cards.

 TIP

If you want to set up a laptop profile for use with both Exchange Server and a peer-to-peer network, create and use personal folders as the delivery point.

Installing Microsoft Mail Postoffice

To use Outlook on a peer-to-peer network, you have to create a postoffice to store messages. The easiest way to do this is to create a Microsoft Mail Postoffice because the programs necessary to create it come with Windows.

First make certain that you have the Microsoft Mail Postoffice feature installed on all of the network computers. Open the Control Panel and look for the Microsoft Mail Postoffice icon.

If you are running Windows 95, Microsoft Mail Postoffice was installed automatically when you installed Microsoft Exchange or Microsoft Messaging. If Microsoft Mail Postoffice is not present, install either of these components now, depending on your version of Windows 95.

Windows 98 does not install Microsoft Mail Postoffice by default and does not offer it as a regular setup option. (Windows 98 does leave an existing Windows 95 version of Microsoft Mail Postoffice on your computer if you installed Windows 98 over your Windows 95 installation.) To install Microsoft Mail Postoffice run the program named wms.exe, which you can find on your Windows 98 CD, in the folder \tools\oldwin95\message\us (for international installations choose the \intl directory instead of \us).

It is strongly recommended that you install Postoffice, regardless of the version of Windows, *before* installing Outlook or Microsoft Office 2000. If you already installed Outlook as a separate program, not as part of Office, rerun the Outlook installation program after installing Postoffice. If you already installed Office 2000, follow these steps after you run wms.exe to update any Office files that might have been affected:

1 Insert the Office 2000 CD in your CD drive.

2 Open the Control Panel.

3 Choose Add/Remove Programs.

4 Select Microsoft Office 2000 and then click Add/Repair.

5 Click the Repair Office button.

6 Choose Repair Errors In My Office Installation.

7 Click Repair, and then wait until the process is completed—it could take some time.

Creating a Postoffice

To set up a workgroup postoffice, you have to pick one computer on the network to store the postoffice. On that computer, follow these steps:

 NOTE

Remember, all of the computers on a peer-to-peer network must use the same workgroup name. Open the Network icon in the Control Panel and check the workgroup name on the Identification tab of the Network dialog box.

1 Create a folder on the machine's hard disk to store the postoffice.

2 Open the Control Panel and then open the Microsoft Mail Postoffice icon.

3 Click Create A New Workgroup Postoffice, and then click Next to see the dialog box shown in Figure 1-7.

4 Type the path of the folder you created to store the postoffice, and then click Next.

FIGURE 1-7.

Wizard for creating and administering a Microsoft Mail Postoffice.

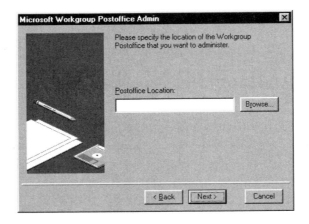

5 Windows creates a folder called Wgpo0000 that contains numerous files and subfolders and asks you to confirm its location. Click Next.

6 Enter your name as the postoffice administrator.

7 Enter a password.

8 Click OK twice.

Sharing the Postoffice Folder

The postoffice you created will store the mailboxes of workgroup network users. You have to now share the postoffice folder so other users can access it.

1 Use My Computer or Windows Explorer to locate the icon for the postoffice folder.

2 Right-click the postoffice icon and choose Sharing from the shortcut menu.

3 Click Shared As.

4 Select the Full Access check box.

5 Click OK.

Adding Postoffice Users

The next step is to add users to the postoffice. This creates a mailbox in the postoffice for each user of the peer-to-peer network. Follow these steps:

1 Open the Control Panel and then open the Microsoft Mail Postoffice icon.

2 Click Administer An Existing Workgroup Postoffice, and then click Next.

3 Type the path of the postoffice if it is not already shown, and then click Next.

4 Enter your name as the postoffice administrator.

5 Enter your password.

6 Click Next to open the Postoffice Manager dialog box, which lists all current users.

7 Click Add User to see the dialog box shown in Figure 1-8.

FIGURE 1-8.

The Add User dialog box.

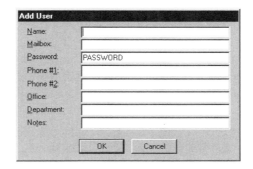

8 Enter the user's name.

9 Enter the user's mailbox name. Other information is optional.

10 Click OK.

11 Give the user the path and name of the postoffice, name of the mailbox, and password.

12 Repeat steps 7 through 11 for each user, and then click Close.

Setting Up an Outlook Profile

Finally, each user must set up a profile to access the postoffice. Here are the steps:

1 Open the Control Panel and then open the Mail icon.

2 If the profile to which you want to add the Microsoft Mail service is not displayed, click the Show Profiles button to display the Mail dialog box, select the profile you want to change, and then click Properties.

3 Click Add on the Services tab of the Properties dialog box.

4 Select Microsoft Mail from the Add Service To Profile dialog box.

5 Click OK to see the dialog box shown in Figure 1-9.

6 On the Connection tab, browse to find the postoffice folder if it isn't already displayed. If the postoffice is on your local computer, it might appear as C:\Postal\wgpo0000. If the postoffice is on another computer on the network, the path will include the computer's name, such as JoesComputer\C\postal\wpgo0000.

7 Click the Logon tab of the dialog box and enter your mailbox name and password.

8 Click OK.

You can change your mailbox password and perform other mailbox functions from within Outlook by choosing Microsoft Mail Tools from the Tools menu.

Using Internet Mail Only

For more information about the Internet Only installation of Outlook, see Appendix A, "Using Outlook for the Internet Only."

If you are going to use Outlook to communicate only on the Internet, and not on a network, you don't have to worry about profiles. Instead, you set up one or more e-mail accounts. You can use more than one account if you have multiple ISP, or you can share a single account with several people.

If you have more than one ISP, you set up a mail service for each. When you create a message, you select which ISP to send it through. You can check all of your ISPs for mail at the same time.

When you share an account, multiple people use the same ISP account, but mail is sent and received under each individual's name. You can even configure Outlook so that each person has a separate set of mail folders.

? SEE ALSO

For detailed information on setting up, using, and sharing mail accounts, see "Setting Up Accounts," on page 227.

When you first run Outlook, choose the Internet Only option, and then follow the dialog boxes shown to create a mail account. The procedure is similar to setting up the Internet E-mail service described in "Setting Up for Internet E-mail," on page 8. If you installed the Corporate/ Workgroup option, you can change to the Internet Only option by setting the Mail Delivery tab on the Options dialog box and then clicking the Reconfigure Mail Support button.

★ TIP

> If you're using the Internet Only option, you can still use the Mail program in the Control Panel to set up and change Internet e-mail accounts.

Setting up mail accounts in Outlook is identical to setting up accounts in Outlook Express. Outlook Express is an e-mail–only program included with Microsoft Internet Explorer, Windows 98, and Office 2000.

Working with Profiles

Once you create a profile, it is still not too late to create a new profile or to add, remove, or modify the properties of the services within an existing profile. If you use your system in more than one place, for example, you might need a separate profile for each location. You might also want a separate profile to send faxes from your computer over a telephone line that you also use for connecting to your mail server. Just be cautious with any changes that you make. An incorrect profile could prevent Outlook from starting or connecting to your network or ISP, or you could potentially lose your Outlook information.

Creating a Profile

You can set up, change, and remove a profile using the Windows Control Panel. You can later change a profile, adding or removing services, from within Outlook itself.

To create a new profile, follow these steps:

1 Open the Windows Control Panel, and then open the Mail icon.

2 If no profiles have been set up on your system, the Mail dialog box will appear. However, if one or more profiles have been set up, you'll see the Properties dialog box for the currently active profile instead. In this case, click the Show Profiles button to display the Mail dialog box, as shown in Figure 1-10.

3 Click the Add button in the Mail dialog box to start creating a new profile using the Inbox Setup Wizard as described in "Developing Your Profile," on page 6.

4 When you're done entering information in the wizard, click Finish to return to the Mail dialog box.

5 In the Mail dialog box, you can choose a default profile in the box labeled When Starting Microsoft Outlook, Use This Profile.

6 Click the Close button.

You can use the Inbox Setup Wizard to create profiles specific to each location from which you use Outlook: office, home, and on the road.

Modifying a Profile

Suppose you signed up for a new online service and want to add it to one or more of your profiles. You also bailed out of an online service that wasn't giving you what you wanted. Your profile is now out of date, so you want to update the online service information. Here's how you do it.

Open the Mail icon in the Control Panel window to open the Properties dialog box. If the profile you want to change is not displayed, click the Show Profiles button to display the Mail dialog box, select the profile

FIGURE 1-10.

The Mail dialog box.

you want to change, and then click Properties. The Services tab of the Properties dialog box, shown in Figure 1-5, on page 12, lists all of the services in the profile you've selected.

Use the Services tab on the Properties dialog box to make changes as follows:

- Click Add to install a new service to the current profile. Fill in the dialog boxes that appear to help you configure the service.

- Click Copy to copy the selected service to another profile.

- Select a service and click Properties to view or edit its settings.

- Select a service and click Remove to delete the service from the profile.

Click OK when you're finished modifying the profile. If you want to make changes to another profile, click Show Profiles and repeat the entire process. Click Close in the Mail dialog box when you've finished.

Notice that the Properties dialog box also contains two other tabs: Delivery and Addressing. You can use these tabs to make additional changes to your profile.

On the Delivery tab, you can change the location to which your mail is delivered. If your profile includes two or more services that support mail with the same address type (for example, Microsoft Exchange and Internet Mail), you can specify the order in which those services should process outgoing mail.

On the Addressing tab, you can specify which address list to display when you first open the address book, where to save new entries in your address book, and in which order to search address lists for recipient names.

 TIP

If you want to edit the profile you're currently using, you don't have to use the Control Panel. While working in Outlook, choose the Services command from the Tools menu.

Using a Different Profile

If you have more than one profile set up, you can select which profile to use when you start Outlook or Windows Messaging.

Open the Windows Control Panel, and then open the Mail icon. Click Show Profiles, and then open the list labeled When Starting Microsoft Outlook, Use This Profile. Choose the profile you want to use by default, and then click Close.

From within Outlook you can set Outlook to use a particular profile all the time or let you choose a profile each time you start the program.

To use the same profile all the time, do this:

1 In Outlook, choose the Options command from the Tools menu, and then click the Mail Services tab if it isn't already displayed.

2 Select the Always Use This Profile check box, and then select the profile from the drop-down list.

3 Click OK.

If you prefer, you can choose a profile at the start of each Outlook session. For this option, follow these steps:

1 In Outlook, choose the Options command from the Tools menu, and then click the Mail Services tab if it isn't already displayed.

2 Select the Prompt For A Profile To Be Used check box.

3 Click OK.

Once the Prompt For A Profile To Be Used check box is selected, you'll need to select a profile in the Choose Profile dialog box each time you start Outlook. *See "Logging On to the Network," on page 26.*

⭐ **TIP**

If you have set up Outlook to prompt you to select a profile each time you start the program, you can click the New button in the Choose Profile dialog box to create or modify a profile.

Removing a Profile

Now suppose that your situation changes and you no longer need all of the profiles that you created. For example, perhaps you no longer have access to the network and you want to delete the profile that includes the Microsoft Exchange service. To simplify your Outlook life, you can remove the unwanted and unnecessary profiles.

To remove a profile from the Control Panel, follow these steps:

1 Open the Mail icon in the Control Panel window.

2 In the Properties dialog box, click the Show Profiles button.

3 Select the profile you want to remove.

4 Click the Remove button, and then click Yes when asked whether you want to remove this profile.

5 Click Close.

CHAPTER 2

Discovering Outlook

Once you have Microsoft Outlook 2000 installed and your profiles (or mail accounts) created, you're ready to use this versatile program. In this chapter you'll learn how to communicate with Outlook, how to customize the Outlook window, and how to use Outlook Assistants to manage your mail.

Logging On to the Network

In Chapter 1, "Preparing for Outlook," you learned how to start Outlook. If you are logged on to your network, Outlook knows who you are and doesn't ask for your logon name and password. Outlook connects you to your e-mail server—either Microsoft Exchange Server or your workgroup postoffice. *See the sidebar "The Lines Are Down! What Now?" opposite, for a different situation.*

 **TIP**

> **Requesting a Password**
>
> If you want to have Outlook request a logon password every time you start the program, do the following: Start Outlook, and choose Services from the Tools menu. In the Services dialog box, select Microsoft Exchange Server and click the Properties button. In the Microsoft Exchange Server dialog box, click the Advanced tab, open the Logon Network Security list and choose None. If you want to log on automatically again, choose NT Password Authentication from the list.

If your computer is part of a network but you're not logged on, you'll see a dialog box asking for your logon name, domain name, and password. (You won't see the Domain field in the dialog box if your workstation has been disconnected from the network.) Enter the information requested, and then click OK to log on.

To determine which options you'll be using, Outlook refers to your profile. *You'll find all the details on profiles in Chapter 1; see "Developing Your Profile," on page 6.* If you have only one profile set up, Outlook begins using that profile when you log on, without asking you any questions. But if you have more than one profile set up, and if you have selected the option that prompts you to choose a profile, Outlook displays the Choose Profile dialog box, shown in Figure 2-1. Select the profile you want to use, and then click OK.

If the profile you're using is set up for use away from your network connection, Outlook then displays a dialog box that asks whether you want to connect to the network or work offline.

FIGURE 2-1.
The Choose Profile dialog box.

NOTE

> You can work offline only if you have set up Outlook to use offline folders or personal folders. *See Chapter 1, "Preparing for Outlook," for information on how to do this and the advantages of each method.*

Click the Connect button if the network is available via a direct connection or a dial-up connection and you want to connect to your e-mail server to send and receive messages. If you want to work offline (because the network is down, because you don't have a direct connection to it, or because you want to compose messages or perform other tasks before you connect), click the Work Offline button. When you work offline, you can compose messages for sending later, and you can review any messages that you have stored on your computer

The Lines Are Down! What Now?

Networks and servers are wonderfully bizarre at times. They love to go down (that is, stop working) just to give some beleaguered system administrator something to do—namely, restart the network or server.

If you start Outlook when the server isn't working or when you are not connected to the network, Outlook might start normally but some services might not be available. You will not, for example, be able to send or receive mail from the network or work with public folders (public folders are located on the server).

In some cases, you might see a dialog box reporting that the network is unavailable. Click the Retry button to attempt a connection with the server again, or click Work Offline to start Outlook without access to network service.

If you're set up to connect to a workgroup postoffice, but the computer storing the postoffice is not available, you'll see this dialog box:

Click here to try
connecting again to a LAN.

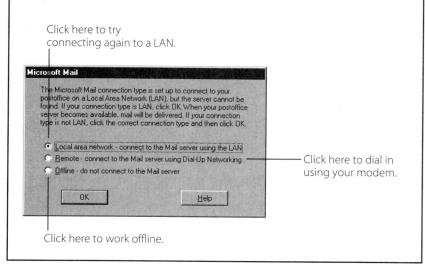

Click here to dial in
using your modem.

Click here to work offline.

(rather than on your e-mail server). Later you can connect to the network or online service to send your messages and to receive any messages that are waiting for you.

Looking at Outlook

When Microsoft Outlook starts up, you'll see your Inbox folder displayed, as shown in Figure 2-2. The name of the open folder appears in the Folder Bar, and the contents of that folder are shown below it. The preview pane at the bottom of the window shows the contents of the message selected in the list above. Outlook folders, arranged vertically in the left pane, are convenient places to store messages and other types of Outlook information.

 **TIP**

> If the preview pane is not displayed on your screen, choose Preview Pane from the View menu. Choose AutoPreview from the View menu to display the first three lines of every message directly under each item.

Understanding the New Outlook Interface

You work with Outlook as you would with any Windows-based application, using the menu bar and toolbars to carry out tasks. Outlook

FIGURE 2-2.

The Outlook window with the Inbox folder open.

Folder Bar   Folder contents

Outlook Bar   Status bar   Preview Pane

2000, however, offers the intelligent menus and toolbars that are part of the new Office 2000 interface, which means that only the most commonly used functions appear on menus and toolbars. If you do not see the command you want on a menu, pause on the menu briefly or point to the down arrow at the bottom of the menu to see additional choices. When you select a command from the expanded menu, Outlook assumes that you'll want to use the same command again and displays it on the abbreviated menu the next time you open it.

More
Buttons

The same rules apply to toolbars. On the right end of each toolbar you'll see the More Buttons downward-pointing arrow, shown in the margin here.

SEE ALSO

For details about customizing toolbars, see "Customizing Toolbars and Menus," on page 44.

Click More Buttons to see whether additional buttons are available and to display the Add Or Remove Buttons command, which you can use to customize the toolbar. If you select a button from the menu that appears, Outlook assumes you'll be using this button again and adds it to the toolbar. Being able to access more buttons than can appear on the screen is particularly useful in windows that display two toolbars side by side on one line.

Using the Outlook Bar

The Outlook Bar, on the left side of the Outlook window, displays one of two or three groups of folders. The number of groups and their names depend on how you installed Outlook. The groups will be called Outlook Shortcuts, My Shortcuts, and Other Shortcuts, or just Outlook, Mail, and Other. Don't worry about the group names; they work the same way whatever they're called.

TIP

You can also open a folder in a separate window. Right-click the folder icon and choose Open In New Window from the shortcut menu.

When you click a specific group's label, it moves to the top of the Outlook Bar, and the folders in that group appear on the bar. A number in parentheses next to a folder name indicates the number of *unread* messages in the folder, not necessarily the total number of items in the folder. To open a particular folder, just click it. You can easily add folders, Web site addresses, or documents to any of the three groups. *For details, see "Customizing the Outlook Bar," on page 35.*

If the group contains many folders you'll see small up and down arrows on the Outlook Bar, which you can click to scroll through the complete folder display.

Exploring the Outlook Shortcuts Group

When you start Outlook, the Outlook Shortcuts group is displayed by default. In this group you'll find these standard Outlook folders: Outlook Today, Inbox, Calendar, Contacts, Tasks, Notes, and Deleted Items.

The Outlook Today folder displays a handy page of frequently used features, as shown in Figure 2-3. You'll see a summary of any calendar events scheduled for the day, the number of unread messages in your inbox, unfinished messages in your drafts folder, and unsent messages in your outbox, as well as any assigned tasks that need to be performed. Click the Calendar, Mail, or Tasks headings to see more information. If you need to look up information about someone in an address book, such as a telephone number, enter the person's name in the Find A Contact text box on the Standard toolbar and then press Enter.

Click the Customize Outlook Today icon to open the Outlook Today Options page, which displays these settings:

- **Save Changes.** Save your options and return to the Outlook Today page.

- **Cancel.** Returns to Outlook Today without saving your changes.

FIGURE 2-3.
The Outlook Today window presents summary information and frequently used commands.

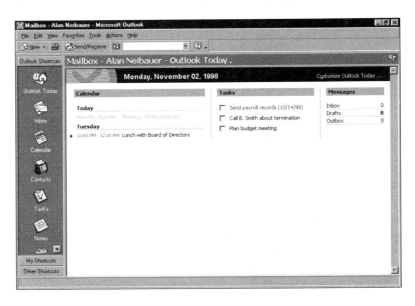

Getting Started

- **When Starting, Go Directly To Outlook Today.** Choose this option to start in the Outlook Today window rather than the Inbox.

- **Choose Folders.** Click this button to select which folders appear under the Mail icon in Outlook Today.

- **Show This Number of Days In My Calendar.** Select the number of calendar days to display on the Outlook Today window including the current day. The default is five days, but only days with appointments will appear.

- **In My Task List Show Me.** Choose whether to display a list of all of your active tasks (the default) or just the current day's tasks and whether to include tasks that have no assigned due date.

- **Sort My Task List By.** Choose how to sort the task list in Outlook Today on up to two fields.

- **Styles.** Choose the overall appearance of the Outlook Today page.

Here's a summary of the other folders in the Outlook Shortcuts group:

(?) SEE ALSO

For details about working with messages, see Chapter 5, "Sending and Receiving Messages."

- **Inbox folder.** Use this folder, shown in Figure 2-2, on page 28, to read messages you've received and haven't moved to another folder or deleted. You can also reply to messages from this folder, forward messages to another destination, and create and send new messages.

- **Calendar folder.** Use this folder to make and keep track of your appointments and, depending on how you've arranged the window, a list of tasks you have recorded.

(?) SEE ALSO

For more information about setting up and working with your list of contacts, see Chapter 13, "Organizing Your Contacts."

- **Contacts folder.** Use this folder to store names, addresses, telephone numbers, e-mail addresses, and other information about people you deal with.

(?) SEE ALSO

For more information about setting up and working with your list of tasks, see Chapter 12, "Managing Your Tasks."

- **Tasks folder.** Use this folder to compile a list of projects and the tasks that are involved in each project. You can describe and categorize each task, record its due date, track its status, and, if you're lucky, assign the task to someone else. You can sort the list in various ways—for instance, by category or by the name of the person assigned the task.

For more information about the Notes folder, see Chapter 15, "Making Notes."

For more information about the Deleted Items folder, see Chapter 16, "Managing Folder Contents."

- **Notes folder.** Use this folder to record notes about anything you like: meetings, personal reminders, comments, and or any bit of useful information.

- **Deleted Items folder.** Use this folder to retrieve items that you've deleted from other folders. Outlook automatically moves items you delete from other folders to this folder. As long as you don't delete the items from the Deleted Items folder, you can always restore them to their original location. (To erase all items from this folder permanently, right-click the folder on the Outlook Bar and choose Empty "Deleted Items" Folder from the shortcut menu.)

Removing Deleted Messages Automatically

You can set up Outlook to automatically remove the messages in the Deleted Items folder when you exit Outlook. Choose Options from the Tools menu, and then select the Other tab, if it isn't already displayed. Select the Empty The Deleted Items Folder Upon Exiting check box, and then click OK.

Exploring the My Shortcuts Group

When you click My Shortcuts on the Outlook Bar (it might be called Mail on your system), you see at least these four standard folders: Drafts, Outbox, Sent Items, and Journal. There might be additional folders, depending on how you set up Outlook.

- **Drafts folder.** This folder stores messages that you are not yet ready to send. They might be messages that you have not completed, or those that you are holding to send at a later time. You can open a message in the Drafts folder to complete and send it.

- **Outbox folder.** This folder temporarily holds messages you've sent but that have not yet been transmitted to your e-mail server for delivery. When you're connected to your server, messages stay in your Outbox folder for only a short time. If you're working offline, the Outbox folder holds your sent messages until you're connected again. Then, depending on how Outlook is set up, outgoing mail might be sent automatically, or it might wait in the Outbox folder until you use the Send And Receive command.

- **Sent Items folder.** This folder contains copies of messages you've sent. Use this folder to verify that you've sent a message, check the date you sent it, refresh your memory of its contents, or possibly to resend a message.

SEE ALSO

For more information about your journal, see Chapter 14, "Keeping A Journal."

■ **Journal folder.** Use this folder to record various actions you've taken, such as sending and receiving messages, assigning tasks (and the responses), creating documents in other Microsoft Office applications—even making phone calls. You can track the actions on a timeline, and you can sort the list of journal entries in different ways.

You might also see an item titled Outlook Update in this group. This is not a folder but a URL link. If you have an Internet connection available and you click this link, Outlook can update itself automatically by downloading new features and program fixes.

Exploring the Other Shortcuts Group

The third group on the Outlook Bar is labeled Other Shortcuts, or sometimes just Other. The folders you see in this group, and even whether the group appears on the Outlook Bar or not, depends on your computer setup and how you installed Outlook. Here are some of the folders typically found in this group.

NOTE

You can add other disk folders, as well as Outlook folders, to the Other Shortcuts group. *For details, see "Customizing the Outlook Bar," on page 35.*

SEE ALSO

For more information about viewing disk contents in Outlook, see "Opening Documents or Starting Programs from Outlook," on page 478.

■ **My Computer.** This folder displays the same icons you see when you open the My Computer icon on your desktop. Use it to switch to any disk drive on your computer or to any network drive to locate and open any folder, file, or document.

■ **My Documents.** This folder contains the same shortcuts as the My Documents folder on the Windows 98 desktop (or the My Documents folder in Windows 95, if you have one). If, like me, you keep most of your documents in the My Documents folder or in a subfolder inside it, you can use My Documents to find and open most any file or document that you want to work on. When you open a file or document from the Outlook window, Windows starts the application that was used to create the document.

SEE ALSO

For information about using Outlook for remote mail, see Chapter 9, "Using Outlook Remotely and Offline."

■ **Personal Folders.** Use this icon on the Outlook Bar to access personal folders if they are part of your profile. Setting up personal folders was discussed in Chapter 1, "Preparing for Outlook."

For details about adding shortcuts, see "Adding Items to the Favorites Folder," on page 466, and "Using Public Folder Favorites," on page 525.

For more information about public folders, see Chapter 19, "Managing Folders."

- **Favorites Folder.** This folder is a shortcut to the Favorites folder on your hard disk. The items in this folder also appear on the Favorites toolbar of your Office shortcut bar (if you have set it up) and are also in the Favorites list you see in Microsoft Internet Explorer. You can set up and click the items in the Favorites folder to quickly jump to any disk folder or file, application, or World Wide Web site (URL).

- **Public Folders.** These folders contain messages on the Microsoft Exchange Server that other network users can access. You can post a message to a public folder to ask questions, provide answers, state opinions and facts, or attach documents. Public folders are intended to present and record public discussion of a specific topic.

- **Microsoft Outlook.** Click this icon to connect to the Internet and learn more about Microsoft Outlook.

Displaying Web Sites

While you'll use the Inbox primarily to display incoming messages, you can also use it to see and navigate through the Internet or a company intranet. In a way, Outlook acts as a Web browser, much like Microsoft Internet Explorer and other Web browsers.

Using the Web Toolbar

One way to display a Web site is to right-click any toolbar and select Web from the shortcut menu to see the Web toolbar shown in Figure 2-4. Type the address of the site in the Location box and press Enter. If you are not connected to the Internet, Outlook dials up your ISP. It connects to the site and displays it in your Inbox. You use the buttons on the Web toolbar to navigate the Web, just as you would the corresponding buttons in Internet Explorer.

If the Web site is already listed on your Favorites menu, click the down arrow to open your Favorites list, and click the site to connect to the Internet and open the site in the Inbox.

Creating Folder Home Pages

Another way to display a Web site is to associate it with a folder. When you open the folder, you can choose to display the associated Web page or the folder contents. Folder Home pages are most useful when

FIGURE 2-4.
The Web toolbar.

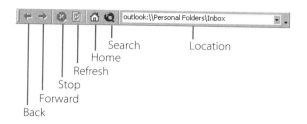

you're working on a corporate intranet. The intranet administrator can set up Web sites with useful information, reminders, or messages that you should be aware of. There might be a site, for example, that introduces new staff or customers. The site might be associated with the Contacts folder so you get a report of changing personnel each time you open that folder.

To create a folder home page, follow these steps:

1 Right-click the folder's icon on the Outlook Bar, and choose Properties from the shortcut menu.

2 In the dialog box that appears, click the Home Page tab to see the options in Figure 2-5, on the next page.

3 Enter the full URL of the Web site page you want to display.

4 If you want the Web site page to display the first time you click this folder icon, select Show Home Page By Default For This Folder.

5 Click OK.

If you didn't select Show Home Page By Default in step 4 above, you will always see the folder contents instead of the Web site when you click the folder icon. Even if you did select Show Home Page By Default in step 4, once you click the folder icon a second time you will see only the folder contents from then on. In either case, to see the Web page associated with the folder icon, choose Show Folder Home Page from the View menu.

Customizing the Outlook Bar

Since the Outlook Bar is so handy, it's helpful to customize it for the way you like to work. You can change its appearance and add or remove groups and folders, or you can choose not to display the bar. You can even add documents and favorite Web sites to the Outlook Bar

FIGURE 2-5.

The Home Page tab of the Notes Properties dialog box.

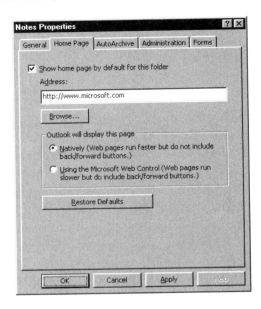

so you can launch them with a click of the mouse. Let's look at these features now.

Turning the Outlook Bar Off and On

There might be times when you find that the Outlook Bar takes up too much valuable screen space. You might, for example, want to leave as much room as possible to display messages or items in other folders. To use the entire width of the Outlook window for the folder contents list, you can turn off the Outlook Bar using either of these methods:

SEE ALSO

For details about how to widen columns and change the size of the parts of the Outlook window, see "Changing Column Width," on page 546.

- Choose Outlook Bar from the View menu.

- Right-click the Outlook Bar (but not on a folder icon on the bar), and then choose Hide Outlook Bar from the shortcut menu.

To turn the Outlook Bar back on, choose Outlook Bar from the View menu again.

Changing the Size of Icons on the Outlook Bar

If the Outlook Bar contains more folders than can be displayed at one time, you can bring the hidden ones into view by using the small arrows at the top and bottom of the scroll bar. As an alternative, you can make the folder icons smaller to see more of them at a time.

To reduce the size of the folder icons, right-click the Outlook Bar (but not directly on a folder icon), and choose Small Icons from the shortcut menu. To return the icons to large size, right-click the Outlook Bar again, and choose Large Icons from the shortcut menu.

Adding a Folder or Document to the Outlook Bar

You can add any Outlook folder, disk folder, or file to any group on the Outlook Bar. For example, you can add a Word document so that clicking it on the Outlook Bar starts Word and displays the document. If you add a disk folder, clicking it displays the folder contents directly in the Outlook window.

The easiest way to add a disk folder or file is to drag it onto the Outlook Bar. Here's how:

1 If Outlook is maximized (that is, it occupies your full screen), size it smaller by clicking the Restore button (the middle of the three small buttons on the right side of the title bar). You can then drag a corner of the Outlook window to shrink it until you can see the Windows desktop in the background.

2 On the Outlook Bar, click to open the group to which you want to add the folder or file.

3 Locate the file or folder you want to add. You can use My Computer or Windows Explorer to find the item, or it may be a shortcut on your desktop. Adjust window sizes so you can see both the folder or file and Outlook.

4 Drag the folder or file onto the Outlook Bar. As you move the mouse onto the bar, you'll see a horizontal line indicating where the item will be placed.

5 When the item is where you want it to appear, release the mouse button.

You can also add an Outlook folder or disk folder to the Outlook Bar using a dialog box. Just take these steps:

1 Select the group on the Outlook Bar to which you want to add the folder.

2 Right-click an empty area of the Outlook Bar (don't click a folder icon) and choose Outlook Bar Shortcut from the shortcut menu

that appears. You will see the Add To Outlook Bar dialog box shown in Figure 2-6.

3 Open the Look In list, and choose Outlook to add an Outlook folder or choose File System to add a folder from your disk or the network.

4 Choose the folder from the Folder Name list or from the large text box list, or type the folder name directly in the Folder Name box. Folders that contain subfolders are indicated in the list with a plus sign—click the plus sign to expand a folder.

5 Click OK.

Adding a Web Site to the Outlook Bar

When you add a Web site to the Outlook Bar, clicking it displays the site directly in the Inbox window. If you are not connected to the Internet, Outlook launches your Web browser, dials up your ISP, and connects to the site (unless you've configured Outlook *not* to connect automatically).

To add a Web page to the Outlook Bar, first open the Web site as you learned in "Displaying Web Sites," on page 34. Then, right-click a blank area of the Outlook Bar, choose Outlook Bar Shortcut To Web Page from the shortcut menu, and then click OK in the message box that appears. The Web site will appear as a shortcut in the My Shortcuts group.

Removing an Icon from the Outlook Bar

To remove an icon from the Outlook Bar, follow these steps:

1 Switch to the group on the Outlook Bar from which you want to remove the icon.

FIGURE 2-6.

The Add To Outlook Bar dialog box.

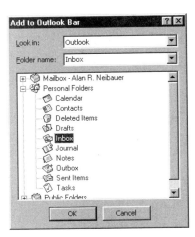

2 Right-click the icon you want to remove.

3 Choose Remove From Outlook Bar from the shortcut menu.

4 Click Yes when asked whether you're sure you want to remove the folder icon.

Removing an icon from the Outlook Bar doesn't remove the actual item the icon represents from your disk. *If you actually want to delete a folder, for example, see "Removing a Folder," on page 522.*

Renaming an Icon on the Outlook Bar

The icons on the Outlook Bar are shortcuts to the actual items. You can change the name of any icon that appears on the Outlook Bar.

Changing the name of an icon on the Outlook Bar does not change the name of the item itself on your disk.

Here's how to rename an icon on the Outlook Bar:

1 Right-click the icon you want to rename.

2 Choose Rename Shortcut from the shortcut menu. The icon's name becomes active (highlighted).

3 Type or edit the name of the icon, and then press the Enter key.

Adding a Group to the Outlook Bar

You might find that you'd like to add another group (or several more groups) to the Outlook Bar. You can easily add a group by following these steps:

1 Right-click an empty area of the Outlook Bar.

2 Choose Add New Group from the shortcut menu. Outlook adds a group label and activates it for naming.

3 Type a name for the new group, and then press the Enter key.

You can now add shortcuts to folders, documents, and Web sites to your new group.

Renaming a Group on the Outlook Bar

If you want to change the name of a group on the Outlook Bar, take these steps:

1 Right-click the label of the group you want to rename.

2 Choose Rename Group from the shortcut menu. Outlook activates that group label for renaming.

3 Type a new name for the group, and then press the Enter key.

Removing a Group from the Outlook Bar

If one of the groups on the Outlook Bar is no longer useful to you, you can remove it from the bar. Simply right-click the label of the group you want to remove, choose Remove Group from the shortcut menu, and click Yes when asked whether you're sure you want to remove the group.

Customizing the Outlook Window

Outlook allows you to customize the appearance and functionality of the main Outlook window to fit the way you work and the tasks you perform most often. You can choose whether to hide or display such components as the preview pane, Folder List, the Outlook toolbars, and the status bar. You can also add, remove, rename, resize, or reposition various elements in the Outlook window.

Displaying the Folder List

As you work with Outlook, you'll be opening folders to add, display, or edit various types of information. If the icon for the folder is shown on the Outlook Bar, just click it to open the folder. Not every folder, however, is listed on the Outlook Bar, and you might have to open another group or scroll through the group to display the folder you want to open.

For quick access to all of your folders, display the Folder List, which is shown in the following illustration. You can set the list to stay open on the screen or to close automatically after you select a folder.

To open the Folder List, choose Folder List from the View menu. Repeat this command to hide the list, or click the Close button on the Folder List title bar.

 NOTE

> You can add a folder to the Outlook Bar from the Folder List. Drag the folder from the list until a horizontal line appears where you want to position the folder on the Outlook Bar, and then release the mouse button.

To display the Folder List temporarily, follow these steps:

1 Click the name of the folder that's currently open on the Folder Bar to display the Folder List. On the top right of the list, where the Close button is on the Folder List shown previously, you'll see an icon of a push pin.

2 Make a selection or click elsewhere to close the Folder List.

To keep the Folder List open, click the push pin at the top of the list.

 NOTE

> Right-click a folder on the Folder Bar to display a drop-down menu of folder commands.

Displaying the Status Bar

The status bar at the bottom of the Outlook window shows helpful information. In many windows, the status bar displays the number of items in the open folder and the number of unread items. In some form windows, the status bar might have been set up to display messages indicating what you should type or choose in a form field.

If none of this information is important to you—if you never or only rarely look at the status bar—you might want to hide it to gain some extra space in the window. To hide or display the status bar, choose

Status Bar from the View menu. If you don't see the command, wait until the menu expands or click the down arrow at the bottom of the menu to expand it immediately.

Changing List Widths

Displaying the Outlook Bar, the Folder List, the list of the folder's contents, and preview pane all at one time can be useful, but it doesn't leave a lot of room on the screen. You can change the size of each of these elements to suit your needs. Reducing the width of the Outlook Bar and Folder List, for example, leaves them on screen and gives you more room to read messages.

? SEE ALSO

The Calendar folder has additional sections that you can size. For details, see "Adjusting the Calendar Display," on page 331.

To change the size of any of these elements, drag the border between it and the list next to it. Position the mouse pointer over the border so that the pointer changes to a two-headed arrow, and then drag the border to the position you want. For example, you can change the size of the Outlook Bar by dragging its right border. Drag the border to the left to reduce the width of the bar or to the right to increase its width. To change the height of the preview pane, drag the border between it and the message list above.

Working with Toolbars

Clicking the toolbar buttons gives you a fast, easy way to take specific actions or perform common tasks. You can turn Outlook's toolbars on and off, you can reposition them, and you can change the size of the toolbar buttons.

Outlook contains three toolbars that you can use with any folder and two more that are available from some of the folders:

- You'll see a version of the Standard toolbar in every folder you open in Outlook. The buttons on the Standard toolbar change for each type of folder or folder item. The Standard toolbar buttons contain the tasks that you are most likely to perform on the type of folder or item you've selected.

- The Advanced toolbar contains an additional set of useful buttons, which vary depending on the folder you have open.

- The Web toolbar contains tools for launching your Web browser in your Outlook window and navigating the Internet, including buttons to open your home page and search the Web and a text box in which to enter the address of a site you want to open.

- The Remote toolbar contains buttons for running a remote mail session. *See "Checking Out the Remote Toolbar," on page 295, for details.* The Remote toolbar is available only in folders where it is relevant, such as the Inbox and other mail folders.

- The Formatting toolbar is available whenever you are working with any item (except notes) that contain text, such as an e-mail message, a meeting request, a task item, or a journal entry, and provides the most common formatting tasks.

- The Clipboard toolbar lets you store up to 12 items in the clipboard that you can paste elsewhere. This toolbar, common to all Office 2000 applications, is only available when you are working in a window in which you can enter text or graphics.

- The Form Design toolbar can only be selected when you are designing a custom form, as you will see in Chapter 22, "Designing and Using Forms."

- The Response toolbar is only displayed when you create a custom response action for a form, as you will see in Chapter 23, "Programming with Forms."

Displaying and Moving Toolbars

In most cases, Outlook displays the toolbar appropriate for the function you are performing. When you are composing a message, for example, Outlook displays two toolbars, the Standard toolbar and the Formatting toolbar, one above the other or side by side, as shown here:

Move handle

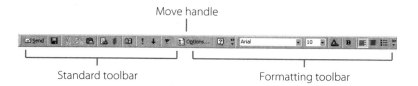

Standard toolbar   Formatting toolbar

You can easily display or hide toolbars and change their position on the screen to suit your tastes and working habits.

Turning Toolbars Off and On

Obviously, toolbars take up a certain amount of window space. You can turn off a toolbar if you'd prefer to use this space to see more folders or folder items, and you can later turn it back on.

Only the names of toolbars that apply to the current folder or to the open folder item appear on the Toolbars submenu or on the Toolbars shortcut menu.

■ Point to Toolbars on the View menu, and then click the toolbar you want to turn off or on. (A check mark in the box beside the toolbar means it is currently turned on.)

■ Right-click any toolbar. On the shortcut menu, click the toolbar that you want to turn off or on.

■ Right-click any toolbar, select Customize from the shortcut menu, and then click the Toolbars tab. Select the check boxes for the toolbars that you want to display. The Form Design and Response toolbars are only available from this dialog box.

If all the toolbars are turned off, right-click the menu bar to display the Toolbars shortcut menu, where you can select the toolbars you need.

Changing the Position of a Toolbar

You might find toolbars more convenient to use in some other position on the screen. Placing the Standard and Formatting toolbars in a message window one above the other uses more space but makes them easier to use because all of the buttons will be visible without scrolling. To move a toolbar, drag it by the *move handle,* located at the left edge of each toolbar. Move the mouse over the handle until the pointer changes to a four-headed arrow, and then click and drag the toolbar to a new location.

Drag a toolbar to the top, bottom, left, or right edges of the window to attach it to the edge and to display its buttons all in one line. You can also position the toolbar within the window so it *floats* as a small window. Having the toolbar float is useful if you can't see all of the buttons on screen in one line. (If the Outlook window is not maximized, you can even drag a toolbar outside the Outlook window.) When a toolbar is floating, you can change its size in much the same way as you change the size of a window, by dragging a side or corner of its window. The buttons will rearrange themselves to fit the shape of the toolbar you create.

Customizing Toolbars and Menus

The toolbars provided by Outlook are useful, but they might not offer all of the features you use often. For example, you might want to quickly set up an appointment from within any folder with a single click of the mouse, but the Appointment button is not on the Standard toolbar in every window.

You can add and delete features from toolbars and menus, create your own custom toolbars, and change the icons on toolbar buttons. To start the process, use one of these methods:

- Point to Toolbars on the View menu, and then click Customize.

- Right-click a toolbar, and then choose Customize from the short-cut menu.

- Choose Customize from the Add Or Remove Buttons list.

The Customize dialog box, shown in Figure 2-7, on the next page, contains three tabs:

- Use the Toolbars tab to display or hide a toolbar; create, rename, or delete a custom toolbar; or reset the menu bar or an Outlook toolbar by removing any custom buttons that you added and restoring Outlook buttons that you removed.

- Use the Commands tab to add features to menus and toolbars.

- Use the Options tab to change the appearance of menus and toolbars and to remove any buttons you added using the More Buttons feature or by selecting a command from an expanded menu.

Adding Buttons to a Toolbar or Menu

You can easily add a feature to a menu or toolbar. Choose the category of the feature in the Commands tab of the Customize dialog box, and then drag the specific feature to where you want it to appear, as explained in the following steps:

1 If you want to add a button to a toolbar, make sure the toolbar is displayed; if you want to add a command to a list of menu items that appears when your Calendar is open, for example, open the Calendar folder first (remember, commands in menus and buttons on toolbars change according to the context).

2 Now open the Customize dialog box using one of the methods described above.

3 Click the Commands tab, shown in Figure 2-7, on the next page.

4 In the Categories list, select the category that contains the feature you want to add.

5 In the Commands list, select the feature you want to add.

FIGURE 2-7.
The Commands tab of
the Customize dialog
box.

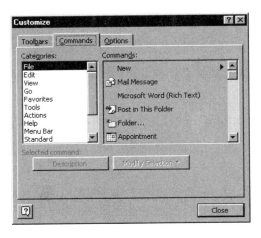

FIGURE 2-7.
The Commands tab of the Customize dialog box.

6 Drag the feature to its new location on the toolbar or menu. As you drag over the toolbar or menu, an icon of a button with a plus sign moves with the mouse and an insert bar appears to guide you. If you drag over a menu, the menu will drop down so that you can position the new feature exactly where you want it.

7 Release the mouse button to drop the feature into place.

Deleting and Changing Buttons and Menu Commands

You can also delete features from a menu or toolbar, change their position, and customize how they appear. First display any tab of the Customize dialog box, and then use either of these techniques:

■ To remove a feature, drag it off of the menu or toolbar.

■ To change the position of a feature, drag it to another location on the menu, toolbar, or to another menu or toolbar.

You have to be particularly careful when dragging a menu command off of the menu. When the Customize dialog box is displayed, pointing to a command on the menu bar, such as the items File or Edit, and dragging, will move the entire menu. To select a specific command on a menu for dragging, follow these steps after the Customize dialog box is displayed:

1 Click the menu name, and then release the mouse. The menu will open and display its commands.

2 Drag the specific menu command away from the menu.

To customize a toolbar button or menu command, right-click it (while the Customize dialog box is displayed) to open a shortcut menu similar to the one shown here for a message's Reply button. The functions of the shortcut menu commands are described in Table 2-1.

TABLE 2-1.   Customizing Buttons and Menu Commands

Command	What the Command Does
Reset	Restores the item to its default status
Delete	Removes the item from the menu or toolbar
Name	Determines the name displayed on the menu, button, or ScreenTip; place the & symbol before the character you want underlined as a keyboard shortcut
Copy Button Image	Copies the button's image to the clipboard
Paste Button Image	Inserts the button's image from the clipboard onto the menu or toolbar
Reset Button Image	Restores the default button image
Edit Button Image	Lets you customize the button image
Change Button Image	Displays a list of alternative images

(continued)

TABLE 2-1.   *continued*

Command	What the Command Does
Default Style	Uses the default style of display for the item
Text Only (Always)	Displays only the name of the feature, no icon, in toolbars and menus
Text Only (In Menus)	Displays only the name of the feature on menus
Image And Text	Displays both the name and icon of the feature
Begin A Group	Inserts a vertical bar to separate toolbar buttons or a horizontal bar to separate menu commands
Assign Hyperlink	Assigns a Web page or document to open when you click the button or menu command

The Edit Button Image option on the shortcut menu opens the Button Editor, shown in Figure 2-8, which you can use to design your own button icons.

To alter the button image, choose a color, and then click or drag in the Picture area to draw with that color. To erase pixels (make them transparent), click the Erase button and then click or drag over the pixels you want to erase. To delete the entire image and start with a blank

FIGURE 2-8.
The Button Editor
dialog box.

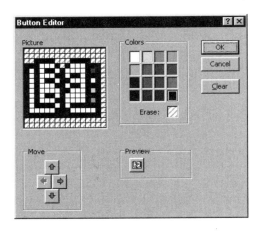

button, click Clear. You can also click one of the arrow buttons to move the image within its frame.

Setting Menu and Toolbar Options

Use the Options tab of the Customize dialog box, shown in Figure 2-9, to change the way toolbar buttons appear and the way menus are displayed.

The Options tab also lets you make these toolbar and menu settings:

- **Standard And Formatting Toolbars Share One Row.** If you want these toolbars to appear side by side, select this check box.

- **Menus Show Recently Used Commands First.** Clear this check box if you want to see a complete list of menu commands when you open a menu. Otherwise, the menu will include only your most recently used commands.

- **Show Full Menus After A Short Delay.** This check box is available only if you select the previous check box. If selected, the complete list of menu commands will appear after a short delay. If this check box is cleared, you'll need to click the arrow at the bottom of each collapsed menu to expand it manually.

- **Reset My Usage Data.** If you've been allowing Outlook to add and remove commands from the menus as you've used or not used them, clicking this button returns all the menus to their initial state and starts the process over again. Advanced menu commands that were hidden initially will be hidden again, and standard menu commands that were hidden because you didn't use them will be made visible again.

FIGURE 2-9.

The Options tab of the Customize dialog box.

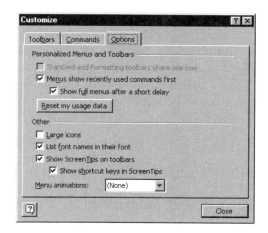

 This option will not reset any customizations that you made to the commands on menus or buttons on toolbars—use the Reset command on the Toolbars tab for that.

- **Large Icons.** Select this check box to replace the standard buttons with much larger ones for easier viewing.

- **List Font Names In Their Font.** If this check box is selected, the name of each available font is displayed using the font itself, so you can see how it appears before you select it and start using it. If you clear this check box, all fonts will be listed using the normal menu font.

- **Show ScreenTips On Toolbars.** If this check box is selected, ScreenTips will pop up on your screen when you position the mouse pointer over a toolbar button, helping you learn what each button does.

- **Show Shortcut Keys In Screentips.** This check box is available only if you select the previous check box. If this check box is selected, the ScreenTip will show shortcut keys for each command (such as Ctrl+P for the Print button).

- **Menu Animations.** Use this list to select the way drop-down menus appear. The default is No Animation, in which the menu just appears when you click the menu bar. You can also select to have menus unfold from the upper left to the lower right corner, slide down like a window shade, or open using the two styles randomly.

Creating a New Toolbar

In addition to customizing Outlook's existing toolbars, you can create entirely new ones. You do this by creating a new blank toolbar and then dragging features to it as you learned earlier. To create a new toolbar, open the Customize dialog box, and then follow these steps:

1 Click the Toolbars tab.

2 Click New.

3 In the box that appears, type a name for the toolbar (the default suggestion is Custom 1), and then click OK to display a small blank toolbar.

4 Click the Commands tab.

5 Drag the desired features to the new toolbar.

6 Click Close.

The toolbar will now be listed on the Toolbars submenu or shortcut menu. To delete a custom toolbar, point to Toolbars on the View menu, choose Customize, click the toolbar in the list on the Toolbars tab, and then click Delete.

Organizing Messages

Outlook provides two ways to help you work with messages that come to your Inbox: the Rules Wizard and the Out Of Office Assistant. The Rules Wizard can be set up to automatically sort messages or to forward or reply to messages that you always treat the same way. For those times when you're out of the office, you can set up the Out Of Office Assistant to tell people who send you messages that you are away, when you'll be back, and whom to contact or what to do during your absence. The Out Of Office Assistant can also automatically sort, move, forward, and delete messages while you are away.

Managing Your Mail with the Rules Wizard

Your Inbox can easily become flooded with messages and other items. You can, of course, attend to each item manually, deleting it or moving it to another location. But sometimes there's a category of messages that you want to act on in a specific way, such as deleting all messages from a certain sender, or moving all messages about a certain subject to a new folder. You can use the Rules Wizard to automatically delete, forward, reply, move, and perform several other actions on items arriving at your Inbox.

Creating a Rule

To create a rule, follow these steps:

1 Choose Rules Wizard from the Tools menu to display the dialog box shown in Figure 2-10, on the next page.

2 Click the New button to open the page shown in Figure 2-11, on page 53.

3 Select the general type of rule you want to create from the Which Type Of Rule Do You Want To Create? list. The types of rules are explained in Table 2-2, on page 54. For example, if you want to

? SEE ALSO

To quickly create a rule using the information in a specific message, see the sidebar "Creating Rules with Organize," on page 58.

Getting Started

FIGURE 2-10.

The Rules Wizard.

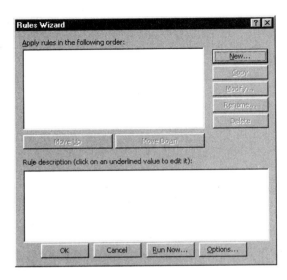

place an e-mail message from a particular recipient in a folder other than the Inbox, select Move New Messages From Someone.

The Rule Description box displays the logic or action of the rule. The description will change and enlarge as you select specific actions from other Rules Wizard pages.

 **NOTE**

If you are using Outlook with Microsoft Exchange Server, you must be online to use the Rules Wizard.

In some cases, the description will contain values, which appear as underlined text. This means that you must click the underlined value to further refine the rule. If you select the Move Messages Based On Content rule, for example, you'll see the description shown here:

Apply this rule after the message arrives
With <u>specific words</u> in the subject or body
Move it to the <u>specified</u> folder

This means you have to click *specific words* to enter the text you want the rule to check for and then click *specified* to choose the folder in which to place the message. If you see the words People Or Distribution List underlined in the description, it means you must click it to select a specific sender or group of senders to use for the rule.

4 After you've chosen the type of rule, click Next.

FIGURE 2-11.

Use this page of the Rules Wizard to create a new rule.

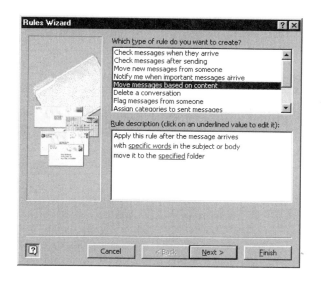

5 On the Which Condition(s) Do You Want To Check? page, you select the conditions that decide whether the rule will be applied to a particular message. Most rules can be applied only when certain conditions are met, such as when a message is addressed to you or when certain words appear in the subject. The options offered by the Rules Wizard depend on the type of rule you are creating. In most cases, you can select more than one option to create rather sophisticated rules. For example, you could create a rule that checks messages to determine whether they are from the sender named Dave Olshina, have to do with budgets, and contain attachments. The list of possibilities is rather long, so a sampling is described in Table 2-3, on page 56.

6 After you select the conditions, click Next again.

7 The next page of the Rules Wizard asks What Do You Want To Do With The Message? and lets you specify the actions that will be taken for messages that meet the conditions of your rule. For example, if you want to send an automatic reply to a message, select Reply Using A Specific Template. A few of the other actions you might choose include deleting the message, forwarding it to a list of recipients, playing a sound, or moving to a folder you specify. Click Next after making your choices.

8 The next page of the wizard asks whether you'd like to make any exceptions to the rule you've created. For example, after specifying that all messages from a certain sender be deleted, you could add an exception such as "except if it has an attachment." After selecting any exceptions you want to add, click Next.

9 You've now completed the rule, and the Rules Wizard asks you to enter a name for the rule and asks whether you want to apply the rule now to existing messages or merely add it to your list of rules to apply to new messages as they are received. If there are any underlined values (such as a specific template) shown in the description that you haven't defined yet, you will have to click them now and complete the definition.

10 Click Finish and the new rule appears in the list of completed rules.

TABLE 2-2. General Types of Rules to Apply

Setting	What the Rules Wizard Acts On
Check Messages When They Arrive	Performs some action when a message is received
Move New Messages From Someone	Automatically places new messages from a sender into a specified folder
Notify Me When Important Messages Arrive	Displays a specified notice when a message with a specified priority arrives
Move Messages Based On Content	Places a message containing specified text into a selected folder
Delete A Conversation	Deletes a message containing specified text in the subject
Flag Messages From Someone	Applies a selected flag for a set number of days when a message is received from a specified sender or group
Assign Categories To Sent Messages	Assigns a category to sent messages based on the recipient
Assign Categories Based On Content	Assigns a category to arriving messages based on the contents
Move Messages I Send To Someone	Moves sent messages into specific folders based on the recipient
Stop Processing All Following Rules	Stops applying any other selected rules once the conditions of this rule are met
Check Messages After Sending	Performs some action after you send a message

If you have more then one rule, the rules will be performed in the order in which they are listed in the box. To change the order of a rule, click it and then click either Move Up or Move Down depending on where you want to place the rule in the list.

You can also use the Rules Wizard dialog box to copy, modify, rename, or delete rules. For additional control over how rules are applied, click the Options button to display the dialog box shown in Figure 2-12.

The Update Exchange Server area of the Options dialog box determines when the rules you create are updated on the server. When you choose Automatically, rules that you create or change are applied immediately. Choose Manually when you want to control when new or changed rules are put into effect. The rules will be applied when you click Update Now.

 NOTE

As your collection of rules grows, you'll want to give some consideration to the order in which they're applied. Placing a rule of lower priority above one of higher priority might result in your mail being processed in an unexpected and unwanted way. You might want to step through the process by thinking of a particular type of message you might receive and testing your rules order from the top to bottom to see where the imaginary message would end up. If the result is not what you intended, you might need to change the order in which your rules are applied or modify the content of one or more rules.

Use the Import And Export section of the dialog box to save your rules to a file on your disk or to retrieve a set of rules that you already saved.

Normally, the rules you create are applied only to new messages as they are received or sent. To apply the rules to existing messages, click

FIGURE 2-12.
The Rules Wizard Options dialog box.

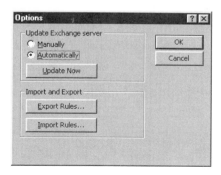

TABLE 2-3. Rules Wizard Options for Selecting Conditions

Setting	What the Rules Wizard Acts On
From *People Or Distribution List*	Items from a particular sender or group of senders
Sent To *People Or Distribution List*	Items sent to a particular recipient
Sent Only To Me	Items addressed only to you
Where My Name Is In The Cc Box	Items with your name in the Cc box
With *Specific Words* In The Subject	Items that include the specified text in the Subject box
With *Specific Words* In The Body	Items that contain the specified text somewhere in the message body
Marked As *Importance*	Items marked with a specified priority
Which Has An Attachment	Items that have attachments

Run Now in the Rules Wizard dialog box to see the options shown in Figure 2-13.

Select the check boxes for the rules you want to apply, and then choose the folder to apply the rules to. You can select only one folder at a time,

FIGURE 2-13.
The Run Rules Now dialog box.

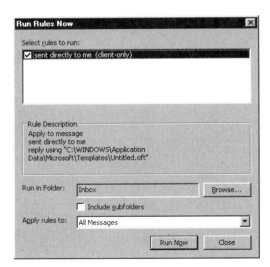

but if you select a higher level folder you can choose to apply the rules to messages in the subfolders as well. You can also choose to apply the rules to all messages, read messages only, or unread messages only in the selected folder(s). Click Run Now to apply the rules.

Rules Wizard Automatic Replies

One popular use of the Rules Wizard is to send an automatic reply to every message received. Before using this feature, you should create the message you want to use as the automated reply. This can be a simple message with some standard text reporting that you've received the sender's message and will be responding when appropriate.

To create the template, create a message, as you will learn how to do in Chapter 5, "Sending and Receiving Messages," and then open the message in either the Outbox or Sent Items folders. Choose Save As from the File menu, and type a title for the message. Open the Save As Type list, choose Outlook Templates (*.oft), and then click Save.

Now you can create the rule, and click a specific template to display this dialog box:

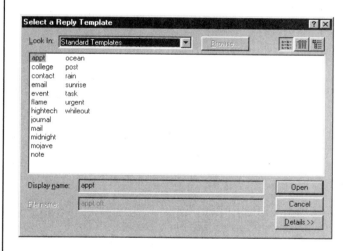

1 Open the Look In list and select User Templates In File System.

2 Select the template you want to use.

3 Click Open.

When you complete and select the rule, Outlook will send the automatic message in response to those meeting the rule's conditions.

Creating Rules with Organize

Outlook includes Organize, a timesaving feature that helps you manage folders and folder items. Using Organize, you can quickly create a rule without going through all of the Rules Wizard pages. You'll learn about Organize features throughout this book. Here's how to use it to create a rule:

1 Select the Inbox folder or another folder containing e-mail messages, such as Drafts, Sent Items, Deleted Items, or Outbox. Look for a folder containing a message to which you'd like to apply a rule. Perhaps you'll find a type of message in your Inbox that you want sent to your Deleted Items folder automatically.

2 Select the message and then click Organize on the toolbar to display the panel shown here:

4 Select From or Sent To.

5 Enter the name of the sender or recipient if necessary.

3 Click here if not already selected.

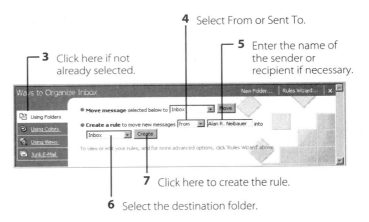

7 Click here to create the rule.

6 Select the destination folder.

The rule will be inserted into the Rules Wizard list and turned on. If you'd like to modify the rule you can quickly access the Rules Wizard from the Organize pane by clicking Rules Wizard.

Using the Out of Office Assistant

When you're away from your office—on vacation, for example—and you want people who write you to know that you're not available for a while, use the Out Of Office Assistant to automatically reply to each message you receive. You can also use the Out Of Office Assistant to create a set of rules for performing actions on messages. The basics of the rules are similar to using the Rules Wizard, although the pages differ.

> **NOTE**
>
> You can use the Out Of Office Assistant only if you are using Outlook with Microsoft Exchange Server and you have the Exchange Extensions add-in installed. *For information about installing add-ins, see "Add-in Manager," on page 103.*

To set up the Out Of Office Assistant, take these steps:

1 Choose Out Of Office Assistant from the Tools menu. You might have to expand the menu. The Out Of Office Assistant appears, as shown in Figure 2-14.

2 Click I Am Currently Out of The Office to turn on the Out of Office Assistant.

3 Type the message you want the assistant to send.

4 If you want the message sent to all the people who send mail to you, you can finish now by clicking OK. Each person who writes to you will receive the same message the first time they write. The mail they send will be routed according to the rules set up in the Rules Wizard. However, if you want to process the messages that arrive during your absence more individually, continue with the next step.

5 Click the Add Rule button, and the Edit Rule dialog box will appear, as shown in Figure 2-15, on the next page. Use this dialog box to set up rules for the types of items you want the Out Of Office Assistant to act on and the actions it should take for those items. The fewer settings you make in the When A Message Arrives section of the dialog box, the fewer steps the Out Of

FIGURE 2-14.
The Out of Office Assistant.

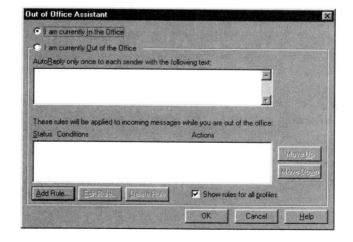

FIGURE 2-15.

The Edit Rule dialog box.

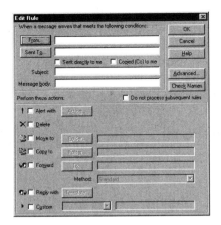

Office Assistant will need to take, and the faster your mail will be processed.

6 Click the Check Names button in the Edit Rule dialog box to check names you've entered in the From and Sent To boxes against the entries in your address book. Here's how it works:

- If Outlook finds a matching name, it underlines the name and turns it into a link to the address book entry.

- If you type a partial name, such as just a first name, Outlook will complete the name with the full listing from the address book.

- If Outlook locates multiple matches, such as several persons with the same first name, you'll be asked to select the correct name from a list.

- If Outlook does not find a match, it asks if you want to create a new address listing.

7 In the event that the Edit Rules dialog box doesn't give you enough options to process your mail in your absence, click the Advanced button to open the Advanced dialog box, shown in Figure 2-16. Consult Table 2-4, on page 62, for a description of these advanced items. When you have set up the Advanced dialog box, click OK to close it and return to the Edit Rule dialog box.

⭐ **TIP**

You can choose settings in the Advanced dialog box even without making any settings in the Edit Rule dialog box.

FIGURE 2-16.

The Advanced dialog box.

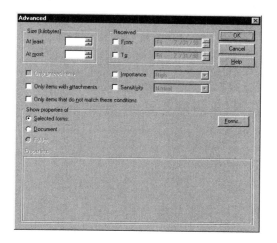

8 After you return to the Edit Rule dialog box, having selected the kinds of items you want the Out Of Office Assistant to act on, you need to specify the actions you want the Out Of Office Assistant to take for these items. In the lower portion of the Edit Rule dialog box, choose the actions that should be taken for this set of items.

9 When the settings are complete, click OK in the Edit Rule dialog box to accept all the settings and return to the Out Of Office Assistant dialog box. If you want to specify different actions for other types of items, you can click Add Rule, identify a new set of messages, and select the appropriate actions. Repeat this procedure for each type of message that you want the Out Of Office Assistant to take care of—closing the Edit Rule dialog box and returning to the Out Of Office Assistant dialog box each time.

10 Finally, when you've finished setting up the rules you want, click OK in the Out Of Office Assistant dialog box.

When the Out Of Office Assistant is turned on, the next time you start Outlook (if you connect to your e-mail server), you'll see a message telling you that the Out Of Office Assistant is on and asking whether you want to turn it off. Click Yes to turn off the Out Of Office Assistant; click No to leave it turned on.

The rules stay intact so that you can use them the next time you're out of the office without having to set them up again. Out Of Office Assistant rules are inactive as long as the assistant is turned off.

TABLE 2-4. **Advanced Dialog Box Options for Out of Office Assistant**

Setting	What the Out Of Office Assistant Does
Size At Least	Acts on items that are larger than the size you set
Size At Most	Acts on items that are smaller than the size you set
Received From	Acts on items received after the date you set (for items between two dates, also set a Received To date)
Received To	Acts on items received before the date you set (for items between two dates, also set a Received From date)
Only Unread Items	Acts on items you haven't read yet
Only Items With Attachments	Acts on items that contain attachments (files or messages)
Importance	Acts on items set to the level of importance you specify—High, Normal, or Low
Sensitivity	Acts on items set to the level of sensitivity you specify—Normal, Personal, Private, or Confidential
Only Items That Do Not Match These Conditions	Uses the reverse of all your settings in both the Edit Rule and Advanced dialog boxes
Show Properties Of Selected Forms	Displays fields in the forms you select with the Forms button
Show Properties Of Document	Displays document properties
Show Properties Of Folder	Displays folder properties.

Out of Office Automatic Replies

In addition to, or instead of, sending the generic reply you enter in the AutoReply text box of the Out Of Office Assistant dialog box to every-one who contacts you while you're away, you can choose to send one or more automatic replies tailored for each type of message you've created rules for in the Out Of Office Assistant. To send custom messages, follow these steps:

1 Open the Out Of Office Assistant dialog box.

2 Select a rule from the lower text box and click the Edit Rule button.

3 In the Perform These Actions area of the Edit Rule dialog box, select the Reply With check box, and then click the Template button to display the window shown in Figure 2-17.

4 Click To or type additional names in the text box if you want to send this reply to other people in addition to the sender.

5 Type an appropriate reply message.

6 Close the Template window.

7 Click Yes in the message box to save your changes.

⭐ **TIP**

> **Using the Assistant**
> You can set up the Out Of Office Assistant in advance and then turn it on and off as needed. You can leave rules you create intact so that you have to set them up only once. You can, of course, change the rules at any time to better suit your needs.

When you are out of the office and a message arrives, Outlook uses the template for the reply. It inserts the word "Re:" and the original subject line as the reply's subject and sends the message.

FIGURE 2-17.
Use this window to create a template for automatic replies.

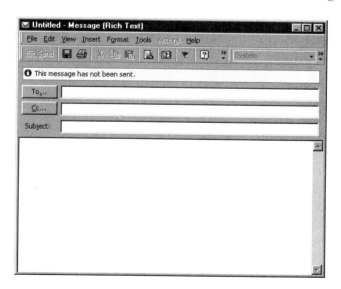

In this chapter you've learned how to get around in Outlook and some ways to customize it to your liking. By taking advantage of the Rules Wizard and the Out Of Office Assistant, you'll be able to automate mail handling tasks, whether you're in the office or far away on vacation. You might not even be missed! In the next chapter you'll learn to set up and customize Outlook's Inbox, Calendar, and other important folders.

CHAPTER 3

Setting Outlook Options

You can start Microsoft Outlook and begin using it exactly as it was installed on your computer. But just as you can customize the appearance of the Outlook window, as you learned in Chapter 2, "Discovering Outlook," you can also customize the way Outlook works. By setting options, you can fine-tune Outlook for the way you like to work, making it more efficient and comfortable.

Accessing Outlook Options

You use the Options command on the Tools menu to access all of the settings that you can customize. In fact, the Options dialog box contains as many as eight tabs, and several of the tabs have buttons that display one or more dialog boxes of additional options. This indicates just how much you can customize Outlook—the way it works and the way it looks.

NOTE Not all of the dialog box tabs and options described in this chapter will be available if you set up Outlook with the Internet Only option or if you are not connected to Exchange Server.

Here's the general procedure for adjusting options:

1 Choose Options from the Tools menu.

2 Click the appropriate tab.

3 Set the options you want to adjust.

4 Click OK.

TIP When you want to set options on more than one tab, you can click Apply instead of OK to apply your changes right away and keep the dialog box open.

Using the Preferences Tab

The Preferences tab of the Options dialog box, shown in Figure 3-1, lets you access a variety of options for controlling various Outlook features. There are a few options you set directly on the tab, but most you access using the provided buttons.

Setting E-mail Options

Click the E-mail Options button on the Preferences tab to access a wide variety of options for controlling how e-mail is received, sent, and managed. The options are shown in Figure 3-2.

Message Handling

Your choices in the Message Handling section determine what happens when you move, reply to, forward, or send a message.

FIGURE 3-1.
The Preferences tab of the Outlook Options dialog box.

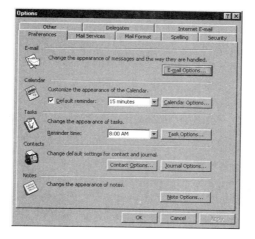

After Moving Or Deleting An Open Item. As part of the process of deleting or moving a message that you've just read, Outlook must close the message window. What should Outlook do after closing the window? You can choose one of the following three options:

- Open The Previous Item is the standard setting. With this option selected, the previous message in the folder (the one listed just before the open one in the item list) is opened when you delete or move the current message.

- Open The Next Item opens the next item in the folder.

- Return To The Inbox is the setting to use if you want to return to the Inbox folder instead of opening another message.

FIGURE 3-2.
The E-mail Options dialog box.

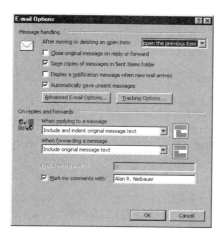

Close Original Message On Reply Or Forward. After you send a reply or forward a message, Outlook leaves open the original item's window by default. This setting is handy if you like to read through all your messages and dispose of them as you go ("disposing" includes replying to and forwarding messages), continuing to move up or down the message list after you send a reply or forward a message. However, if you're working on a few scattered messages, you might want to select this check box to close the original message.

Save Copies Of Messages In Sent Items Folder. For your own recordkeeping, you might want to have copies of the messages you send. By default, Outlook puts a copy of every message you send in your Sent Items folder. If you prefer to be more selective about which messages you keep, clear this check box. If you do so, remember to add yourself to the Cc box for any messages that you want to keep for your records.

Display A Notification Message When New Mail Arrives. If you select this check box, Outlook will display a message on the screen reporting that new mail has been received.

Automatically Save Unsent Messages. By default Outlook saves messages you're working on every three minutes. If this check box is selected, Outlook saves the messages in the Drafts folder.

On Replies And Forwards

The options in the On Replies And Forwards section determine how the contents of the original message appear when you reply to or forward it.

When Replying To A Message. Because replies to messages have a conversational context (the reply takes place as part of a conversation among correspondents), the standard Outlook setup is to include a copy of the original message in the reply. Also, to distinguish the original message from the reply, Outlook indents the original message. This setting is listed as Include And Indent Original Message Text. You have these additional choices for dealing with the original message in replies:

- The Do Not Include Original Message option omits the original message from your reply.

- The Attach Original Message option includes the original message as an attachment, which appears as a message icon. This choice saves space in the message window but requires you and the recipient to double-click the attachment to read it.

- The Include Original Message Text option includes the original message in the reply but does not indent it.

- The Prefix Each Line Of The Original Message option adds the prefix character before each line of the original message. When you select this option, you can then choose the prefix character, such as <, >, :, or |, to list a few common choices.

When Forwarding A Message. When you forward a message, you naturally want to include the original message text. Outlook is initially set up to simply include that text using the Include Original Message Text option. You have these three other choices for how to forward the message:

- The Attach Original Message option includes the original message as an attachment, which appears as a message icon that you and the recipient must double-click to read.

- The Include And Indent Original Message Text option indents the original message text.

- The Prefix Each Line Of The Original Message option adds the prefix character before each line of the original message. Prefix Each Line With lets you choose the prefix character.

Mark My Comments With. When you're replying to or forwarding a message with the original message included, you might want to stick comments into the middle of the original message text. When you do, Outlook inserts a label that identifies you as the commentator. The label looks something like this:

> *[Alan Neibauer]*

You can change the name that appears in the comment label by changing the name in the Mark My Comments With box. If you don't want your comments labeled, clear this check box.

▶ NOTE

If you are using the Internet Only setup, you can also choose Automatically Put People I Reply To In and then choose a folder (usually your Contacts folder) for automatically recording the addresses of people to whom you reply.

Advanced E-mail Options

Click the Advanced E-mail Options button in the E-mail Options dialog box and the Advanced E-mail Options dialog box will open, giving you four more categories of settings, as shown in Figure 3-3.

Save Messages

The options in the Save Messages section control how your messages are saved.

Save Unsent Items In.   By default, when you choose Save from the File menu while composing a message, the unsent message is stored in the Drafts folder. You can choose another folder here, such as the Inbox.

AutoSave Unsent Every.   Select this check box to automatically save unsent messages at the number of minutes you specify. Clear this check box if you don't want to use the AutoSave feature.

In Folders Other Than The Inbox, Save Replies With Original Message.   If you select this check box, when you reply to a message from any folder other than the Inbox, your replies will be stored in the folder from which you're replying. If you sort your mail into various folders by sender or subject, you might find it useful to also keep the replies you write in these same folders.

Save Forwarded Messages.   Select this check box to save messages that are forwarded. Clear this check box if you don't need to save copies of forwarded messages.

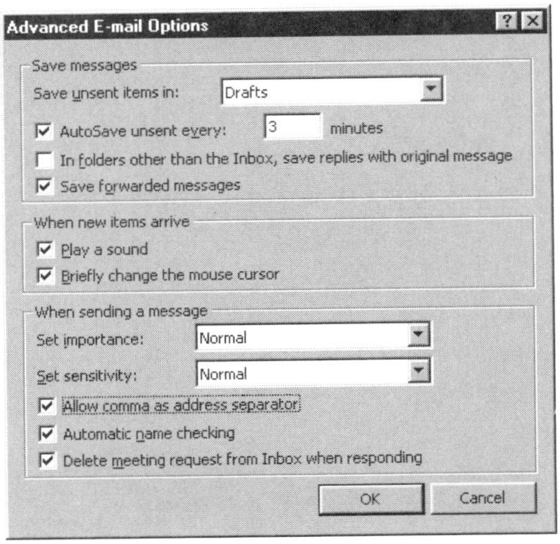

FIGURE 3-3.

The Advanced E-mail Options dialog box.

When New Items Arrive

You can choose how (and whether) you want Outlook to notify you when a new message arrives in your inbox.

Play A Sound. Select this check box to hear a beep when new messages arrive. (It is selected by default.) If you have a sound card installed in your computer, you can set the new-message sound to any .wav file. Open Sounds in the Control Panel and set the New Mail Notification item to the file you want played when your mail arrives. Clear this check box to receive your mail silently.

Briefly Change The Mouse Cursor. Select this check box to see the mouse pointer change briefly to an envelope when new messages arrive. (This check box is selected by default.)

When Sending A Message

Use the settings in the When Sending A Message section to control how your messages are sent.

Set Importance. Use this option to set the priority for your messages. Most messages you send are of normal importance. (Outlook uses Normal as the standard setting.) If all or most of your messages require top priority, select High from the drop-down list. Or, if all or most of your messages can be read at any time without compromising your work or the recipient's work, select Low.

A message that you send with High importance displays a red exclamation mark to the left of its envelope in the message list; a message with Low importance displays a blue downward-pointing arrow. Your e-mail administrator might have set up your e-mail server to deliver messages sent with High importance faster than those sent with Normal or Low importance.

Set Sensitivity. Use this option to specify the nature of your messages. Most messages you send are not particularly sensitive. (Normal is the standard sensitivity setting in Outlook.) If a message requires a different level of sensitivity, you have three other choices: Personal, Private, or Confidential.

- The Personal setting displays the word *Personal* in the Sensitivity column of the message list.

- The Private setting displays the word *Private* in the Sensitivity column of the message list. This option prohibits recipients from changing your original message when they reply to it or forward it.

■ The Confidential setting displays the word *Confidential* in the Sensitivity column of the message list. Confidential sensitivity notifies the recipient that the message should be treated according to the policies about confidentiality that your organization has set up.

> The Sensitivity column is not displayed in the message list by default. *To select which columns are displayed, see "Adding Columns from the Field Chooser," on page 544.*

Allow Comma As Address Separator.   When this check box is selected (as it is initially), names in the To, Cc, and Bcc boxes of a message header can be separated with a comma as well as a semicolon.

Automatic Name Checking.   When this check box is selected, Outlook checks the names in the To, Cc, and Bcc boxes of a message header against your address books. If a name doesn't appear in at least one of your address books, Outlook marks the name with a wavy red underline. You can ignore this underline as long as you're sure that the e-mail address is correct. You can also use the underline as a signal for you to add the name to your personal address book. If you find the underline annoying, you can clear the check box. You can then check a name manually when you want, either by clicking the Check Names button on the Standard toolbar or by pressing Alt+K.

Delete Meeting Request From Inbox When Responding.   When this check box is selected, Outlook will delete a meeting request from your inbox after you send a response to it; if you accept the meeting request, Outlook will also enter the meeting in your calendar.

This completes our survey of the Advanced E-mail Options dialog box. When you've made your selections, click OK to return to the E-mail Options dialog box.

Tracking Options

If it's important that most of your messages be received and read right away—or if you would at least like to have a record of when most of your messages were received and read—you can turn on Outlook's tracking options. If you need this information only for specific messages, you can adjust the tracking options in the Properties dialog box of the message or on the Message Options dialog box. To make these settings for all messages, click the Tracking Options button on the E-mail Options dialog box to display the Tracking Options dialog box, shown in Figure 3-4.

The first section of this dialog box applies to messages traveling over a network as well as Internet mail systems that support receipts.

Process Requests And Responses On Arrival. Leave this check box selected to have Outlook automatically process all message requests and responses.

Process Receipts On Arrival. If the sender of a message has asked for a receipt when you receive the message, leave this check box selected so Outlook automatically returns a received receipt.

After Processing, Move Receipts To. Select the folder to place delivery and other receipts after they have been processed.

Delete Blank Voting And Meeting Responses After Processing. If recipients of your meeting or voting requests respond without further comments for you to read, selecting this check box moves their response messages to the Deleted Items folder after the response is tracked and processed.

Request A Read Receipt For All Messages I Send. If you want to know when a recipient has opened your message, select this check box. Outlook will send a notification to your inbox of the date and time the recipient opened your message.

Request A Delivery Receipt For All Messages I Send. If you like to know when messages have been delivered to the recipients, select this check box. When your message arrives in the recipient's mailbox,

FIGURE 3-4.
The Tracking Options dialog box.

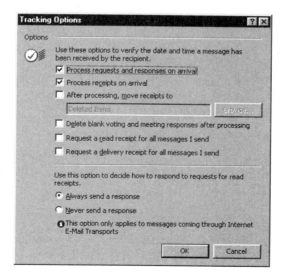

Outlook delivers a message to your inbox indicating the date and time the message was received.

Not all Internet Service Providers provide delivery and read receipts.

The second section of this dialog box applies to mail you receive from others with receipt requests attached. It only applies to messages you receive over the Internet, and it only functions if the ISP supports this feature.

Always Send A Response. Directs your mail server to send a read response when you retrieve your messages.

Never Send A Response. Directs your mail server not to send a read response.

If you are using the Internet Only setup, you can also choose Ask Me Before Sending A Response to control when receipts are sent.

Setting Calendar Options

The Calendar section of the Preferences tab of the Options dialog box lets you set up the calendar work week, your working hours, the standard reminder time for appointments, the font for dates, and the display of week numbers. You can also designate which calendar file to use, choose a time zone, add holidays to your calendar, and adjust some advanced scheduling options.

When you've set up an appointment, Outlook sends you a reminder before the appointment's start time. By default, Outlook reminds you fifteen minutes beforehand. To change this lead time for your reminder, select a preset time from the drop-down list next to the Default Reminder check box or type in the specific number of minutes you prefer. You have a wide range of choices, from a few minutes to several hours or even two days. You can turn off reminders by clearing the Default Reminder check box.

To set the other Calendar options, click the Calendar Options button to display the dialog box shown in Figure 3-5.

Calendar Work Week

You can specify your standard work week schedule for your Outlook calendar. You can indicate which days of the week you work, the first workday of the week, and the first workday of a new year.

FIGURE 3-5.
The Calendar Options
dialog box.

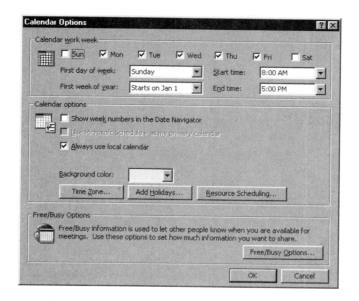

Workdays. By default, Outlook's calendar sets up Monday through Friday as standard workdays. If your workdays are different, you can simply select the check boxes for the days that reflect your own workweek.

First Day Of Week. Outlook also initially designates Sunday as the first day of a full week, although you can change this by selecting a day from this drop-down list. (In some European countries, for example, Monday is considered the first day of the week.)

First Week Of Year. This option allows you to specify exactly when your work calendar starts a new year: January 1, the first four-day week in January, or the first full (five-day) week in January.

Start Time and End Time. A workday can start at various hours. Many people start at 8:00 AM, others at 9:00 AM. My father started work at 4:30 AM. Flextime systems in modern companies can mean that individuals start work at various times during the day. You can set the start time and end time for your own workday so that your calendar can indicate to others the timeframe in which you might be available for meetings. You can open the Start Time and End Time lists to set hours and half-hours throughout the entire day, or you can set custom times (for example, 8:45 AM or 9:10 PM) by typing them in the boxes.

Calendar Options

The options and buttons in the Calendar Options section control a variety of settings for working with your calendar in Outlook.

Show Week Numbers In The Date Navigator. Select this check box to number the weeks from 1 to 52 in the calendar.

Use Microsoft Schedule+ As My Primary Calendar. If you are switching to Outlook from Microsoft Schedule+ and you still need to use Schedule+ because some members of your organization haven't yet switched to Outlook, select this check box. Outlook displays the appointments, tasks, and events that you set up in Schedule+, but it doesn't include your contacts. When this check box is selected, people who are still using Schedule+ can see your appointment schedule when they're trying to arrange a meeting.

> If you choose to use Microsoft Schedule+, you cannot use the Outlook Contacts folder as an address book. *See the sidebar "Why Isn't the Show This Folder Check Box Available?" on page 538.*

Always Use Local Calendar. Leave this check box selected to use the local calendar for Outlook events. This option is unavailable in the Internet Only installation.

> If you are using the Internet Only setup, you will see the additional option Send Meeting Requests Using iCalendar By Default. This lets you share meeting schedules and requests over the Internet rather than over a local area network running Microsoft Exchange Server.

Background Color. This setting determines the background color for work hours in the calendar.

Time Zone. Many people travel with their computers all the time. When you're on the road in another time zone, it's convenient to have that time zone's clock visible so that you can set appointments and task times to fit your location. Outlook gives you the means to set your current time zone and to show a second time zone. You can just swap the two zones when you travel from one to the other. Click the Time Zone button on the Calendar tab to open the Time Zone dialog box, shown in Figure 3-6.

- In the Time Zone dialog box, select your current time zone from the drop-down list in the Time Zone box. In the Label box, type a label that represents the time zone; for example, you might use PT for Pacific Time, or you might want to enter the name of the city. This label will appear above the time slots adjacent to the appointment slots on your calendar. If you want Windows to

FIGURE 3-6.
The Time Zone dialog box.

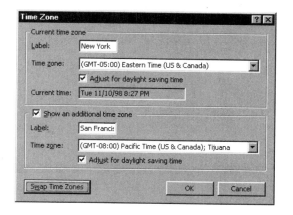

automatically adjust your computer clock and your calendar when daylight saving time begins and ends, leave the Adjust For Daylight Saving Time check box selected.

■ When you travel to another time zone and plan to use your calendar there, you can set up a second time zone for the calendar. To set it up, select the Show An Additional Time Zone check box and complete the Label and Time Zone boxes just as you did for your current time zone. On your calendar, time slots for this second time zone will appear to the left of the time slots for the current time zone.

■ When you move into the second time zone and it becomes your current time zone, you can swap the zones. To do this, simply click the Swap Time Zones button. When you return home and want to switch back, click the Swap Time Zones button again. When you swap time zones, the time slots for the current time zone move next to the appointment slots on your calendar. You can turn off the display of the second time zone by clearing the Show An Additional Time Zone check box in the Time Zone dialog box.

Add Holidays.   The Calendar Options section also contains a button named Add Holidays. The Outlook calendar is initially set up to indicate the holidays observed in the country for which your computer is set up. If you also observe (or simply want to be informed about) holidays in other countries, click the Add Holidays button. From the Add Holidays To Calendar dialog box, select the check boxes for those countries or religions whose holidays should appear on your calendar. Adding holidays for other countries makes particularly good sense if you do any business internationally—this way, you'll know when businesses in other nations are likely to be closed.

Resource Scheduling. The Calendar Options section also contains the Resource Scheduling button, which sets up how Outlook should process meeting requests that are sent to you. You can choose to automatically accept meeting requests and process cancellations, decline requests that conflict with your calendar, and decline recurring meeting requests.

You can also give other users permission to view and edit your calendar, and to schedule resources, even when you are working offline.

You must also give other users permission to view and edit your calendar for the above features to work while you're offline. To do this, click the Set Permissions button. When the Calendar Properties dialog box opens, click the Permissions tab and add the names of those people who should have access to your calendar for scheduling purposes.

Free/Busy Options

The Free/Busy Options section of the Calendar Options dialog box lets you inform other people when you have time available for meetings. Click the Free/Busy Options button to determine just how much information about your schedule you want to provide. You'll see the dialog box shown in Figure 3-7.

Set the number of months of your calendar to publish on the network and set the interval at which the information is updated on the network.

 NOTE

You can also designate a Web site to use for storing your Free/Busy information and another Web site to search for the Free/Busy information of other users.

FIGURE 3-7.
The Free/Busy Options dialog box.

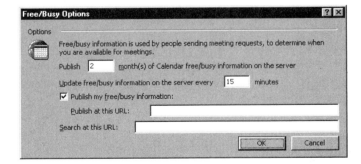

Settings Tasks Options

The Tasks section of the Preferences tab of the Options dialog box provides settings for task reminders. Outlook will remind you of your tasks for the day at the time you select.

Click the Tasks Options button to choose the display colors for overdue and completed tasks.

Setting Contact Options

When you enter the name of a contact in the Contacts folder, Outlook records the name in two ways. It displays the contact's full name in First Middle Last order, but it organizes the names in the folder in Last, First order.

To change how full names are displayed by default and how contacts are organized, click the Contact Options button on the Preferences tab. In the dialog box that appears, you can select a Full Name and a File As choice.

Setting Journal Options

Outlook can be set up to record journal entries each time you create, open, close, or save any Microsoft Office file (a file created in Microsoft Access, Microsoft Excel, Microsoft Office Binder, Microsoft PowerPoint, or Microsoft Word). Click the Journal Options button on the Preferences tab of the Options dialog box to determine which activities you want to record in your journal. The Journal Options dialog box appears, as shown in Figure 3-8.

FIGURE 3-8.
The Journal Options dialog box.

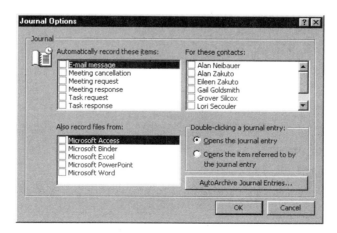

Automatically Record These Items. Select the appropriate check boxes to have Outlook automatically record journal entries for e-mail messages, meeting cancellations, meeting requests, meeting responses, task requests, and task responses that are sent to or received from the contacts you select in the For These Contacts list.

For These Contacts. The items that you selected to be recorded automatically will only be recorded if they were sent to or received from contacts selected in this section. So select the check box for each contact for whom you want to record these items. This list includes only the names listed in your Contacts folder. If you have no contacts set up, this list is empty. If a name you want to select is not listed, click OK in the Options dialog box, add the new contact, and then return to this dialog box.

Also Record Files From. Decide for which Office programs you want to record file actions (creating, opening, closing, and saving a file) and clear the check boxes of those you don't want to record. Other programs that are compatible with Microsoft Office might also appear in this list.

Double-Clicking A Journal Entry. Select what should happen when you double-click a journal entry. Outlook can either open the journal entry form itself or open the item associated with the entry (an e-mail message, a PowerPoint file, and so on). The setting you choose here for the double-click action also determines what is opened when you choose Open from the File menu in the Journal folder window, when you right-click a journal entry and choose Open from the shortcut menu, and when you press Ctrl+O.

AutoArchive Journal Entries. Click this button to open the Journal Properties dialog box, and then click the AutoArchive tab where you can change AutoArchive settings. *For details, see Chapter 18, "Archiving Folder Items."*

Setting Notes Options

Click the Note Options button on the Preferences tab of the Options dialog box to establish the format you prefer to use for new notes.

Color. Set the color of new notes in this box. Your choices are Blue, Green, Pink, Yellow (the standard color), and White.

Size. Select the standard size for notes in this box. Your choices are Small, Medium, and Large.

Font. To change the font for the text of notes, click this button to open the Font dialog box, where you can adjust the settings to your preference.

Using the Mail Services Tab

The Mail Services tab of the Options dialog box, shown in Figure 3-9, lets you choose profiles and fine-tune your profile mail services.

Selecting a Startup Profile

The options in the Startup Settings area of the Mail Services tab let you control which profile Outlook will use when it starts.

(?) SEE ALSO

For more details about profiles, see "Logging On to the Network," on page 26, and "Developing Your Profile," on page 6.

Prompt For A Profile To Be Used. If you switch between two or more profiles because you connect to several online services, or if you travel with your computer and you sometimes connect to your e-mail server from a remote site, you might want to select the Prompt For A Profile To Be Used option. When this option is selected, Outlook displays the Choose Profile dialog box each time it starts, allowing you to select the profile you want to use for the current session.

Always Use This Profile. If you use only one profile, select the Always Use This Profile option, and then select the profile name from the list next to the label. This option is most useful when your computer is always in one place and you always use the same profile.

FIGURE 3-9.

The Mail Services tab of the Options dialog box.

Setting Mail Options

If you have more than one mail service set up, you can determine which to check for new mail by default. In the Mail Options section of

---

Internet Only Mail Delivery Options

If you are using the Internet Only setup, you will see the Mail Delivery tab instead of the Mail Services tab, with a set of options designed especially for Internet mail access.

The Accounts button opens a dialog box in which you can set up and edit your Internet accounts.

The following Mail Account options control when your messages are sent and received:

- **Send Messages Immediately When Connected.** Select this check box to transmit your mail as soon as you click Send.

- **Check For New Messages Every __ Minutes.** Select this check box to determine the intervals at which Outlook will check your ISP accounts to determine whether any new mail has been received.

The following Dial-Up options determine how Outlook connects to your mail accounts:

- **Warn Before Switching Dial-Up Connection.** Select this check box to be asked before Outlook disconnects from one dial-up account and dials another, which might be necessary when you have more than one ISP account from which you're gathering mail.

- **Hang Up When Finished Sending, Receiving, Or Updating.** Select this check box to disconnect from your ISP automatically, usually after dialing in automatically.

- **Automatically Dial When Checking For New Messages.** Select this check box to have Outlook connect to the ISP when checking for new mail without asking for confirmation from you. Use this to update your mail periodically even when you're away from your computer. Be sure to also set the previous command to disconnect automatically after each dialup.

- **Don't Download Messages Larger Than __ KB.** This check box lets you set a maximum message size, above which the messages are not downloaded (but are left on the server so you can download them later if you want).

The Reconfigure Mail Support button lets you switch Outlook to the Corporate/Workgroup setup.

the Mail Services tab, select the check box for each service that you want Outlook to check for messages.

Synchronizing Folders

If you want to access your Exchange Server Outlook information when the network is down or when you're traveling, you can create offline folders (before you disconnect from the server). Offline folders store a copy of your messages and appointments on your local computer. To ensure that your offline folders have the latest information from the server, and vice versa, you must regularly *synchronize* the folders when you are online, either over a network or over a telephone line. During synchronization, Outlook exchanges the data between the server and your offline folders so that both have the most current information.

SEE ALSO

For details about synchronizing offline folders, see "Synchronizing Folders," on page 283.

In the Mail Services tab, select the Enable Offline Access check box to activate the capability to synchronize folders. Clear this check box only if you prefer to manually synchronize your offline folders (with the Synchronize command on the Tools menu) while you're online. You can synchronize folders manually any time you're online, even if this check box is selected, by choosing Synchronize from the Tools menu.

If you select When Online, Synchronize All Folders Upon Exiting, Outlook synchronizes all your offline folders with your server folders when you exit Outlook. This way, your offline folders are consistent with your online folders when you start to work offline.

The remaining two options set up Outlook to synchronize your folders at intervals you choose, both online and offline. When you select the offline option, Outlook will attempt to connect to the server at the interval you choose and synchronize the folders.

The Offline Folder Settings button lets you choose which folders you want to use offline and create smaller groups of offline folders for faster synchronizing. You'll learn more about these options in Chapter 9, "Using Outlook Remotely and Offline."

Reconfiguring Mail Support

Click the Reconfigure Mail Support button on the Mail Services tab to change the e-mail service you selected when setting up or first starting Outlook.

Using the Mail Format Tab

On the Mail Format tab of the Options dialog box, shown in Figure 3-10, you select the format for your messages. You can also choose to use Microsoft Word as your e-mail editor, which means you'll have available all of Word's formatting capabilities to create attractive-looking messages.

Selecting a Message Format

In the Message Format section of the Mail Format tab, the Send In This Message Format list lets you choose the default format for your mail messages. You can select either HTML or Microsoft Outlook Rich Text to send formatted documents, or Plain Text for messages without formatting. Select HTML to send messages to a wide variety of users, complete with fonts, colors, and other decorative features. Select Rich Text to provide a lesser degree of formatting in e-mail messages for recipients whose e-mail software can't read HTML. Also select Rich Text for sending meeting requests or task assignments over a Microsoft Exchange Server network. Choose Plain Text if you know your recipient's e-mail system cannot accept formatted messages.

> When sending replies, Outlook always uses the format of the original message to ensure that the reply can be read when received.

Once you select the default format, choose the message editor. The editor determines the options that will be available when you create a message. Select the Use Microsoft Word To Edit E-mail Messages check

FIGURE 3-10.
The Mail Format tab of the Options dialog box.

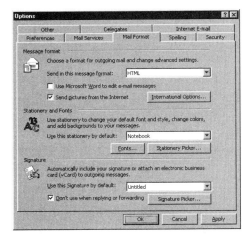

box to use Word as your editor. When you create a message, Windows launches Word and displays a message window with the same toolbars and menu options available in Word itself. You can then use tables, formulas, fields, and Word's wealth of formatting features. However, the Send In This Message Format option determines what formatting is actually sent with the message. If you choose Plain Text, for example, fonts and other formatting you applied in Word will not be sent with the message, even though the formatting appears when you compose your e-mail message.

If you clear this check box, you can still create attractive formatted messages when not using Plain Text, but with fewer options.

> **NOTE**

> You can also choose to use Microsoft Word for individual messages, rather than as the default. *You'll learn more about this in Chapter 5, "Sending and Receiving Messages."*

If you select HTML format, you can also choose Send Pictures From The Internet. If the check box is selected, pictures or graphics you place in your mail that are links to images on the Internet or a corporate intranet will be sent as links, making your mail messages smaller and faster to send. But if your recipient doesn't have access to the Internet or your corporate intranet, you should clear this check box; then the graphics will be included in the mail message, making the message larger but complete within itself.

Click the International Options button to choose character sets for foreign-language messages. The International Options dialog box includes the Use English For Message Headers option. If you're using a version of Outlook for a language other than English, selecting this option directs Outlook to translate the labels in the message header (To, Subject, From, and Sent) into English. You'd want to select this check box only if you are sure that all the recipients of your messages read English. Clear this check box to keep message header labels in the language of the version of Outlook you're using.

Selecting Templates, Stationery, and Fonts

The second set of options on the Mail Format tab let you select the default font or page design for new messages. The options shown depend on the message format you've selected and whether you use Word as the e-mail editor. In fact, when you use Word as the e-mail editor, you do all of your formatting from within Word—all of the options in the dialog box are unavailable. If you select the HTML format and choose not to use Word as the editor, you can choose Font and Stationery options. If you choose Plain Text or Microsoft Outlook Rich Text Format, only the Fonts button will be available.

Fonts

To select a default font for all new messages, click the Fonts button. In the dialog box that appears, you can choose a font for new messages, replies, forwarded messages, and plain text messages. You can also choose to use your selected font rather than stationery fonts when using a stationery design.

Stationery

Stationery in Outlook, like paper stationery, is a preformatted design consisting of a background picture and perhaps a special design, font, and text. Figure 3-11, for example, shows a message using the Baby News stationery. Outlook includes a number of attractive stationery designs, and you can also create your own.

> You can also choose to use stationery for individual messages, rather than as the default. *You'll learn more about this in Chapter 5, "Sending and Receiving Messages."*

To choose a stationery to use for all new messages, make your selection from the Use This Stationery By Default list. To use no stationery

FIGURE 3-11.
A message using the Baby News stationery.

and start with a blank message, select <None>. The Stationery Picker button lets you create and edit stationery designs.

Attaching a Signature

A signature is a standard closing that you can attach to your messages. You can also attach a *vCard*, a special attachment that contains information from your address book listing. After you create one or more signature files, select the file to use for all messages from the Use This Signature By Default list. You create and modify signature files using the Signature Picker. You can only use the Signature options in this dialog box when you are not using Word as your e-mail editor. *Word has its own signature feature, which you'll learn about in Chapter 5.*

Using the Internet E-mail Tab

The Internet E-mail tab of the Options dialog box, shown in Figure 3-12, lets you control the encoding style for mail you send over the Internet and how Outlook checks for new Internet mail.

Mail you send over the Internet must be *encoded*—converted to a format that the various computers that make up the Internet can handle. You can select from two formats: MIME (Multipurpose Internet Mail Extensions) and uuencode (UNIX-to-UNIX encoding).

If you choose MIME, you can select to actually use no encoding, Quoted Printable, or Base64. In most cases you can choose MIME with its default settings. MIME is widely used, feature-rich, and compatible with most mail readers. Uuencode might be preferable if you communicate with people using a text-based mail program on the UNIX

FIGURE 3-12.

The Internet E-mail tab of the Options dialog box.

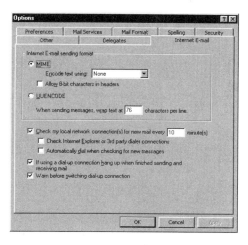

platform or any text-based program that doesn't support MIME. You can also choose to include certain characters in headers without encoding them.

The When Sending Messages Wrap Text At __ Characters Per Line option sets the length of lines. Some older e-mail systems cannot handle lines that are over 80 characters. Setting lines at between 72 and 76 characters allows room for indentations and prefix characters.

Selecting the Check My Local Network Connection For New Mail Every __ Minute(s) check box will check your mail server for new mail at regular intervals.

If you connect to the Internet through a modem, the Check Internet Explorer Or 3rd Party Dialer Connections check box will check mail using the connections already established with Internet Explorer or another browser.

You can have Outlook dial the connection if you are not already online by selecting the Automatically Dial When Checking For New Messages check box.

You can also have Outlook automatically disconnect and hang up when it has finished sending and receiving mail by selecting the If Using A Dial-Up Connection Hang Up When Finished Sending And Receiving Mail check box.

Finally, you can have Outlook ask you before it hangs up one dial-up connection to dial up another one (if you have more than one ISP account for retrieving messages) by selecting the Warn Before Switching Dial-Up Connection check box.

Using the Spelling Tab

When you check the spelling of messages, Outlook compares the words in your message text with a dictionary file. If the spelling checker can't find the word in its dictionary, it shows you the word in a dialog box and gives you a chance to correct the spelling, ignore the word (because it's a special word or a proper name), or add the word to the dictionary.

On the Spelling tab of the Options dialog box, shown in Figure 3-13, you'll find options for checking the spelling of messages and for how (and when) the check should be conducted.

FIGURE 3-13.
The Spelling tab of the
Options dialog box.

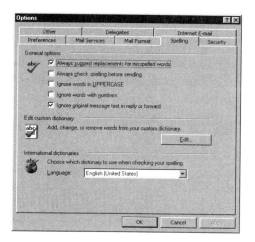

Setting General Options

By default, Outlook suggests correct spellings for misspelled words. It also checks numbers, words that include numbers, and words that are written in all capital letters, as well as any original text in replies and forwarded messages. You can ask the spelling checker to ignore any or all of these types of information in message text.

Always Suggest Replacements For Misspelled Words. If you don't want Outlook to automatically suggest correct spellings for words not included in the dictionary file it uses, clear this check box. When this check box is cleared, you must click the Suggest button in the Spelling dialog box to get a suggestion from the spelling checker. If you prefer to always have a suggestion to work from, leave this check box selected.

Always Check Spelling Before Sending. If you're someone who always likes to check spelling before sending a message, Always Check Spelling Before Sending is for you. If you select this check box, Outlook checks the spelling in your message text after you click the Send button but before the message is sent.

Ignore Words In UPPERCASE. To tell the spelling checker to ignore words that are written in all capital letters, select the Ignore Words In UPPERCASE check box. The spelling checker then ignores words such as UNIX.

Ignore Words With Numbers. To tell the spelling checker to ignore numbers, select the Ignore Words With Numbers check box. The spelling checker will then ignore words that contain a mix of numbers and letters (such as WSJ010846) and words that consist entirely of numbers (such as 123456789 or the 97 in Office 97).

Ignore Original Message Text In Reply Or Forward.   The spelling checker is set up to ignore the original text included in replies and forwarded messages. If you want Outlook to check the spelling in the original text, clear this check box.

Using a Custom Dictionary

Proper names, jargon, and technical words might be properly spelled but not found in the dictionary file. Rather than have the spelling checker report these words as possible errors, you can add them to a custom dictionary when they are first encountered.

If you click the Edit button, a Windows Notepad window opens displaying the contents of the custom dictionary, one word per line. Edit the file to add or delete words, and then choose Save from the File menu in Notepad to save your changes.

You can purchase additional dictionaries to use for checking spelling. If you have one of these dictionaries you'd like to use, choose it from the Language list in the International Dictionaries section of the Spelling tab.

Using the Delegates Tab

The Delegates tab of the Options dialog box is used to give other people permission to perform Outlook tasks on your behalf. You might assign your assistant, for example, to act as a delegate on your behalf when you are out of the office or to handle certain types of requests and actions. These options, shown in Figure 3-14, are only available when using Microsoft Exchange Server.

The Delegates box lists those people you have designated as your delegates. Use the buttons along the right side of the Delegates box to change the list or to change the types of permission you grant to a delegate.

 NOTE   You can only set the permissions for delegates if you are using your Exchange mailbox as the delivery point, not when using personal folders.

FIGURE 3-14.

The Delegates tab of the Options dialog box.

Adding Delegates

To add a delegate to your list, follow these steps:

1 Click the Add button on the Delegates tab to open the Add Users dialog box, where you can select the names of people you want to assign as delegates.

2 In the Type Name Or Select From List box of the address book, type the name of someone in your address book, or select names from the list below the box.

3 Click Add, and then click OK to open the Delegate Permissions dialog box, shown in Figure 3-15, on the following page.

4 For each folder (Calendar, Tasks, and so forth), open the list box to its right and choose permissions for that folder.

5 Select or clear the check box that determines whether your delegate receives copies of meeting requests sent to you.

6 Select or clear the check box that determines whether Outlook notifies your delegate of the permissions you granted.

7 Select or clear the check box that determines whether your delegate sees items marked private.

8 Click OK.

FIGURE 3-15.

The Delegate Permissions dialog box.

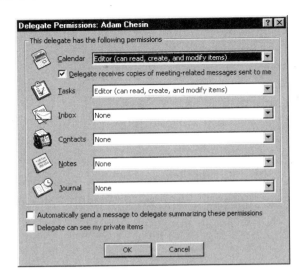

Removing Delegates

To remove a delegate from your list, simply select the name of the delegate in the Delegates box and click the Remove button. Outlook does not ask you to confirm deletion of a delegate.

Granting Permissions

When you want to change the level of permissions for a delegate, take these steps:

1 Select the name of the delegate in the Delegates box.

2 Click the Permissions button.

3 Change the permission settings in the Delegate Permissions dialog box (shown in Figure 3-15).

4 Click OK in the Delegate Permissions dialog box.

If you type or select more than one name as a delegate, the Delegate Permissions dialog box shows the phrase <Multiple Delegates> in its title bar. The permissions you set apply to all the delegates you selected. To set permissions for individuals, either add them one at a time or add them all at once and then change permissions for each one with the Permissions button. See "Granting Permissions," above.

Setting Delegate Properties

The Properties button displays the Properties dialog box for the name you select in the Delegates box. The Properties dialog box shows address book information, such as the delegate's e-mail name, title, and so on.

Sending Requests Only to Your Delegate

If you have arranged for a delegate to keep track of your calendar, you can take yourself off the meeting-request-and-response carousel. To set this up, take these steps:

1 In the Delegate Permissions dialog box, give the delegate you have chosen to take care of your calendar Editor permission for your Calendar folder.

2 Select the Delegate Receives Copies Of Meeting-Related Messages Sent To Me check box.

3 Click OK in the Delegate Permissions dialog box.

4 On the Delegates tab, select the Send Meeting Requests And Responses Only To My Delegates, Not To Me check box.

Using the Security Tab

(?) SEE ALSO

For information about installing add-ins, see "Add-In Manager," on page 103.

On the Security tab of the Options dialog box, shown in Figure 3-16, you'll find options for encrypting your messages, adding your digital signature to messages, setting your security file, changing your security password, setting up advanced security, logging off advanced security, and sending security keys. Security provides a layer of protection for your messages.

There are two levels of protection, as follows:

■ Encryption ensures that only someone who logs on to the e-mail server as a valid recipient can read your message. Without encryption, your messages are sent as readable text.

■ A digital signature assures the recipient that you are really the person who sent the message—in other words, that the message is not some bogus transmission sent by a pernicious computer hacker—and that the message has not been altered along the way.

FIGURE 3-16.

The Security tab of the Options dialog box.

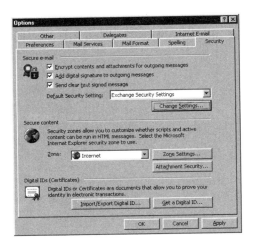

In order to use these features, however, you must have a security certificate that verifies who you are to others. There are two types of certificates available in Outlook—an Exchange certificate to use over the network and a S/MIME certificate that you use over the Internet.

Getting a Digital Certificate

To get a digital certificate, follow these steps:

1 Choose Options from the Tools menu, and click the Security tab.

2 Click Get A Digital ID.

3 If you're not connected to a security-enabled Exchange Server network, you can only obtain a digital ID over the Internet. Clicking Get A Digital ID will launch your Web browser and connect you to a site that provides information on security certificates. In this case, skip ahead to "S/MIME Internet Security," opposite.

4 If the Get A Digital ID dialog box appears, choose Get A S/MIME Certificate From An External Certifying Authority if you want to get a security certificate for use over the Internet. Select Set Up Security For Me On The Exchange Server if you want an Exchange Key Management Server to assign you a digital ID.

Exchange Server Security

To get an exchange certificate, your network administrator must have security running on the server and must give you a special password, called a *token*. When you chose Exchange security in step 4 above, the Set Up Advanced Security dialog box should have appeared. Now follow these steps:

1 Type the token given to you by the network administrator in the Token text box.

2 Accept your keyset name if it appears, or correct it if necessary in the Keyset Name box.

3 Click OK to close the Setup Advanced Security dialog box and process your request for a digital ID.

4 When a message appears telling you that your request for security has been sent to your Exchange server, click OK.

5 Click OK again on the Security tab.

In a few moments (depending on how busy the server is), your Exchange server will send you an e-mail message verifying your token. When you open the message, a dialog box appears reporting that Outlook is writing the Exchange signing key to your system. Click OK to display a box reporting that Outlook is writing the encryption key to your system. Click OK again. The message appears reporting that you are now security enabled. This means that the certificate has been added to Outlook and you now send and receive encrypted and digitally signed messages.

 NOTE

> Once you enroll in Exchange security you do not have to do it again, unless you are notified by your system administrator to enroll with a new token.

S/MIME Internet Security

To use Internet security, known as S/MIME, you have to get a certificate from a third-party company by registering on their Web site. Most companies charge a small fee for their certificate services, although many offer a free trial period.

When you select Get A S/MIME Certificate From An External Authority in the Get A Digital ID dialog box, Outlook launches your Web browser and connects you to the appropriate site. Follow the instructions on the screen to apply for a digital certificate. In most cases, after you apply you'll be notified by e-mail that your certificate is ready and you'll have to connect to a Web site to accept it. When the site verifies your certificate, it will download and install it on your system so you are ready to send and receive secure messages.

Changing Security Settings

If you are on a network and connected to the Internet, you can have both types of security certificates. In the Security tab of the Options dialog box, choose the setting to use as the default from the Default Security Setting list.

If security is not yet set up for you, click the Setup Secure E-mail button on the Security tab of the Options dialog box to open the Change Security Settings dialog box, shown in Figure 3-17. Once security is set up, the button is labeled Change Settings. Use it to adjust the settings if you have problems using security procedures. Generally, the settings in the Security Settings Name and Secure Message Format boxes should match. That is, if you are using the Exchange security setting you should also use the Exchange secure message format.

The following options in the Change Security Settings dialog box determine when each type of security is used:

Default Security Setting For This Secure Message Format. If you select this check box, these settings will be used by default for the format listed above in the Secure Message Format text box. If you chose the S/MIME format, for example, the settings will be used when you send a secure message using S/MIME. Select this check box if you want to use different settings when sending S/MIME and Exchange Security secure messages.

FIGURE 3-17.
The Change Security Settings dialog box.

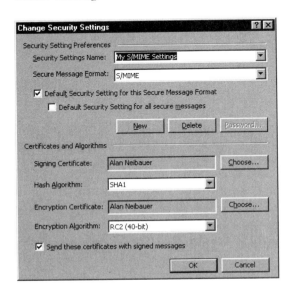

Default Security Setting For All Secure Messages. Selecting this check box will apply these settings to all types of secure messages.

Send These Certificates With Signed Messages. Choose this option to send a copy of your certificate with secure messages. The recipient will be able to use the certificate to send you encrypted messages. You cannot clear this check box when using Exchange Server security.

> You can obtain more than one certificate. Click the Choose buttons in the Change Security Settings dialog box to select the certificate to use for your digital signature and for encrypted messages. You can also click the Choose buttons to display information about the certificate.

Securing Contents

E-mail messages using HTML formatting can also contain *active content*—elements that have the potential to run programs and perform operations on your computer. While it is unlikely that you will receive such a message, it pays to be careful. The Zone setting in the Secure Content area of the Security tab lets you control how active content is handled in both e-mail messages and attachments.

Selecting and Changing Zones

You can select from four zones: Internet, Local Intranet, Trusted Sites, and Restricted Sites. The Internet and Local Intranet zones offer a medium level of security that will warn you before active content is accepted and run. The Trusted Sites zone offers a low level of security and assumes that the sites are trusted to have proper content. The Restricted Sites zone offers a high level of security that simply excludes any active content. To change the degree of security in a zone, click the Zone Settings button to see the dialog box shown below, and then follow these steps:

1 Choose the zone you want to change.

2 If your choice is not Internet, click Sites and designate the sites that are trusted or to be restricted or specify how to deal with intranet sites.

3 Slide the bar to set the security level.

4 Click OK.

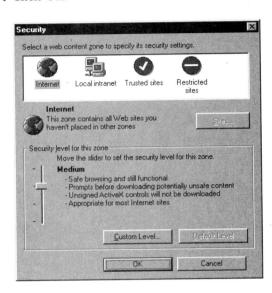

If you choose the Custom level of security, you can then click Settings and choose to enable, disable, or warn for each of a list of specific types of content.

Securing Attachments

Active content can also be found in message attachments. Again, it is highly unlikely that you will receive an attachment with dangerous content, but by default, you will be warned of the potential problem when you save or open some attachments. If you do not want to receive this warning, click the Attachment Security button on the Security tab of the Options dialog box, choose None in the dialog box that appears, and then click OK.

Exporting and Importing Digital IDs

Security certificates are stored on your computer's hard disk. You can make a copy of the certificate on a floppy disk to transfer it to another computer, or as a backup in the event the security file becomes damaged. For example, suppose you use different computers at home and at the office. If you downloaded your S/MIME certificate at the office, you can make a copy of it to use at home.

To save your certificate, follow these steps:

1 Click Import/Export Digital ID on the Security tab of the Options dialog box.

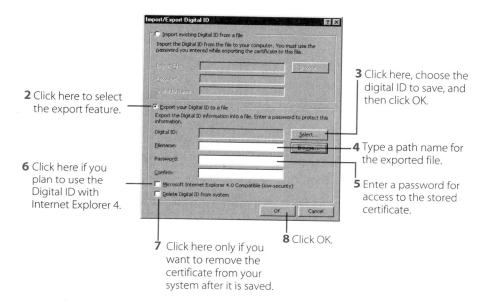

2 Click here to select the export feature.

3 Click here, choose the digital ID to save, and then click OK.

6 Click here if you plan to use the Digital ID with Internet Explorer 4.

4 Type a path name for the exported file.

5 Enter a password for access to the stored certificate.

7 Click here only if you want to remove the certificate from your system after it is saved.

8 Click OK.

If you later need to restore the saved digital ID, choose Import Existing Exchange Or S/MIME Security Information at the top of this dialog box. Enter the path and name of the file to import, the password you saved it with, and the keyset if you are importing an Exchange certificate, and then click OK.

Using Security

To use security with all messages, select the encryption and digital signature check boxes on the Security tab of the Options dialog box.

- Select the Encrypt Contents And Attachments For Outgoing Messages check box to encrypt your messages. Without encryption, your messages are sent as readable text.

- Select the Add Digital Signature To Outgoing Messages check box to add a digital signature to each message you send so your recipient can be sure that the message originated from you.

■ Select the Send Clear Text Signed Message check box if you want recipients who cannot read S/MIME signatures to be permitted to read your message.

? SEE ALSO

You'll learn more about sending and receiving secure messages in Chapter 5, "Sending and Receiving Messages."

You can, of course, clear the encryption and digital signature check boxes on the Security tab, as explained earlier. If you do so, you can encrypt a single message or add your digital signature to a single message by clicking the Options button on the Standard toolbar when composing a message, and then selecting the Encrypt Contents And Attachments check box or the Add Digital Signature To Outgoing Message check box. You can also clear these check boxes to turn off security for an individual message.

When you are sending an encrypted message over the Internet, you must have the recipient's public key stored with his or her address in your address book. If you do not have this information, or if a Microsoft Exchange Server recipient doesn't have security set up, you'll see a message box telling you so. You then have two choices for delivering the message:

■ Click the Send Unencrypted button to send the message anyway. When encryption is turned on, this is the only way to send a message to a recipient who doesn't have advanced security.

■ Click the Cancel button if you decide not to send the message to someone who doesn't have advanced security.

Using the Other Tab

On the Other tab of the Options dialog box (shown in Figure 3-18), you'll find "other" options for how Outlook should act in general. You'll also find buttons for adding additional programs that work with Outlook and for setting the appearance and operation of the preview pane.

Select the Empty The Deleted Items Folder Upon Exiting check box if you want Outlook to empty your Deleted Items folder each time you exit Outlook. If you prefer to clear out your Deleted Items folder more selectively, be sure that this check box is cleared.

FIGURE 3-18.

The Other tab of the Options dialog box.

Setting Advanced Options

Advanced options offer additional ways to set how Outlook acts. Click the Advanced Options button in the General area of the Other tab to determine how Outlook acts on startup, to specify how notes are displayed, and to access more advanced customization features. The options are shown in Figure 3-19.

General Settings

Use this area of the Advanced Options dialog box to set some overall ways for Outlook to work. In addition to selecting which folder displays when you start Outlook, you can set the options shown on the next page.

FIGURE 3-19.

The Advanced Options dialog box.

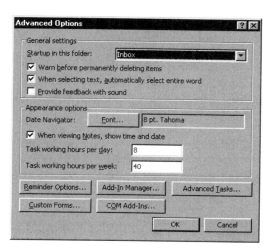

Warn Before Permanently Deleting Items. If this check box is selected, Outlook prompts you to confirm that you want to permanently delete items from the Deleted Items folder when you empty the folder or when you manually delete an item from it. (This check box is selected by default.) When you see the message, click Yes to delete the items or click No to keep the messages in your Deleted Items folder. (If your Deleted Items folder contains subfolders or remote message headers you'll see a slightly different message.) If you don't want this warning, clear this check box.

When Selecting Text, Automatically Select Entire Word. When you're editing a message and need to select text that includes a space, as soon as you select a single character beyond the space, Outlook selects the entire word. This setting can be handy if you usually select entire words. But if you need to select parts of two neighboring words, you will find this option frustrating and disruptive. If necessary, you can clear this check box to turn it off.

Provide Feedback With Sound. Select this check box if you want Outlook to produce a sound for such actions as deleting a message or opening a file. If you don't have a sound card in your computer, the sound will be a simple beep. If you have a sound card, you can set the sound for each action by selecting the .wav file you want Outlook to play when that action occurs. You set up these sounds through the Sounds icon in the Windows Control Panel.

Appearance Options

Use these settings to control some aspects of the Outlook display.

Date Navigator. Choose the font to use with monthly calendars in the Calendar folder.

When Viewing Notes, Show Time And Date. Select this check box to display the time and date with notes in the Notes folder.

Task Working Hours Per Day. Set the number of working hours per day to use for tasks.

Task Working Hours Per Week. Set the number of working hours per week to use for tasks.

Reminder Options

Click the Reminder Options button in the Advanced Options dialog box to set how Outlook should notify you when a reminder you've set for a task or an appointment comes due. The options are as follows:

Display The Reminder. Select this check box to have Outlook display a reminder message. When the reminder appears, you can close it if you don't need further reminding, you can reset the reminder to appear again after an interval you specify, or you can edit the task or appointment. *For details, see "Setting a Reminder," on page 313, and "Setting a Task Reminder," on page 375.*

Play Reminder Sound. Select this check box to have Outlook play a sound to notify you that a task or an appointment is due. If you don't have a sound card, you'll hear a beep. If you do have a sound card, you can set the reminder sound to any .wav file by typing its full pathname in this box or by clicking the Browse button to find the file.

Add-In Manager

Click the Add-In Manager button in the Advanced Options dialog box to install add-in programs, which provide additional functionality to Outlook. Outlook comes with several add-ins, sometimes called extensions, for features such as NetMeeting, Exchange, and Internet Mail. Add-ins can also be third-party programs. Some add-ins are installed when you set up Outlook. To use certain Outlook add-ins (including Digital Security over your network), you must be running Outlook with Microsoft Exchange Server. If you need to install another of Outlook's add-ins or want to use a third-party add-in, you can install it from the Add-In Manager dialog box by following these steps:

1 Clear the check boxes of add-ins you don't want to use.

2 Click Install to select additional add-ins. A typical Office installation will contain an Add-Ins folder within the Office folder, in which you might find additional add-ins.

SEE ALSO

For information about the add-ins that come with Outlook, see Outlook Help.

3 Select the add-in you want to install and choose Open. The add-in will be added to the list and the check box will be selected.

4 Click OK when finished.

Advanced Tasks

The Advanced Tasks button in the Advanced Options dialog box opens the Advanced Tasks dialog box, which contains these three settings for handling tasks:

Set Reminders On Tasks With Due Dates. Select this check box if you want Outlook to automatically issue a reminder for a task that has a due date. The reminder will appear on the due date at the time you set in the Reminder Time box. You can change the reminder date and time in the task item window.

Keep Updated Copies Of Assigned Tasks On My Task List. When you assign a task to someone else, you might want to receive updates on the task status as it changes. Select this check box to keep a copy of the task in your task list so that Outlook can update the task status as it changes.

Send Status Reports When Assigned Tasks Are Completed. When this check box is selected, you will receive a status report when the person to whom you have assigned a task marks the task as completed.

Custom Forms

SEE ALSO

For more information about creating and using forms, see Part VI, "Working with Forms."

The Custom Forms button on the Advanced Options dialog box helps you manage Outlook forms. Forms are an integral part of Outlook. You use them to send and read messages, to set and request appointments, and to respond to meeting and task requests. Every folder item window in Outlook is actually a form. In addition, Outlook provides tools for you to create custom forms. In some cases, these forms might be set up by a forms designer in your company. In other cases, you or a colleague might create a special form for your own purposes. To make forms work, you need to set aside some temporary storage space for them on your computer. Also, you can install forms that are included in form libraries to use in your work. For dealing with the necessary aspects of form life in Outlook, click the Custom Forms button to open the Custom Forms tab, shown in Figure 3-20. You can also use this tab to change your Microsoft Windows NT and Windows 2000 network

FIGURE 3-20.
The Custom Forms tab.

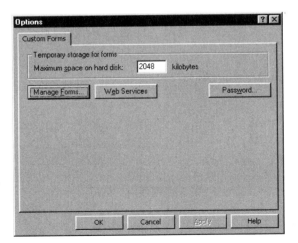

password, give permissions for other users to send your mail, and set several features of Outlook's Web services.

 NOTE

The Custom Forms option is not available with the Internet Only setup.

To prevent forms from taking up hard disk space that you need for other work, you can limit the amount of space Outlook can use for temporarily storing forms. In the Maximum Space On Hard Disk box, type a number (in kilobytes) for the amount of space you want to set aside for temporary form storage. If you use many different forms frequently and have plenty of free space on your hard disk, you might change this value to a higher number. Otherwise, the default setting (which depends on your system) is probably appropriate. When Outlook has filled the space you've set aside, it removes the oldest form stored in temporary storage to make room for the newest form you're using. (No forms are ever permanently deleted in this process.)

Manage Forms. Outlook downloads forms for reading messages when you need them. But when you want to use a form to send a message, you'll need to have the form installed. That's where the Manage Forms button comes into play. The Forms Manager dialog box helps you copy, update, and remove forms. To manage forms, do the following:

1 Click the Manage Forms button on the Custom Forms tab. The Forms Manager dialog box will appear, as shown in Figure 3-21.

2 Click the left Set button to add more forms.

FIGURE 3-21.
The Forms Manager dialog box.

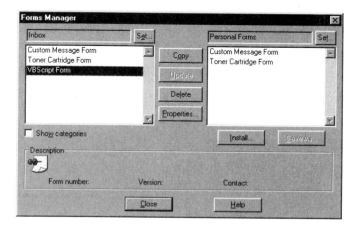

3 In the dialog box that appears, select the library that contains the forms from the Form Library list or select the folder that contains the forms from the Folder Forms Library list.

4 Click OK.

5 When you've returned to the Forms Manager dialog box, select the forms that you want to add from the list at the left.

6 If the folder shown in the text box to the right is the folder to which you want to copy the forms you've selected, proceed to step 7. Otherwise, click the right Set button and adjust the folder first.

7 Click Copy. When Outlook has finished copying the forms, their names appear in the list at the right.

8 To copy forms from other folders, repeat steps 2 through 7.

9 Click the Close button in the Forms Manager dialog box.

Web Services. Communicating over the Web offers some unique challenges because of the variety of formats available and the way information is transmitted.

Click the Web Services button on the Custom Forms tab to set these options in the Web Services dialog box:

- **Use Outlook Web Access To Open Messages Not Understood By Outlook Client.** If Outlook receives a form that it does not recognize and is not able to display, you can set Outlook to display the form in HTML format on your Web browser. When you select this check box, you have to enter the path to your Web server and specify if you want to be notified before each such form is opened.

- **Activate Web Forms Link On Actions Menu.** You can add a command to the Actions menu that jumps to a library of HTML forms. When you choose to add this command to the menu, you must specify the path to the server where the forms are stored.

Password. In some organizations, you might be required to change your password according to a certain schedule. Even if you aren't required to do this, it's a good idea to change your network password regularly, at least once every 60 days or so. Doing so helps maintain network security.

To change Your Windows NT or Windows 2000 password, click the Password button on the Custom Forms tab to open the Change Windows NT Password dialog box, and then follow these steps:

1 Type your network username in the Username box.

2 Type your network's domain name in the Domain box.

3 Type your current password in the Old Password box.

4 Type your new password in the New Password box.

5 Type the new password again in the Confirm New Password box.

6 Click OK.

COM Add-Ins

Using Outlook and other Office applications, you can develop programs of your own using such languages as Microsoft Visual Basic Script and Microsoft Visual Basic for Applications. These Component Object Module (COM) add-ins further extend the power and customization of Outlook. The COM Add-ins section of the Advanced Options dialog box lets you install such COM components.

Setting AutoArchive Options

SEE ALSO

You need to take additional steps to set up automatic archiving, especially for folders that don't contain e-mail messages. For details, see Chapter 18, "Archiving Folder Items."

E-mail and other items quickly accumulate in your folders, just as fast as paper can accumulate on your desk. The AutoArchive feature will automatically move older items to special folders so they do not clutter up the Inbox folder and other folders that you use often.

To set up the AutoArchive feature, click the AutoArchive button on the Other tab of the Options dialog box. In the AutoArchive dialog box that appears (see Figure 3-22) you set the time span between archiving, ask for a prompt when archiving starts, direct Outlook to delete items after they're archived, and set the file that you want Outlook to use for archives.

FIGURE 3-22.
The AutoArchive dialog box.

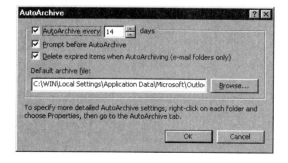

Internet Only Fax Options

The Internet Only setup installs its own fax software and service. When using this setup, you'll also see a Fax tab on the Options tab.

The options on this tab let you specify your name, company, fax telephone number, voice telephone number, and station identifier. You can also select from several sample templates to use as a cover page.

Other options let you select and configure your modem and set Outlook to automatically answer incoming calls after a specified number of rings. You can also specify whether you want Outlook to retry dialing after unsuccessfully sending a fax, as well as the number of retries and the time between each redial.

AutoArchive Every __ Days. To specify the time interval at which automatic archiving should take place, choose the number of days (1–60) in this box. Clear this check box to prevent all automatic archiving.

Prompt Before AutoArchive. Clear this check box if you don't want a prompt before the AutoArchive process begins. Otherwise, when the time period specified for AutoArchive is reached, you will see a dialog box asking if you want to AutoArchive at that time. Select Yes to archive or No to skip archiving for the time being, and if you don't want to be prompted in the future, select the check box labeled Don't Prompt Me About This Again.

Delete Expired Items When AutoArchiving (E-mail Folders Only). When this check box is selected, expired items are deleted from e-mail folders during the AutoArchive process. If you don't want items to be deleted, clear this check box.

Default Archive File. This box lists the file used to hold your archives. You can select a different file for your archives if you want. To locate or create another archive file in your file system, click the Browse button.

Setting Preview Pane Options

The preview pane is a handy area to quickly review messages. Click the Preview Pane button on the Other tab of the Options dialog box to display these options for setting the operation and appearance of the pane:

Mark Messages As Read In Preview Window. Selecting this check box will mark a message as read after it appears in the preview pane for the number of seconds you specify. When marked as read, the message will no longer be displayed in bold and it will not be counted as an unread message next to the folder display in the Folder List.

Mark Item As Read When Selection Changes.   Selecting this check box will mark a message as read when you move from it to another message.

Single Key Reading Using Space Bar.   Selecting this check box conveniently lets you use the spacebar to scroll through a message to read it and then automatically move to the next message in your list.

Preview Header.   You can choose the font used to display the text in the preview pane header, which includes such information as the From and Subject fields.

In this chapter, you learned many ways to customize the way Outlook works. You may want to wait until you've used Outlook a while before changing options so you have a better understanding of the effects of your choices. Then, take your time as you work through the Options dialog box, limiting your changes so you can better gauge Outlook's performance. In the next chapter, you'll learn how to use the Outlook Address Book in preparation for sending and receiving mail.

Using Address Books

The Address Book lets you easily address e-mail messages and other Microsoft Outlook items such as meeting and task requests. Instead of typing an address each time you want to send something you simply select it from the appropriate address list. In fact, if you're on a network, the addresses of other network users will appear in the Address Book automatically.

Network users will have more than one address list. If you are on an Exchange Server network, you'll have an address list with recipients on your domain, along with a global address list for your entire organization. On a peer-to-peer network, you have the postoffice address list of other network users. You'll also have a personal address book for e-mail addresses of people not on the network, and maybe an offline address book so you can address messages when you are not connected to the network. You'll also probably have an Outlook address book, which is created automatically from entries in your Contacts folder.

Unless you are a network administrator, however, you cannot add addresses to your domain, organization, or postoffice lists.

Opening the Address Book

Address
Book

To open the Address Book, choose Address Book from the Tools menu, press Ctrl+Shift+B, or click the Address Book button on the Standard toolbar—the button is displayed when the Inbox, Outbox, Outlook Today, Sent Items, Drafts, or other mail folder is open. The Address Book opens and displays the names from whichever address list is set up as your default.

You can change the default address list using the Services dialog box; choose Services from the Tools menu to open this dialog box. Click the Addressing tab and select the list you want to see first from the Show This Address List First list.

Figure 4-1 shows a typical Address Book window displaying names from the global address list maintained by Exchange Server for an entire organization.

Switching Address Lists

When you want to get an address to send e-mail or for another purpose, you'll have to select the relevant address list. After opening the Address Book, if the list that appears is not the one with the information you need, do the following:

1 Open the Show Names list to display the available address lists.

FIGURE 4-1.

The Address Book displaying a global address list.

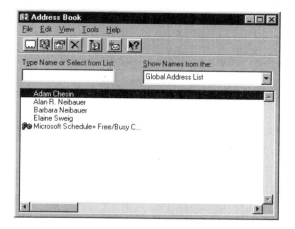

2 Select the list you want to open, as shown below. The names contained in the selected address list will then appear in the Address Book window.

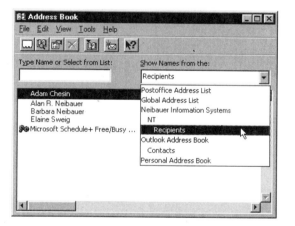

 NOTE

Select Recipients to see addresses on your local Exchange Server domain, or select Postoffice Address List for addresses on your peer-to-peer network.

Finding People

If you are on a large network, or have a lot of contacts or other addresses, finding one name in the list can be time-consuming and even tiresome. Rather than scroll through the list to locate a name (which is of course one way to do it), you can have Outlook search for a listed name for you. To find a name in an address book, take these steps:

1 Choose Address Book from the Tools menu, or click the Address Book button on the Standard toolbar.

2 In the Show Names box, select the address list you want to look in.

NOTE

Internet Only users can also locate e-mail addresses using online search directories. *See "Using E-mail Directories," on page 239.*

3 Type the beginning of the name in the Type Name Or Select From List box. Outlook highlights the first name that matches what you've started to type. If you press Enter, that person's address information will be displayed.

Adding a Personal Address Book to Your Profile

Chances are you'll already have a personal address book because it is usually created when you set up a profile. If you do not have a personal address book, however, you can add one to a profile at any time by following these steps:

1 Choose Services from the Tools menu.

2 On the Services tab, click the Add button.

3 In the Add Service To Profile dialog box, select Personal Address Book, and then click OK.

4 In the Personal Address Book dialog box, enter a name for the personal address book in the Name box.

5 In the Path box, enter the path of the personal address book file, or click the Browse button to locate a personal address book file that already exists. Personal address books are maintained in files with the .pab extension.

6 Click OK in the Personal Address Book dialog box, and then click OK again in the message box that appears.

7 Click OK in the Services dialog box, and then exit and restart Outlook.

To add a personal address book to a profile other than the one you are currently using, open the Mail icon in the Microsoft Windows Control Panel. On the Services tab, click Show Profiles. On the General tab, click the profile you want in the Profile box, click Properties, and then follow steps 2 through 7 above.

NOTE

To locate a person without first opening the Address Book, simply type the name of the person in the Find A Contact text box on the Standard toolbar and press Enter. If the name is found in any of your address lists the person's contact information will appear. If more than one name matches a partial entry you've entered, such as the first few letters of a name, the Choose Contact dialog box will open and display all the possible matches, from which you can choose the one you want. If no matches are found, a message box will tell you so.

Adding an Address

When you first start using Outlook, your address lists will include the people on your network. Because an ever-increasing number of people around the world now use e-mail regularly, you'll develop "pen pals" as well as professional contacts with whom you'll want to exchange messages. You can, of course, simply type an e-mail address in each message you send, but e-mail addresses are singularly weird. It's really hard to remember them, and equally hard to get the syntax or spelling correct.

To avoid confusion, to reduce memorization, and to make sure you use the correct e-mail address every time, you should add names and addresses to your personal address book or to your Outlook Contacts folder. (When you add a contact entry with an e-mail address, the entry is automatically added to your Outlook address book.) You can add new names, change names, and remove names as often as you want.

Think of your personal address book as your "little black book." In your address books, you keep the name and "address"—an e-mail identification, a fax number, or any other electronic identification—of each of your correspondents.

To add a name and address to your personal address book or Contacts folder, do the following:

1 Choose Address Book from the Tools menu, or click the Address Book button on the Standard toolbar.

New Entry

2 Click the New Entry button on the Address Book toolbar to open the New Entry dialog box, shown in Figure 4-2, on the next page.

3 Open the list labeled Put This Entry In The and choose either Personal Address Book or Contacts. Unless you're a network administrator, you won't be able to add an address to the other lists.

II

Working with Electronic Mail

FIGURE 4-2.

The New Entry dialog box.

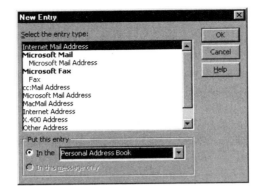

4 From the Select The Entry Type list select the type of address you want to enter. The types listed depend on your profile and the list you selected in step 3. If you chose to add the name to the Contacts folder, for example, you'll have two choices—New Contact and New Distribution List. Figure 4-2 shows the many choices available when I selected Personal Address Book. Depending on your system, you might not have all of the same options.

5 Click OK.

The next dialog box you see varies according to the type of entry you selected. For most new entries, you'll enter information such as the name to display in the address book and the e-mail address. The example in Figure 4-3 is based on selecting the Internet Mail Address type for the Personal Address Book.

If you don't see an Internet mail option, you can enter an Internet mail address by choosing Other as the Entry type and then typing *SMTP* in the E-mail Type box that appears in the New Other Address Properties dialog box.

1 In the Display Name box, type the name as you want it to appear in the address book.

2 In the E-mail Address box, type the e-mail address, such as alann@worldnet.att.net.

3 Select the check box labeled Always Send To This Recipient In Microsoft Outlook Rich-Text Format if you want to send meeting and tasks requests to other Outlook users over the Internet.

4 Fill in the boxes on the other tabs with as much information as you want. For example, the Business tab provides boxes for a

FIGURE 4-3.

The New Internet Mail Address Properties dialog box.

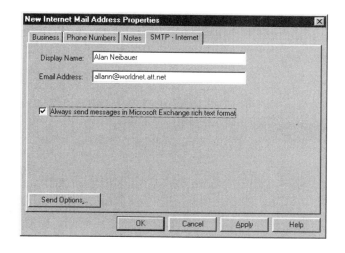

mailing address and phone number. The Phone Numbers tab contains boxes for multiple phone numbers, including a box for the person's fax number. If you want to send a fax to this person, be sure to enter the fax telephone number.

5 Click OK.

Copying an Address to the Personal Address Book

You can easily add to the personal address book an address already in another address list, such as Contacts. Just follow these steps:

1 Choose Address Book from the Tools menu, or click the Address Book button on the Standard toolbar.

2 Select the address list containing the name you want to add from the Show Names list.

3 Click the name in the list.

4 Click the Add To Personal Address Book button on the Address Book toolbar.

5 Close the Address Book dialog box. The listing is now duplicated in your personal address book.

SEE ALSO

For information about setting up a fax entry, see Chapter 6, "Sending and Receiving Faxes."

When you add a name and address, Outlook requires only that you fill in the Display Name and adress boxes. You can leave the fields on the other tabs blank and fill them in later by double-clicking the name in the Address Book window, or by using the Properties button on the Address Book toolbar. Clicking the Properties button displays the same dialog box that you saw in Figure 4-3, on page 119.

 TIP

> If you communicate with other Outlook users over the Internet, make sure you select the Always Send To This Recipient In Microsoft Outlook Rich-Text Format check box. Then you can send them Outlook items, such as meeting and tasks requests, which will be properly formatted when they open them in their own Calendar or Tasks folders.

Using Internet Encoding Methods

When you add an entry to your personal address book, you will often be adding an address for someone with whom you exchange e-mail over the Internet. Depending on your Outlook setup, you can use the Send Options button in the New Address Properties dialog box to select options for how to send messages and attachments to your Internet correspondents.

Different e-mail systems use different encoding methods for sending attachments and formatting across the Internet. These methods allow you to send whole documents, as well as files in other formats, through e-mail. The three most commonly used encoding methods are MIME (Multipurpose Internet Mail Extensions), which allows you to send highly formatted documents; uuencode, which converts binary files to text; and (for Macintosh files only) BinHex (binary-hexadecimal). The standard encoding method for Outlook is MIME. If an e-mail address in your address book uses uuencode, select that option for the e-mail address.

For addresses that use MIME, you can select various formats for the body of your messages: Plain Text, HTML (Hypertext Markup Language—the encoding for World Wide Web pages), or both.

Using Distribution Lists

Do you know a bunch of people to whom you send e-mail regularly? You probably think you have to remember everybody's name every time. And you have to type or select all those names every time. Too slow. Too prone to errors. Too boring!

Instead, you can group any number of addresses together into a distribution list. When you select the list as the message recipient, the message is sent to every member of the group at one time. You can have any number of lists, and you can store them in either your personal address book or the Contacts folders—regardless of the source of the entries.

Outlook provides the tools you need to create personal groups, to edit a personal group (to add and delete names), to delete personal groups, and to give a personal group a new name.

Creating a Personal Address Book Distribution List

Once you've decided to set up a personal group, the steps are easy. You simply name the group, open the address book or books that contain the names you need, and select the names.

The steps are slightly different depending on where you want to store the list, however. So, let's start with storing the list in the personal address book.

1 Open the Address Book.

2 Click the New Entry button on the Address Book toolbar to open the New Entry dialog box.

3 Choose Personal Address Book from the Put This Entry In The list box.

4 Select Personal Distribution List in the Select The Entry Type box, and then click OK. Outlook opens the New Personal Distribution List Properties dialog box, as shown in Figure 4-4, on the following page.

5 In the Name box, type a name for the list. Make it a name that helps you identify the group, such as Bowling League.

6 Click Add/Remove Members to open the Edit Members Of dialog box, shown in Figure 4-5, on the following page.

7 Use the Show Names box to select the list containing the names you want to add to this personal group. You can switch to a different address list at any time if you want to add names from several different lists.

8 Select the names you want to add to the group from the list on the left side of the dialog box. To add more than one name at a time, hold down the Ctrl key as you click the names. These

FIGURE 4-4.

The New Personal Distribution List Properties dialog box.

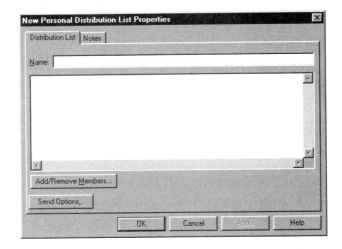

names don't have to be listed consecutively. To add several consecutive names, select the first name, hold down the Shift key, and then click the last name. Outlook selects all the names from the first to the last that you clicked.

9 Click the Members button. The selected names now also appear in the Personal Distribution List box. (If you added someone by mistake, click the name and press the Delete key. They will *not* be removed from your address list, only from the distribution list you're creating.)

10 When you've finished adding members to your personal distribution list, click OK in the Edit Members Of dialog box.

FIGURE 4-5.

The Edit Members Of dialog box.

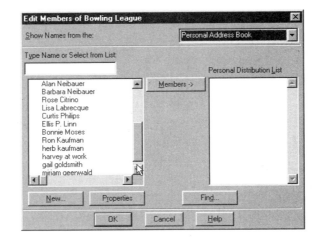

TIP

You can add new names to your personal address book as you're creating a personal distribution list. To do so, click the New button in the Edit Members Of dialog box and follow the steps in "Adding an Address," on page 117. You can also change the information for a person by selecting the name and clicking the Properties button in the Edit Members Of dialog box.

11 In the New Personal Distribution List Properties dialog box, you can click the Notes tab and enter any information that you want about this personal group. When the properties for this new personal distribution list are all set, click OK. The new personal distribution list now appears in your personal address book with a "group" icon next to the name, as shown here:

     Bowling League

Creating a Contacts Distribution List

You can also create a distribution list and store it in the Contacts folder. Here's how:

1 Open the Address Book.

2 Click the New Entry button on the Address Book toolbar to open the New Entry dialog box.

3 Choose Contacts from the Put This Entry In The list.

4 Select New Distribution List in the Select The Entry Type box, and then click OK. Outlook opens the window shown in Figure 4-6, on the next page.

5 Type a name for the group in the Name box.

6 Click Select Members.

7 In the Select Contacts dialog box that appears, select the names to add to the list just as you learned for creating a personal address book distribution list, and then click OK.

8 Click Save And Close.

The distribution list will appear as an item in your Contacts folder.

Editing a Distribution List

People come and people go. From time to time, a personal distribution list changes. New people want to be in your club; others want out.

FIGURE 4-6.

The Distribution List window.

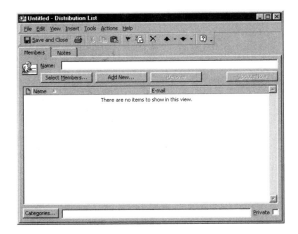

(And there are always a few you just want to throw out!) For your distribution list to be fully useful all the time, you need to be able to add and remove names as things change.

To add a name to an existing personal distribution list, follow these steps:

1 Open the Address Book.

2 In the Show Names list, choose the location of the distribution list, either a personal address book or the Contacts folder.

3 Select the distribution list you want to change.

4 Click the Properties button on the Address Book toolbar.

Properties

5 Click the Add/Remove Members button for a personal address book distribution list, or the Select Members button for a Contacts distribution list.

6 In the Show Names box, select the address list that contains the name you want to add, select the name from the Type Name Or Select From List box, and then click the Members button or the Add button.

7 Click OK.

To remove a name from a personal distribution list, follow these steps:

1 Repeat steps 1 through 4 in the preceding procedure. For a personal address book distribution list, click the Add/Remove Members button.

2 Now select the name or names you want to remove from the list. Press the Delete key for a personal address book distribution list, or click Remove for a Contacts distribution list.

3 If you removed members from a personal address book distribution list, click OK in the Edit Members Of dialog box, and then click OK in the Properties dialog box. For a Contacts distribution list, just click Save And Close.

 **NOTE**

> If you change an e-mail address for a person in a Contacts distribution list, open the list, select the name of the person, and click Update Now.

Deleting a Distribution List

Sometimes groups disband—not even the Beatles lasted forever, though one fears that the Rolling Stones might. When you no longer want or need a personal distribution list, you can remove it from your personal address book or Contacts folder.

To delete a personal distribution list, take these steps:

1 Open the Address Book.

2 In the Show Names list, choose the location of the distribution list, either the personal address book or the Contacts folder.

3 Select the distribution list you're removing and then click the Delete button on the Address Book toolbar.

4 When Outlook asks whether you want to permanently remove the selected users from the address book, click Yes. (The distribution list will be removed, but the individuals will remain in your address list.)

5 Close the address book.

Renaming a Distribution List

Maybe a group changes its colors; maybe a group changes its mind; maybe you just want to use a different group name for whatever reason. Outlook provides a way to change the name of a personal distribution list without much trouble.

To rename a personal distribution list, do the following:

1 Open the Address Book.

2 In the Show Names list, choose the location of the book, either your personal address book or Contacts folder.

3 Select the name of the personal distribution list you're renaming, and then click the Properties button on the Address Book toolbar.

4 Type the new name for the personal distribution list where the old name appears in the Name box, and then click OK for a personal address book distribution list or Save And Close for a Contacts folder distribution list.

The Address Book is an important tool for sending e-mail, whether through a network or over the Internet. In this chapter, you learned how to add addresses and distribution lists. In the next chapter you'll put the Address Book to good use as you learn to send and receive e-mail using Outlook's many enhanced mailing features.

Sending and
Receiving Messages

Whether or not you're on a network, communicating by e-mail has become almost as popular as using the telephone and postal service. When you're connected to a network, you often need to exchange messages with other persons in your office and within your organization. With an ever-increasing number of people on the Internet, you can also exchange messages with business associates, friends, relatives, and even strangers around the world.

Working with Message Windows

You create an e-mail message in a message window, and in Microsoft Outlook you have two choices: Outlook's own standard message window and the Microsoft Word e-mail window. Both windows let you create and format mail, although the Word e-mail window offers a wider variety of formatting options.

Using the Standard Message Form

The default setting for the Workgroup/Corporate installation is to use Microsoft Outlook Rich Text as the mail format and the standard Outlook e-mail editor, shown in Figure 5-1. The Formatting toolbar is unavailable when you're in the To, Cc, and Subject lines but available when you're typing your message. This toolbar, by the way, will be a little different if you're using HTML mail format, and it will be unavailable if you're typing your message using Plain Text format.

 **NOTE**

The default mail format for the Internet Only installation is Plain Text using the standard message editor. You can change to Word as the e-mail editor and select either HTML or Microsoft Outlook Rich Text as the format.

FIGURE 5-1.
Outlook's standard message form.

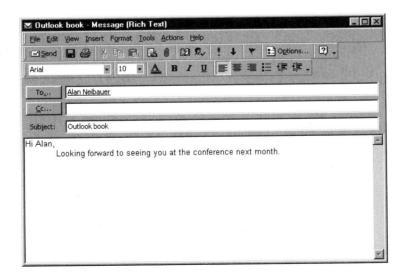

Selecting Microsoft Word as Your Mail Editor

If you prefer, you can use Microsoft Word to compose a new message or to read, reply to, or forward a message. By choosing Word as your mail editor, you can incorporate tables, formulas, and fields in your message and use Word's entire array of formatting features when composing a message.

To set up Word as your editor, you must first have Word installed. Then follow these steps:

1 Choose Options from the Outlook Tools menu to open the Options dialog box.

2 Click the Mail Format tab.

Choosing the Format for Specific Messages

Regardless of your choice for the default mail format and editor, you can change these settings for individual messages.

Rather than clicking the New Message button on the toolbar to start a new message, point to New Mail Message Using on the Actions menu. The menu that appears lists any recent stationery you've used along with a More Stationery button for choosing another type. Below that you will see options to use HTML (no stationery), Microsoft Outlook Rich Text, Plain Text, Microsoft Office, or Microsoft Word (HTML). The final option might be called Microsoft Word (Rich Text) instead if you've chosen Microsoft Outlook Rich Text in the Mail Format tab of the Options dialog box.

The Microsoft Office choice offers additional options that vary depending on other applications installed on your system. These might include Microsoft Access Data Page, Microsoft Excel Worksheet, Microsoft PowerPoint Slide, and Microsoft Word Document. These options let you use these other Office applications to create the contents of the message. Choose Microsoft Excel Worksheet, for example, if you want to send a worksheet as the message, rather than as an attachment.

The differences between selecting Microsoft Word (HTML) and Microsoft Word Document from the Microsoft Office menu are subtle. If you choose Microsoft Word (HTML), you'll be able to use Outlook features such as Signatures and Personal Stationery to create your message, and when you save the message it is stored in Outlook's Drafts folder. If you choose Microsoft Word Document from the Microsoft Office menu, you'll create a Word document that will be inserted into the message. Saving the message stores it as a Word file on your hard disk, and you will not have access to Outlook's unique message features.

3 Select the Use Microsoft Word To Edit E-mail Messages check box.

4 Click OK to close the Options dialog box.

With Word as your e-mail editor, the message window is similar to the standard message window, but you have Word's formatting and table features available from the menu bar.

Sending a Message

It's easy to create a new e-mail message—and Outlook gives you lots of options for protecting, formatting, delivering, and tracking your message, as well as for drawing attention to the message and adding attachments to it.

Creating a New Message

The fastest and easiest way to send a message is simply to type the text and click the Send button. In this basic case, your message looks tidy but unspectacular, and it also requires the least effort.

You can create a new message from any folder in Outlook. From the Inbox, Outbox, or Drafts folders, you click the New Mail Message button as described in the steps that follow. From another folder, click the down arrow on the Standard toolbar's New button (the first button on the left) and select Mail Message. (The full name and icon of the New button depend on the folder you have open.)

To send a simple message from a mail folder, do the following:

1 Click the New Mail Message button on the Standard toolbar.

2 In the new message window, which you saw in Figure 5-1, on page 128, click the To button to display the Select Names dialog box, shown in Figure 5-2. You use the Select Names dialog box much like the Address Book you learned about in Chapter 4, "Using Address Books."

3 Select the address book you want to use from the Show Names list box.

FIGURE 5-2.
The Select Names
dialog box.

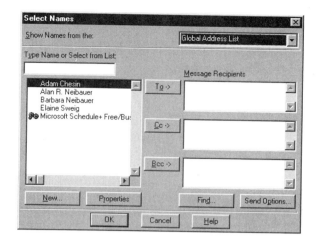

4 In the Type Name Or Select From List box, type the name or part
of a name of the recipient, or select a name from the list below.

When you type the beginning of a name in the Type Name box,
Outlook scrolls the list of addresses to the first name that matches
the letters you've typed. You can then scroll further, if you need to,
to find the name you want. You can also select a distribution list
from either the personal address book or from the Contacts list to
send the message to a group of people. To select more than one
addressee, hold down the Ctrl key and click each name.

5 Click the To button for the main addressees, and click the Cc or
Bcc boxes to send copies to others. The name or names you've
selected will appear in the boxes to the right of each button.

The names you place in the Bcc (blind carbon copy) box will
not be visible to other recipients of the message, or to one another,
while the names you place in the Cc box will be visible. (If the Bcc
button and box are not visible in the message window, you can
display them by selecting Bcc Field from the View menu.)

6 Click OK when you've chosen all the addressees.

7 In the message window, click in the Subject box and type a brief
description of the subject of your message.

8 Click in the message area, or press the Tab key to move to the
message text area, and then type your message.

 9 When your message is ready to send, click the Send button.

> If you do not complete your message and are not ready to send it, choose Save from the File menu. Outlook stores the message in the Drafts folder, unless you've specified another folder. To complete the message, open the Drafts folder in the My Shortcuts group, and then double-click the message in the message list. Click Send when you are ready to send the message.

Sending Mail with Multiple Accounts

You can send and receive e-mail over the Internet using multiple accounts. You can also share a single mail account, perhaps with members of your family, so mail goes out under the name of the person who wrote it. How you do so depends on whether you've installed Outlook using the Corporate/Workgroup option or the Internet Only option.

If you have more than one ISP and are using the Corporate/Workgroup option, create an Internet E-mail service in your profile for each account. When you are ready to send mail, choose Send/Receive from the Tools menu, and then click the account you want to use on the submenu that appears. To share an account with another member of the family, follow these steps:

1 Create an address book listing in the personal address book for each family member sharing your e-mail address—use your e-mail address.

2 In the message window, choose From Field from the View menu. This inserts the From box above the To box.

3 Click From and select the name of the family member sending the message.

4 Complete the message as usual, and click Send.

5 Choose Send And Receive from the Tools menu.

When the message arrives, the name you selected in the From field will be shown as the sender.

If you set up Outlook using the Internet Only option, you can create and use more than one e-mail account, as you'll learn how to do in Chapter 7, "Using Outlook Express." If you are sharing an account with other members of the family, each person uses the same e-mail address but has his or her own username. While you have to select one account as the default to use for new messages, you can change the account for specific messages. After you write the message, do *not* click Send. Instead, point to Send Using on the File menu and choose the account to use when sending the message. When the message arrives, the name assigned to the account appears as the sender.

> Using the Internet Only setup, you can also select the account in the Send Message Using list in the Message Options dialog box.

Typing Recipient Names and Addresses

Instead of clicking the To button in the message window to address your message, you can directly type the names of the recipients, or their Internet e-mail addresses. To send the message to more than one person, separate the names with a semicolon.

> To send mail to numeric-style CompuServe e-mail addresses, substitute the comma in the numeric address with a period (for example, to send mail to member 70365,770 use the address 70365.770@compuserve.com). With America Online addresses, remove any spaces between words in screen names—send mail to AOL User by addressing it to AOLUser@aol.com.)

When you send mail, Outlook checks all the recipients that you entered in the To and Cc headers to make sure that your mail can be delivered. It underlines names that correspond to persons in your address book and Contacts folder who have network mailboxes or Internet e-mail addresses, and it uses the actual e-mail addresses when transmitting messages. It also underlines an Internet e-mail address not included in your address book if it is typed in the proper format, *name@service.something*.

If Outlook cannot find a name or finds multiple matches or an incomplete Internet address, it displays the Check Names dialog box, shown in Figure 5-3, on the following page. (To check the recipients before sending the message, click the Check Names button on the Standard toolbar or choose Check Names from the Tools menu.)

Outlook lists any possible matches for the name you typed. If one of the names is correct, select it and click OK. You can also click Properties to see the address book listing for the selected name.

If the name is not listed, or Outlook has no suggested name, you can either search the address book or create a new listing for the name you typed. To search the address book click the Show More Names button. To create a new listing, select the Create A New Address For option, and then click OK.

FIGURE 5-3.
The Check Names dialog box checks addressees against your address book.

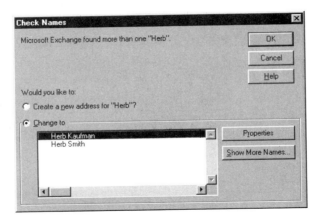

Sending Your Messages

What happens when you click the Send button depends on how your system is set up and to whom the mail is addressed. Mail sent to recipients on your Exchange Server or workgroup postoffice is transmitted immediately. Mail to Internet recipients, however, is stored in the Outbox until you dial in and connect. To actually send the mail, click the Send/Receive button on the Standard toolbar. Outlook sends any mail in the Outbox and checks for new mail waiting for you.

> Users of the Internet Only installation of Outlook have the option to send e-mail immediately as well as to store it in the Outbox.

If you have more than one mail service set up, the Send/Receive command will transmit all of your mail and check for mail on all of the services. If you want to send mail using a particular service point to Send/Receive on the Tools menu (of the Outlook window, not the message form window), and then choose the service you want to use.

SEE ALSO

To save a message in another format, such as an Outlook template, see "Saving Messages in Files," on page 169.

When you send a message, Outlook automatically saves a copy of it in the Sent Items folder. To check your sent messages, open the My Shortcuts group, and click the Sent Items folder.

Sending a Protected Message

When you want to ensure the privacy of your messages, you can encrypt them. When you want to assure your recipients that *you* actually sent the messages they received in your name and that the messages weren't tampered with during transit, you can digitally sign them. You can both encrypt and digitally sign a message.

Swapping Security Certificates

In order to send encrypted mail, you need the security certificate of the recipient. To send protected messages over your network, swapping security certificates isn't necessary—it's part of setting up Microsoft Exchange Server. To send an encrypted message over the Internet, however, people to whom you want to send encrypted messages must first send you a message that is digitally signed and includes their certificate. You then add their certificate to your address book so you can later send them encrypted mail. You'll have to follow the same procedure to receive encrypted messages from others, so here are the steps:

1 Choose Options from the Tools menu, and select the Security tab.

2 Click the Change Settings button.

3 In the Security Setting list, make sure you select the setting for Internet security (the Secure Message Format box will most likely indicate S/MIME when you've chosen the Internet security setting), not Exchange Server security.

4 Select the Send These Certificates With Signed Messages check box.

5 Click OK in each dialog box.

Now when you send the recipient a message that is digitally signed, as you'll learn how to do next, your security certificates will be sent as well. When your message arrives, the recipient can double-click the message to open it, right-click on your name, and then choose Add To Contacts from the shortcut menu. This creates an address listing for you that also contains your public key. The recipient can then use this public key to read future secure messages that you send. The key is called public because there is another portion of your certificate, the private key, that always remains on your system. Messages are secure because each message requires an exact match between the private key on one system and the public key on the other system before the message can be read.

Encrypting and Digitally Signing Messages

? SEE ALSO

For information about reading an encrypted message or checking a digital signature, see "Reading a Protected Message," on page 164.

If you want to encrypt or digitally sign all messages that you send, choose Options from the Tools menu, select the Security tab, and select both the Encrypt Contents And Attachments For Outgoing Messages check box and the Add Digital Signature To Outgoing Messages check box. (Again, this assumes that you've set up security as described in Chapter 3, "Setting Outlook Options.")

II

Working with Electronic Mail

If you don't want to use these security features for all messages that you send, you can still encrypt or digitally sign individual messages by following these steps:

1 Create the message.

2 Click the button labeled Options on the Standard toolbar. You might have to expand the toolbar to display the button.

3 In the Security area of the Message Options dialog box, select the Encrypt Message Contents And Attachments check box to encrypt messages and the Add Digital Signature To Outgoing Message check box to send your digital certificate. You can choose one or both types of security.

4 Click Close.

5 Click Send.

6 If the message is protected with Microsoft Exchange security, one of three things will happen:

- If your security level is set to the default Medium level, a message appears reporting the level of security. Click OK to send the message.

- If your security level is set to Low, the message is sent immediately.

- If your security level is set to High, you must supply a password to send the message. Type your password and then click OK.

If any of the intended recipients of your encrypted message do not have security set up or you do not have their certificates, you'll see a message box telling you that the recipients cannot process encrypted messages. To send the message anyway, click the Send Unencrypted button. The message then goes out without protection.

Stamping Your Signature

Have you ever received a message with a few standard closing lines at the end of it? Maybe the sender's name, an e-mail address, a postal address, and some pithy saying? Would you like to add such lines at the end of your messages? Outlook gives you the Signature command to do just that. Your closing is then added automatically to your new messages, and optionally to replies and forwarded messages.

You can create as many signatures as you want, and then select the one to use by default for all messages. You can also override the default with a more appropriate signature for individual messages. Here's how to choose a signature or set up your first signature when you are composing a message:

NOTE

> The instructions given here are for the standard Outlook message window. *For details on using Word as your e-mail editor, see the sidebar "Using Word as the E-mail Editor," on page 149.*

Signature

1 Click the message area of the message window.

2 Click the Signature button on the message window's Standard toolbar, or point to Signature on the Insert menu. If you have already created one or more signatures, select one from the list that appears (or click More to see signatures that aren't displayed) to insert it into the message.

3 If you haven't created any signatures, click More. A dialog box will appear, informing you there are no signatures on file and asking if you want to create one now. Click Yes.

　　If you have already created a signature and want to create an additional one, return to the Outlook window, select Options from the Tools menu, select the Mail Format button, click the Signature Picker button, and then click New.

4 In the Create New Signature dialog box, shown in Figure 5-4, on the following page, type a name to describe the signature you're about to create.

5 Choose to start with a blank signature, use an existing one as a template, or use another file as a template.

6 Click Next to display the Edit Signature dialog box, shown in Figure 5-5, on the following page.

FIGURE 5-4.

The Create New Signature dialog box.

7 In the large text box, type the text you want to appear in the signature. Use the Font button to change fonts, and the Paragraph button to align text or add bullets. You can also click Clear to start over, or click Advanced Edit to use another program to create the signature. *See "Sending Business Cards," opposite, for more information on vCard options.*

8 Click Finish when you're done, or click the OK buttons to close the various dialog boxes if you created the signature through the Tools menu.

9 If this is your first signature, it appears in your message form automatically. If this is an additional signature you just created, return to the message form, click the Signature button, and select the new signature. For future messages you can choose the same

FIGURE 5-5.

The Edit Signature dialog box.

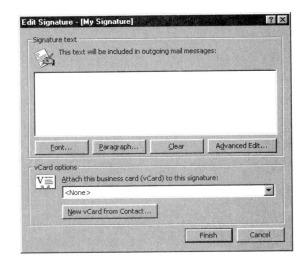

signature again from the menu that appears when you click the Signature button on the message window's Standard toolbar, or you can choose Signature from the Insert menu.

Using the Signature Picker

If you want to choose a signature to use for all messages, set it as the default on the Mail Format tab of the Options dialog box, shown in Figure 3-10, on page 84. You can also click the Signature Picker button on this tab to create, edit, or delete signatures.

To select a default signature, choose it from the Use This Signature By Default list. Once you select a signature, the Don't Use When Replying Or Forwarding check box is selected by default. If you want to include your signature in these messages as well, clear the check boxes. If you change your mind and decide not to use any signature by default, choose <None> in the list.

To create, edit, or delete signatures, click the Signature Picker button. In the Signature Picker dialog box that appears, you can choose to edit or remove an existing signature or create a new one.

If you selected a default signature, the next time you send a message, Outlook automatically adds your signature at the end of the message. If you chose to include your default signature on replies and forwards, Outlook places the signature above the copy of the message you are responding to or forwarding.

Sending Business Cards

Outlook lets you send an electronic version of your business card, called a *vCard*, as an attachment to your mail messages. This card includes information from your own listing in your address book. When you include it as a signature, recipients can read the information and add it to their address book with a few clicks of the mouse—so it's better than sending recipients an actual printed card.

Sending Your Own vCard to Others

Most of the time, you'll be sending your business card with a message. This is accomplished by attaching your vCard to one or more signatures. To add your vCard to one or more of your signatures, take these steps:

1 Choose Options from the Tools menu, and then select the Mail Format tab.

2 Click Signature Picker.

3 Select the signature to which you want to attach your vCard and click Edit. If you want to create a new signature for your vCard, click New instead and then follow the instructions in "Stamping Your Signature," on page 136.

4 In the Edit Signature dialog box, click the New vCard From Contact button. If you already have a vCard, you can select it from the Attach This Business Card list.

5 In the Select Contacts To Export As vCards dialog box, find your own listing from the appropriate address list, and click Add.

6 If you want to edit the information about yourself that will be sent to others as part of your vCard, click the Properties button and make your edits. Click Save And Close when you're done.

7 Click OK, and you will see your name listed in the Attach This Business Card list.

8 Click OK to close each of the three dialog boxes. Your vCard will now be included as part of your signature on all messages in which you include the signature.

Forwarding Another Person's vCard

Occasionally you might want to send someone's contact information to a third party. Rather than manually typing the person's phone number and other information in an e-mail message, you can quickly forward complete information as a vCard to the party who needs it. Just follow these steps:

1 Select Contacts from the Outlook Bar.

2 Select the name of the person whose vCard information you want to send.

3 From the Action menu, select Forward As vCard.

4 Include any message you want to send with the vCard, and then click Send.

Receiving a vCard and Adding It to Your Address Book

When you receive a message that includes a vCard (or when a message you send with a vCard is opened by the recipient), a paper clip icon appears in the preview pane, indicating an attachment. If the message is opened in its own window, a business card icon will appear in the attachment area at the bottom of the message form. To add the vCard information to your address book, take these steps:

1 Select the paper clip icon in the preview pane header and click the filename that appears, or right-click the business card icon in the message form and click Open.

2 When the Opening Mail Attachment dialog box appears, select Open It and click OK.

3 When the Properties dialog box opens, you will be able to view the information sent to you in the vCard attachment, but you cannot change it. Click the Add To Address Book button on the Personal tab.

4 The Properties dialog box appears again. Now you can edit the information you see just as you can any other address book entry. Click OK and the contact information will be added to your Outlook Contacts list in the Address Book.

 If you try to save a vCard you receive and that person is already listed in your address book, you see a message asking whether you want to update the existing contact with the new contact. If you answer no, the address listing is not changed. If you answer yes, the new information is merged into the existing information you already have on file. You can also send updated information about yourself to others. Just attach your vCard to a message that tells the recipients something like, "My address information has changed. Please add my updated vCard to your Address Book." The recipient won't have to manually search for which information is new and won't introduce any errors by manually typing in the new information.

Formatting Text

A plain text message is quick and easy, but you might want to decorate the message's text a little, just to make it livelier. Outlook provides several ways to enhance the appearance of your mail messages.

You can use some basic text decorations to format a message, you can add background colors and pictures, and you can create electronic stationery for special events and effects.

 NOTE

Text formats are not available when you are using Outlook's Plain Text message format.

Applying Basic Text Formats

To apply basic formats to selected text in a message, use the buttons and boxes on the Formatting toolbar, which is available when you click in the message area. If you're using Outlook as your e-mail editor, the buttons on the toolbar vary slightly between Rich Text and HTML formatted messages. Here's the toolbar when using the HTML format:

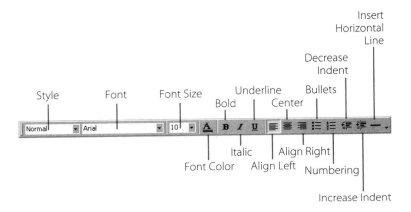

When you're using Microsoft Outlook Rich Text format, the toolbar does not include the Style, Numbering, and Insert Horizontal Line buttons.

> As with a word processing program, you can choose a format for text you are about to type, or you can select existing text and apply formatting to it.

You can add text formats to HTML messages by selecting a style from the Style list. Choose from the list on the far left of the Formatting toolbar, or point to Style on the Format menu and select the style you want. The list offers 16 options in addition to the normal text format. Most styles apply more than one type of formatting. The Heading 1 style, for example, formats text as Arial, 24-point, and bold.

The Font and Paragraph commands are also available on the Format menu in the message window. In the Font dialog box, you can select fonts, font sizes, bold, italic, underlining, and color. The Paragraph dialog box provides options for adding bullets and for setting paragraph alignment.

Changing the Default Font

Outlook uses default fonts for new messages, text you type when replying to or forwarding messages, and plain text messages. Each of these message types can use different default font settings. Set the default fonts by choosing the Fonts button on the Mail Format tab of the Options dialog box, as described in "Selecting Stationery and Default Fonts," on page 148.

Adding Pictures and Backgrounds

If you are using the HTML mail format, you can add a graphic, a color background, or fill the background with a repeating graphic to create even more eye-appealing mail messages. The graphic can be an animated file that moves on the message, such as the animated GIF graphics common on the Internet.

To insert a graphic in an HTML message, follow these steps:

1 Click in the message where you want the graphic to appear.

2 Choose Picture from the Insert menu to see the dialog box shown in Figure 5-6.

3 Type the path and filename of the graphic you want to use in the Picture Source text box, or use the Browse button to locate it.

4 Type any text in the Alternate Text box that you want to appear as the image is loading onto the recipient's screen or when the image cannot be displayed on a reader's system.

5 Select an alignment for the graphic if you want it to appear somewhere other than at the location of the insertion point.

6 Enter the image's border thickness in pixels (use 0 for no border).

7 Enter the horizontal and vertical spacing between the picture and text, in pixels.

8 Click OK.

The picture will appear at the position you designated.

FIGURE 5-6.
The Picture dialog box.

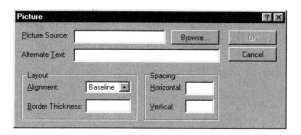

To change the position of the graphic, click in the middle of the figure and drag it to a new location. The mouse pointer appears as a four-directional arrow. You can only drag the graphic within text, not to areas below the last text line.

To change the size of the graphic, click on the picture. A dotted border with eight small boxes, called handles, will appear. Point to one of the handles so the mouse pointer appears as a two-directional arrow and drag to resize the picture as follows:

- Drag a center handle on the left or right border to change the width of the graphic.

- Drag a center handle on the top or bottom border to change the height of the graphic.

- Drag a corner handle to change both the width and height.

You can also add a background to the entire message. To color the background, point to Background on the Format menu, select Color, and then choose a color from the menu that appears. To completely fill the background with a picture, point to Background on the Format menu and select Picture. In the dialog box that appears, enter the path and name of the picture or click Browse to locate it. When you click OK, the picture will be tiled in the background—duplicated as many times as necessary to fill the message window both horizontally and vertically. This works particularly well for a very small image that creates a textured background for your message when tiled. The small image only needs to be sent once and will add very little delay in your mail being sent over the network or the Internet.

Using Stationery

Stationery lets you design a message format and then use it as the default for all your messages or just for selected messages. Outlook includes a number of attractive stationery designs ready for you to use. You can edit these designs or create your own.

Selecting a Message Stationery

To format a specific message using one of Outlook's stationery designs, start a new message by pointing to New Mail Message Using on the Actions menu. The menu that appears includes a list of any stationery designs you've already used, as well as the More Stationery option.

If the stationery you want to use is listed in the menu, click it. Otherwise, click More Stationery to see the Select A Stationery dialog box, shown in Figure 5-7. Choose a stationery design to see it in the Preview window. If there is a scroll bar in the Preview window, scroll through the window to see more of the design. If there is no scroll bar, the image will tile, or repeat itself, to fill the message area. Choose the design you want, and then click OK.

NOTE Regardless of the default message format, choosing a stationery from the Actions menu creates a message in HTML format.

Some designs contain both background graphics and sample text. You can change the text as you would in any other message—just position the insertion point and insert or delete text as desired.

TIP Click Get More Stationery to launch your Web browser, connect to the Web, and download additional stationery designs.

Selecting a Default Stationery

You can also select a stationery design to use as the default for all new messages. It can be one of the designs provided with Microsoft Outlook or one that you create yourself. To select the default stationery, follow these steps:

1 Choose Options from the Tools menu.

2 Click the Mail Format tab.

FIGURE 5-7.
The Select A Stationery dialog box.

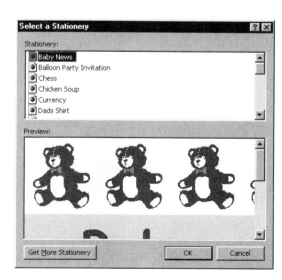

II

Working with Electronic Mail

3 Select a design from the Use This Stationery By Default list.

> You can only choose stationery as described here if you use HTML and the standard Outlook mail editor. *To use stationery with Word mail messages, see the sidebar "Using Word as the E-mail Editor," on page 149* .

4 Click OK.

Use the Stationery Picker button to create, edit, and delete stationery forms. The Stationery Picker is essentially the same as the Select A Stationery dialog box shown in Figure 5-7, on the previous page. It lists all of your stationery, including the ones provided by Outlook and those you create yourself, and contains additional buttons labeled Edit, Remove, and New.

Creating Stationery

If you have your own message design that you want to use frequently, save it as a stationery file. You can then use it as the default stationery or select it for individual messages by pointing to New Mail Message Using on the Actions menu and selecting it from the list that appears.

You can create new stationery from scratch or use an existing stationery file or HTML file as a template. You can also edit a stationery file, changing the graphics, color, or font used for its default text. To create or edit stationery, follow these steps:

1 Choose Options from the Tools menu.

2 Click the Mail Format tab.

3 Click Stationery Picker. If it is unavailable, select HTML and do not choose Word as the e-mail editor at the top of the dialog box.

4 Click New to create a new stationery. (If you want to edit an existing design, select it from the list, click Edit, and then skip to step 8.)

5 Enter a name for the new stationery in the Create New Stationery dialog box.

6 You now have to choose from three options, just as you did when you created a new signature. Click Start With A Blank Stationery to start from scratch, click Use This Existing Stationery As A Template to choose an existing stationery as a starting point, or click Use This File As A Template to pick an existing HTML file to start with, and then click Next.

7 If you chose to use an existing piece of stationery or an HTML file, a sample of it appears in the preview pane of the Edit Stationery dialog box, shown in Figure 5-8. Otherwise the preview pane will be empty.

8 Use the Change Font button to select a default font for messages you compose using this stationery.

9 To insert a picture into the design, select the Picture option and choose a picture from the list, or click Browse to locate one. The picture will be tiled to fill the entire message background.

10 To choose a background color, select the Color option and select a color from the list. You can select either a picture or color for the background but not both.

11 To use a blank background, select the option labeled Do Not Include A Background In This Stationery.

12 Click OK, and then click OK again to return to the Mail Format tab of the Options dialog box. The new stationery will now be included with your other stationery in the Use This Stationery By Default list box.

13 To use the new stationery as the default, select it from the list and click OK to close the Options dialog box. If you don't want to use a stationery by default for every message, set the list box to None.

FIGURE 5-8.
The Edit Stationery dialog box.

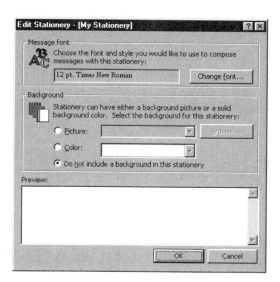

II

Working with Electronic Mail

You can always select a stationery for an individual message by pointing to New Mail Message Using on the Actions menu and selecting the stationery you want from the submenu.

Selecting Stationery and Default Fonts

Most stationery designs include their own default font. You can choose to use the font associated with the stationery or to use the same default font for all messages. To do this, click the Fonts button in the Mail Format tab of the Options dialog box.

In the Message Fonts section of the Fonts dialog box that appears, you can choose the default fonts to use for new messages, for replying to and forwarding messages, and for reading and composing plain text messages. Click the Choose Font button next to each type of message and select a font from the box that appears.

The Stationery Fonts section of the Fonts dialog box also lets you choose one of these three options:

- **Use The Font Specified In Stationery (If Specified).** Select this option to let the stationery font override the font selected in the Message Fonts section of this dialog box.

- **Use My Font When Replying And Forwarding Messages.** Select this option to use the stationery font for new messages and the font chosen in the Message Fonts section for replies and forwarded messages.

- **Always Use My Fonts.** Select this option to make the font chosen in the Message Fonts section always override the stationery font.

Saving Messages as Stationery

When you design a new piece of stationery using the Stationery Picker, you are *not* given the opportunity to enter and format text that you want to appear each time you use the stationery, such as a title or your name and address. If you want to include text in a piece of new stationery, take these additional steps:

1 Start a new message using the stationery design you want to add text to.

2 Insert and format the text in the message as you want it to appear with each copy of the stationery.

3 Choose Save As from the File menu.

4 Make sure that HTML is chosen in the Save As Type list.

5 Enter a filename and then click Save.

6 Close the message.

7 Choose Options from the Tools menu.

8 Click the Mail Format tab.

Using Word as the E-mail Editor

When you choose to use Word as your e-mail editor, you have all of the formatting capabilities of Word available to you, as well as such message options as voting buttons and receipts.

While the signature and stationery features will be unavailable in the Mail Format tab of the Options dialog box, you can still use these features from within the Word message itself.

When you open the Word message window, choose Options from the Word Tools menu, and click the General tab. Then click the E-mail Options button to display the E-mail Options dialog box shown here.

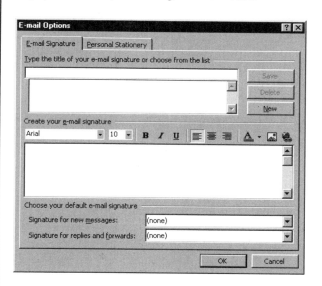

Use the E-mail Signature tab to create one or more signatures that you'd like to add to Word mail messages, and then choose the signature to use for new messages and replies and forwards.

Use the Personal Stationery tab to select a theme for messages. Each theme specifies a collection of styles for text and the background. Many of the themes are identical to the stationery designs. You can also choose a theme by selecting Theme from the Format menu.

II

Working with Electronic Mail

9 Click Stationery Picker.

10 Click New to create a new stationery.

11 Enter a name for the stationery.

12 Click Use This File As A Template, click Browse, and then select the HTML file you saved in step 5.

13 Click Next to display the Edit Stationery dialog box.

14 Click OK.

You can now use the stationery as you would any other.

Setting Message Options

Outlook sets up your new messages according to the options selected on the tabs of the Options dialog box. However, you might want to change the standard settings for a specific message. To do this, click the Options button on the message window Standard toolbar, or choose Options from the View menu, to display the options shown in Figure 5-9.

 SEE ALSO

For information about setting up standard options on the tabs of the Options dialog box, see Chapter 3, "Setting Outlook Options."

The settings you choose in the Message Options dialog box apply only to the message you're currently working on. Any changes you make here do not affect the standard settings on the tabs of the Options dialog box.

Use these options to set the level of importance and sensitivity, to include voting buttons in the message, or to have replies to your e-mail sent to another e-mail address. You can also specify a folder other than Sent Items in which to store the sent message.

Message Settings

The first set of options in the Message Options dialog box lets you designate how important or sensitive a message is.

Importance

The default importance level for your messages is set in the Options dialog box (accessed by choosing Options from the Tools menu), but sometimes you might want to send a message with a different level of importance. Suppose, for instance, that you need to send an urgent message about a deadline change to members of your project team. It's important that they notice and read the message right away. You can click the Options button on the message window Standard toolbar and select High in the Importance box. When Outlook delivers that message, it adds a red exclamation mark to the left of the envelope in the recipient's message list, alerting the recipient that this is an important message. (Depending on how your e-mail server is set up, a High

FIGURE 5-9.

The Message Options dialog box.

Message Options

Message settings
Importance: Normal
Sensitivity: Normal

Security
☐ Encrypt message contents and attachments
☐ Add digital signature to outgoing message

Voting and Tracking options
☐ Use voting buttons:
☐ Request a delivery receipt for this message
☐ Request a read receipt for this message

Delivery options
☐ Have replies sent to: Select Names...
☑ Save sent message to: Sent Items   Browse...
☐ Do not deliver before:
☐ Expires after:

Contacts...
Categories...

Close

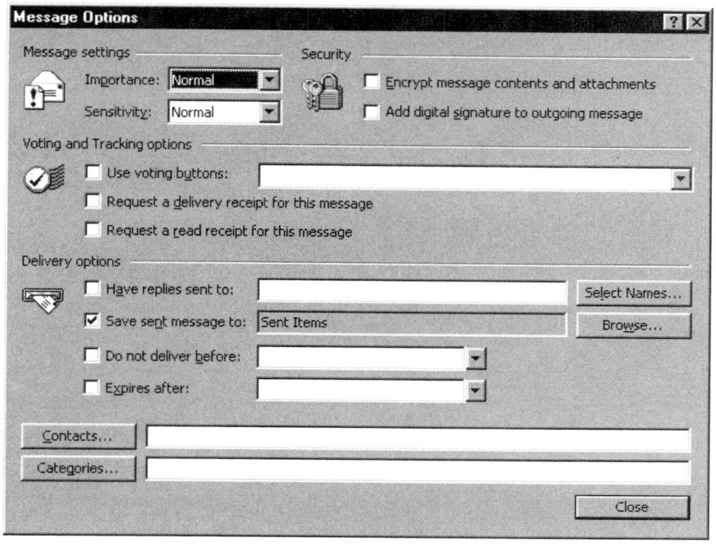

importance message might also be delivered faster than messages with Normal or Low importance levels.)

Likewise, if you've just heard a funny story that you'd like to pass along to a friend, but you know that your friend is busily working to complete a project, you can set a Low importance level for your message. When the message arrives, the recipient sees a blue downward-pointing arrow next to the envelope in the message list and knows that this message can wait until the project's work is done.

 TIP

> You can click either the Importance: High button (the red exclamation mark) or the Importance: Low button (the blue down arrow) on the Standard toolbar in the message window to quickly set the importance level for an individual message. If you change your mind and want to return the importance level of the message to Normal, click that toolbar button again.

Sensitivity

If a specific message requires a different level of sensitivity than you set as the default for all messages, you can designate this level in the Message Options dialog box. The four levels of sensitivity are Normal, Personal, Private, and Confidential.

II

Working with Electronic Mail

For information about
changing the column
display, see "Setting Up
Columns," on page 544.

Outlook shows the corresponding label—*Normal, Personal, Private,* or *Confidential*—in the Sensitivity column of the recipient's message list, provided that the Sensitivity column is displayed. If the Sensitivity column is not displayed, the recipient will see that the message has been marked Personal, Private, or Confidential when she or he opens the message to read it.

The Personal designation is informational only. The Private designation prevents recipients from altering your original message if they reply to it or forward it. The Confidential sensitivity level notifies recipients to treat the message according to your organization's policies about confidentiality.

Security Options

The second set of options in the Message Options dialog box lets you encrypt the message and add your digital signature to it, assuming you have already set up these features on the Security tab of the Options dialog box.

Voting and Tracking Options

The Voting And Tracking Options area of the Message Options dialog box helps you get responses to questions using voting buttons and ask for receipts when your mail has been delivered or read.

> **NOTE**
>
> To use voting buttons with Internet e-mail, the recipient's e-mail address must be set to use Microsoft Exchange Rich Text format. See "Adding an Address," on page 117. Voting buttons are not available using the Internet Only installation.

Did you ever send a message that asked people to respond to a proposal or an invitation? If you haven't yet, you probably will sometime during your e-mail lifetime. Outlook makes it possible to give your recipients an easy way to send a response to your proposal or invitation: voting buttons. When you select the Use Voting Buttons option in the Message Options dialog box, you'll see three choices in the drop-down list—Approve;Reject, Yes;No, and Yes;No;Maybe—which correspond to these three sets of voting buttons:

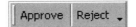 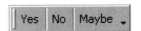

Select the set of buttons you want to include in your message, and send the message. (You will not see the buttons on your screen when you are composing the message, but they *will* appear with the message in your Sent Items folder.) When Outlook delivers the message, the recipients will see the buttons in the message window, along with the instruction *Please respond using the buttons above.*

NOTE

The buttons and the explanatory text will not appear in the preview pane of the message window, so you might want to include an instruction in your message to open this message and respond by clicking one of the voting buttons.

SEE ALSO

To find out how to use a voting button in a message you receive, see "Replying Through Voting Buttons," on page 168.

You can even create your own set of voting buttons. Instead of selecting one of the choices in the list, replace the text that appears in the list box by typing in new text with the voting button names you want to use. Separate the names with semicolons, and don't include any spaces: for example, *Fish;Chicken;Vegetarian* for meal choices or *Tuesday; Thursday* for selecting a meeting day. When your message is delivered, it will display your custom buttons.

When the recipient responds using the voting buttons, you'll receive an e-mail informing you of his or her selection. Read the e-mail to see the response and any additional comments. The message in your Sent Items folder will now be marked with a special icon indicating that responses have been received. When you open the message it will contain a Tracking tab that lists all recipients and the status and date of their replies, as well as any delivery and read receipts, as shown in Figure 5-10.

The default tracking options for your messages are set on the Preference tab of the Options dialog box, using the E-mail Options button. *See "Tracking Options," on page 72.* But if you want to set a different

FIGURE 5-10.
The Tracking tab lets you keep track of votes, message delivery, and read receipts.

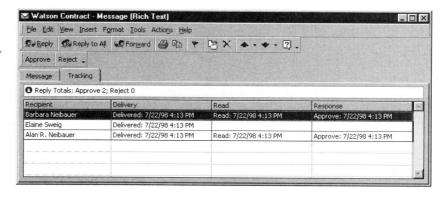

tracking option for a specific message, you can do so in the Message Options dialog box.

To have Outlook notify you when your message arrives in the recipient's mailbox, select the Request A Delivery Receipt For This Message check box. To have Outlook notify you when the recipient has opened your message, select the Request A Read Receipt For This Message check box. You can choose either or both of these options.

When your message arrives (or when the recipient opens it), Outlook delivers a message to your Inbox conveying this information, and adds the information to the tracking tab, as shown in Figure 5-10, on the previous page

NOTE

The Internet Only setup only allows you to request a read receipt. The dates the messages were retrieved by the recipients appear on the Tracking tab of the sent message.

Delivery Options

The Delivery Options area of the Message Options dialog box determines where replies to messages are delivered, where sent messages are stored, when messages are sent, when messages expire, and which categories are assigned to the message.

Have Replies Sent To

When you send a message that requests replies, you might want the replies to go to an e-mail address other than your own. For example, you might invite staff members to a staff party but want your assistant to receive the replies in order to set up a list of attendees or to supply a proper attendance figure to the caterer.

To have the replies to your message sent to another e-mail address, take these steps:

SEE ALSO

For another way to let recipients send their responses to a different e-mail address, see "Including an E-mail Link," on page 161.

1 In the Message Options dialog box for the message, select the Have Replies Sent To check box.

2 Type the e-mail address, or click the Select Names button. Clicking the Select Names button displays the Have Replies Sent To dialog box, where you can select the name or names of those who should receive the replies. (Outlook includes your e-mail name in this box by default. To delete your name, select it and press the Delete key.)

Save Sent Message To

You might want to save an occasional message in a folder other than the Sent Items folder. At other times, you might not want to save a particular message at all. You make both of these adjustments with the Save Sent Message To option as follows:

- To tell Outlook not to save the message, deselect the Save Sent Message To check box.

- To save a message in a different folder, click the Browse button, select the folder where you want the message saved, and then click OK in the Select Folder dialog box.

If you want to save your message in a folder that doesn't yet exist, follow these steps:

1 Be sure that the Save Sent Message To check box is deselected, and then click the Browse button.

2 Select the folder you want your new folder placed within.

3 Click the New button.

4 In the Create New Folder dialog box, type a name for the new folder in the Name box.

5 Click OK in the Create New Folder dialog box, and then click OK in the Select Folder dialog box.

Do Not Deliver Before

Some messages are time sensitive—either they can't be delivered before a specific date, or they expire after a certain date, or both. To set up a delayed delivery, select the Do Not Deliver Before check box and type or select the earliest date on which the message should be delivered.

Expires After

If the message is time sensitive because it becomes irrelevant after a certain date, set an expiration date for the message by selecting the Expires After check box, and then type or select an expiration date for the message.

 NOTE

You can use delayed delivery only if you are running Outlook with Microsoft Exchange Server.

II

Working with Electronic Mail

Categories

SEE ALSO

For more information about categories, see "Working with Categories," on page 549.

A handy way to organize messages is to group them into categories. By assigning a message to a category, you can match it up with other messages that belong to a specific project, an activity, a group, or any other designation. This lets you collect similar items for easy review and retrieval. To assign a message to a category by using the Message Options dialog box, follow these steps:

1 While writing or editing the message, open the Options dialog box and click Categories to display the box shown in Figure 5-11.

2 Select the check boxes for the categories you want to assign the message to.

3 To create a new category, type it in the large text box, and then click Add To List.

4 Click OK.

 ## Contacts

In addition to categories, mail and other Outlook items such as tasks can be associated with one or more contacts listed in the Contacts folder. You can then quickly list all of your Outlook activities that relate to the contact by opening the Activities page of the contact's listing.

To associate an e-mail message with a contact, click the Contacts button. In the dialog box that appears, click the contact's name and then click OK or Apply. To associate multiple contacts at one time, hold down the Ctrl key while you click their names.

FIGURE 5-11.
The Categories dialog box.

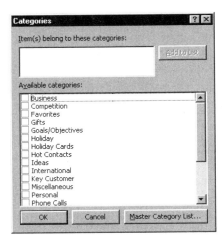

Setting Message Properties

Additional aspects of your messages can be controlled through the Properties dialog box. From the message window, choose Properties from the File menu. (You might have to expand the File menu to see the Properties option.) On the General tab of the Properties dialog box, you can set these options:

- Importance

- Sensitivity

- Do Not AutoArchive This Item

- Save Copy Of Sent Message

- Read Receipt Requested

- Delivery Receipt Requested

- Send Options

On the Security tab of the Properties dialog box, you can choose to encrypt the message and add a digital signature, and you can choose the security settings to use.

Flagging a Message

Even though you can make a Subject line informative and can include instructions within message text, you still might find it useful to add a "flag" to a message. A message flag is a line that appears in the message header that has information about the nature of the message or that requests a response to the message.

ⓘ Call as soon as possible

You set a message flag with the Flag For Follow Up command on the Actions menu of the message window. Here's how to set a message flag:

1 Choose Flag For Follow Up from the Actions menu, or click the Flag button on the Standard toolbar, to display the Flag For Follow Up dialog box shown in Figure 5-12, on the following page.

2 Choose a flag message from the Flag To list box, or type your own message.

Working with Electronic Mail

FIGURE 5-12.

The Flag For Follow Up dialog box.

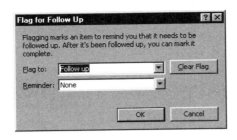

3 If you want to set a due date, enter it in the Reminder text box, or click the down arrow to choose a date from the calendar that appears.

4 Click OK.

In the recipient's message list, a flagged message displays a flag beside its icon (assuming the Flag Status column is displayed). When the flag is red, the recipient hasn't yet responded. When the flag is white, a response has been made.

To remove a message flag, click the Clear Flag button in the Flag For Follow Up dialog box.

Sending Files as Attachments

Have you ever mailed a cover letter accompanied by other documents? These other documents are called attachments because they are attached to a letter that introduces them. You can also send attachments with e-mail messages. An attachment is a file on your disk that you want to send to the recipient of the e-mail. The attachment can be anything that you'll find on your disk such as:

■ Microsoft Office documents

■ Graphics, sound, movie, and other multimedia files

■ Data files from other word processors, spreadsheets, and database programs

■ Programs and fonts, if you have the licensing rights to share with others

The contents of an attachment do not appear on the screen with the message but are shown as an icon. The recipient can easily open the attachment to display its contents, play the sound or movie, or run the executable program. You can attach files of any sort to any message you send, whether it is a new message, a forwarded message, or a reply.

The easiest way to send a file is to drag it from the Windows desktop or Windows Explorer and drop it onto the message window. To do this, you'll have to arrange the message window to see both it and the source of the file at the same time.

You can also attach a file using the Insert File command, by following these steps:

1 Click the Insert File button (the paper clip) on the message window Standard toolbar, or choose File from the Insert menu.

2 In the Look In box, select the disk and the folder that contains the file, or select an item from the Outlook Bar style box on the left side of the dialog box.

3 Select the file or files you want to attach.

4 Select the Attachment option in the Insert File dialog box to retain the file's natural structure. It will be displayed in the message as an icon, which the recipient can open in the program used to create the file.

5 Click OK.

In the Outbox folder next to the message, you'll see a paper clip icon under the Attachment column (the column marked with a paper clip in the header). This lets you know that the message includes one or more attachments.

If you have a plain text file stored on disk (for example, a file saved in Windows Notepad), you can either add it as an attachment or insert the text of the file directly into the message by clicking the Text Only option in the Insert File dialog box.

Adding Links

Outlook provides a way to add two types of links to a message. A link is a clickable object. The recipient can click the object to launch their Web browser and jump to a Web site or to open a message window all set up to send a reply to the recipient you designate.

Sending a URL in a Message

SEE ALSO

To find out how to use a URL in a message, see "Working with Links," on page 166.

If you've been surfing the World Wide Web and found a Web site you want to share with someone, the easiest way to do so is to send the Web site address (URL) to your friend. To get the URL into a message, you can either type it or copy and paste it.

In fact, if the URL begins with *www*, you can even leave off the *http://* designation. For example, if you type *www.microsoft.com* and then press the Spacebar or Enter key, Outlook automatically formats the URL as a link to the Web page, right before your eyes, displaying it something like this:

www.microsoft.com

The URL is easily recognized because it is formatted with an underline and appears in color.

If the URL does not start with *www*, type *http://* or *ftp://* (for a file transfer protocol address) along with the remainder of the address. When you're done, the text will be formatted as a link: underlined and in color.

You can also change the type of a link, from *http:* to *https://* or *gopher://*, for example, by changing its properties. Right-click the link and choose Properties from the shortcut menu. In the dialog box that appears, choose the new type of link from the Type list.

While the Internet requires a complete URL to find a site, the format of the address might be confusing to mail recipients. Rather than display the URL in the message itself, you can use more familiar or descriptive text as a link for the reader to click to move to a location on the net. Here's how:

1 Select the text that you want to serve as a link. It can be text that you've already typed in the message or a separate note telling the recipient when to click. For example, if you want the user to jump to the Microsoft Press Web page, you could type *Click here to learn more about Microsoft Press,* and then select this text.

2 Choose Hyperlink from the Insert menu.

3 In the dialog box that appears, open the Type list and choose the type of link.

4 In the URL text box, enter the complete URL of the address.

5 Click OK.

The hyperlink will appear formatted with an underline and in color.

Including an E-mail Link

From time to time, you might want to send a message that offers your recipients an e-mail address to which they can send questions or comments rather than sending their replies to you. For example, let's say you want to encourage your friends to send a message to the President of the United States at *president@whitehouse.gov.*

SEE ALSO

For an alternative way to have responses to a message sent to another e-mail address, see "Have Replies Sent To," on page 154. To find out how to use an e-mail response link, see "Working with Links," on page 166.

To make it easy for your recipient to do this, just type the e-mail address you want the recipient to contact, such as *alann@worldnet.att.net.* When you press the Spacebar or Enter key after the address, Outlook formats the address as a link, underlined and in color.

Outlook automatically creates what is known as a Mailto link. If you right-click the link and choose Properties, you'll see that the URL starts with *mailto:* as in

> mailto:alann@worldnet.att.net.

You do not have to type *mailto:* yourself, and it will not appear in the message. When the recipient clicks the link, a new message window will open with the address already in the To section.

Attaching Messages

Usually, to send a copy of a message to someone—even lots of someones—you just forward the message. That's fine if you want to send only *one* message. But suppose you want to forward several related messages all at one time? For that, you need to attach messages to your new message. You can attach other messages to any message you send, even if the message you're sending is itself a forwarded message or a reply.

To attach existing messages to the message you're working on, take these steps:

1 Choose Item from the Insert menu in the message window to see the Insert Item dialog box, shown in Figure 5-13, on the next page.

2 Select the folder containing the items you want to attach.

3 Select the items you want to attach. Depress the Ctrl key to select multiple, nonadjacent items, or the Shift key to select a contiguous range of items.

4 Click the Attachment in the Insert As section to attach each message as an icon and preserve its original format.

5 Click OK.

II

Working with Electronic Mail

FIGURE 5-13.
The Insert Item dialog box.

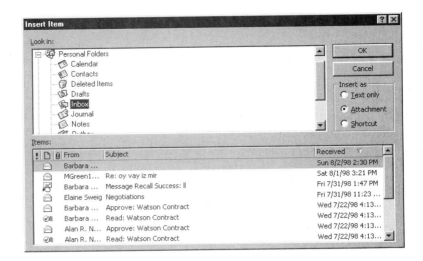

Reading a Message

When an e-mail message arrives in your Inbox, you can read and respond to it, forward it to others, view or open attachments, and respond using URL or e-mail links. Mail messages that you receive over the Microsoft Exchange Server network are automatically inserted into your Inbox. To receive messages from the Internet, you have to use the Send/Receive command, or you have to set up Outlook options to check for mail automatically at regular intervals.

By the way, if you are connected to a network using Microsoft Exchange Server, the network administrator might have established limits to the messages that your mailbox accepts. Your mailbox can be set to accept or reject messages from specific recipients or those over a certain size. If you feel you are not getting all of your messages, consult your network administrator.

> **? SEE ALSO**
>
> To learn how to automatically dispatch incoming messages that you don't want to read to the dustbin or to other places in Outlook or your file system, see "Organizing Messages," on page 51.

As you learned earlier in this chapter, a mail message can contain text that you read in the message window as well as attachments, links to a World Wide Web page (a URL), an e-mail response link, or voting buttons.

You can read a mail message in the preview pane or in a separate window. If the preview pane is not displayed, choose Preview Pane from the View menu.

To quickly read mail message text when the preview pane is displayed, click the message in the Inbox message list. If part of a long message falls below the bottom of the preview pane, scroll through the message window to read the rest of the message. To see the first three lines of messages directly in the message list, choose AutoPreview from the View menu.

Recalling, Replacing, or Resending a Message

Suppose you sent a message to your project team on a Microsoft Exchange Server network but inadvertently included the incorrect date of the next team meeting. Rather than send an entirely new message, you can do one of the following:

- Recall the message you've already sent, removing it from the recipient's inbox.

- Resend the same message after correcting or updating it.

You can only recall or replace messages to recipients who are logged on and using Outlook and who have not already read the message or moved the message out of their Inboxes.

First find the message you've already sent by opening the My Shortcuts group on the Outlook Bar, opening the Sent Items folder, and double-clicking the sent message to open it.

To recall or replace the message, follow these steps:

1 Open the message and choose Recall This Message from the Actions menu of the message window.

2 In the Recall This Message dialog box, do one of the following:

- To recall the message, select the Delete Unread Copies Of This Message option, and then click OK.

- To replace the message with another, select the Delete Unread Copies And Replace With A New Message option, and then click OK. In the new message window that appears, type the new message, and then click the Send button.

3 To receive a notification about the success or failure of recalling or replacing the message for each recipient, select the Tell Me If Recall Succeeds Or Fails For Each Recipient check box.

To simply resend the message (rather than recall or replace the message), follow these steps:

1 Open the message and choose Resend This Message from the Actions menu of the message window.

2 In the message window that appears, make any necessary changes, and then click the Send button.

II

Working with Electronic Mail

If you are using the Internet Only installation and selected Ask Me Before Sending A Response in the Tracking options, Outlook asks you if you want to send a receipt when you open a message that requests one. Select Yes to send the receipt or No to not send a receipt.

To read the message in its own window, simply double-click the message line in your Inbox's message list. If you want to add the sender's name to your address book, right-click the person's name in the open message, and then choose Add To Contacts or Add To Personal Address Book. Choose Properties from the shortcut menu if you just want to see the sender's e-mail address.

TIP

Once you've opened a message in its own window, you can use the Previous Item and Next Item buttons on the message window Standard toolbar to move from message to message (the buttons with the large up- and down-pointing arrows). Adjoining each of these buttons is a small down arrow that you can click to see a list of commands that let you move more quickly to the messages you want to read. For example, you can move to the next or previous message from the same sender or to the next or previous unread message.

Reading a Protected Message

To read a protected message, double-click the message line in your Inbox's message list. (You cannot read an encrypted message in the preview pane.) If the message is protected with Microsoft Exchange security, one of three things will happen:

SEE ALSO

For information about sending an encrypted or digitally signed message, see "Sending a Protected Message," on page 134.

- If your security level is set to the default Medium level, a message appears reporting the level of security. Click OK to send the message.
- If your security level is set to Low, the message is sent immediately.
- If your security level is set to High, you must supply a password to open the message.

You don't have to do anything special to read encrypted mail over the Internet. For someone to send you encrypted mail, the sender has to have a copy of the public key that comes with your certificate. This means you'll have to send the person your certificate ahead of time. *See "Sending a Protected Message," on page 134.* The message will be decrypted automatically when it arrives in your Inbox.

Adding a Sender's Public Key to Your Contacts Folder

Remember, for you to read encrypted mail sent over the Internet, the sender has to first send you his or her certificate in a digitally signed message.

Creating a Rule

In Chapter 2, "Discovering Outlook," you learned how to create a rule to channel messages using the Rules Wizard. Most of the time, you'll be creating a rule based on a specific sender or subject matter. If you already received a message that meets the conditions for the rule you want to set, you can save yourself time by creating the rule from the message itself. This procedure is somewhat similar to using the Organize button to make a rule based on a specific message *(see the sidebar "Creating Rules with Organize," on page 58)*, but you will have more flexibility in setting up the rule using the method described here:

1 Double-click the message to open it in its own window.

2 Choose Create Rule from the Actions menu. The Rules Wizard appears with the message's sender, recipient, and subject already listed as conditions, as shown here.

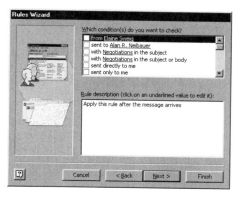

3 Select the conditions that you want to apply.

4 Click Next.

5 Select an action to apply to the rule, and then complete the rule as you learned how to do in Chapter 2.

You can create multiple rules from one message, and you can later delete or change them using the Rules Wizard command on the Tools menu.

Working with Electronic Mail

When an encrypted message arrives, do the following:

1 Double-click the message in the Inbox to open it.

2 Right-click the sender's name and choose Add To Contacts from the shortcut menu that appears.

3 A Contacts form opens, displaying the sender's address book information. Click the Save And Close button on the form's Standard toolbar.

Now the sender's public key is included in your Contacts folder information about that person and the key will be available for decrypting secure messages this sender mails to you in the future. Certificates do not need to be exchanged for secure traffic across a Microsoft Exchange Server network; the network administrator sets up certificates that reside on the server and don't need to be distributed locally to the individuals on the network.

Working with Links

Using a link in a message you've received is perhaps the easiest thing of all. Just click the link.

When you receive a message that contains a URL (a Web site address), you can simply click the URL in the message text to visit the Web site. Windows starts your default Web browser and connects to the Web site. (Depending on your setup, if you connect to the Internet over a dial-up connection, you might have to make the connection manually by selecting the dial-up account from your Dial-Up Networking folder and clicking the Connect button.)

When you receive a message that contains an e-mail response link in the message text, you can send a response, a question, or a comment by clicking the link. Outlook opens a new message addressed to the e-mail address in the response link and with the Subject line set up for you to fill in. All you have to do is add your message text, and then click the Send button.

Replying to a Message

Frequently a message provokes you to respond. So what do you do? Send back a reply. You can direct your response only to the person who sent the message, or if it was sent to more people than just you, you can respond to everyone who received it as well as the sender.

To reply to a message, do the following:

1 Select the message line in the message list, or open the message.

2 To reply to only the person who sent the message, click the Reply button on the Standard toolbar. To also reply to the entire audience (all those who received the original message), click the Reply To All button (also on the Standard toolbar).

3 Type your response anywhere in the message area. (Outlook positions the insertion point at the top of the message area, above the original message.) You can type your response at the top, at the bottom, or anywhere within the original message. You can format the text and add any other stuff just as you can for a new message.

4 Delete any parts of the original message that you don't need to send back.

5 Click the Send button on the message window's Standard toolbar.

When you open the original message again, you'll see a notice reporting that you've replied to the message. Click the notice to open your reply.

 TIP

> If you modify the original message and the Mark My Comments With option is selected, Outlook puts your name in square brackets at the leading edge of your changes. *For ways to change this behavior, see "Mark My Comments With," on page 69.*

You'll notice that if the message is not in Plain Text format, Outlook indents the original message when you reply either to the sender or to all those who received the message. Also, Outlook includes the entire original message in the reply. If you'd like to change the way Outlook handles replies, you can choose Options from the Tools menu, click the Preferences tab, click the E-mail Options button, and then adjust the settings in the E-mail Options dialog box. You can set up Outlook so that original messages are not indented in your replies. You can also choose to exclude the original messages from your replies, or you can opt for including them as attachments rather than as text. In addition, you can select different font effects for your replies. *For details about these options, see "Using the Internet E-mail Tab," on page 87.*

Working with Electronic Mail

TIP

Too often, people simply add their comments to a message they've received and then reply to everyone who received the original message. After half a dozen replies to everyone, the message gets quite long. Most of this extra baggage isn't really necessary, so it's best to throw away the excess. Keep the message short and crisp for the sake of your hard disk and for the sake of the e-mail system's performance.

Replying Through Voting Buttons

When you receive a message over the server that contains voting buttons, simply click the button that corresponds to your vote. Outlook displays a dialog box asking whether you want to send the response now or edit your response first.

If you select Send The Response Now, Outlook immediately sends the message without opening a reply form. The message arrives with your response inserted in front of the original Subject line—for example, *Approve: Special Offer.*

If you select Edit The Response Before Sending, Outlook opens a reply message addressed to the proper e-mail address and with the Subject line and original message text included. You can add additional comments if you like. Then click the Send button to send your reply. The message arrives with your response inserted in front of the original Subject line.

Replying to a Message Flag

When you receive a message with a flag and a due date, you can easily record your response to the flag when you've finished taking the action the flag requests:

1 Open the message.

2 Click the Flag button on the Standard toolbar.

3 Select the Completed option in the Flag For Follow Up dialog box.

4 Click OK.

The flag area of the message displays the date on which you marked the action completed. You now have a record that you can store in an Outlook folder.

> ⓘ Call as soon as possible
> Completed on Sunday, August 02, 1998 2:32 PM.

Forwarding a Message

 SEE ALSO

To set up Outlook to automatically forward messages of interest, see "Managing Your Mail with the Rules Wizard," on page 51.

Let's say someone has sent you a really important message. You think that other people might want or need the information in the message, even though they weren't originally recipients. In this case, you can forward the message to other interested parties.

To forward a message, follow these steps:

1 Select the message line in the message list, or open the message.

2 Click the Forward button on the message window Standard toolbar.

3 In the To box, add the names of those who should receive the message. Remember that you can use group names, too. *See "Using Distribution Lists," on page 120, for information about personal groups.*

4 If you want to add your own remarks to the message, type your comments anywhere in the message area.

5 Delete any parts of the original message that you don't want to send on.

6 Click the Send button.

Saving Messages in Files

Even though Outlook automatically saves a copy of your messages in the Sent Items folder, there might be a message that is so important or useful that you'll also want to save it in a file that you can open in another application.

To save a message in a file, do this:

1 Select the message from the message list, or open the message. You can save several messages in the same file by selecting all of them in the message list at the same time.

2 Choose Save As from the File menu to open the Save As dialog box.

3 If you select a single message, Outlook creates a name for the file by using the Subject line of the message. If you select more than one message, you need to enter a name for the file in the File

Name box. You can select a different disk or select a different folder if you want by using the Save In box.

4 In the Save As Type box, select the format for the file you want to save.

5 Click the Save button.

Saving Message Attachments

When you receive a message with an attachment that is a file, you might decide that you want to save the attachment. If a message has more than one file attached, you can save one, some, or all of the files. You can open and save attachments from either the message list or from the open message window.

Saving Attachments from the Message List

In the message list, a paper clip displayed next to the message name indicates one or more attachments to the message, and you'll also see the paper clip in the preview pane header, if you have it displayed. Click the icon in the preview pane to see the names and sizes of the attached files.

Preview pane header.

Click here to see attachments.

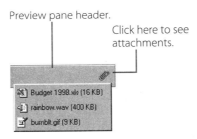

Click the filename that you want to open to see the Opening Mail Attachment dialog box, which has two options: Open It and Save It To Disk. This dialog box will not appear, by the way, for some types of files, such as text and audio files—instead the file will be opened immediately.

Click Save It To Disk to store the file in a location of your choice.

NOTE

> Depending on the recipient's mail reader and its settings, the Attachments icon might appear next to messages that contain a graphic, stationery background, or signature, even though these items are displayed by Outlook within the message itself. Even Outlook sometimes displays the Attachment icon for items displayed in the message body.

What happens when you click Open It depends on the type of file you're opening. Files such as Word documents and Excel worksheets are opened in their respective applications. Media files, such as audio and video files, are played. To properly open a file of a given format, you must have the application installed on your system and it must be registered in Windows as associated with the file extension of the file you're opening. For example, to have a .bmp file open in Microsoft Paint, you need to have Paint installed and to have the .bmp extension associated with that application.

You can also choose to save all or some of the files attached to a message using the File menu. With this technique, however, you won't see the Opening Mail Attachment dialog box. Here's how:

1 Select the message in the message list. A message with an attachment shows a paper clip on its message line, if you have the Attachment field column turned on.

2 Choose Save Attachments from the File menu. The menu that appears lists each of the attachments as well as the option All Attachments.

3 Select the attachment you want to save, or choose All Attachment to save them all.

4 If you choose to save one attachment, you'll see the Save Attachment dialog box, where you can select the location and filename for the attachment.

5 To save additional individual attachments, repeat steps 1 through 4. If you choose to save all attachments, Outlook displays the Save All Attachments dialog box, shown on the following page.

II

Working with Electronic Mail

6 All the attachments are initially selected. Click any of the attachments that you *do not* want to save to deselect them. Select multiple attachments by holding down the Ctrl key when you click.

7 Click OK to display the Save All Attachments dialog box.

8 Choose the folder where you want to store the attachments, and then click OK.

Saving Attachments from the Message Window

When you open a message by double-clicking it, attachments included with it are shown as icons below the message text. Depending on the message format, the icons may also appear in the preview pane.

Double-click an icon to display the Opening Mail Attachment dialog box, and then choose to open or save the attachment. If a message has multiple attachments, choose Save Attachments from the File menu to display the Save All Attachments dialog box. Hold down the Ctrl key and deselect any of the attachments that you do not want to save, and then click OK. Next choose the folder where you want to save the attachments, and then click OK.

Managing Junk Mail

As Internet e-mail becomes increasingly popular, you will likely receive a greater amount of junk e-mail, or *spam* as it is often called. Junk e-mail is any unsolicited messages about sales, offers, Web sites, or any other subject that you are not interested in. If left unmanaged, junk e-mail can quickly clog your Inbox.

Outlook lets you build a list of junk mail addresses—the e-mail addresses of persons or companies whose messages you identify as junk mail. You can automatically delete this e-mail, channel it into a special folder, or mark it with an identifying color on the message list. You'll need to set up this feature before you can use it, after which a couple of mouse clicks will route the junk out of your Inbox.

Channeling Junk and Adult Content Mail

One way to channel junk mail is by creating a rule in the Rules Wizard. The rule would instruct Outlook to look for incoming mail from persons on the junk mail list and perform some action on it, such as deleting the mail or moving it to a certain folder. *See Chapter 2, "Discovering Outlook," for a detailed discussion of the Rules Wizard.*

You can also channel junk mail using the Organize button by following these steps:

1 Click the Inbox folder.

2 Click the Organize button on the Standard toolbar.

3 Click Junk E-mail to see the options shown in Figure 5-14.

4 Select the types of junk mail you want to move by choosing Move from the first box on each line.

FIGURE 5-14.

Working with junk mail.

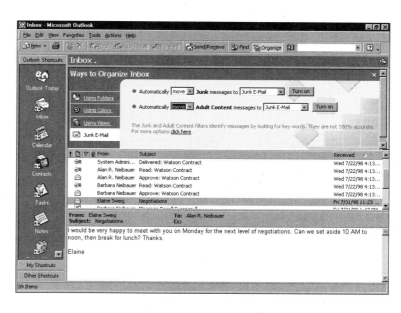

II

Working with Electronic Mail

5 Open each folder list and select Junk E-mail, Deleted Items, or Other Folder.

6 You can refine the junk e-mail rules and download updated filters by clicking the *click here* link.

7 Click Turn On to activate the movement of junk e-mail to the selected folders. (The button then changes to Turn OFF, and you can click it if you no longer want to channel junk e-mail to the designated folder.)

8 If you do not yet have a Junk E-mail folder, Outlook will ask whether you want to create it. Select Yes to create the folder at that time. A message box will appear and ask whether you want to add a shortcut for the folder to your Outlook Bar (unless you've previously turned off this message box). However, the Junk E-mail folder will always be visible in the Folder List.

9 Click the Close box on the Organize pane to remove it from the Inbox.

 NOTE

If Outlook treats mail that you do want to receive as junk mail, use the *click here* link to channel the mail to another location.

Color Coding Junk Mail

Rather than moving or deleting junk e-mail, you can choose to display it in a special color to set it apart from other mail. Just choose Color rather than Move in step 4 on page 173, and then select the color from the second list box.

Adding a Sender to the Junk E-mail List

The Junk E-mail feature, once set up, applies rules to automatically move or color junk and adult content e-mail. For messages that you consider junk that still make it into your Inbox, follow these steps to add the sender's address to the junk e-mail list:

1 Right-click a message from the offending sender in the Inbox.

2 Point to Junk E-mail on the shortcut menu and then choose either Add To Junk Senders List or Add To Adult Content Senders List.

3 You can also click the message, point to Junk E-mail on the Actions menu, and then choose Add To Junk Senders List or Add To Adult Content Senders List. From now on, all mail from this

sender will be automatically routed or colored according to your settings for junk and adult content e-mail.

Managing the Junk Senders List

Rather than wait until a junk e-mailer sends you a message, you might want to add his or her address to the Junk Senders list in anticipation. You might also want to remove an address from the Junk Senders list if you decide that the sender's messages might have some value after all.

You manage your junk e-mailers with the Edit Junk Senders dialog box. Follow these steps:

1 Click the Inbox folder.

2 Click the Organize button on the Standard toolbar.

3 Click Junk E-mail.

4 Click the *click here* link.

5 Click Edit Junk Senders to display the following dialog box. (To manage the Adult Content Senders list, click Edit Adult Content Senders instead.)

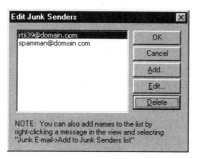

6 Select the address of the person you want to edit or delete, or click Add to manually enter another e-mail address.

ON THE WEB

Outlook applies a built-in set of rules to determine what is junk mail, in addition to the e-mail addresses you add to the Junk senders list and to the rules you create in the Rules Wizard. You can download additional rules to filter out even more unwanted messages by clicking the Outlook Web Site link in step 5 above. The link takes you to *http://officeupdate.microsoft.com/articles/junkmail.htm*, where you can download junk mail rules from third-party providers.

Working with Electronic Mail

TIP

Making Exceptions for Good Junk

You can't delete any of the built-in rules that Outlook applies to determine junk or adult content e-mail. But as you discover mail flagged by Outlook as junk or adult content that you want to treat as normal mail, you can stop Outlook from flagging those particular senders in the future. To do so, open the Rules Wizard from the Tools menu, and turn on the Exception List rule. In the lower part of the dialog box, click Exception List to open the Edit Exception List dialog box. Any e-mail addresses you enter here will be ignored by Outlook's built-in junk and adult-content filtering rules.

7 Click Edit to change the selected address, or click Delete to remove it from the list (which means that new mail from the sender will appear in your Inbox again).

8 Click OK to finish.

You certainly won't use all of the features you learned about in this chapter for every e-mail message, but all of them are important tools. The more e-mail you send, the more comfortable you'll be with these features, and the more use you'll find for them. In the next chapter, you'll learn how to send and receive faxes, and then you'll learn how to send and receive e-mail over the Internet with Outlook Express.

CHAPTER 6

Sending and Receiving Faxes

S ending faxes is a popular form of communication. The trouble with a stand-alone fax machine is that you need to print your message before you can send it. If your computer has a fax modem installed, you can create your message on the computer and then use Microsoft Outlook to send the fax to its destination.

Installing Fax Service

To send and receive faxes using the Internet Only installation, see the sidebar "Using Internet Only Fax Service," on page 195, and Appendix A, "Using Outlook for the Internet Only."

If you use Windows 95, the fax service is installed automatically when you install Microsoft Exchange or Microsoft Messaging. If not, you have to install Microsoft Fax from the Windows CD. Use the Add/Remove Programs option in the Windows Control Panel, select the Windows Setup tab on the Add/Remove Programs Properties dialog box, and select the Microsoft Fax component.

Windows 98 does not install fax service by default and does not offer it as a regular setup option. (Windows 98 does leave an existing Windows 95 version of Microsoft Fax on your computer if you installed Windows 98 over your Windows 95 installation.) To install the fax files, you have to run a program called Awfax.exe. You can find it on your Windows 98 CD, in the folder \tools\oldwin95\message\us (for international installations choose the \intl directory instead of \us).

It is strongly recommended that you install the fax service, regardless of which version of Windows you're running, *before* installing Outlook or Microsoft Office 2000. If you already installed Outlook as a separate program, not as part of Office, rerun the Outlook installation program after installing the fax software. If you already installed Office 2000, follow these steps after you run Awfax.exe to update any Office files that might have been affected:

1 Insert the Office CD in your CD-ROM drive.

2 Open the Control Panel.

3 Choose Add/Remove Programs.

4 Click Microsoft Office 2000 and then click Add/Repair.

5 Click the Repair Office button.

6 Choose Repair Errors In My Office Installation.

7 Click Repair, and then wait until the process is completed—it could take some time.

Setting Up a Fax Profile

If you had fax service installed before you installed Outlook, you might have already added it to your profile using the Inbox Setup Wizard described in Chapter 1, "Preparing for Outlook." If not, you need to add fax service to your Outlook profile before you can send or receive faxes. Just follow these steps:

1 If you want to add fax service to the profile you're currently using while working in Outlook, choose Services from the Tools menu.

To add fax service to a profile other than the one you're using, open the Control Panel window, open the Mail icon, and then click the Show Profiles button. Select the profile you want to change, and then click the Properties button. When the Properties dialog box appears, be sure that the Services tab is showing and that the name of the profile you want to change appears in the title bar.

To add a profile, follow the steps outlined in "Creating a Profile," on page 19.

2 Click the Add button on the Services tab.

3 In the Add Service To Profile dialog box, select Microsoft Fax, and then click OK.

4 A message asks whether you are ready to supply your name and fax number. Click Yes.

5 When the User tab of the Microsoft Fax Properties dialog box appears, as shown in Figure 6-1, fill in as much of the information as you can. You *must* provide your fax number on the User tab.

6 If more than one modem is available to you, click the Modem tab, select the modem you'll be using, and then click the Set As Active Fax Modem button.

7 Fill in the other information and select options as required. *For detailed information, see "Setting Fax Options," on the next page.*

FIGURE 6-1.
The User tab of the Microsoft Fax Properties dialog box.

SEE ALSO

For information about setting up fax addresses, see the sidebar "Adding Fax Addresses to Your Address Book," on page 188.

8 When you've finished setting the fax properties, click OK in each of the open dialog boxes. If Outlook is running, you'll see a message telling you that you can't use the service until you log off and restart Outlook. The next time you start Outlook, you will be able to send and receive faxes.

To send a fax, you must first set up at least one fax address. Then you simply send your message to that address. Outlook sends the message by fax rather than through e-mail.

Setting Fax Options

There are quite a few settings you can make when adding fax service to a profile. You can later make or change settings by editing the profile from the Control Panel's Mail applet or from within Outlook by choosing Services from the Tools menu. You can also point to Microsoft Fax Tools on the Tools menu and choose Options from the submenu.

Let's take a more detailed look at the settings in the Microsoft Fax Properties dialog box now.

Setting Message Options

On the Message tab of the Microsoft Fax Properties dialog box, shown in Figure 6-2, you can select when you want Outlook to send your faxes, you can choose a standard message format, and you can set up a default cover page.

Time To Send. You can designate when Outlook should normally send your faxes.

- If you select the As Soon As Possible option, Outlook sends the fax right away if you're using a network-connected fax service and you're connected to the network. Outlook also sends the fax right away if you're working offline with a profile that has no online services but you have a fax modem in your computer. If you're working offline with a profile that includes an online service, Outlook sends the fax as soon as you connect to the online service that handles faxes.

- If you select the Discount Rates option, Outlook sends faxes only during the hours when your telephone rates are discounted. To set the hours of discounted rates, click the Set button. In the

FIGURE 6-2.

The Message tab of the Microsoft Fax Properties dialog box.

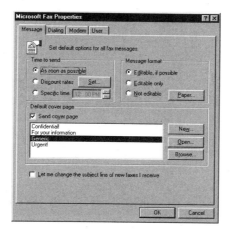

dialog box that appears, set the starting and ending times of the discount period and then click OK.

■ If you select the Specific Time option, Outlook holds faxes until the time you specify in the box.

Message Format.   You can decide whether you want your recipients to receive faxes in a form they can edit. To be editable, your fax must be sent to another computer. If all of your faxes are sent to paper fax machines, you'll want to choose the Not Editable option; choose the Editable Only option if you always send your faxes to computers. The Editable, If Possible option sends the fax in editable format if it goes to a Microsoft Fax–enabled computer but otherwise sends it as a conventional bitmap fax image, not editable but printable as a graphic on a stand-alone fax machine.

The Paper button lets you specify the paper size and image quality for faxes that are sent to stand-alone fax machines. Follow these steps to set the Paper options:

1 Click the Paper button to open the Message Format dialog box shown in Figure 6-3, on the following page.

2 Select the paper size according to the destination of most of your faxes.

3 Select the image quality. The setting Best Available will send at the highest resolution the receiving fax machine can handle. If transmission speed is more important than quality, you can choose the Draft setting instead.

FIGURE 6-3.
The Message Format
dialog box.

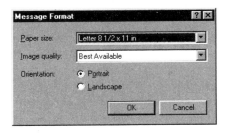

4 Select the orientation. Portrait is the usual choice, where the paper is oriented taller than it is wide, 8½ inches wide by 11 inches tall for letter-size paper.

5 Click OK.

Default Cover Page. This section of the Microsoft Fax Properties dialog box lets you specify whether a cover page is sent along with the fax itself. If you don't want to send cover pages with your faxes, clear the Send Cover Page check box. If you do want to send cover pages with your faxes, select the Send Cover Page check box and then select the style of the cover page. The Confidential, For Your Information, and Urgent styles add these labels to the fax cover page.

You can create a new cover page, change the design of one of the four listed cover pages, or choose a different cover page that's stored elsewhere on your system as follows:

■ When you click the New button, Outlook starts the Fax Cover Page Editor with a blank sheet on which you can design your own cover page.

■ When you click the Open button, Outlook starts the Fax Cover Page Editor and opens the cover page you selected in the list. You can then rearrange it to suit your needs and save it when you're done. It's usually easier to start with an existing cover page design, save it under a new name, and modify it to suit your needs. This way the various fields of information you're likely to need will most likely be available for you to work with.

■ Click the Browse button to locate and open a cover page file not listed, such as one stored on your network server.

If someone gives you a fax cover page file, copy it to the folder in which Windows is installed. That's where Outlook looks for cover page files when you open the Microsoft Fax Properties dialog box. The cover page files use a .cpe filename extension. If you want to remove a fax cover page from the list in this dialog box, move the file to a folder other than the Windows folder.

Let Me Change The Subject Line Of New Faxes I Receive. If you receive faxes on your computer, you might want to change the subject line of an incoming fax to make it more descriptive of an action you must take or a point you want to note. In Outlook when you select the folder where you keep your faxes, the subject lines are displayed just like the subject lines of your mail messages are displayed when you select the Inbox. If you want to be able to change the subject lines of incoming faxes, select the check box labeled Let Me Change The Subject Line Of New Faxes I Receive.

Setting Dialing Options

On the Dialing tab of the Microsoft Fax Properties dialog box, shown in Figure 6-4, you can set up the locations from which you send faxes, create a list of telephone numbers with toll prefixes, and specify how Outlook should handle retries when a fax doesn't go through on the first attempt.

FIGURE 6-4.
The Dialing tab of the Microsoft Fax Properties dialog box.

II

Working with Electronic Mail

Dialing Properties. Click this button to open the Dialing Properties dialog box. In this box, you select your dialing location, area code, calling card information, and the type of dialing.

If you dial a network or other e-mail or fax service from the same telephone all the time, you need to set up only one location. If you dial from several telephones, you need to set up a location for each telephone for which the dialing is different.

To create a new location for dialing, click the New button in the Dialing Properties dialog box. In the Create New Location dialog box, type the location name, and then click OK to return to the Dialing Properties dialog box, where you can set up the properties for the new location.

Toll Prefixes. Click this button to open the Toll Prefixes dialog box, which is useful for people living in areas where certain numbers within the local area code require that you dial the area code along with the local number. If you live in such an area, you can tell Outlook to dial the area code even though it is the area code within which you reside. To do so, follow these steps:

1 Click the Toll Prefixes button on the Dialing tab of the Microsoft Fax Properties dialog box to display the dialog box shown here:

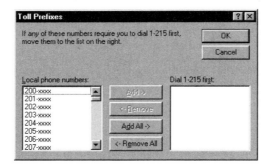

2 In the Local Phone Numbers list, select the prefixes for which the area code must be dialed.

3 Click the Add button to add the prefixes to the Dial list. You can also click Add All to include all of the prefixes. Use Remove and Remove All to remove prefixes from the Dial list.

4 Click OK.

If most prefixes in your area code require that you dial the area code, click Add All in the Toll Prefixes dialog box, and then remove the few prefixes that *don't* require the area code.

Retries. For various reasons, a fax does not always get to its destination—a busy line, no fax machine answer, a faulty connection, or a glitch in the receiving machine. You can decide how many times Outlook should try to get your fax through to the recipient—simply set the number in the Number Of Retries box on the Dialing tab. You can also decide how long you want Outlook to wait between retries. Because the most common problem with sending a fax is probably a busy line, you might want to wait the two minutes initially set up in Outlook. To specify a different waiting period, set the number of minutes in the Time Between Retries box.

Setting Modem Options

The Modem tab of the Microsoft Fax Properties dialog box, shown in Figure 6-5, lets you select the modem Outlook will use for faxes and set the options for that modem.

Adjusting Modem Properties

You can set up your modem to answer incoming calls, and you can adjust the modem speaker volume and set your call preferences. To set modem properties, select your fax modem from the Available Fax Modems list, and then click the Properties button. You can then change the settings in the Fax Modem Properties dialog box, shown in Figure 6-6, on the next page.

FIGURE 6-5.

The Modem tab of the Microsoft Fax Properties dialog box.

FIGURE 6-6.
The Fax Modem
Properties dialog box.

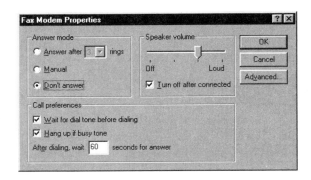

The Answer Mode section lets you specify how your modem should answer incoming calls:

- **Answer After __ Rings.** If you use your telephone line primarily for fax reception and you want your computer fax modem to automatically answer every incoming call, select the Answer After option and set the number of rings the fax modem should allow before it answers. If you use the line only for faxes, you can set the number of rings to one. The standard setting of three rings gives you a chance to answer in case you occasionally receive voice calls on this line. This setting also ensures that you're not answering a single-ring call made in error.

- **Manual.** If you use your telephone line for both voice and fax and you want to manually switch on fax reception, select the Manual option. When a call comes in and you hear the fax warble, click the Answer Now button in the Microsoft Fax Status window. *See "Receiving a Fax," on page 193.*

- **Don't Answer.** If you don't want your fax modem to ever answer an incoming call, select this option. You should select this option if you receive your faxes from a fax service or a stand-alone fax machine.

Clicking the Advanced button in the Fax Modem Properties dialog box displays a dialog box in which you can set more options for fax transmission and reception.

Adding a New Modem

If the modem you want to use is not listed on the Modem tab of the Microsoft Fax Properties dialog box, you can add it. You can add either a local modem (a modem in your computer or attached to it) or a network modem.

To add a modem, take these steps:

1 Click the Add button on the Modem tab to open the Add A Fax Modem dialog box.

2 Select a local modem or a network fax server.

3 Click OK.

4 If you selected a local fax modem, work through the Install New Modem Wizard. If you selected a network fax server, type the share name of the modem and click OK.

Sharing a Modem

If your organization has fewer modems than computers, you might need to share your modem with others. When your modem is shared, the people to whom you give the proper permissions can send their faxes through your modem. To share your modem with other users on the network, follow these steps:

1 Click the Modem tab of the Microsoft Fax Properties dialog box, and then select the check box labeled Let Other People On The Network Use My Modem To Send Faxes.

2 If the Select Drive dialog box appears, select the drive on your local machine that you want the network fax service to use, and then click OK.

3 Click the Properties button to set up sharing. Outlook displays the NetFax dialog box shown in Figure 6-7, on the next page.

4 Make sure that Shared As is selected, and change the share name if needed.

5 Use the Access Type section to select the type of access users will have to the faxes folder:

  • Select Read-Only to limit others to viewing faxes. If you select this option, you can also require a password by specifying it in the Read-Only Password box.

  • Select Full to allow others full access to the fax server folder. If you want to restrict access to those with a password, enter the password in the Full Access Password text box.

II

Working with Electronic Mail

FIGURE 6-7.
The NetFax dialog box.

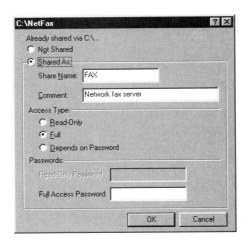

- Select Depends On Password if you want some users to have full access and others to have read access only to the faxes folder. If you select this option, enter two different passwords in the Read-Only and Full Access Password boxes.

6 Click OK.

Adding Fax Addresses to Your Address Book

In Outlook you have three ways to set up a fax address, two of them in your address book and one on the spot. You can add a fax number to an e-mail address in your personal address book or to a contact entry in your Contacts folder, which becomes an entry in the Outlook Address Book. *For information about setting up entries in your address books, see "Adding an Address," on page 117, and "Setting Up Contacts," on page 400.*

Follow these steps to set up a fax address in your personal address book:

1 Choose Address Book from the Tools menu.

2 In the Address Book dialog box, select your personal address book from the Show Names From The box, and then click the New Entry button.

3 In the New Entry dialog box, select your personal address book from the Put This Entry In The list. The entries in the Select The Entry Type list will change accordingly. Depending on how you set up Outlook, the list might include the type FAX.

4 If you see the FAX type, select it and click OK; otherwise select Other Address and click OK.

> **Adding Fax Addresses to Your Address Book** *continued*
>
> **5** If you selected FAX, the New Fax Properties dialog box opens. Enter an identifying name for the fax recipient in the Name To Show On Cover Page box, and enter the recipient's fax number.
>
> If instead you selected Other Address, the New Other Address Properties dialog box appears. From the New - Address tab enter the recipient's name and fax number in the Display Name and E-mail Address boxes, and then enter FAX as the E-mail Type.
>
> **6** Fill in additional information as you want on the remaining tabs of the dialog box, and then click OK.
>
> To address a fax on the spot (useful for a one-time fax message), fill in the recipient's name and fax number in the second page of the Compose New Fax Wizard, as explained in the next section, "Sending a Fax."

Setting User Options

You were introduced to the User tab of the Microsoft Fax Properties dialog box at the beginning of this chapter, when you added the Microsoft Fax service to your profile. It contains your sender information, and the information you supply here can appear on your fax cover sheet and can be used by recipients as your return fax address.

Sending a Fax

When you've set up your fax service and modem, you're ready to send a fax. You have two ways to do this—by using Outlook's Compose New Fax Wizard or by addressing a message to a fax recipient from your address book and clicking Send.

The Compose New Fax Wizard lets you send a cover page with a note and attached files. Here are the steps for using the wizard:

1 Choose New Fax Message from the Actions menu. Outlook starts the Compose New Fax Wizard, shown in Figure 6-8, on the next page.

FIGURE 6-8.

The Compose New Fax Wizard.

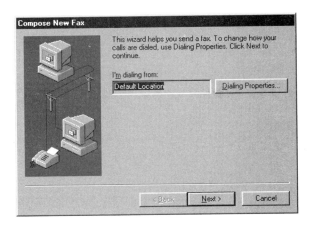

2 Click the Dialing Properties button if you need to change your dialing location or how the call is dialed.

3 Click Next.

4 On the second page of the wizard, use these methods to select the fax recipients:

- Click the Address button if you've added the recipients to your address book, as described in the sidebar "Adding Fax Addresses to Your Address Book," on page 188. (Since contacts may have several e-mail addresses and phone numbers, the contact's name will be repeated for each in the address book, followed by its type. Choose the name followed by Business Fax, Home Fax, or Other Fax, depending on where you want the fax sent.)

- Type the recipient's name in the To box, and select the appropriate country from the drop-down list. Type the recipient's fax number, and select the Dial Area Code check box if needed. Then click the Add To List button.

Repeat these procedures for each recipient if the fax is being sent to several people.

5 Click Next.

6 Choose whether to include a cover page.

7 For a cover page, select the style.

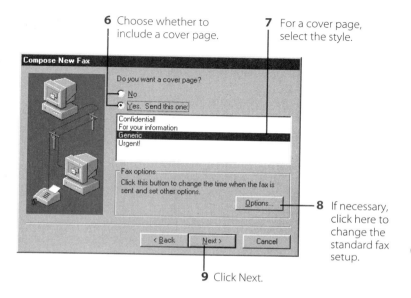

8 If necessary, click here to change the standard fax setup.

9 Click Next.

10 Type a subject line.

11 Type an optional note. (This could be the entire message.)

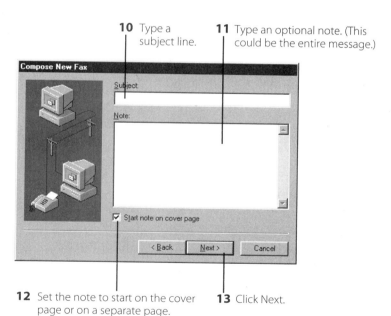

12 Set the note to start on the cover page or on a separate page.

13 Click Next.

14 On this page of the wizard, you can add a file to the fax by clicking the Add File button. In the dialog box that appears, select the file you want to include and click Open. Repeat this procedure for each file that you want to send in your fax. The files will appear as icons in your message.

15 Click Next.

16 On the Finish page of the Compose New Fax Wizard, click the Finish button.

To send a fax using Outlook's message window instead of the Compose New Fax Wizard, you must have the fax recipients set up with a fax address in your address book. *See the sidebar "Adding Fax Addresses to Your Address Book," on page 188, for information about how to do this.* Then follow these steps:

1 Click the New Message button, as if you were starting a new e-mail message.

2 Click the To button, select the address book you need from the Show Names From The box, and then select the fax recipient or recipients from the address list. When selecting a contact, be sure to select the name followed by Business Fax, Home Fax, or Other Fax, depending on where you want to send the fax. Click OK in the Select Names dialog box.

3 In the message window, enter a subject and a message as you would for a regular e-mail message. You can format the message and add attachments as you can for other messages.

4 To change the options used to send this fax, choose Send Options from the File menu to see options similar to those shown in Figure 6-2 (page 181). Choose your settings from the dialog box, and then click OK.

5 When you're finished composing the fax message, click the Send button.

6 You'll see the Microsoft Fax Status dialog box, informing you of the status of the fax as Outlook prepares the fax message, initiates the fax modem, and then sends the fax.

> **NOTE**
>
> To quickly create a fax address from within the message window, choose the Fax Addressing Wizard from the message window's Tools menu. Enter the recipient's name and fax number, click Add To List, and then click Finish.

If you set up a number of faxes to send, you might want to know which fax is being sent and how many more are in the fax queue. To check the status of outgoing faxes, do the following:

1 Point to Microsoft Fax Tools on the Tools menu, and choose Show Outgoing Faxes to see a list of outgoing faxes.

2 To cancel an outgoing fax, select it from the list and then choose Cancel Fax from the File menu. If the fax message remains on your Outbox after you've cancelled it, delete it from the Outbox yourself.

Receiving a Fax

You can set up Outlook to receive faxes in your Inbox. Before you can receive faxes, however, you must perform the following two actions:

- Set up your modem to answer incoming calls by selecting one of the Answer Mode options in the Fax Modem Properties dialog box. *See "Setting Modem Options," on page 185.*

- Decide whether you want to be able to change the subject line of the faxes you receive. On the Message tab of the Microsoft Fax Properties dialog box, select (or clear) the check box labeled Let Me Change The Subject Line Of New Faxes I Receive. *See "Setting Message Options," on 180.*

> If you usually have Outlook set up to receive faxes and you want to discontinue doing so, select Don't Answer as your Answer Mode option.

After you complete these two actions, you're ready to receive a fax. How you do this depends on the Answer Mode option you've chosen:

- If you selected the Answer After option, simply let Outlook answer the call and receive the fax.

- If you selected the Manual option, when a call comes in and you pick up your phone and hear the fax warble, click the Answer Now button in the Microsoft Fax Status window and hang up the phone after Outlook has answered the call.

> If the Microsoft Fax Status window does not appear when the telephone rings, click the Fax icon in the System tray (at the right end of the Windows taskbar).

Received faxes appear in your Inbox, just as e-mail messages do. You can then treat the faxes just as you treat any folder item in Outlook.

Retrieving a Fax from a Service

If you have your faxes sent to a fax service instead of directly to your computer, you can request that the service send your faxes to you. To request faxes from your fax service, follow these steps:

1 Point to Microsoft Fax Tools on the Tools menu, and then choose Request A Fax from the submenu. You'll see the first page of the Request A Fax Wizard, shown in Figure 6-9.

2 Select to receive all available faxes or just a specific fax. If you chose a specific fax, enter the title of the fax and your password, if applicable.

3 Click Next.

4 In the dialog box that appears, type the name of the fax service in the To box, and select the appropriate country from the drop-down list. Type the fax service's fax number, and select the Dial Area Code check box if needed. Then click the Add button. (Alternatively, you can click the Address Book button to select the fax service.)

5 Click Next.

6 Select the time you want Outlook to send the request. The options are As Soon As Possible, When Phone Rates Are Discounted, and A Specific Time.

7 Click Next.

8 Click the Finish button.

FIGURE 6-9.

The Request A Fax Wizard.

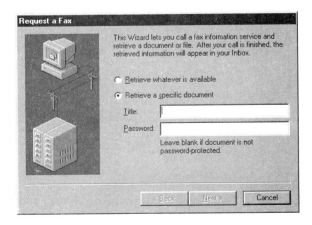

9 When the faxes arrive, receive the faxes as described in the previous section, "Receiving a Fax," on page 193.

That concludes our coverage of using Outlook's faxing services from the Corporate/Workgroup installation. Most features work similarly if you're using the Internet Only installation of Outlook except that a different fax program is installed automatically with the Internet Only installation, the Symantec WinFax Starter Edition. See the sidebar that follows for more details. In the next chapter, you'll learn how to use an entirely different program to send and receive e-mail—Outlook Express.

Using Internet Only Fax Service

If you installed Outlook with the Internet Only setup, Outlook provides its own fax service automatically and adds a Fax tab to the Options dialog box.

Use the Fax tab of the Options dialog box to set up your fax modem as described in the sidebar "Internet Only Fax Options," on page 108. Outlook might also begin the Outlook Fax Setup Wizard, which asks for your personal information, how it should receive and send faxes, and whether to include a cover page.

To send a fax, start a new message as you would normally.

To address a fax to a person in the Contacts folder who has a fax number, enter the name of a recipient and complete the message. Then click the Options button, open the Send Message Using list and choose Symantec WinFax Starter Edition. Close the Message Options dialog box and click Send.

You can also send a fax by typing a fax number in the To box using the form *FAX@555-5555*. If you need to dial a number to reach an outside phone, use the syntax *FAX@9w555-5555*. In this case, 9 is the number to reach an outside line, and the letter *w* tells Outlook to wait for a dial tone before dialing. Complete the message as you would any other but do *not* click Send. Instead, choose Send Using from the File menu and click Symantec WinFax Starter Edition.

For additional information, see Appendix A, "Using Outlook for the Internet Only."

Working with Electronic Mail

II

CHAPTER 7

Using Outlook Express

Microsoft Outlook Express is a full-featured application provided with Microsoft Internet Explorer and Microsoft Office 2000 that lets you send and receive e-mail over the Internet and subscribe to and trade messages with newsgroups. You can even use it with multiple e-mail accounts or to share a single account with several people. It is really quite a bonus.

Sending and receiving mail in Outlook Express is similar to sending and receiving mail in Outlook itself. So if you've read Chapter 5, "Sending and Receiving Messages," you're well on your way to using Outlook Express. Because Outlook Express is different from Outlook in many ways, however, don't skip this chapter even if you're an experienced Outlook user. You may still want to use Outlook Express for your Internet e-mail, and you'll need a basic understanding of how the program works to trade messages with newsgroups.

Starting Outlook Express

To start Outlook Express, open its icon on your desktop, or click Start, point to Programs, point to Internet Explorer, and click Outlook Express. If you already have Internet e-mail set up with Outlook, Outlook Express should start and be ready for you to send and receive mail.

Outlook and Outlook Express

You can, of course, have both Outlook and Outlook Express on your computer at the same time, and you can send and receive Internet e-mail with either program. If you are using the Corporate/Workgroup installation of Outlook, the programs maintain their own separate set of address books and folders such as the Inbox and Outbox. While you can import Outlook Express addresses and mail into Outlook, the programs do not automatically share the information. With the Internet Only installation, the two programs can share a single address book, if you like, but the mail folders will still be separate.

If you want to send meeting requests and task assignments to other Outlook users over the Internet, you have to use Outlook for such e-mail. If you primarily use Outlook for communicating over your network, and keep your Internet mail totally separate, you may find Outlook Express more convenient and somewhat faster.

You also have to decide which program, Outlook or Outlook Express, to use as your default mail program with Microsoft Internet Explorer. This is the mail program used when you select to send or receive mail from within the browser. To select the default program, open Internet Explorer, choose Internet Options from the Tools menu, and then click the Programs tab to see these options in the Messaging area:

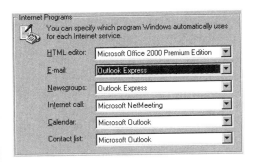

From the E-mail list, choose which program to use—Outlook or Outlook Express, and then click Close. If you choose to use Outlook Express as your default, you won't be able to access your Exchange address book and messages when sending mail from Internet Explorer.

When you do not have e-mail set up, launching Outlook Express might open the Internet Connection Wizard, which you can use to tell Outlook Express how to connect to the Internet to check your mail and newsgroups. If you've been using a Web browser or another mail program and you already have a dial-up account established, you can select the same account. You can also create a new dial-up connection for an existing account, or you can start from scratch and select an Internet provider right online, from the comfort of your own home or office. *To learn how to set up an e-mail account for Outlook Express see "Setting Up Accounts," on page 227.*

Running Outlook Express

Once you've completed the Internet Connection Wizard and each time you start Outlook Express, you might see the message shown here:

Outlook Express doesn't automatically connect to your Internet service provider (ISP) when you first start it. If you have more than one ISP account, choose the one you want to use from the Connect To list, and enter your username and password. To avoid having to enter your password each time you open Outlook Express, select the Save Password check box. And, if you don't want to see this message box each time you start Outlook Express, select the Connect Automatically check box—Outlook Express will then connect to your ISP when you open the program. Now let's take a look at the Outlook Express window, shown in Figure 7-1, on the next page.

Below the menu bar is the toolbar. You use the buttons on the toolbar to create, send, and receive messages, to work with your address book, and to connect to your ISP. The buttons on the toolbar depend on the folder being displayed, but you can create, get, and send mail from any

FIGURE 7-1.
The Outlook Express window.

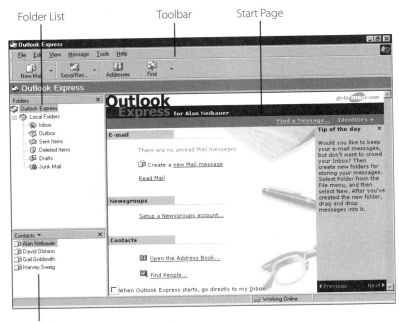

Folder List   Toolbar   Start Page

Contacts List

folder in Outlook Express. You can also customize the buttons on the toolbar to your preference.

> **NOTE**
>
> The Send/Receive button on the toolbar is unavailable if you haven't set up an Internet account.

Like Outlook, Outlook Express stores messages in folders, shown in the folder list on the left side of the window. Unlike Outlook, Outlook Express shows the folder list by default where Outlook would display the Outlook Bar. When you select a folder from the folder list, Outlook displays its messages in the larger pane to the right. Below the folder list is another panel displaying the Outlook Express address book. (If it's not visible, you can turn it on by choosing Layout from the View menu, selecting the Contacts check box, and then clicking OK.) You'll learn how to use this to quickly send mail to a person in the address book.

> **NOTE**
>
> Even though the address book is labeled Contacts, it does not contain the entries from your Outlook Contacts folder unless you are sharing address books and running the Outlook Internet Only installation.

When you start Outlook Express you'll see the start page. (To return to the start page later on, click Outlook Express at the top of the folder list.)

The Go To MSN.COM button at the top right of the window lets you connect to Microsoft's online service. The Switch Identities and Add New Identity options let you use Outlook Express with more than one person or mail account. You'll learn more about identities later in this chapter. Along the right side of the window you may see a panel showing a handy tip of the day. If this is turned off, you'll see the word *Tip* in the upper right corner of the screen. Click this to display the tip of the day. You can browse through additional tips by clicking the Previous and Next buttons at the bottom of the Tip window.

The other options on the start page perform these functions:

- **Create A New Mail Message.** Click this to open a new message window to create an e-mail message.

- **Read Mail.** Click this to open the Inbox folder so you can read mail that you've already received.

- **Set Up A Newsgroups Account.** Click this to set up newsgroups.

- **Open The Address Book.** Click this to open the address book in a separate window.

- **Find People.** Click this to locate people by searching your address book or by searching popular online e-mail directory services.

If you want Outlook Express to automatically start in the Inbox rather than on the start page, select the check box at the bottom of the screen labeled When Outlook Express Starts, Go Directly To My 'Inbox.'

Using the Outlook Express Address Book

The address book in Outlook Express is a simpler version of the one in Outlook, but it offers many of the same capabilities. You can, for example, organize addresses into groups and initiate online conferences if Microsoft NetMeeting is installed.

To access the address book, click the Addresses button on the toolbar, or choose Address Book on the Tools menu.

You can quickly enter a new listing by clicking the Contact button above the Contacts list and choosing New Contact from the menu that appears.

Create a new contact, folder, or group.

Edit the selected listing.

Remove the selected listing.

Find a person's address.

Print one or more addresses.

Send an e-mail message or make an Internet call.

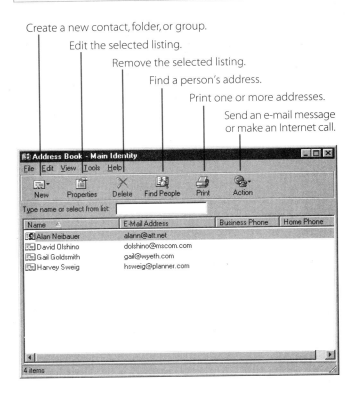

The Outlook Express address book only has one address type, and you cannot access addresses on your network server or in Outlook itself, although you can import from some other address sources (by selecting Import from the File menu). To create a new listing, click New on the Address Book toolbar and choose New Contact from the menu that appears. Figure 7-2 shows the Address Book form for creating a new address or editing an existing one.

Here's how to create a listing:

1 Type the person's first, middle, and last names in the appropriate text boxes. The full name appears automatically in the Display box as you type. You can change how the name will appear in the address book by typing something different in the Display box.

2 Enter an optional nickname in the Nickname box.

3 Type the e-mail address in the E-Mail Addresses box.

4 Click Add.

5 You can enter additional e-mail addresses for the same person by repeating steps 3 and 4. Select the main address you want to use for e-mail and then click the Set As Default button.

6 If a person's e-mail system does not allow him or her to read formatted messages, select the check box labeled Send E-Mail Using Plain Text Only.

Use the remaining tabs of the dialog box to record home and business information, add notes and see group membership (on the Other tab), enter dial-up and server information for NetMeeting conferencing, and record digital IDs to send encrypted mail.

If you are using Outlook's Internet Only installation, Outlook and Outlook Express can share a single address book. In Outlook Express, open the Address Book, and then choose Options from the Tools menu in the Address Book toolbar. Select the check box labeled Share Contact Information Among Microsoft Outlook and Other Applications, and then click OK.

Setting Up Groups

You often want to send the same e-mail message to several individuals, such as members of a project team or a group of friends. You can create one or more groups in Outlook Express and then add members to

FIGURE 7-2.
The Properties dialog box for entering or editing an address listing.

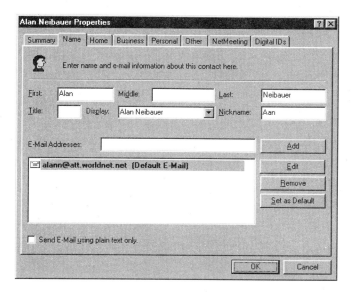

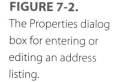

it. To send a message to the members of the group, just select the group name in the address book rather than the names of each individual recipient.

To create a group, click the New button on the address book toolbar, and then choose New Group from the menu to display the dialog box shown in Figure 7-3.

1 Type a name for the group in the Group Name box.

2 Click Select Members to choose group members from your address book. You can quickly add additional members not in your address book by entering their names and e-mail addresses in the Name and E-Mail boxes and clicking Add.

3 To add a contact to the group and your address book in one step, click New Contact, and then create the address book entry.

4 Click OK.

FIGURE 7-3.
The Properties dialog box for creating a new group.

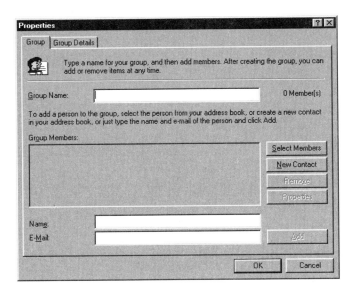

You can also delete a selected member of the group using the Remove button or display a member's information by clicking Properties.

Use the Group Details tab of the Properties dialog box to specify a street address, phone number, and Web site address for the group. Click the View Map button to connect to Microsoft Expedia Maps on the Internet to see the address on a map.

You'll see the group icon in the list of address book names. You can also choose Folders And Groups from the View menu to see your groups in the folder list, as shown here.

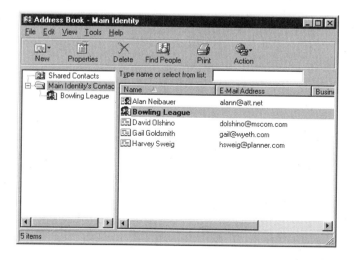

To quickly list the members of the group, click the group icon in the folder list and the list appears. After selecting a group in the folders list, click Contacts to again display the full address book.

Once you've created a group, you can "drag" new people into it. Here's how:

1 Make sure that groups are shown in the folder list by choosing Folders And Groups from the View menu.

2 Click Contacts, or another folder, to display the individual entries within it.

3 Drag the name you want to add to your group from the address book list to the group icon in the folder list.

Creating Address Book Folders

In addition to collecting persons in groups, you can organize addresses into folders. While you cannot automatically send mail to everyone in a particular folder in quite the way you can to a group, folders can help you organize addresses that have something in common. Address book folders work similarly to folders on your hard disk.

To create a folder, click the New button on the Address Book toolbar, and then choose New Folder from the menu. In the box that appears, type a name for the folder. If you want to share the folder with all identities using Outlook Express, select the Share This Folder With Other Identities check box. Click OK to finish. Folders appear in the folder list under the identity, like this:

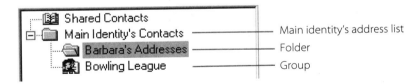

If you selected to share the folder with other identities, the folder will appear under the Shared Contacts item in the folder list. To add a new name to the folder, select the folder in the folder list, and then choose New Contact after clicking the New button. You can also drag existing names from one folder to another, which removes them from the origi- nal location.

> To send an e-mail message to all the addresses in a folder, select the folder, click the first name in the list of addressees, hold down the Shift key, and click the last name in the folder. Then, with all the names selected, click the Action button on the toolbar. Choose Send Mail from the menu that appears, and a new message window will open with all the names placed in the To box.

Sending Mail

Sending Internet mail in Outlook Express is just as easy as sending mail using Outlook, if not easier. To start a message by choosing the recipi- ent first, use one of these techniques:

- Double-click the name in the Contacts list.

- Click the name, or group name, in the address book, click Actions on the Address Book toolbar, and choose Send Mail from the menu.

The message window appears with the message already addressed to the recipient, as shown in Figure 7-4. If you selected a group name or multiple addressees, the message will be addressed to every person selected.

FIGURE 7-4.
The New Message window.

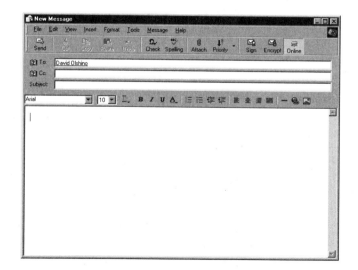

You can also open the message window and then select the recipient using these steps:

1 Click the New Mail button on the Outlook Express toolbar.

2 Click the icon next to the To text box to open the Select Recipients dialog box.

3 Select the address list containing the person or persons you want to address the message to.

4 Type a name (or part of one) or choose a name from the list. You can choose multiple recipients by holding down the Ctrl key as you click each name.

5 Click the To button.

6 Select names to add to the Cc or BCc boxes if you want to send carbon copies or blind carbon copies to other recipients.

7 Click OK.

Once the message is addressed, complete and send it as follows:

1 In the message window, click in the Subject box and type a brief description for the subject of your message.

2 Click in the message text area, or press the Tab key to move to the message text area, and then type your message.

3 When your message is ready to go, click Send.

TIP

> If you do not complete your message or are not ready to send it, select Save from the File menu to store it in the Drafts folder, and then close the message without clicking Send.

Before you click Send, you can also mark your message as having either low or high priority. When you select either of these options, a special icon will appear on the recipient's screen so they know how important you feel the message is. Click the Priority button on the toolbar and choose from these options:

Making Sure Your Messages Are Sent

Clicking Send might or might not actually send your message. It all depends on how Outlook Express is set up.

If Outlook Express is set up to send messages immediately and to automatically dial, it will connect to your ISP, if you are not already online, and send your message. Otherwise, it merely adds the message to the Outbox and displays a dialog box reporting that you still have to send the mail. After you've seen this dialog box a few times, you'll probably want to select the Don't Ask Me This Again check box to stop it from displaying.

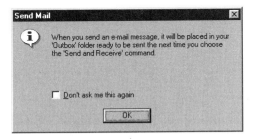

To further remind you that you have mail to go out, the name of the Outbox folder is shown in bold and you'll see the number of unread Outbox messages.

  To send the mail in your Outbox, click the Send/Receive button on the toolbar. This sends any mail you have ready to go and checks for new mail at the same time. If you want to send mail without looking for new messages, click the small arrow next to the Send/Receive button and choose Send All from the menu. Choose Receive All from the menu to get new mail without sending the mail in your Outbox.

As Outlook sends your mail and checks for new messages waiting for you, you'll see a dialog box reporting its progress. Click the Details button in the box to expand it, as shown in Figure 7-5.

Outlook will first send any mail that you've composed and then download any mail that's waiting for you. If you have mail, the word Inbox in the folder list is displayed in bold and followed by the number of messages that you have not yet read.

CAUTION

Do not select the Hang Up When Finished check box if you use Outlook Express as the default mail program with Internet Explorer. If Outlook Express sends and receives mail in the background while you are browsing, your dial-up connection will be terminated and so will your browsing.

If you want Outlook to disconnect from your ISP after it has received messages, select the Hang Up When Finished check box. Otherwise you can select Work Offline from the File menu. Outlook Express will ask if you'd like to disconnect before going offline. Click Yes to disconnect. You can also disconnect directly from Windows by closing the dial-up networking connection.

Copies of all sent messages are stored in the Sent Items folder so you have a record of your communications.

Typing E-mail Addresses

Instead of looking up a recipient in the address book, you can type the name or e-mail address of the recipient in the To section of the New Message window. To send the same message to more than one recipient, separate the names with a semicolon.

FIGURE 7-5.

Sending and receiving mail.

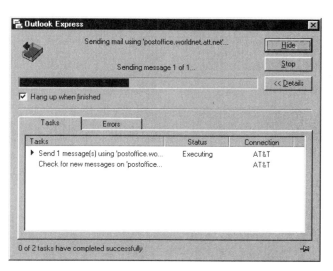

Working with Electronic Mail

SEE ALSO

For more information about the Check Names dialog box, see "Typing Recipient Names and Addresses," on page 133.

As long as the recipient's name or e-mail address is in your address book, you only have to type enough characters to distinguish it from any other name in your address book. As you type, Outlook Express scans the address book for an entry that starts with those characters and displays it highlighted on screen. If the name or e-mail address is correct, just move on and continue composing your message. If it is not, continue typing additional characters until Outlook Express finds the match you want. When Outlook Express recognizes the name, you can immediately type a semicolon and begin typing another name. While Outlook Express automatically expands names against the entries in your address book, it doesn't automatically check whether you've entered an e-mail address for each of them in the E-mail Addresses box of their Properties dialog box. To confirm that all of your recipients have an e-mail address in the address book, click the Check button on the toolbar. Outlook Express will look up the names in the address book. Names that have an e-mail address associated with them will be underlined. If Outlook finds a name without an e-mail address, it will underline and display the name in red. If Outlook cannot locate the name, you'll see the Check Names dialog box.

TIP

You can also set up Outlook Express to search for recipients in online directories. *See "Finding People," on page 241.*

Adding a Signature

While your e-mail address automatically appears on all of your messages, you may want to identify yourself even more by including a standard signature closing. In Chapter 4, "Using Address Books," you learned how to use a signature in Outlook. Signatures work the same way in Outlook Express, except you set them up differently.

To set up a signature in Outlook Express, follow these steps:

1 Choose Options on the Tools menu, and click the Signatures tab to see the options in Figure 7-6.

2 Click New to create a signature. The notation Signature #1 appears in the Signatures box.

3 Click Rename to highlight Signature #1, and then change the name as desired.

4 Click in the large box under Edit Signature and type the text of the signature. Alternatively, you can click the File option button and use Browse to select a file to append to your messages.

FIGURE 7-6.

The Signatures tab of the Options dialog box.

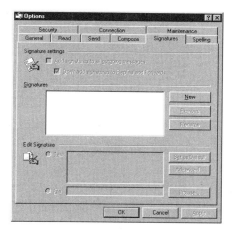

5 Repeat this procedure to create any additional signatures, and then select the one to use by default from the list in the Signatures box and click Set as Default.

6 Select the check box labeled Add Signatures To All Outgoing Messages.

7 Select or clear the check box labeled Don't Add Signatures To Replies And Forwards according to whether you want the signature to be added to all your messages only to your original messages.

The signature you pick for the default will be used for all of your mail and newsgroup messages, and for all of your accounts. If you want, you can choose a different signature for each account. In the Signatures dialog box, click the signature you want to use for a specific account, such as all newsgroup messages, and then click the Advanced button to display the Advanced Signature Settings dialog box:

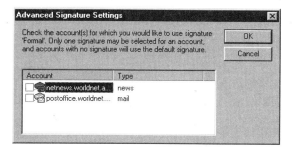

Select the check box for each account you want to use this signature with, and then click OK. Accounts not assigned any specific signature will continue to use the default signature, if any.

The next time you compose a new message, Outlook Express inserts the signature text into the message area. For replies and forwards, Outlook Express adds the signature above the copy of the message you are responding to or forwarding. Just type your message above the signature text.

You can also choose to insert your signature manually in selected messages. Follow all of the steps above to create the signature but do not select the check box labeled Add Signatures To All Outgoing Messages in step 6 on the previous page. When you want to add your signature to an e-mail message, move to the end of the message and choose Signature from the Insert menu to see a list of signatures that you created. Select the signature you want to add to the message.

Creating a Virtual Business Card

As you learned in Chapter 5, "Sending and Receiving Messages," a vCard is an electronic business card containing contact information from your address book. When you include your own vCard as part of your signature, recipients can read the information and add it to their address books with a simple click of the mouse. Follow these steps to add your vCard to your outgoing messages:

1 Choose Options from the Tools menu, and click the Compose tab to see the options shown in Figure 7-7.

2 Select the Mail check box in the Business Cards section to set up a card for e-mail messages; click the News check box to set up a card for newsgroup messages.

3 Open the list next to the check box you enabled and select your name from the list of contacts that appears. To change your address book listing, click Edit.

4 Click OK.

The next time you send a message, Outlook Express will add your business card as an attachment. When you compose a message, you'll see an icon indicating that the card is attached. If you do not want to include the card with a specific message, click the icon and choose Delete from the menu that appears. Choose Open from the same menu if you want to edit the address book listing.

FIGURE 7-7.

The Compose tab of the Options dialog box.

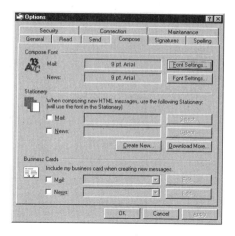

? SEE ALSO

To learn how to read a business card that you receive with a message, see "Reading and Saving Business Cards," on page 222.

You can also add the business card on a message-by-message basis. Follow the steps on page 212 to select your name for the card, but clear the Mail and News check boxes before closing the Options dialog box. When composing a message, choose My Business Card from the Insert menu. Outlook Express will insert the business card for the listing you chose on the Compose tab of the Options dialog box.

Formatting Messages

Outlook Express lets you format messages in much the same way as Outlook, but with some differences. You can use the Formatting toolbar and the Format menu to add pizzazz to your text, and you can also add stationery and graphics files. To insert graphics, use the Picture command on the Insert menu or the Insert Picture button on the far right of the Outlook Express Formatting toolbar. To add a background picture, color, or sound, choose Background on the Format menu. When you select Sound from the submenu that appears, for example, you can select a sound file, such as a midi file, to play once or continuously as the recipient reads the messages.

> NOTE

Formatting is only available if you use the HTML format rather than plain text for the message. Select Rich Text (HTML) from the Format menu of the New Message window to use this format for a specific message. To make this the default format, choose Options from the Tools menu of Outlook Express and select HTML from the Send tab of the Options dialog box. While most browsers can now read HTML messages, many newsgroups still require plain text format. You can set the default format for mail and newsgroups separately in the Options dialog box.

Changing the Default Font

Do you find yourself changing the font of every message because you just don't like the default font displayed by Outlook Express? Save yourself some time and choose another font, font size, or style as the new default. Follow these steps to change the default font:

1 Choose Options from the Tools menu, and click the Compose tab.

2 Click the Font Settings button next to the Mail box to change the font settings for e-mail messages; click the Font Settings button next to the News box to change the font settings for newsgroup messages.

3 Choose a font, font style, size, effects, and color from each Font dialog box.

4 Click OK twice.

The selected font will now be used with all new messages. You can, of course, use the Formatting toolbar or Font command on the Format menu to choose a different font for individual messages, and you can select a new default font whenever you want.

Using Stationery

While Outlook Express and Outlook do not share address books or mail folders, they do share stationery. In fact, new stationery that you create with one program will be available to the other. Even so, the techniques for selecting stationery differ.

Composing a Message with Stationery

You may want to send most messages without a stationery design. Stationery does add to the time it takes to send and receive a message, and not all recipients are able to see background designs and graphics.

When you want to send a message using a stationery design, you can select it before or while you're composing the message.

To start a new message with a stationery design, use these steps:

1 Click the small arrow on the New Mail button on the toolbar, or point to New Message Using on the Message menu.

2 Select one of the listed stationery designs and start your message, or click Select Stationery to see the Select Stationery dialog box.

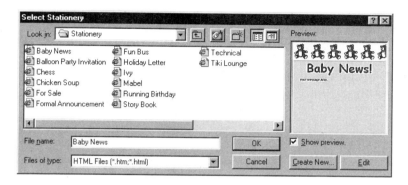

3 Select a stationery design. You'll see what it looks like in the Preview panel. You can also use the navigation buttons in the dialog box to locate and choose any HTML file.

4 Click Open.

Remember, some stationery designs, such as Baby News, contain formatted text as well as a background pattern and pictures. You can edit or delete the formatted text if you do not want it in your message.

If you already started a message without stationery and decide you want to add it, choose Apply Stationery from the Format menu, and then select a stationery design or More Stationery from the list.

Choosing a Default Stationery

Now suppose you have a great stationery design that you want to use for all your messages. Rather than choose it each time you send a message, set it as the default. Here's how:

1 Choose Options from the Tools menu, and click the Compose tab.

2 Select the Mail check box in the Stationery section to set up a card for e-mail messages; click the News check box to set up a card for newsgroup messages.

3 Click the Select button next to the check box you enabled, choose the design from the Select Stationery dialog box, and then click OK.

4 Click OK.

Choosing Something Other Than the Default

Just because you select default stationery doesn't mean you *have* to use it for every new message. You may want to send a formal message to a business associate, a letter of complaint, or some other message that you just don't want formatted with the default stationery design. You may want to select a different design or just send a message with a plain background. It's your choice.

- To send a message with a plain background, click the small arrow on the New Mail button and choose No Stationery from the list.

- To send a message with different stationery, just select it using the techniques explained above. *See "Composing a Message with Stationery," on page 214.*

> Selecting a stationery design from within the message might cause the new stationery to be superimposed on your default stationery or any other design you selected before you started the message. While this might make for an amusing or creative message, you might have to start your message over if you don't like the effect.

Creating Your Own Stationery

Life is full of choices and so is Outlook Express. Rather than simply selecting one of the stationery designs supplied in Outlook Express, you can create your own. You can have Outlook Express guide you through the process, create and use an HTML file as a template, or download new stationery from the Internet. Whatever new stationery you create will be listed along with those provided by Outlook Express so you can easily choose it.

Follow these steps to create your own stationery:

1 Choose Options from the Tools menu, and click the Compose tab.

2 Click Create New to open the Stationery Setup wizard.

3 Click Next to display the options shown in Figure 7-8.

4 Choose to use a picture or color as the background, or both. For a picture, choose one from the list, or click Browse and locate a graphics file to use. For a color, choose the color you want from the list. Click Next when you're done.

5 Choose a default typeface, size, and color for the text you will type in messages using this stationery, and then click Next.

FIGURE 7-8.

The Stationery Setup wizard.

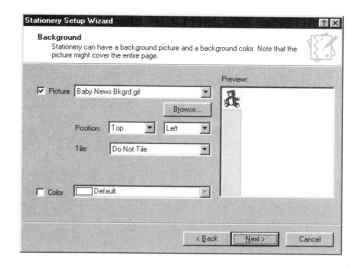

6 Set the left and top margins to position where the text will fall on your stationery design. Some stationery contains borders or other elements that you won't want your text to overprint. Use the Preview box to position text, and then click Next.

7 Type a name for the stationery, and then click Finish.

You can choose your design from the Select Stationery Dialog box, just as you would select one of the built-in stationery patterns.

> **NOTE**
>
> If you installed the Microsoft Office 2000 suite, you can also edit any of the stationery designs listed in the Select Stationery box. Choose the design you want to customize, and then click the Edit button. Windows opens Microsoft Word with the selected stationery design. Make any changes to the design, and then click the Save button on Word's Standard toolbar.

Adding "Other Stuff" to Messages

E-mail is e-mail, regardless of what program you use to create it. Outlook Express offers the same capabilities as Outlook to include "other stuff" in your messages. You can include text from a file that you previously created, URL and mail links, and attachments. Again, the concepts are the same as for Outlook, it's just the procedures that differ.

Adding Text from a File

If you have an HTML file or a plain text file stored on disk (for example, a Web page that you downloaded from the Internet or a file saved in Windows Notepad), you can insert the file as part of your message. Since Office 2000 programs can save their files in HTML format, this means you can include any document created in Office 2000 and saved as a Web page. The document appears as part of your message, complete with all of its formatting.

 TIP

You can always copy and paste text from a word processing program or other application into the Outlook Express message window.

To insert a file into a message, follow these steps:

1 Place the insertion point in the message where you want the text from the file to appear.

2 Choose Text From File on the Insert menu to display the Insert Text File dialog box.

3 Choose either Text Files (*.txt) or HTML Files (*.htm;*.html) from the Files Of Type list, depending on the type of file you want to include.

4 Locate and select the file to insert.

5 Click Open.

 TIP

Advanced users can also embed HTML files containing JavaScript or VBScript code into their messages using the Text From File command on the Insert menu.

Including Links in Messages

A link is a clickable object. If you want the recipient to be able to click a URL in your message and visit a particular Web site, add a URL link. To make it easy for the recipient to send an e-mail to someone, add an e-mail link in your message.

As with Outlook, just type addresses in the proper format or type a URL link, starting with either *www* or *http://.* When you follow the entry with a punctuation mark, a space, or press the Enter key, Outlook Express recognizes and formats the address as a link, underlined and in color.

If you need to change the type of link, from *http:* to *ftp:*, for example, right-click the link and choose Properties from the shortcut menu to change the type of link or address. You can also select any text not automatically recognized as a link and choose Hyperlink from the Insert menu to convert it to a link.

Sending Attachments

There will be times when you want to send a recipient more than just a message. You may want to send someone a document that you've created with Word, a sound file that you've recorded, a picture, or perhaps another file that you've found on the Internet.

As with Outlook, the easiest way to send a file is to drag it from the Windows desktop into the message window. Arrange the Outlook Express and message windows so you can see the Windows desktop, and then locate the file using My Computer or Windows Explorer. Then drag the document you want to attach to the text area of the message window. You'll see the heading Attach after Subject in the message header, followed by the name and size of the attached file.

You can also send one or more attachments, by following these steps:

1 Start a new message, and click the Attach button on the toolbar or choose File Attachment from the Insert menu.

2 Select the file you want to attach.

3 Click the Attach button.

4 Complete your message and click Send.

Sending a Web Page

If you want to send a copy of a Web page, not just its address, click the down arrow to open the New Mail list on the Outlook Express toolbar and choose Web Page. In the Send Web Page dialog box that appears, enter the URL of the page and click OK.

Outlook Express then downloads the page from the Internet, connecting to your ISP if necessary, and inserts the Web page as the contents in a new message window (depending on your setup, you might need to manually connect to your ISP first). Just add the recipient's address, a subject, and other text you want to appear above or below the Web page (if you really want to, you can even type within the Web page), and then click Send.

When you view the message in the preview pane, a paper clip icon indicates that the message contains an attachment. Click the paper clip and you see a list of the attachments. Graphics files that can be displayed by Outlook Express, such as .gif and .jpg types, are listed with a check mark in their icon to indicate they are also displayed at the bottom of the message. Animated .gif graphics even appear animated in the message window. Files that are attached without being displayed are listed without a check mark.

If you want graphics to appear at a specific location in your message, use the Picture command on the Insert menu to place them. You can also choose to have multiple graphics attachments appear as a slide show with buttons to move from one to the other, or choose not to show graphics at all. *See "Read Options," on page 234.*

Getting Mail

Sending mail is only half the fun—getting mail is the other. To get new mail, click the Send/Receive button or choose Send/Receive from the Tools menu. If you are working offline, click Yes in the dialog box that appears. Outlook Express will send any messages in your Outbox and then download any messages waiting for you. A dialog box will display its progress.

If you have mail, the word Inbox in the folder list is displayed in bold and followed by the number of messages that you have not yet read. If you are viewing the start page, you'll also see a note reporting the number of unread messages.

Remember, if you want Outlook Express to disconnect from your ISP after it has received messages, select the Hang Up When Finished check box. Otherwise you'll have to hang up by selecting Hang-Up from the File menu or by clicking the Hang-Up button on the start page toolbar. You can also disconnect from your ISP by closing the Windows dial-up connection that appears on your screen or on the taskbar.

Reading Mail

The mail in your Inbox won't do you much good until you read it. To read your mail, click Read Mail on the start page or click Inbox in the folder list.

The Outlook Express window then appears as shown in Figure 7-9. Click a message to display it's contents in the preview pane, or double-click the message to read it in a separate window. (If your window appears

FIGURE 7-9.

The Outlook
Express Inbox.

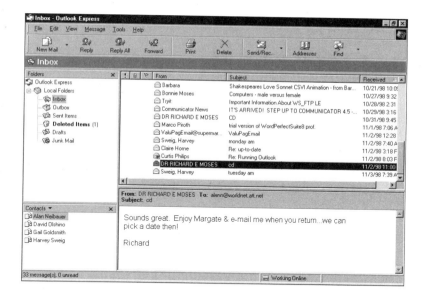

differently or is missing the preview pane, you can adjust the display by choosing Layout from the View menu. *See "Changing the Window Layout," on page 250.*)

 TIP

> To add the sender's address to your address book, double-click the message to display it in a separate window, and then right-click the sender's name and choose Add To Address Book from the shortcut menu that appears.

Saving Attachments

In the message list, a paper clip icon next to the message name indicates attachments, and you'll see a paper clip in the preview pane header. Click the icon to see the names and sizes of the attached files. Click the filename that you want to open to see the Open Attachment Warning dialog box. The box will not appear, by the way, for some types of files, such as text and audio files—these files will be opened (or played) immediately.

Select Open It from the dialog box to display the contents of the file in the associated application. Select Save To Disk to store the file in a location of your choice. Click OK.

NOTE

> You might also see a paper clip icon next to a message name if the message contains a graphic or stationery background, even when it does not have an attachment.

 SEE ALSO

To save attachments using the File menu, see "Saving Attachments from the Message Window," on page 172.

If you double-click a message to open it in its own window, the Attach box in the message header displays each attached filename with an icon and the file size. Double-click the icon to display the Open Attachment Warning dialog box, or right-click for a menu that lets you open, save, or print the file. If too many attachments are included in the message to fit on one line, you'll see small scrolling arrows at the right end of the line to enable you to bring the other attachments into view.

Reading and Saving Business Cards

If a message you receive includes a business card, you'll see a Rolodex card icon in the preview pane header. Click the card icon to display the Open Attachment Warning dialog box. If you double-click the message to open it in its own window, you'll see the card icon in the header area. Click the icon and choose Open from the menu to display the Open Attachment Warning dialog box.

Most likely you'll want to add business card information you receive to your Outlook Express address book. To do so, follow these simple steps:

1 From either the preview pane or the opened message, open the business card as just described.

2 You can view (but not change) the information in the Properties dialog box for the opened card and then click the Add To Address Book button to insert the contents of the card as a listing in your address book.

3 The Properties dialog box for the card appears again, this time as viewed from your address book. Notice that you can now edit any of the contents if you want, just as you can any other entry in your address book. Click OK to save the contents to your address book and close the Properties dialog box.

4 If there is already an address book listing for the person you're adding, an additional dialog box appears, asking whether you want to update the contents of the old listing. This new feature merges newer data over older data but leaves existing fields that don't have newer information as they were. In most cases you will want to click Yes to merge the data.

The entry is now added to your Outlook Express address book.

Replying to and Forwarding Messages

If you want to respond to the person who sent you a message, use the Reply feature. To send a message you received to another person, use the Forward feature. These features work similarly to the same features in Outlook.

To respond to the sender, click the Reply button on the Standard toolbar. To reply to the entire audience (all those who received the original message), click the Reply All button (also on the Standard toolbar).

To forward a message, click the Forward button.

When a message is open, you can also reply to or forward it using the Reply, Reply All, or Forward buttons on the message window's toolbar.

 NOTE

Once you reply to a message, Outlook Express indicates that a reply has been sent by adding a return arrow to the open envelope icon displayed next to the message in the Outlook Express message list.

Setting Up Mail Security

The security measures available in Outlook Express are similar to those in Outlook but are designed for Internet mail, not Exchange mail. While the security concepts are the same, there are some important differences, so let's look at Outlook Express security in some detail.

Security Zones

You can set rules for the type of content that Outlook Express accepts in HTML messages by using security zones. These settings also apply to Web sites you visit in Internet Explorer, so changing the settings in one program will change them for the other program as well.

II

Working with Electronic Mail

There are two zones that you can select:

- Internet Zone offers less security but allows greater access to sites on the Internet.

- Restricted Sites Zone is more secure but may prevent you from accessing certain sites.

To select the zone, choose Options from the Tools menu and click the Security tab. Then click the option button for the zone you want to use, and click OK. You can customize the zone settings from within Internet Explorer, not Outlook Express.

Digital IDs

You can also secure your e-mail message using a digital ID (also called a certificate). A digital ID lets you prove to recipients that the message actually came from you, and it allows others to send you encrypted mail. Before you can use a digital ID, however, you have to obtain one over the Internet from one of the organizations that provide them. These organizations also periodically verify that your digital ID is still valid.

 NOTE

Outlook Express shares Internet S/MIME security certificates with Outlook.

Getting Your Own Digital ID

When you apply for a digital ID, you'll have to complete an online form and then wait until you get a response from the company. You will receive instructions for obtaining and downloading the security certificate.

To get a digital ID directly from within Outlook Express, follow these steps:

1 Choose Options from the Tools menu.

2 Click the Security tab.

3 Click Get Digital ID.

Outlook Express launches Internet Explorer and connects to a page on the Microsoft Web site that lists certifying authorities from which you can get a digital ID. Choose one, and then follow the directions you see on screen and those you receive with your confirmation by e-mail.

Associating the ID with Your Account

Once you get your ID, either through Outlook or Outlook Express, you have to associate it with your account. This lets Outlook Express know what ID to use with digitally signed messages. Follow these steps:

1 Choose Accounts from the Tools menu.

2 Select the account you want to associate with the ID, and then click Properties.

3 Click the Security tab to display the dialog box shown in Figure 7-10.

4 Select the Use A Digital ID When Sending Secure Messages check box.

5 Click the Digital ID button. You'll see a dialog box listing certificates installed on your system.

6 Choose the certificate to use, and then click OK.

7 Click OK to close the Properties dialog box.

A digital ID is made up of two codes, called keys. The public key is the code you send to people who you want to be able to send encrypted messages to you. The private key is stored on your computer, and it must be present in order for you to read encrypted messages. You should make a backup copy of your private key—if the key is lost, you will not be able to sign your mail with the ID or read encrypted mail.

FIGURE 7-10.

The Security tab of the Properties dialog box.

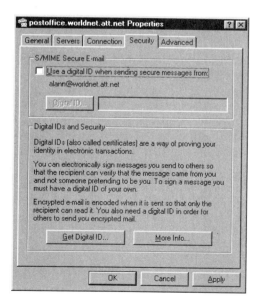

Working with Electronic Mail

Make a backup copy of the certificate from Outlook. *See "Exporting and Importing Digital IDs," on page 98.*

Sending a Digital Signature

When you want the recipient to be sure that the message came from you, send the message with a digital signature. When you are composing a message, apply a digital signature by clicking the Digitally Sign Message button or by choosing Digitally Sign from the Tools menu. The Digitally Signed icon will appear in the message header.

A red ribbon indicates the sender digitally signed the message.

Similarly, if a message you receive includes this red ribbon, you know the message is digitally signed. You will also see a special screen before the message is displayed. Click Continue to read the message. To avoid doing this for every digitally signed message you receive, select the Don't Show Me This Help Screen Again check box before clicking Continue.

Swapping Keys

In order to send encrypted mail, you must know the public key of the recipient and it must be part of the entry for that person in your address book. In order for you to receive encrypted mail, the sender must have your public key.

To send your public key, just send a digitally signed message. To get a key, ask the sender to send you a digitally signed message.

When you receive the digitally signed message, add the key to your address book by following these steps:

1 Click the message in the Inbox.

2 Choose Properties from the File menu.

3 Click the Security tab.

4 Click the Add Digital ID To Address Book button. You'll see a dialog box informing you the digital ID was added to all contacts that matched the e-mail address or that a new contact was added if no matching name was found in your address book.

5 Click OK to close the message box, and click OK again to close the Digital Sign dialog box.

You can verify whose public keys you have on file by opening the address book and looking for the digitally signed icon next to the entries' names. You can send encrypted mail to these people.

> You can select to digitally sign and encrypt all messages automatically from the Security tab of the Options dialog box.

Sending and Receiving Encrypted Mail

While it sounds like something out of a James Bond movie, there are good reasons to encrypt mail. In these days of computer networks, it is quite possible for e-mail to be seen by someone other than the intended recipient. Encryption makes sure that only the person to whom you sent it reads the message.

To encrypt a message, click the Encrypt Message button or choose Encrypt from the Tools menu. Outlook Express adds the Encrypt icon (a blue padlock) to the message header to indicate an encrypted message.

When you receive an encrypted message, Outlook Express confirms that you have the recipient's public key and then automatically decrypts the message.

Setting Up Accounts

When you first start Outlook Express, you have the opportunity to set up your connection, mail, and news accounts. You can also set up the accounts or change the specifics of the accounts later from within Outlook Express.

Outlook Express can manage multiple accounts. If you plan to use more than one e-mail account on your computer, for example, you can set up all of them. You can then send and receive mail through one or all accounts at the same time. Each account can have its own name and dial into its own ISP.

You can also set up Outlook Express to share one account with other members of your family by establishing each as a separate identity, as described on the next page. Each identity is associated with a complete set of folders so each has its own Inbox, Outbox, and so on.

Changing Account Setup

There are a lot of reasons why your e-mail account can change. You may get fed up hearing busy signals from your ISP, so you switch to another provider and need to change your mail server and dial-up connection service. You may just want to change your e-mail password or the name of your service that appears in the Internet Account dialog box and in the dialog box that opens when sending and receiving mail.

NOTE

> If you change Internet service providers, you will probably have to make changes to your dial-up connection using the Dial-Up Networking resource in Windows. Make those changes and then adjust your Outlook Express account as described here.

Because things in life change, you are not tied to the original setup that you created when you first ran Outlook Express. To change account information, just start Outlook Express and follow these steps:

1   Choose Accounts from the Tools menu to display the Internet Accounts dialog box, shown in Figure 7-11.

2   Select the Mail tab of the dialog box and then click the account you want to change.

3   Click the Properties button.

4   Change the desired settings in the Properties dialog box, using the appropriate tabs:

   - Change your user information or e-mail address on the General tab.

FIGURE 7-11.
The Internet Accounts dialog box.

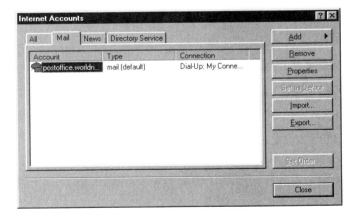

- Change the name of the incoming or outgoing mail servers and your logon name and password on the Servers tab.

- Change the dial-up connection on the Connection tab.

- Set security for the account on the Security tab.

- Set server port numbers, timeouts, and delivery rules (for advanced users only) on the Advanced tab.

5 Click OK.

Adding New Mail Accounts

Outlook Express (and Outlook when you're using the Internet Only installation) can be set up to use any number of e-mail accounts. You can also share a single account so every member of your family, for example, can send and receive mail under his or her own name.

 TIP

To share an account with other members of your family, create an identity for each person, as you will learn how to do next. If you use the Internet Only setup of Outlook, you can share an account by creating additional mail accounts as explained here. Use the same e-mail address and server name, just change the username and the name used for the service in the Internet Connection Wizard. You'll have to use the same account name and password, however, to log on to your mail server.

To add a mail account to Outlook Express, follow these steps:

1 Choose Accounts from the Tools menu.

2 Click Add.

3 Click Mail on the submenu to start the Internet Connection Wizard.

4 Complete the steps in the wizard and then click Finish in the final dialog box.

All your accounts will be listed in the Accounts dialog box. The default account will be used automatically for all mail that you send. You can tell which account is the default by looking for the word *(default)* in the list of accounts. Use the Set As Default button to select another account as your default.

II

Working with Electronic Mail

Identities

You can share one mail account with other members of your family by creating an identity for each person.

To create an identity, choose Identities from the File menu, and choose Add New Identity. In the box that appears, type a name for the identity and then click OK. You'll be asked whether you want to switch to that identity. If you select Yes, a new set of Outlook Express folders appears. Now create accounts for the identity by choosing Accounts from the Tools menu. If you are sharing one e-mail account, use the same account information but type the name of the family member when the Internet Connection Wizard asks for the display name.

You can choose which identity to use as the default when you start Outlook Express, and you can switch identities to send and receive mail. Choose Identities from the File menu, and choose Manage Identities to see this dialog box, listing the identities you've created:

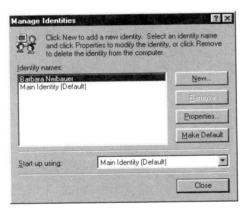

Decide which identity to use as the default, and then click the Make Default button. You can also choose which identity to use when you start Outlook Express by choosing it from the Start Up Using list. Select Ask Me from the list if you want to choose the identity when you start Outlook Express.

Use the Properties button in the Manage Identities dialog box to change the identity name. You can also create a new identity or delete an existing one.

To switch identities after Outlook Express has started, choose Switch Identity from the File menu, click the identity in the box that appears, and then click OK.

 **NOTE**

> If you are sharing one e-mail account with more than one user, choosing the Send/Receive command sends just the mail for the current identity but downloads all mail waiting on the ISP's server. Later in this chapter you'll learn how to automatically sort arriving mail for each person into separate folders. *See "Organizing Messages with Message Rules," on page 245.*

Setting Message Options

Outlook Express is set to send and receive messages using popular default settings. You can change these settings if you don't like the way Outlook Express operates or if you want to customize it for your own personal tastes.

To change the default settings, choose Options on the Tools menu to see the Options dialog box.

 NOTE

> You already learned about the Signatures tab of the Options dialog box. *You'll learn about the Layout tab in "Customizing the Toolbar," on page 249. (See Figure 7-22, on page 251.)*

General Options

The General tab of the Options dialog box, shown in Figure 7-12, lets you designate some general ways in which Outlook Express works.

When Starting, Go Directly To My 'Inbox' Folder. Select this check box to have the Inbox folder open rather than the start page when you start Outlook Express.

FIGURE 7-12.
The General tab of the Options dialog box.

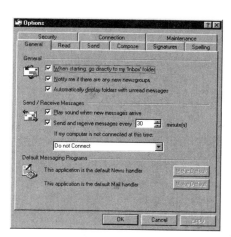

Notify Me If There Are Any New Newsgroups. Select this check box to display a message when you access your newsgroup server if any new newsgroups have been added since your last visit.

Automatically Display Folders With Unread Messages. Select this check box to expand folders and make bold folder names that contain unread messages.

Play Sound When New Messages Arrive. When this check box is selected, a sound will play when new messages are downloaded. When this check box is clear, you will still see an icon in the status bar reporting that you have new mail.

Send and Receive Messages Every __ Minutes. If you want Outlook Express to automatically check for messages at regular intervals, select this check box and set the number of minutes between attempts. When you're working online, your mail is checked at the interval you specify.

If My Computer Is Not Connected At This Time. This setting determines whether Outlook Express automatically connects at the interval specified for checking mail. The choices include always connecting, never connecting, and connecting if Outlook Express is not in Work Offline mode.

Default Message Programs. If you have more than one mail program or newsreader set up on your system, you can choose to make Outlook Express the default. (If Outlook Express *is* the default and you want to make another program the default, such as Outlook, you would use the Connection tab to make that change, as described in "Internet Connection Settings," on page 237.)

Send Options

Use the Send tab of the Options dialog box, shown in Figure 7-13, to determine how and when your messages are sent.

Save Copy Of Sent Messages In The 'Sent Items' Folder. Clear this check box only if you are certain you will not need copies of your sent mail.

Send Messages Immediately. Select this check box to send each message as soon as you click the Send button in the New Message window. Otherwise the message is placed in the Outbox.

Automatically Put People I Reply To In My Address Book.   Select this check box if you want the address of the recipient to be inserted in your address book when you send a reply.

Automatically Complete E-mail Addresses When Composing. Select this check box if you want Outlook Express to try to complete the name or e-mail address that you start to type in the New Message window.

Include Message In Reply.   Select this check box to insert the text of the original message in your reply.

Reply To Messages Using The Format In Which They Were Sent. Select this check box to automatically reply in the same format (HTML or plain text) as the original message.

International Settings.   Click this button if you want to set the language encoding for your outgoing messages.

Mail Sending Format.   These options determine whether messages are sent in HTML or as plain text. The default is HTML because this allows for rich formatting and is compatible with most e-mail programs. If most of your recipients cannot read HTML or if you don't care about formatted messages, select Plain Text. If only a few of your recipients can't read HTML, leave this setting as HTML. Then go to your address book, open the Properties dialog box for each recipient who needs to receive e-mail messages as plain text, and select the Send E-mail Using Plain Text Only check box for each of these recipients. The Settings buttons let you specify more detailed settings for each format, if necessary.

FIGURE 7-13.
The Send tab of the Options dialog box.

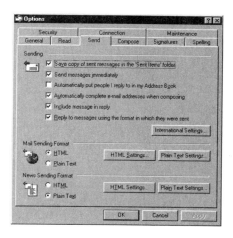

II

Working with Electronic Mail

News Sending Format. These options determine whether news messages are sent as HTML or plain text. Plain Text is selected by default.

Read Options

The options on the Read tab of the Options dialog box, shown in Figure 7-14, determine how and when your incoming mail is read.

Mark Message Read After Displaying For __ Seconds. Select this check box to automatically mark a message as read after you've reviewed it in the preview pane for the number of seconds you specify in the box.

Automatically Expand Grouped Messages. Select this check box to display all the messages in the message thread. If this is not selected, only the first message of each message thread is displayed, with a small plus-sign icon that you can click to expand and display the remaining messages for the thread.

Automatically Download Message When Viewing In The Preview Pane. Select this check box to have the preview pane display each news message as you select it, just like it displays mail messages you select. If you clear this check box, press the Spacebar to display the message.

Show ToolTips In The Message List For Clipped Items. Select this check box to display information about an item in the message list when you point to the item.

FIGURE 7-14.
The Read tab of the Options dialog box.

Highlight Watched Messages With The Color __. Select a color to easily identify any messages you have marked to watch.

Get __ Headers At A Time. Select this check box to limit the number of newsgroup headers downloaded at one time to the number (up to 1,000) that you specify here. If this check box is not selected, all message headers will be downloaded.

Mark All Messages As Read When Exiting A Newsgroup. Select this check box only if you want all your news messages marked as read when you leave the newsgroup, even messages you have not actually opened.

Fonts. Click the Fonts button to set the font that will be used to display plain text messages received in various languages.

International Settings. Click the International Settings button to set the language encoding for incoming messages.

Spelling Options

The Spelling tab of the Options dialog box, shown in Figure 7-15, lets you control how the spelling of words in your message is checked. The options are the same as those discussed in Chapter 2, "Discovering Outlook," for Outlook itself, with two additions. You can choose to ignore the spelling of Internet addresses, and you can edit the custom dictionary by inserting names and other words that you know are correct but that are not contained in Outlook's dictionary.

FIGURE 7-15.
The Spelling tab of the Options dialog box.

Security Options

The Security tab of the Options dialog box, shown in Figure 7-16, lets you control how active content you receive in HTML messages is handled, as discussed in "Setting Up Mail Security," page 223. You can also choose to digitally sign and encrypt your outgoing messages, and you can connect to the Internet to receive a digital ID.

Use the Advanced button on the Security tab to choose an encryption method, and whether you want to automatically send a decrypted copy of secure messages to yourself.

FIGURE 7-16.

The Security tab of the Options dialog box.

Connection Options

Use the options on the Connection tab of the Options dialog box, shown in Figure 7-17, to determine how your connections are handled.

Ask Before Switching Dial Up Connections. If this check box is selected and you have more than one dial-up account, Outlook Express will ask whether you want to try another account when the first is not working. Also, if you are connected with one dial-up account but have chosen an action (such as sending mail or accessing a news server) linked to a different dial-up account, it will ask your permission before automatically disconnecting from the first connection to dial the second.

Hang Up After Sending And Receiving. If this check box is selected, Outlook Express automatically terminates the connection when all messages have been sent and received and all newsgroup messages have been downloaded.

FIGURE 7-17.

The Connection tab of the Options dialog box.

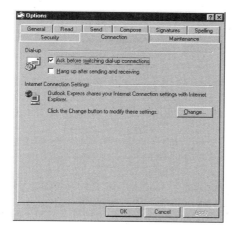

Internet Connection Settings.   Click the Change button if you need to change any of the Internet settings established in Internet Explorer. Your Internet connection settings are shared by both Outlook Express and Internet Explorer.

Signatures Options

Use the Signatures tab of the Options dialog box (shown previously in Figure 7-6, on page 211) to create default signatures for mail and news messages.

Compose Options

Use the Compose tab of the Options dialog box (shown previously in Figure 7-7, on page 213) to set the default font, stationery, and business card.

Maintenance Options

The options on the Maintenance tab of the Options dialog box, shown in Figure 7-18, on the following page, are used less frequently than the others and should be changed with caution. They determine how newsgroup messages are handled and whether logs are maintained of your Outlook Express activities.

Empty Messages From The 'Deleted Items' Folder On Exit.   Select this check box to delete the messages you've moved to the Deleted Items folder automatically when you exit Outlook Express.

Purge Deleted Messages When Leaving IMAP Folders. Some mail servers let you store messages on the server, in addition to your own computer. This check box lets you delete messages from the server.

Compact Messages In The Background. Select this check box to delete wasted space from folders while you perform other Outlook Express activities.

Delete Read Message Bodies In Newsgroups. Select this check box to delete newsgroup messages after you read them.

Delete Messages __ Days After Being Downloaded. Select this check box to automatically delete newsgroup messages after a specified number of days from their receipt.

Compact Messages When There Is __ Percent Wasted Space. Select this check box to delete wasted space from folders when it reaches the percentage you specify.

Clean Up Now. Click this button to compact your folders and delete the newsgroup messages.

Store Folder. Use this button to see and change the path of the folder where Outlook Express stores your information. The folder shown contains two subfolders: Mail, which holds all of your e-mail folders; and News, which stores your newsgroup messages.

Troubleshooting. Select these check boxes to make a log of commands sent to your news and mail services, which can be useful for troubleshooting communication problems.

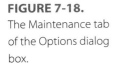

FIGURE 7-18.
The Maintenance tab of the Options dialog box.

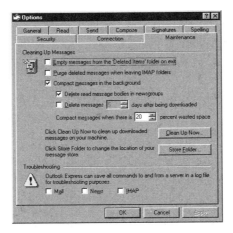

Using E-mail Directories

You know that Outlook Express can complete a recipient's name that you start to type. It does so by checking the address book for names with matching characters. You can also set up Outlook Express to check online directories as well, such as Bigfoot and Switchboard. If Outlook Express cannot find the e-mail address for a name in your address book, it can then search one or more of the online directories before reporting that it cannot find a match. You can also use online directories to look up e-mail addresses whenever you want.

Checking for Addresses

To access an online directory service, you have to first set it up for your account. Follow these steps to set up one or more online directories:

1 Choose Accounts from the Tools menu.

2 Click the Directory Services tab to see a list of the services already set up.

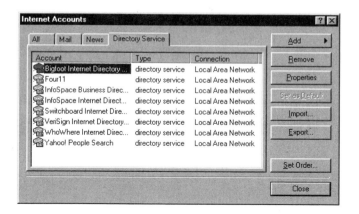

3 Click the service that you want to use, and then click Properties to open the dialog box shown in Figure 7-19, on the next page.

4 Select the check box Check Names Against This Server When Sending Mail.

5 Repeat steps 3 and 4 for other directory services you want to check.

Unless you get specific instructions for setting up a directory service, leave the other options in the Properties dialog box set to their defaults. The Server Information section, for example, determines how the

FIGURE 7-19.

The General tab of the Properties dialog box.

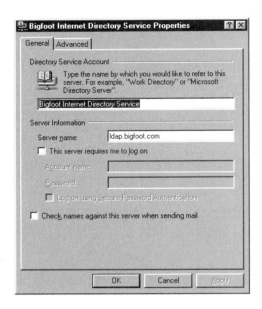

directory service is accessed. It includes the directory's Internet name, and any login information that might be required. Some services, for example, require you to register to receive an account name and password.

If you set up more than one service, you can determine the order in which they are checked for e-mail addresses. To do this, follow these steps:

1 In the Accounts dialog box, click the Directory Services tab.

2 Click Set Order to display the Directory Services Order dialog box listing the services that will be checked, arranged in the order they will be checked. If you haven't selected the Check Names Against This Server check box for any of the services as described above, the list will be empty.

3 Click a service whose position you want to change.

4 Click the Move Up button to access the service before others, or click Move Down to access the service after the others.

5 Click OK.

As additional directory services become available, you can add them to the directory list. You'll need to get the directory's Internet server name (called the LDAP server) from your ISP. If the server requires you to log on, you'll also need an account name and password. When you have the information, open the Accounts dialog box, click Add, and choose Directory Service to start the Internet Connection Wizard. Follow the steps in the wizard dialog boxes to complete the installation.

Finding People

In addition to using the online directories to automatically locate e-mail addresses when composing messages, you can check them anytime you need to look up an e-mail address. You can use any of the following methods to search any directory service listed in Outlook Express, even if you haven't selected the service for automatic e-mail address checking as described above:

1 Open the address book and click the Find button on the toolbar to open the Find People dialog box, shown in Figure 7-20.

2 Select a service to use for the search in the Look In list box.

3 Type the full or partial name of the person you're searching for in the Name box on the People tab. Alternatively, you can type an e-mail address you have to look up the person's name or other information on file. If necessary, you can carry out a more complex search using the Advanced tab.

4 Click Find Now to start the search.

Any matches that are found will be displayed in the text box at the bottom of the dialog box, as shown in Figure 7-20. If the first service you use doesn't come up with a match, just switch to another service in the Look In box and search again.

FIGURE 7-20.

The Find People dialog box.

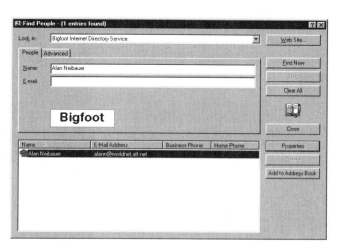

You can also use the Find People dialog box to do the following:

- Click the Properties button to display any other available information about the person, such as address and telephone number.

- Click the Add To Address Book button to insert the name and e-mail address of the person in your address book for future reference.

- Click the Web Site button to open the directory service's Web site on the Internet, where additional options might be available.

When you search your local address book rather than an online directory, the Find People dialog box also lets you search by address, phone number, or any text in the address book listing. When it locates a name, you can also select Delete to remove it from your address book.

Working with Folders

Outlook Express folders serve as storage containers for messages, much like the Windows folders store files. The initial folders provided by Outlook Express serve specific purposes:

- **Inbox.** This folder stores messages that you receive.

- **Outbox.** This folder stores messages ready to be sent.

- **Sent Items.** This folder stores messages that you have sent.

- **Deleted Items.** This folder stores messages you have marked to delete.

- **Drafts.** This folder stores items that you are working on.

- **Junk Mail.** This folder stores mail that Outlook Express has deleted from the Inbox and designated as junk mail.

This arrangement of folders is convenient, but it might not serve all of your purposes. You might need additional folders to store messages for other accounts, for example, or you might want to subdivide a folder and create subfolders to organize messages further. Your Sent Items folder, for example, could contain a subfolder for each of your clients.

Working with folders is very easy. Your folders are organized in a hierarchy much like the directories on your hard disk. At the top of the hierarchy is the Outlook Express folder. All of the other folders are contained within it. Clicking the Outlook Express folder shows the start page.

To add a folder, follow these steps:

1 Right-click any folder in the list and choose New Folder from the shortcut menu that appears. The Create Folder dialog box appears showing the current folders.

2 In the Folder name text box, type a name for the new folder.

3 From the list of folders, choose the folder that you want to contain the new one if it isn't already selected.

4 Click OK.

Folders that contain subfolders are marked with a plus sign. Click the plus sign to expand the listing; a minus sign is then displayed and the names of the subfolders are shown. Click the minus sign when you want to collapse the display so the subfolders no longer appear.

To delete a folder, right-click its name—expanding the folder that contains it if necessary—and then click Delete on the shortcut menu. Click Yes in the message box that appears to confirm the deletion, which moves the folder to the Deleted Items folder. To rename a folder, right-click it and choose Rename from the shortcut menu. In the box that appears, enter the new name and then click OK.

You cannot rename or delete the default folders: Inbox, Outbox, Sent Items, and Deleted Items.

Working with Messages in Folders

You should organize your messages in a way that makes them most convenient for you. For example, create a special folder for important messages, and move messages into the folder for safekeeping. You can flag important messages that require some sort of follow-up, and delete messages that you no longer need.

To delete a message, for example, click it and then click the Delete button on the toolbar or just press the Delete key. Outlook Express moves the message into the Deleted Items folder, just in case you later change your mind. When you're really sure you do not need the message, open the Deleted Items folder and delete the message from there.

NOTE

If you have set Outlook Express to delete items from the Deleted Items folder each time you close Outlook Express, be sure you really don't want the deleted items before exiting. This option can be turned on and off in the Maintenance tab of the Options dialog box.

Flag a message when you want to be reminded to take some action on it later on. To flag a message, click the Flag column to its left—under the icon of a flag—or select the message and then choose Flag Message from the Edit menu. Outlook Express places a flag icon next to the message header to make it easy to see. Remove the flag using the same methods.

You can move, copy, and delete messages from your folders, as well as flag them. You do not have to leave messages in the folders where Outlook Express puts them.

To move a message to another folder, follow these steps:

1 Expand the folder list, if necessary, to see the folder where you want to place the message.

2 Open the folder containing the message.

3 Click the message you want to move.

4 Drag the message to the destination folder in the folder list.

When you release the mouse, the message will be removed from its original folder and placed in the new folder.

> You don't even have to open a subfolder before moving an item to it. Drag the item you want to move onto the visible "parent" folder, hold it there a moment, and the subfolders will open automatically. Continue to drag the item down to the destination folder, and then drop it in place.

To make a copy of a message in another folder, follow the same steps but hold down the Ctrl key when you release the mouse. You do not have to hold down the Ctrl key as you drag the message.

As an alternative to dragging, you can also move or copy a message using a dialog box. Follow these steps:

1 Right-click the message and choose Move To Folder or Copy To Folder from the shortcut menu. You can also click the message and choose Move To Folder or Copy To Folder on the Edit menu. Outlook Express displays the list of folders.

2 Click the folder where you want to place the message.

3 Click OK.

You cannot drag a message from the Deleted Items folder to the Outbox. If you accidentally delete a message from your Outbox that you want to send, double-click it in the Deleted Items folder and click the Send button when the message window opens.

Organizing Messages with Message Rules

In Chapter 2, "Discovering Outlook," you learned how to use the Rules Wizard and the Out Of Office Assistant to organize messages as they are received by Outlook. Outlook Express offers the Message Rules command, which operates similarly and includes additional options and features.

With the Outlook Express Message Rules feature, you can set a rule to apply to all messages or the rule can be based on the contents of the To, Cc, From, and Subject fields or on the account used and the message size. In addition to the Move To, Copy To, Forward To, and Reply With actions, you can also tell Outlook Express not to download the message from the server and even to delete it from the server without downloading it.

You can create rules for mail, news messages, and junk mail, and to block mail from specific senders. For example, here's how to control your junk mail:

1 Choose Message Rules from the Tools menu. You'll see the following tabs: Mail Rules, News Rules, Junk Mail, and Block Senders.

2 Select Junk Mail to see the options shown in Figure 7-21.

FIGURE 7-21.
The Junk Mail tab of the Message Rules dialog box.

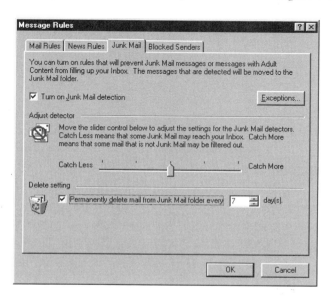

Working with Electronic Mail

3 Select the check box labeled Turn On Junk Mail Detection.

4 Move the slider in the Adjust Detector section to control the aggressiveness with which Outlook Express judges your mail items to be junk. Messages evaluated as junk mail will be inserted into the Junk Mail folder.

5 Click the Exceptions button to exclude specific addresses you enter from being mistakenly classified as junk mail.

6 To delete mail from the Junk Mail folder automatically, select the check box in the Delete Setting section and then set the number of days to wait before deleting the junk mail.

7 Click OK.

If you established any mail or news rules, click Apply Rules Now to apply the rules to messages already in your Inbox.

Customizing the Outlook Express Window

Outlook Express lets you customize its appearance in a number of ways. You can change the size of the panes displayed on screen and choose whether to hide or display such components as the toolbar, status bar, Outlook Bar, and Folder Bar. The Folder Bar is a horizontal bar above the message list that shows the name of the currently open folder.

Viewing Read or Unread Messages

By default, Outlook Express displays all messages in a folder, showing the number of unread messages after the folder name, and displaying the unread messages in bold. If your folders contain a large number of messages, you may find it tiresome to have to scroll to find those that are unread. To display just the unread messages, point to Current View on the View menu and choose Hide Read Messages. Outlook Express will hide read messages from the display. To redisplay all messages, point to Current View and choose Show All Messages.

Changing Message Size

You can change the size of the font used to display messages in the preview pane. Choose Text Size from the View menu, and then choose Largest, Larger, Normal (the default), Smaller, or Smallest. The font appears relative to the font size in which the message was typed. Even

when you choose Smallest, for example, text typed in 24-point type
will appear larger than text in 12-point type.

Working with Columns

You can add additional columns of information to those already displayed in the message list pane, and you can remove any already there
by default. To add and remove columns from the message list display,
follow these steps:

1 Click the folder that you want to change.

2 Choose Columns from the View menu to display the Columns
dialog box.

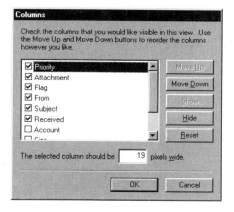

3 Select the check boxes of the columns that you want to display
and clear the check boxes for the columns you want to hide.

4 Click Move Up or Move Down to change the order of the selected
column.

5 Set the width of the columns, if desired.

6 Click OK.

Rearranging Columns with the Mouse

When you want to quickly move a column to a new position in a
folder window, just point to the column heading and drag it to the new
location. As you move the column heading between existing columns,
you'll see a shaded copy of the column heading indicating where the
column will be inserted when you release the mouse button. When
you release the button, the column moves to its new location and the
columns to the right move over to make room.

II

Working with Electronic Mail

Changing Column Width

To change column width with the mouse, first position the mouse pointer along the right edge of the column heading for the column that you want to widen or narrow. Then drag the right edge of the column heading to the right to widen the column. Drag the right edge of the heading to the left to narrow the column.

Sorting and Grouping Messages

When messages are received, they are added to the list of messages already in the Inbox. You can sort the order of messages in the Inbox, or in any folder, by clicking the column headings.

Sorting with the mouse is quick and convenient, and you can sort items in ascending or descending order. (Ascending order, depending on the column selected, means alphabetical, earlier time to later time, or lower number to higher number; descending order reverses these directions.)

You can tell how messages are sorted by looking at the column heading. If you see an up-pointing arrow next to the column name, messages are sorted in ascending order by that column. A down-pointing arrow means messages are sorted in descending order.

If you want to sort the messages based on the information in a different column, click that column heading. Outlook Express uses that column for an ascending sort, displaying the up-pointing arrow. Then each time you click the column heading, Outlook Express reverses the sort direction.

You can also right-click a column heading and then choose either Ascending or Descending from the shortcut menu that appears.

As an alternative to using the mouse to sort columns, you can use the Sort By command on the View menu as follows:

1 Select the folder that you want to sort.

2 Choose Sort By from the View menu.

3 In the menu that appears, choose the column to use for the sort, and choose either Sort Ascending or Sort Descending.

The Current View submenu also offers the Group Messages By Subject command. When you choose this command, messages are arranged by subject and placed under the message that initiated each topic, and indented and ordered according to who responded to whom, and in what order. Organizing messages in this fashion (also referred to as threading messages) allows you to follow the sequence of the conversation (or thread), reply to a specific previous reply, and have your message indented under the one you replied to. This is especially useful for newsgroups, where many people may contribute their thoughts on one subject, and where who is talking to whom about what aspect of the topic can quickly become confusing.

The first message on each subject is listed first and shown with a plus sign. The plus sign indicates that there are later messages on that same subject. Click the plus sign to expand the item, displaying the other messages. They will be indented to show their relationship to the first message. Click the minus sign to collapse the message group.

Changing Pane Size

Gray bars separate the panes that make up the Outlook Express window. To change the size of a pane, just drag one of the bars. When you point to a bar, the mouse pointer will appear as a two-directional arrow.

For example, to enlarge the preview pane, drag the bar that it is between it and the message list up toward the top of the screen. You cannot remove a pane by dragging a bar.

Working with the Toolbar

Chances are you'll be using the Outlook Express toolbar an awful lot. The toolbar buttons give you a fast, easy way to perform common tasks. You can change the size of the toolbar buttons. You can also add new buttons to the toolbar for functions that you perform often.

Removing Text Labels

The default toolbar includes icons as well as text labels describing the button functions. This way, you don't have to worry about memorizing what the icons represent. The text Send/Receive, for example, leaves nothing to the imagination, while the icon on that button might be obtuse for new users.

If you are familiar with the icons and want to make some extra room for messages, you can remove the text labels, cutting the size of the toolbar roughly in half. To remove, or later restore, the text labels, right-click the toolbar and then click Text Labels.

Customizing the Toolbar

While the Outlook Express toolbar includes buttons for the most common functions, you can easily add additional features to the toolbar, such as a button to print a message or to move a message to another folder. You can also remove buttons that you do not use. If you find that you never use the Forward Message feature, for example, you can remove it to make room for another button.

To add or remove toolbar buttons, right-click the toolbar and choose Customize to display the Customize Toolbar dialog box shown here:

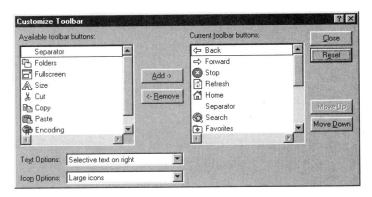

You can now carry out the following customizations:

- To add a button to the toolbar, choose it from the Available Toolbar Buttons list and then click Add.

- To insert a vertical line between buttons, add the Separator item from the Available Toolbar Buttons list.

- To remove a button from the toolbar, choose it in the Current Toolbar Buttons list and then click Remove.

- To change the position of a button, select it in the Current Toolbar Buttons list and then click Move Up or Move Down to move it left or right on the toolbar.

- To restore the original toolbar, click Reset.

Changing the Window Layout

For additional ways to customize Outlook Express, choose Layout from the View menu to display the Window Layout Properties dialog box, shown in Figure 7-22.

The Basic options in the dialog box let you show or hide such screen elements as the Folder Bar and Contacts list. You can even display the Outlook Bar used in Outlook itself.

FIGURE 7-22.
The Window Layout
Properties dialog box.

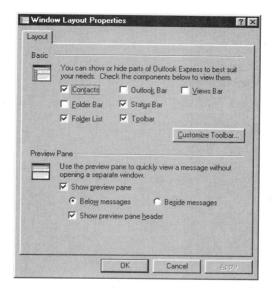

The Preview Pane area turns the pane off and on and controls its position when on. You can position the pane either below or to the right of the message list, and you can display or hide the header, which shows the From, To, and Subject headings of the previewed message.

In the next chapter you'll learn how to use the newsreader features of Outlook Express to read and participate in the thousands of newsgroups on the Internet.

CHAPTER 8

Communicating with Newsgroups

A *newsgroup* is a group of individuals who share a common interest and who exchange messages with each other over the Internet. The collection of messages is also called a newsgroup. When a member *posts*, or sends, a message to the newsgroup, the message can be read and responded to by every other member of the group.

There are thousands of newsgroups, covering almost every imaginable topic—and some you probably couldn't even imagine! There are usually no membership fees or charges beyond what you pay your Internet service provider (ISP) for the Internet connection. You just sign up (*subscribe* in newsgroup parlance) and jump right in. There are even some ISP-like companies that specialize in newsgroup delivery and charge their own membership fee. Some corporations maintain their own newsgroups for employees only; others make their newsgroups available publicly to provide customer support (for example, Microsoft Corporation maintains a public news server with hundreds of newsgroups that support its products). You'll learn how to set up as many news accounts as you want and how to switch between them freely.

Setting Up for Newsgroups

For you to access newsgroups, your ISP must maintain a news server, which is usually one (or several) computers dedicated to receiving multiple news feeds (which are similar to the wire services used by newspapers). These computers are used to download the hundreds of thousands of daily messages sent to the many different newsgroups.

Because of the popularity of newsgroups, it would be hard to find an ISP that doesn't offer such a server. Most ISPs have to make decisions about how many different newsgroups to offer (based both on physical constraints and sometimes decisions about the content) and about how long to retain the messages on each newsgroup. Unlike the World Wide Web, where the ISP is merely the conduit for the pages you call up on your browser, the thousands of news messages in newsgroups must actually be physically downloaded and maintained at the ISP's location on very large hard disks before you can access them. The number, retention, and timeliness of the messages all depend on the resources available to the ISP and the number and quality of the news feeds it subscribes to. Before you can access the newsgroups carried by your ISP, you must set up Outlook to connect to the ISP's news server.

Outlook uses the newsgroup features of Outlook Express as its newsreader. (These features can be run from within Outlook or directly from Outlook Express.) A newsreader is a program that lets you access news servers, subscribe to newsgroups and maintain them according to your preferences, and send and receive newsgroup messages. A newsreader is similar to an e-mail program, except it deals with news servers and newsgroup messages rather than e-mail addresses and e-mail messages. Outlook Express is installed automatically when you install Microsoft Office 2000, as is Microsoft Internet Explorer.

If you already set up Outlook Express as a separate program and configured it for at least one news server, it is ready and waiting. If you did not yet install any news servers, you'll have the chance to do so when you first access the newsreader.

Starting the Internet Connection Wizard

The easiest way to set up your news server is to use the Internet Connection Wizard.

If you are running Outlook, point to Go To on the View menu and choose News. Outlook Express opens and starts the Internet Connection Wizard if you don't already have a news server set up.

You can also start the wizard from within Outlook Express by following these steps:

1 Start Outlook Express.

2 Choose Accounts from the Tools menu.

3 Click Add, and then choose News from the menu that appears.

Completing the Internet Connection Wizard

The Internet Connection Wizard presents a series of dialog boxes in which you define your news server and prepare Outlook Express to communicate with it. The wizard assumes you want to use the same dial-up connection that you have set up for Internet Explorer. You can set up the news account and then later change the dial-up connection to it through the Accounts dialog box or in Internet Explorer.

You can set up separate news accounts for each identity established in Outlook Express.

To complete the Internet Connection Wizard, follow these steps:

1 Type your name as you want it displayed when you post to the newsgroup in the first wizard dialog box and click Next.

2 Type your e-mail address and click Next to see the dialog box shown in Figure 8-1, on the next page.

3 Type the news server name. If your news server requires you to sign on with a password, select the check box labeled My News Server Requires Me To Log On. You might need a username and password for some private newsgroups on company news servers but usually not for ISP news servers, which grant you free access once you log on to the ISP itself.

If you have accounts with two ISPs, each might maintain its own newsgroups and only allow you access when you've dialed up through that particular ISP. In this case, set up two news accounts, one for each ISP, and set each to dial up the appropriate ISP. This way Outlook Express, either automatically or with your confirmation, hangs up from one ISP and redials the second ISP whenever you click one of its newsgroups in the folder list.

Working with Electronic Mail

II

FIGURE 8-1.

The Internet News
Server Name page
of the Internet
Connection Wizard.

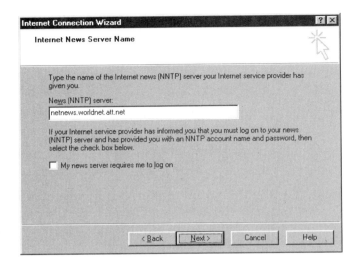

4 Click Next.

5 If you indicated that you need to enter a username and password, the Internet News Server Logon dialog box, shown in Figure 8-2, will appear. Enter the necessary information and then click Next.

6 Click Finish on the final page of the wizard.

7 If you started the wizard from the Tools menu, also close the Accounts dialog box.

FIGURE 8-2.

The Internet News
Server Logon page of
the Internet
Connection Wizard.

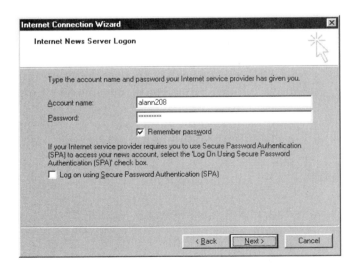

The name of your news server now appears below your mail folders in the folder list.

A message will appear asking whether you want to download newsgroups from the server. *See "Downloading and Subscribing to Newsgroups," on page 258.*

To add an additional newsgroup account, you'll need to know the name of the newsgroup server. Then follow these steps:

1 Point to Go To on Outlook's View menu and choose News, or start Outlook Express.

2 When the newsreader opens, choose Accounts from its Tools menu.

3 Click Add.

4 Click News to start the Internet Connection Wizard.

5 Complete the wizard as described on the previous pages.

When you have more than one news account, you must make one your default news server. In the Internet Accounts dialog box, select that account and click Set As Default.

If you need to update information for a news server account you've already created, follow these steps:

1 Choose Accounts from the Tools menu.

2 On the News tab of the dialog box, select the account you want to change.

3 Click Properties.

4 Change the desired settings.

5 Click OK, and then click Close in the Internet Accounts dialog box.

Downloading and Subscribing to Newsgroups

The easiest way to send and receive messages and regularly participate in newsgroups that interest you is to subscribe to them. *Subscribing* to a newsgroup simply means marking it in Outlook Express so that it is displayed in the folder list. However, before you can select individual groups to subscribe to, you'll have to download to your computer the entire list of newsgroups provided by your news server.

You'll be given an opportunity to download the list of newsgroups when you add or create a news server or the first time you click a news server name in the folder list. Click Yes when you see the following message:

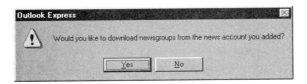

If you're not online when you select to download the newsgroups, you'll see a message asking whether you want to connect now. Click Yes to connect to your news server and download the newsgroup names. Many news servers carry several tens of thousands of newsgroups, so it might take a while to download the list for the first time.

After the newsgroup names are downloaded, you'll see the names in the Newsgroup Subscriptions dialog box, as shown in Figure 8-3, and you won't need to download the complete list again. This list will now appear whenever you click the Newsgroups button after clicking the news server name in the folder list. The button is only accessible when you are viewing messages from a newsgroup.

Once you've downloaded the newsgroup list, you're ready to subscribe to the newsgroups that interest you. To find a group that interests you, click the news server name in the folder list and then click the Newsgroups button to display the available groups. You can scroll through the list looking for groups of interest, but with thousands of groups this could take some time. Instead, enter a word or phrase in

FIGURE 8-3.

The list of all available newsgroups down-loaded from the news server.

Alphabetical listing of all newsgroups carried by the server

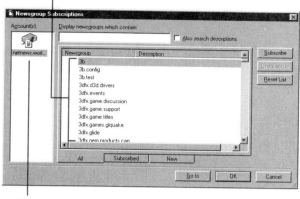

News server

the Display Newsgroups Which Contain list. After a short delay, a filtered list appears showing only groups whose names contain the text you entered. To redisplay all of the groups, delete the text in the box.

To subscribe to a group, double-click its name, or click its name and then click the Subscribe button. If you later want to unsubscribe to the newsgroup, click the Unsubscribe button.

To view just the groups to which you have subscribed, click the Subscribed tab below the list.

From time to time, your news server might add more newsgroups to its list. When this occurs, you'll get a message whenever you log on to the news server asking if you want to download the new names. If you choose Yes, after Outlook Express downloads the new names, you can click the New tab of the Newsgroup Subscriptions dialog box to easily review only the additional newsgroups and subscribe to any that interest you.

 NOTE

To make sure that you are notified when new groups are added, choose Options from the Tools menu, click the General tab of the dialog box that appears, and then make sure the check box Notify Me If There Are Any New Newsgroups is selected.

Receiving Newsgroup Messages

After subscribing to newsgroups, whenever you click the news server name in the folder list, you'll see a list of your subscribed groups along with the total number of messages in each group and the number of those messages you haven't read, as shown in Figure 8-4.

The Synchronization Settings column shows how messages will be downloaded and made available when you are offline. When you synchronize a newsgroup, you can make messages or just their headers available when you are not connected.

Downloading Message Headers

To read newsgroup messages, you have to download them from the server. Because a popular newsgroup can have thousands of messages, many of which may not interest you, Outlook Express usually downloads only the message headers—the titles or subjects of the messages. You can then pick and choose which messages you want to read.

If there is a plus sign in front of the news server name, click it to list the subscribed newsgroups in the folder list, and then click the newsgroup name that you want to read. Any messages or message headers that you already downloaded will be retrieved from the cache and displayed in the message list. You'll see a message on the left of

FIGURE 8-4.
The list of subscribed newsgroups.

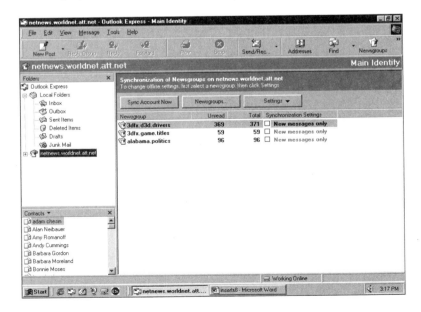

the status bar showing the total number of message headers you've downloaded and the number that are still unread.

If you are online, Outlook will then automatically download up to 300 new message headers. (You can change this number on the Read tab of the Options dialog box.) A message on the left of the status bar will show the number of headers being received, and then the headers will appear in the message list. The list has a column to indicate if the message is flagged, and four headings—Subject, From, Sent, and Size, although you might have to scroll the pane to see them all. If you want, right-click the column names and choose Columns from the shortcut menu that appears. You can add a column that counts the lines in a message (you might not want to retrieve very long messages) or turn off any of the columns you don't want to see.

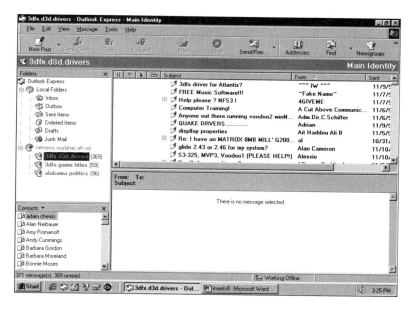

II

Working with Electronic Mail

TIP

Choose Get Next 300 Headers from the Tools menu to download the next set of headers. The number listed in the menu command matches whatever number you selected for the Get __ Headers At A Time option on the Read tab of the Options dialog box, up to 1,000. If you deselected this option, all message headers are downloaded when you first enter the newsgroup, and the menu item will be Get New Headers. Other menu items that don't apply to newsgroups are unavailable.

If you are offline, Outlook might automatically connect to your Internet provider to download message headers. If Outlook does not automatically connect or if you are offline, you can connect to the news server and download new message headers by following these steps:

1 Select the newsgroup in the folder list.

2 Choose Synchronize Item Now from the Tools menu.

Outlook connects to the news server, and then downloads new message headers and displays them in the message list.

To download message headers from all subscribed newsgroups and check your mail server for new incoming mail, choose Synchronize from the Tools menu.

Reading Messages

Now that you've downloaded the message headers, you can read messages that interest you. Messages that you have not read are shown in bold in the header list. Because only the header is actually downloaded by default, you can read the contents' of messages as long as you are online but not if you disconnect.

To read a message, use either of these techniques:

- Click the message header to retrieve and read the message in the preview pane.

- Double-click the message header to open the message in its own window.

If you don't see the preview pane in the newsreader, you can turn it on by selecting Layout from the View menu and clicking the Show Preview Pane Header check box.

You can also flag a message if you want to call your attention to it later on. Click the Flag column next to the message header, or select the header and choose Flag Message from the Edit menu.

When you read a message, its contents will be temporarily stored in your computer's cache memory, so it might be available even after you disconnect. Once the cache is cleared, however, the message contents will no longer be available offline unless you specifically download the message.

Working with Message Threads

A message thread is composed of an original message, all replies to it, replies to the replies, and so on. The thread usually relates to a single topic, though you shouldn't be surprised if messages get way off track as more replies are made.

Threads form a "conversation" about a subject that members are interested in. You can follow the thread to read the conversation in the order in which it actually took place.

Messages that contain threads are indicated with a plus sign in the header list. Threads tend to build up multiple levels with responses to responses and so on, as shown here:

Click here to see
replies to this message.

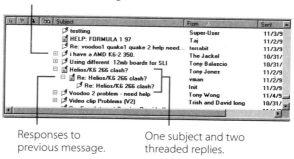

Responses to
previous message.

One subject and two
threaded replies.

A plus sign next to a message means that there are responses—click the plus sign to display them. The plus sign changes to a minus sign. Click the minus sign when you do not want to display the responses. If your messages are not displayed in threads, point to Current View on the View menu and choose Group Messages By Subject.

TIP

> To expand all message threads, choose Options from the Tools menu and click the Read tab. Select the Automatically Expand Grouped Messages check box.

When the thread is collapsed, the message header will be bold if at least one message in the thread is still unread.

Watching and Ignoring Threads

Some message threads will be particularly interesting to you; others won't interest you at all. You can mark threads that you want to read as being *watched*, and threads you are not interested in as being *ignored*.

To watch a thread, click in the thread state column next to its header, so an eyeglasses icon appears. To ignore the thread, click the eyeglasses icon a second time and it will change to a circle with a line through it. Click the icon a third time to remove it:

Watched thread

Ignored thread

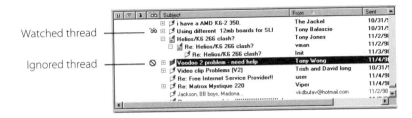

You can also select a message and then choose either Watch Thread or Ignore Thread from the Message menu.

You'll be able to hide all messages that are marked as ignored by pointing to Current View on the View menu and choosing Hide Read Or Ignored Messages. You can create rules to perform special functions on watched columns by choosing Define Views from this same submenu.

Synchronizing Messages

Reading messages while you are online can be time consuming. You could easily run up huge phone bills and ISP charges if you are not on an unlimited plan. By synchronizing messages, you can download the contents of all messages along with their headers. You can choose to automatically download messages, but that can take a long time and you may not even be interested in many of the messages. As an alternative, you can download selected messages and threads and then read them offline.

Reading Messages Offline

If you think you would be interested in every newsgroup message, you can set the newsreader to download both the headers of messages and their contents at the same time. You can then read the messages offline at your convenience. To set up a newsgroup for offline reading, follow these steps:

1 Click the news server name in the folder list.

2 Click a newsgroup name in the large panel on the right.

3 Open the Settings list and choose what you want to download: All Messages, New Messages Only, or New Headers Only.

4 Repeat steps 2 and 3 for each newsgroup you want to set up.

5 When you want to download your messages, choose either Synchronize or Synchronize Item Now from the Tools menu. You can also click the Sync Account Now button.

6 After the messages are downloaded, you can log off and read the messages at your convenience.

Downloading Selected Messages

You will probably find it more efficient to download only the messages that you are interested in reading. You can mark your newsgroups to download just the headers and then review the headers offline to decide which messages to download. This way you don't take up a lot of disk space with uninteresting conversation, and you don't spend a lot of time waiting for the messages to be downloaded.

As you read through the message headers offline, mark those whose contents you are interested in downloading. You can mark an individual message or an entire thread of messages.

To quickly mark a message for downloading, click in the Mark For Offline column (the column with the arrow) next to the message you want to download:

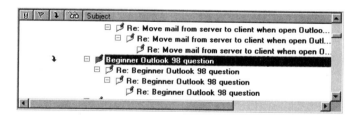

Click in the column of the first message in a thread to download all of the messages in the thread. If you change your mind about downloading the message, click in the column again to remove the icon.

You can also mark messages using these steps:

1 Click a message header you want to read.

2 Point to Mark For Offline on the Tools menu, and then choose Download Message Later. To mark an entire thread to be downloaded, select any message in the thread, point to Mark For Offline on the Tools menu, and choose Download Thread Later.

3 Repeat steps 1 and 2 for each message you want to download.

4 Choose Synchronize from the Tools menu.

5 Disconnect after the messages are downloaded, and then read the messages at your leisure.

To quickly mark a message for download, right-click it, point to Mark For Offline from the shortcut menu, and then select Download Message Later or Download Thread Later. If you mark a thread when it's collapsed (only the first message is displayed with a plus sign next to it), all the messages in the thread will be marked for download.

Displaying Messages

By default, Outlook displays all the message headers. With possibly thousands of messages in a newsgroup, it can take a long time to scan the list looking for ones you want to read.

Rather than display all the headers, you can choose to display certain ones. Point to Current View on the View menu, and then choose from these options:

- **Show All Messages.** This option displays all message headers.

- **Hide Read Messages.** This option displays just messages you have not yet read.

- **Show Downloaded Messages.** This option displays just messages that you downloaded.

- **Show Replies To My Messages.** This option displays replies to messages that you posted.

- **Hide Read Or Ignored Messages.** This option does not show messages that you have read or message threads that you have chosen to ignore.

- **Define Views.** This option lets you filter messages, creating rules that determine which messages are displayed, just as you use the Rules Wizard to create rules in Outlook.

- **Group Messages By Subject.** This option groups messages by their thread.

Just remember to change back to Show All Messages when you want to see all of the message headers!

Changing the Read Status of Messages

As you know, messages you haven't read are shown in bold in the message list. If you want to display all messages, you can take advantage of the bold indicator to scan the list for your unread messages. Once you're sure you are no longer interested in any unread messages in the list, you can mark them all as read. In this way only new messages downloaded later will be shown in bold, and they'll be easy to identify.

To mark all of the messages in a selected newsgroup as read, follow these steps:

1 Point to Current View on the View menu, and then choose Show All Messages.

2 Choose Mark All Read from the Edit menu.

The Edit menu also lets you mark individual messages or an entire thread as read, or you can mark a message as unread.

NOTE

The Catch Up command on the Edit menu lets you mark as read messages that you click or scroll through on the header area.

Finding Messages

When you're interested in messages about a specific topic, you'll find yourself scanning up and down the list looking for a key word or phrase in the headers. But because a newsgroup can contain hundreds, or even thousands of messages, you'll become bleary-eyed long before you reach the end of the list. Rather than straining your eyes by scanning through the message list to find those you are interested in, have the newsreader find messages for you.

TIP

Remember, you can sort messages by clicking the column heading in the message list. To sort by date, for example, click the Sent header to toggle between an ascending and descending sort. If you select Group Messages By Subject on the Current View submenu of the View menu, messages will first be grouped by thread and then sorted within each thread according to the column you click. Deselect Group Messages By Subject to sort purely by the column you click.

The Quick Message Search

Much of the time you'll be looking for messages within a single newsgroup, and you'll want to use a fast method to find them. Follow these steps:

1 Select the Newsgroup from the folder list, and allow the message headers to be downloaded.

2 Press the F3 shortcut key, or point to Find on the Edit menu and choose Messages In This Folder.

3 In the Find dialog box that appears, type the word or phrase in the message header that you want to search for. If you also want to search the contents of messages that have been downloaded, select the Search All The Text In Downloaded Messages check box.

4 Click Find Next, and Outlook will move to the first matching message and display it in the preview pane.

5 Click the Find Next button or the F3 key to move to each successive matching message.

The Advanced Message Search

If you want to search in more than one folder, even through all the mail and news folders in Outlook Express, or if you want to search in a more advanced way, follow these steps:

1 Point to Find on the Edit menu, and choose Message to see the dialog box shown in Figure 8-5.

2 If you don't want to search all your mail and news folders, click Browse to find the folder you want to search; then select Include Subfolders if you also want to search folders within the selected folder.

3 Enter as many specifications as needed. You can locate messages based on whom they are from, the text in the subject or body of

FIGURE 8-5.
The Find Message dialog box.

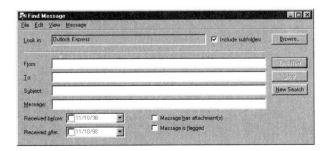

the message, whether they are flagged, and when they were posted. Choose both a Before and After date to find messages posted during a specific period. Select the appropriate check boxes, and then either enter the date or click the down arrow to choose the date from the calendar that appears.

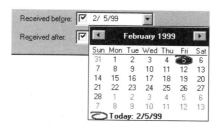

4 Click Find Now.

Outlook Express will find and display all the messages that meet your criteria. Double-click each message you want to read.

Managing Newsgroup Messages

In Chapter 2, "Discovering Outlook," you learned how to create rules for managing messages in Outlook, and in Chapter 7, "Using Outlook Express," you learned how to filter mail messages in Outlook Express. You can also create rules for newsgroup messages.

The quickest way to filter messages is by the sender. Perhaps there's someone who clutters up the newsgroup with meaningless messages or inappropriate material. Just click a message from that person, and choose Block Sender from the Message menu to display the dialog box shown in Figure 8-6.

Choose to block mail, news messages, or both, and then click OK. You can use the same dialog box to block mail from anyone—even if you

FIGURE 8-6.
The Block Sender dialog box.

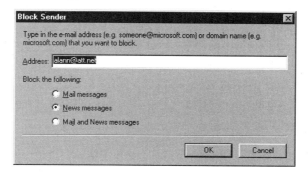

have not yet received a message from the person. Just select Block Sender from the Message menu at any time, and type the person's e-mail address in the Address text box.

If you need to add, remove, or change the e-mail address of a blocked sender, point to Message Rules from the Tools menu and click Blocked Senders List. In the dialog box that appears, you can delete that sender from the list, change the address, or add additional blocked senders.

In addition to blocking messages, you can create rules, much as you learned in Chapter 2 for Outlook messages. To quickly create a rule using the e-mail address contained in a message you've already received, select the newsgroup message and choose Create Rule From Message from the Message menu. You'll see the Rule Editor dialog box, as shown in Figure 8-7.

1 Select the condition for the message.

2 Choose an action.

3 Edit any underlined values.

4 Name the Rule.

5 Click OK.

To create more extensive rules, point to Message Rules from the Tools menu and click either Mail or News, depending on the type of message

FIGURE 8-7.
The Rule Editor dialog box.

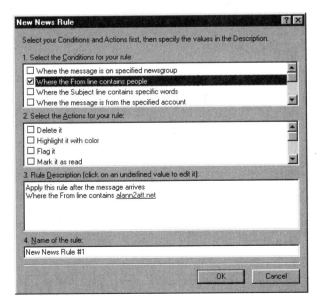

> ### What Happened to My Messages?
>
> What happens if you download a message but it seems to disappear after you read it or a week later? It's not magic; it's just the settings on the Maintenance tab of the Options dialog box that you learned about in Chapter 7, "Using Outlook Express." Several of the options on that tab are specifically designed for newsgroup messages rather than for e-mail.
>
> For example, the tab contains options that let you automatically delete the body of messages after you read them or a specific number of days after they've been downloaded. These options are helpful in cutting down the size of your news folders.
>
> You can also set when your news folders are compacted. When messages are deleted, they are no longer available, but the space occupied by them on your disk is not actually released. Compacting reorganizes the folder and frees up this wasted space. Outlook Express automatically compacts folders when 20 percent of their space is being wasted, but you can change this percentage on the Maintenance tab.
>
> You can also compact the folders and delete messages or headers whenever you want by using the Clean Up Now button on the Maintenance tab. In the dialog box that appears, you choose the news server or newsgroup you want to clean out and then select to compact it, remove messages, or delete both messages and headers.

you want the rule to apply to. Then create the rule just as you learned in "Managing Your Mail with the Rules Wizard," on page 51.

Posting Newsgroup Messages

Sending mail to a newsgroup is very similar to sending regular e-mail. The main difference is that when you post a message, even a reply to someone else's message, you are sending it to the news server, where every reader of the newsgroup can view it.

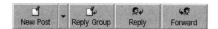

As the text on the buttons above indicates, you can post a new message (start a new thread), reply to the newsgroup (adding it to an existing thread for the entire world to read), reply only to the sender as in a traditional e-mail message, or forward the newsgroup message as an e-mail message to someone else who may be interested in the topic.

From the Message menu you also have the choice Reply To All. This command sends your reply to the newsgroup and by e-mail directly to the sender. Mailing directly to the sender as well as the group is a good way to make sure the sender sees your reply, or sees it sooner, because many people only occasionally visit certain newsgroups but check their e-mail regularly.

When you post a new message or reply to the newsgroup, the To field of the New Message window will contain the name of the group. Do not edit the field. Complete the message, and then click Send in the message window to place it in the Outbox. Finally, click Send/Receive to post the message.

You've now learned how to use two programs to send and receive e-mail—Microsoft Outlook and Outlook Express. If you're on a network, however, you may not always be connected to the network to send messages and work with other Outlook items. In the next chapter, you'll learn how to work offline and remotely when the network is not available or when you're on the road.

CHAPTER 9

Using Outlook Remotely and Offline

I f you're among the adventurous who travel with your computer, you can use Microsoft Outlook anywhere. You may want to connect to your network when you're lodged in a hotel to get your messages and update your calendar. Or you may just want to compose messages that will remain in your Outbox until you send them at some later time when you are connected.

In this chapter, you'll learn how to work with Outlook when you're not physically connected to your network—remotely and offline. For this chapter, working remotely means connecting to the network through a modem and telephone line. There are two ways to work remotely:

- Dialing in just to get your messages through Remote Mail.

- Dialing in and working with Outlook as if you were still in the office. I'll call this *working remotely online*.

Working offline means not being connected at all but working with the Outlook files stored on your disk. You can still compose new messages, you'll just have to wait to send them.

NOTE

To work with Outlook remotely, your system administrator must set up your user account with dial-up access rights so that you can dial in to the network. Contact your system administrator for assistance.

Working Remotely Online

When you work remotely online, you dial into and connect to your network. Then Outlook behaves exactly the same as if you were still in the office connected to the network with a cable.

Setting It Up

To work this way, you don't need to make any changes to an Outlook profile, and you don't have to worry about offline folders. What you do need, however, is to set up Dial-Up Networking in Windows so you can dial in to your network computer. Here's how:

SEE ALSO

See "Setting Up Calling Card Dialing," on page 297, for details about setting up Outlook to dial using your telephone calling card.

1 Open My Computer on the Windows desktop, and then open Dial-Up Networking. If you have not created a Dial-Up Networking connection before, you'll see the welcoming page of the Make New Connection Wizard, and you can skip ahead to step 3. Otherwise, you'll see the Dial-Up Networking window showing any existing dial-up services.

2 If the Dial-Up Networking window appeared, open Make New Connection to see the dialog box in Figure 9-1.

3 Type a name for the connection.

FIGURE 9-1.
The Make New Connection dialog box.

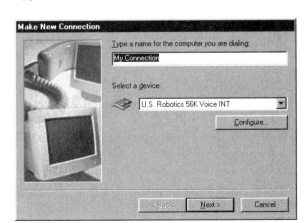

4 Make sure your modem appears in the Select A Device box. If not, open the list and choose your modem.

5 Click Next.

6 On the next screen, enter the area code and telephone number of your network computer.

7 Select the country location of the network server's phone number.

8 Click Next.

9 Click Finish on the final page of the Make New Connection Wizard.

You'll use this new connection in the next section.

Making the Remote Connection

When you're ready to connect to the network computer to work with Outlook remotely, take these steps:

1 Open My Computer on the Windows desktop, and then open Dial-Up Networking.

2 In the Dial-Up Networking window, open the connection you set up to connect to your network dial-up computer. Depending on how Dial-Up Networking is set up, your system might connect automatically or the Connect To dialog box might appear as shown in Figure 9-2. If the dialog box does not appear, skip ahead to step 8.

3 Make sure your user name is correct.

4 Enter your password if the Password box is empty.

FIGURE 9-2.
The Connect To dialog box.

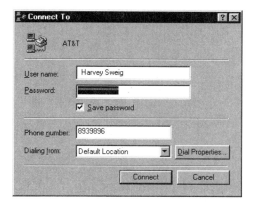

II

Working with Electronic Mail

5 Select the Save Password check box if you don't want to enter your password each time you connect.

6 Check the telephone number and location—edit them if needed.

7 Click Connect.

8 When Dial-Up Networking has established the network connection, start Outlook as you do when you're connected directly to the network.

> Select the Save Password check box in the Connect To dialog box only if your computer is always secure. With this check box selected, anyone can use your Dial-Up Networking connection to connect to the network. If you sometimes leave your computer where it's available to anyone, it's better to clear the Save Password check box. This means you'll have to type your password each time you want to establish a Dial-Up Networking connection, but your network will be much more secure.

Working Offline

When you are away from the office, you may want to compose mail and work with your calendar and other Outlook folders without being connected. I call this *working offline*. To work offline, you need to use either personal folders or Offline folders.

- Personal folders store all of your Outlook information on your own hard disk, even when you're connected directly to the network, and you create them as part of your Exchange Server profile.

- Offline folders are a copy of your server folders. They are maintained on your own machine for use when you're not connected to your network mailbox.

You can decide which to use and learn more about setting up personal folders by reading Chapter 1, "Preparing for Outlook." You must set either personal folders or your server's mailbox as your delivery point. *For information on how to do this, see "Setting the Delivery Point," on page 10.*

NOTE

You can use offline folders only if your e-mail server is Microsoft Exchange Server. If you are connected to a peer-to-peer network you must use personal folders to work offline.

If you already set up Outlook to use personal folders, and they are set as your delivery point when connected to the network, you don't have to make any other preparation.

However, if your delivery point is your network mailbox, you have to take these general steps, which you'll learn how to do in detail in the sections that follow:

1 Set up an offline folder file to store Outlook information on your computer.

2 Download the Offline Address Book so you can address mail while offline.

3 Set up public folder favorites for public folders you want to open offline.

4 Designate other folders for offline use.

5 Synchronize all offline folders.

Setting Up an Offline Folder File

To set up an offline folder file, make sure your Exchange mailbox is set as the delivery point, and then take these steps:

1 Connect to your e-mail server for online work.

2 Choose Services from the Tools menu, select Microsoft Exchange Server in the list of services, and then click Properties.

3 In the Microsoft Exchange Server dialog box, click the Advanced tab.

4 Click the Offline Folder File Settings button on the Advanced tab to see the dialog box shown in Figure 9-3, on the following page.

II

Working with Electronic Mail

FIGURE 9-3.
The Offline Folder File
Settings dialog box.

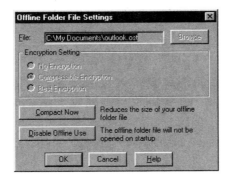

5 Outlook suggests a name for the offline folder file. If you already have offline folders set up from another installation, click Browse to find the file. Offline folders files have .ost extensions.

6 Click OK.

7 When you are returned to the Advanced tab of the Microsoft Exchange Server dialog box, select the Enable Offline Use check box.

8 Click OK to close each dialog box.

You will now see a special icon under each of Outlook's folders in the Outlook Bar and the Folder List indicating that they are available for offline use:

Folders available
for offline use

When you work offline, you can open and view these folders as you would while working online. You can compose messages, move messages, delete messages, and empty your Deleted Items folder—all while you're working offline. New messages you compose won't be sent and you won't receive new messages sent to you, however, until you go online and *synchronize* the folders. Synchronizing means updating the contents of your offline and server mailbox folders so they both contain identical sets of the most up-to-date information.

> **Working Offline with Windows CE**
>
> A variety of handheld computing devices are controlled by the Microsoft Windows CE operating system. Many of these devices also include Pocket Outlook, a special version of Outlook designed for portable devices.
>
> With software and cables provided with the device, or which can be purchased from third-party companies, you can download the Outlook data from your desktop computer into the handheld device for working offline. Once downloaded, you can synchronize the information in much the same way as you can synchronize offline with the server, as explained in this chapter. If you attach your handheld device to a docking station linked to your desktop, you can also automatically synchronize the two devices.

Turning Off Offline Folders

If circumstances change and you don't think you'll be working offline anymore, you can discontinue using offline folders. Here's how:

1 Connect to your e-mail server for online work, either through a network connection or through Dial-Up Networking.

2 Choose Services from the Tools menu, select Microsoft Exchange Server, and then click the Properties button.

3 In the Microsoft Exchange Server dialog box, click the Advanced tab.

4 To discontinue the use of offline folders immediately, clear the Enable Offline Use check box.

To discontinue their use the next time you start Outlook, click the Offline Folder File Settings button and then the Disable Offline Use button. Click Yes when Outlook asks whether you want to continue.

5 Click OK to close each dialog box.

Downloading the Offline Address Book

You're now ready for the next phase of setting up offline folders: downloading the Offline Address Book. When you're working offline, you'll probably want to compose new messages, reply to messages, and forward messages. Before you can specify Exchange Server recipients of your message or place the message in your Outbox to be sent to them later, you need to have the offline address book available. This address book is a local copy of the server's address book, just like offline folders are local copies of the server folders.

To download the offline address book, do the following:

1 Connect to your network and start Outlook.

2 Point to Synchronize on the Tools menu, and choose Download Address Book to open the dialog box shown in Figure 9-4.

FIGURE 9-4.

The Download Offline Address Book dialog box.

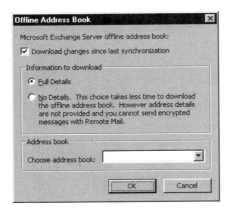

3 Select the level of detail you want for the offline address book. The Full Details option downloads the entire address book. The No Details option downloads only the essentials. This second option is faster, but you won't be able to send encrypted mail remotely.

4 Select an address book to download from the Choose Address Book list.

5 Click OK. You'll see a message that shows you how downloading is progressing. When downloading is complete, you're ready to work with messages offline.

You can later update the offline address book by downloading it again. Select the check box labeled Download Changes Since Last Synchronization to download just the new information, not the entire address book.

Working Remotely with Public Folders

While you're working offline, you can't open public folders, at least not directly, because they're located on the server. Outlook helps you get around this restriction through public folder favorites. If you've already set these up, you're in a good position to take advantage of them during offline work. If you haven't yet set up any public folder favorites, you must do so before you can work with the contents of a public folder offline.

Setting up public folder favorites is quite easy; simply follow these steps:

1 Choose Folder List from the View menu to display the Folder List.

2 Click the plus sign next to Public Folders, and then click the plus sign next to All Public Folders.

3 Select a public folder you want to be able to use while offline.

4 Point to Folder on the File menu, and then choose Add To Public Folder Favorites from the submenu.

5 When the Add to Favorites dialog box appears, the folder you chose will already have been highlighted in the Favorite Folder Name list. Click the Add button. The folder you created will now be listed under the Favorites item under Public Folders in the Folder List. It will contain all of the messages currently in the associated public folder.

6 Click the plus sign next to Favorites under Public Folders.

7 Right-click the folder where you dropped it under Public Folder Favorites, and then click Properties from the shortcut menu that appears.

8 Click the Synchronization tab to see the dialog box shown in Figure 9-5.

9 Under This Folder Is Available, select When Offline Or Online.

10 Click OK.

FIGURE 9-5.

Use the Synchronization tab to set a folder's properties to enable offline access.

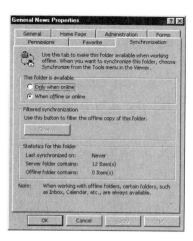

Working with Electronic Mail

This folder is now available for work offline as well as online. If you no longer want a folder to be available for offline work, select the Only When Online option under This Folder Is Available on the Synchronization tab of the Properties dialog box.

> If you'd like, you can also drag a copy of the folder you added to your public folder favorites to your Outlook Bar for more convenient access. The offline folder symbol will appear on the folder's icon in both the Folder List and the Outlook Bar.

Filtering Folders for Offline Work

By default, your offline folders will be complete duplicates of your folders from the Exchange server. Rather than duplicate all of the folder contents, however, you can create a filter to determine what items are copied to your offline folders when they are synchronized. This saves both synchronization time and disk space on your computer. Only items that match the filter will be transferred into your offline folders. Create a filter from the folder's Properties dialog box by following these steps:

1 Right-click the public folder favorites folder you want to filter.

2 Choose Properties from the menu that appears.

3 Select the Synchronization tab on the Properties dialog box.

4 Make sure the When Offline Or Online option is selected. Then click Filter and define any combination of the criteria shown here:

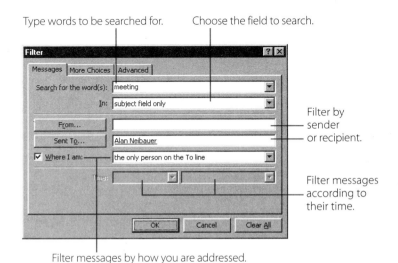

Type words to be searched for.

Choose the field to search.

Filter by sender or recipient.

Filter messages according to their time.

Filter messages by how you are addressed.

5 When you've completed this tab, click the More Choices tab if you want to specify additional criteria. These options let you filter mail based on whether it's read or unread, includes attachments, or has a certain level of importance. You can also choose to match the case when filtering on text and to include messages of a specified size.

6 Click the Advanced tab if you want to specify additional criteria. This tab lets you create custom criteria using fields, a condition, and a matching value.

7 Click OK to close the dialog box and activate the filter.

Synchronizing Folders

After you set up folders for offline use, you need to synchronize the offline folders periodically with their related folders on the Exchange server. During synchronization:

- Any new items in your offline folders are uploaded to your server mailbox.

- Any new items in your mailbox are downloaded to your offline folders.

Outlook synchronizes your offline folders whenever you connect to Microsoft Exchange Server. After a session of working online, you might want to synchronize your folders again.

Synchronizing Offline Folders Manually

Before exiting Outlook, and while you're still connected to your Exchange server, you can synchronize any folders that you have set up to be available offline.

To synchronize a single folder, do the following:

1 Select the folder that you want to synchronize.

2 Point to Synchronize on the Tools menu, and choose This Folder from the submenu.

You cannot synchronize a public folder directly because these are located on the server, not on your local machine. If you want to synchronize a public folder, you must first add it to the public folder favorites and mark it for offline use as explained in "Working Remotely with Public Folders," on page 280, and then choose to synchronize the copy of the folder in public folder favorites.

To synchronize all folders you've set to offline use, point to Synchronize on the Tools menu, and then choose All Folders from the submenu. In either case—synchronizing a single folder or all folders—Outlook displays the progress of its synchronization in the Outlook status bar.

Synchronizing All Offline Folders Automatically

To further help you keep your offline folders synchronized, you can have Outlook automatically synchronize all offline folders with your online (server) folders when you exit Outlook or at periodic intervals.

 On the Mail Services tab of the Options dialog box, you can clear the Enable Offline Access check box if you decide not to synchronize folders automatically.

To synchronize when you exit Outlook, follow these steps:

1 While working online in Outlook, choose Options from the Tools menu, and then click the Mail Services tab.

2 Select the check box labeled When Online, Synchronize All Folders Upon Exiting, and then click OK.

With this check box selected, your offline folders are consistent with your online folders when you start to work offline. Leave this check box clear only if you prefer to synchronize your offline folders manually (by using the Synchronize command on the Tools menu) while you're working online.

On the Mail Services tab, you can also select to automatically synchronize folders at periodic intervals, such as every 60 minutes, in either or both of these ways:

- To automatically synchronize folders when you are online, select the When Online, Automatically Synchronize All Offline Folders check box and set a time interval.

- To automatically connect remotely and synchronize folders, select the When Offline, Automatically Synchronize check box, select All Folders from the list, and then set a time interval.

Offline Folder Settings

You can customize the way offline folders are synchronized using Offline Folder Settings. To access the settings, choose Options from the Tools menu, click the Mail Services tab, and then click the Offline Folder Settings button. Outlook opens the dialog box shown here:

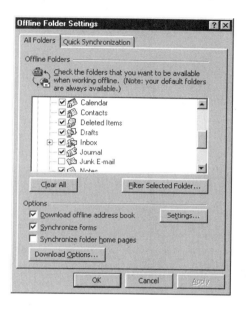

The All Folders tab of the dialog box lets you choose which folders will be synchronized when you choose All Folders from the Synchronize submenu on the Tools menu. Clear the check boxes for the folders you do not want to include.

Other options in the dialog box let you automatically download the offline address book when you synchronize folders and synchronize custom forms and folder home pages.

Clicking Download Options lets you set limits to the messages that are downloaded based on their size. You can choose not to download messages over a certain size but specify exceptions for messages from specific senders, marked with a high priority, or with a certain flag.

The Quick Synchronization tab of the Offline Folder Settings dialog box lets you designate groups of folders that you can synchronize with one click. When you point to Synchronize on the Tools menu, for example, you might see a listing in the submenu labeled Mail And Calendar. Clicking that option automatically synchronizes your mail folders (Inbox, Outbox, and Drafts) and Calendar folders. You use the Quick

Synchronization tab to combine other folders into a group that will also be shown on the submenu.

Starting Outlook Offline

Working in Outlook offline is a simple matter of starting Outlook. Outlook might take a little time before it starts, trying to connect to your network. When it finally gives up, a dialog box appears with these options:

- Click the Retry button to try connecting again, if you are connected.

- Click the Work Offline button if your computer is not connected.

Your personal or offline folders appear, depending on the delivery point set up for the profile.

NOTE

> When you are working offline from your Exchange Server network, you might not be able to send Internet mail through Outlook.

Moving Items to Different Folders

SEE ALSO

To learn how to move items to a different folder, see "Moving a Folder Item," on page 457.

While you're working offline, you might want to move an item to a different folder. This is a simple process: you move the item just as you would when you're connected to your Microsoft Exchange Server. The next time you connect to your server, either remotely or through a network connection, the Microsoft Exchange Server moves the items in the server folders to match the moves you made while you were working offline. This movement of items among folders is part of the synchronization process.

Using Remote Mail

Remote Mail is another option for working remotely, but only when you want to work with your network server's Inbox folder to check or send messages. By default, connecting to your e-mail server with Remote Mail only downloads a list of message headers. A message header is the same information you'd see in the Inbox folder, but not the message itself as you'd see in the preview pane. Remote Mail then disconnects from the server to save you from expensive phone charges.

You mark the messages you want to read and the messages you want to delete and then connect with Remote Mail again. When you reconnect to your e-mail server, Outlook downloads only those messages marked for download, deletes those messages marked for deletion, and disconnects again. You can then read the downloaded messages and perform all the mail tasks—reply, delete, forward, move, and save—that you perform with messages when you're connected to the network. Then you connect again so your replies and forwarded messages can be routed to their destinations.

> **NOTE**

> Use Remote Mail with either personal folders or offline folders, whichever is set as the delivery point in your Outlook profile.

Before you can connect through Remote Mail, you need to perform the following general steps:

1 Download the offline address book while you're connected to your e-mail server. *For details, see "Downloading the Offline Address Book," on page 279.*

2 Set up Remote Mail connections, providing Outlook with information such as your username and password.

3 Set up Remote Mail options, which you can do either online or offline.

Setting Up Remote Mail Connections

Before you can use Remote Mail, you must provide Outlook with information about your remote connection. Follow these steps:

1 Choose Services on the Tools menu, select Microsoft Exchange Server, and then click the Properties button.

2 Click the Dial-Up Networking tab, shown in Figure 9-6, on the next page.

3 Select the option for your Remote Mail connection. You have two choices:

- **Dial Using The Following Connection.** Select this option when you're working offline and you're going to use Remote Mail over a telephone line only. This option starts the dial-up process for you when you run Remote Mail. The connection names that are listed come from the Windows Dial-Up Networking window.

II

Working with Electronic Mail

FIGURE 9-6.

The Dial-Up
Networking tab of the
Microsoft Exchange
Server Properties
dialog box.

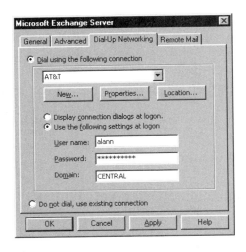

- **Do Not Dial, Use Existing Connection.** Select this option when you want to work offline while you're connected directly to your network (perhaps the network is down for maintenance) or when you've opened a dial-up connection through Windows Dial-Up Networking. This option simply connects to your Microsoft Exchange Server through the existing connection rather than by hanging up and dialing again.

4 If you select the first option above, you can select an existing connection name from the drop-down list, or you can create a new connection by clicking the New button. If you need to modify a connection, click the Properties button. To change the location, click the Location button, and follow the instructions in "Setting Dialing Options," on page 183. You also need to enter your network username, password, and domain.

Setting Remote Mail Options

The options on the Remote Mail tab of the Exchange Server Properties dialog box make it possible for you to save time by screening messages before you download them. Remote Mail can first download message headers only, allowing you to mark them for reading or deletion. You can then download in their entirety the messages that you have marked for reading. Alternatively, you can choose to make one longer connection instead of two shorter ones, and retrieve both headers and messages at one time.

Two options can make Remote Mail work better for you:

- Filtering Remote Mail so that you don't have to see messages you don't care about when you're away from your office

- Scheduling automatic dial-in times so that you can keep your folders current when at home or on the road.

To set Remote Mail options, take the following steps. The specific procedures are detailed in the next two sections.

1 If the Dial-Up Networking tab of the Microsoft Exchange Server properties dialog box is still visible from the previous steps, click the Remote Mail tab to see the options in Figure 9-7. Otherwise, choose Services from the Tools menu, select Microsoft Exchange Server, click the Properties button, and then click the Remote Mail tab.

2 Click Process Marked Items or click Retrieve Items That Meet The Following Conditions, and then click the Filter button to choose the conditions, as described in the next section.

3 Clear the Disconnect After Connection Is Finished check box if you want to stay connected after the messages have been processed. Remember you can incur expensive telephone charges if your call is not local.

4 Click Schedule to set the time of the next connection.

5 Click OK.

FIGURE 9-7.
The Remote Mail tab of the Microsoft Exchange Server Properties dialog box.

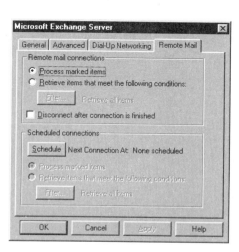

Filtering Remote Mail

A filter sets up conditions that tell the Remote Mail part of Outlook which message headers to download. A filter screens out messages you don't want to deal with and passes through only those message headers that you do want to see. This means shorter connection times while Remote Mail downloads the message headers and shorter work sessions for you because you aren't wading through extraneous messages.

Here's how to set up a Remote Mail filter:

1 Return to the Remote Mail tab of the Microsoft Exchange Server dialog box by choosing Services from the Tools menu, selecting Microsoft Exchange Server, and then clicking the Properties button.

2 In the Remote Mail Connections section of the dialog box, select the Retrieve Items That Meet The Following Conditions option, and then click Filter to open the Filter dialog box:

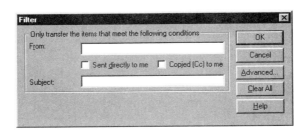

3 Fill in any or all of the four criteria, which can limit your remote mail transfers to messages from certain people, with a certain subject, and sent or copied directly to you.

4 Click Advanced to see more options.

5 In the Advanced dialog box, set up any additional conditions you want, such as accepting items of certain sizes, items within a certain range of dates, items set with a specific level of importance or sensitivity, and unread items, items with attachments, or items that *don't* match the conditions you've set here or in the previous Filter dialog box. You can set criteria in the Advanced dialog box without setting any conditions in the Filter dialog box, or you can set conditions in both boxes.

To receive all your Remote Mail items, don't set any filter conditions in the Filter dialog box—when you close the Filter dialog box, the phrase next to the Filter button will read *Retrieve All Items*.

6 Click OK to close each of the open dialog boxes.

Notice the check box in the Advanced dialog box labeled Only Items That Do Not Match These Conditions. Selecting this check box reverses all the other conditions you set up in the Filter and Advanced dialog boxes. For example, if you select this check box and the Only Unread Items check box, only items that you have already read will be delivered to you.

It's a simple matter to turn off a Remote Mail filter—click Process Marked Items on the Remote Mail tab. This preserves your filter but deactivates it. It can be restored at any time by clicking Retrieve Items That Meet The Following Conditions again.

To remove the filter entirely, follow these steps instead:

1 Click the Filter button on the Remote Mail tab.

2 In the Filter dialog box, click the Clear All button, and then click OK.

Clicking the Clear All button clears both the Filter and the Advanced dialog box settings. The label beside the Filter button on the Remote Mail tab changes to Retrieve All Items. To make it clear that you aren't using any filter, you can select the Process Marked Items option, but with the filter turned off, either option will retrieve marked items.

Scheduling Remote Mail Connections

When you're away from your network connection, you might want to connect with Remote Mail at a specific time or at specific intervals or both. With Remote Mail scheduling, you can set the time and interval you want Outlook to use to dial in and connect.

To set up a dial-in schedule for Remote Mail, follow these steps:

1 Choose Services from the Tools menu, select Microsoft Exchange Server, click the Properties button, and then click the Remote Mail tab.

II

Working with Electronic Mail

2 Click the Schedule button.

3 Select this check box to connect at a specific time, and then set the time.

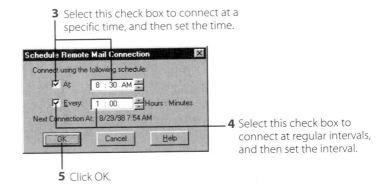

4 Select this check box to connect at regular intervals, and then set the interval.

5 Click OK.

6 In the Scheduled Connections area of the Remote Mail tab, select the Process Marked Items option to have Outlook process all marked items, or select the Retrieve Items That Meet The Following Conditions option to set up a filter. Click the Filter button in the Scheduled Connections area, and then complete the filter as just explained in "Filtering Remote Mail," on page 290.

7 Click OK to close each of the open dialog boxes.

Running Remote Mail

To use Remote Mail, follow these steps:

1 Start Outlook and select your profile if you're asked.

2 If you're asked whether you want to connect to your server or work offline, click the Work Offline button. This message is displayed only if you selected Choose The Connection Type When Starting on the General Tab of the Microsoft Exchange Server Properties dialog box.

3 Point to Remote Mail on the Tools menu, and then choose Connect from the submenu. Alternatively, you can click the Connect button on the Remote toolbar. *See "Checking Out the Remote Toolbar," on page 295.* Outlook starts the Remote Connection Wizard, as shown in Figure 9-8.

4 Select the service connection you want to make. If you want the option of changing your dial-up settings before connecting, also select the Confirm Before Connecting check box.

FIGURE 9-8.
The Remote
Connection Wizard.

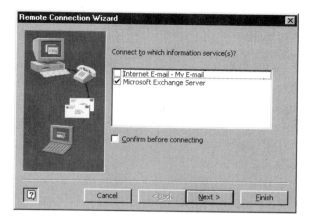

5 Click Next to proceed to the next page of the wizard, as shown in Figure 9-9, on the following page.

6 To download and send all messages, select the Retrieve And Send All New Mail option. To limit the remote connect options, select the Do Only The Following option, and then choose the tasks you want to carry out. The specific actions you can choose will vary.

7 Click the Next button, if it's available, or the Finish button. For example, if you selected the Confirm Before Connecting check box on the first Remote Connection Wizard page, click the Next button on the second page, and select your location settings.

8 You'll see messages telling you that your computer is dialing and then that your computer is connecting to your server. When the connection is established, you can work with messages using Remote Mail.

Breaking the Remote Mail Connection

Outlook doesn't keep a persistent Remote Mail connection by default. Remote Mail does its work and then disconnects in order to save you phone charges.

If you want to break the connection yourself before Remote Mail finishes, click the Disconnect button on the Remote toolbar or point to Remote Mail on the Tools menu, and then choose Disconnect from the submenu.

FIGURE 9-9.

Use this page to select which messages to transfer while connected.

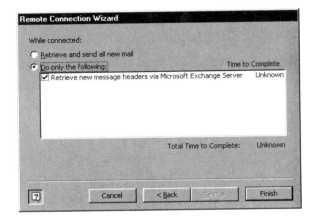

If you don't want Remote Mail to disconnect automatically, you can do the following:

1 Choose Services from the Tools menu, select Microsoft Exchange Server, and then click the Properties button.

2 Click the Remote Mail tab.

3 Clear the Disconnect After Connection Is Finished check box.

4 Click OK.

Working with Remote Mail

When the Remote Mail connection is made, Outlook performs the following actions in the order listed:

■ Sends any messages you have set up to send—new messages, replies, forwards, and task and appointment responses.

■ Downloads the complete text of messages for the message headers you've marked for downloading (or downloads all new items if you've selected that option).

■ Downloads message headers for messages that aren't already in the Inbox in your personal folders.

■ Deletes messages from the Microsoft Exchange Server that you marked for deletion while offline.

■ Disconnects the Remote Mail connection.

You can now read and work with the new messages you received, mark new message headers for downloading, or delete messages or message headers.

Checking Out the Remote Toolbar

Outlook provides the Remote toolbar, which contains buttons for Remote Mail commands. Figure 9-10 shows the name of each button on the Remote toolbar.

FIGURE 9-10.
The Remote toolbar.

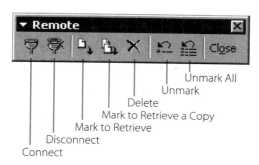

To display the Remote toolbar, use one of the following methods:

- Point to Remote Mail on the Tools menu, and then choose Remote Tools from the submenu.

- Right-click a visible toolbar, and then click Remote on the shortcut menu.

- Point to Remote Mail on the Tools menu, and then drag the band at the top of the submenu into the Outlook window.

- Point to Toolbars on the Tools menu, and then choose Remote.

To close the Remote toolbar, you can use any of these methods:

- Point to Remote Mail on the Tools menu, and then choose Remote Tools from the submenu.

- Right-click a visible toolbar, and then click Remote on the shortcut menu.

- If the Remote toolbar is floating in the Outlook window, click the Close box on the upper-right corner of the toolbar.

II

Working with Electronic Mail

Marking Messages for Downloading

Marking a message header for retrieval tells Remote Mail that you want to download the complete text of that message so that you can read and respond to it. Here's how to mark a message header for retrieval:

1 In the Inbox message list, select the messages you want to download. To select more than one message, hold down the Ctrl key as you click each message.

2 Click the Mark To Retrieve button on the Remote toolbar. Alternatively, you can point to Remote Mail on the Tools menu, and then choose Mark To Retrieve from the submenu.

The messages are now marked and ready to download the next time you connect to your Exchange server.

If you accidentally mark a message header for a message that you don't want to download, select it and click the Unmark button to unmark it. If you want to unmark all message headers, click the Unmark All button.

Connecting Remotely with Peer-to-Peer Networking

If you are using Outlook on a peer-to-peer network, access remote mail functions by choosing Microsoft Mail Tools from the Tools menu. The submenu that appears lets you change your mailbox password and perform these other tasks:

- **Download Address Lists** lets you copy the postoffice address list to your computer so you an access it when working offline.

- **Schedule Remote Mail Delivery** lets you set the time when Outlook will dial-in and connect to the network. You can select to dial-in at a regular interval—every so many hours or minutes, weekly at a certain day and time, or once at a specific time.

- **Set Dialing Location** lets you specify your phone number and dialing rules.

- **View Session Log** shows the dates and times you connected to the network, both over the network and remotely, as well as the items sent, received, and downloaded.

If you use separate profiles for Remote Mail and for connecting to your e-mail server over a network, use the Mark To Retrieve A Copy toolbar button or command rather than Mark To Retrieve. Mark To Retrieve A Copy puts a copy of the message in your remote mail folder Inbox and leaves the message in your e-mail server Inbox. This way when you later connect to the network, the folders designated as your delivery point in the profile will contain the originals of your messages.

Deleting Messages When You Work Remotely

If you no longer want to keep a message, you can mark the message header for deletion. To delete a message header and the message from your e-mail server, simply select the message header, and then click the Delete button on the Remote toolbar. The message moves to your Deleted Items folder.

When you connect to your e-mail server, Outlook completes the deletion.

To delete the messages in their entirety after they've been downloaded, use the Delete button on the Standard toolbar. As with online messages, deleting offline messages sends them to the Deleted Items folder.

Setting Up Calling Card Dialing

You might want to charge your dial-up calls to a telephone calling card to save money, to have your business calls reimbursed by your employer, or for another reason. That's easy to set up. Here's what you do:

The instructions and illustrations shown here are for Windows 98. The appearance of the My Locations and Calling Card dialog boxes will differ slightly with Windows 95, Windows NT 4.0, and Windows 2000.

1 From within Outlook, choose Services from the Tools menu, select Microsoft Exchange Server, click Properties, click the Dial-Up Networking tab, and then click Location. Outlook opens the Dialing Properties dialog box, which displays the My Locations tab, shown in Figure 9-11, on the following page.

FIGURE 9-11.

The My Locations tab of the Dialing Properties dialog box.

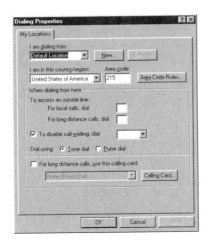

2 Select the check box labeled For Long Distance Calls, Use This Calling Card.

3 Open the list box under that check box and select the specific type of calling card you want to use. If yours is not listed, skip ahead to "Creating a New Calling Card Entry," on page 299.

4 Click the Calling Card button to open the dialog box shown in Figure 9-12 (with Windows 95 or Windows NT, the button is labeled Change).

5 Confirm that your card is listed in the top box. If not, open the list and select it.

FIGURE 9-12.

The Calling Card dialog box.

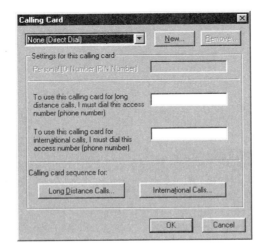

6 Enter your PIN number in the Personal ID Number text box, if applicable to the card type you've chosen.

7 The proper access numbers for long distance calls and for international calls should be shown in the appropriate text boxes. Edit the numbers shown if necessary.

8 Some calling cards require a special series of steps to make a connection. After dialing the calling card number, for example, you might have to wait until a tone sounds or for a certain number of seconds to dial the destination number or PIN number. These steps should already be defined for your card, but you can check them by clicking the Long Distance Calls and International Calls buttons.

9 Click OK to close each of the open dialog boxes.

Creating a New Calling Card Entry

If the type of calling card you want to use isn't listed in the My Location or Calling Card dialog boxes, you can add it to the list. To add a new calling card, follow these steps:

1 From the My Locations dialog box, click the Calling Card button or the Change button, whichever is present.

2 In the Calling Card dialog box, click the New button.

3 In the Create New Calling Card dialog box that appears, type a name for your calling card, and then click OK.

4 A message appears reminding you that you have to set up the card by entering access numbers and dialing rules for long distance and international calls. Click OK.

5 Now complete the calling card information as described in the steps above. Since you're defining a new card, you'll have to enter the access numbers and calling card sequences yourself.

6 Click OK to close each of the open dialog boxes.

The previous six chapters have concentrated on using Outlook and Outlook Express to communicate with others. You've learned how to work with address books, send and receive mail over a network and the Internet, send and receive faxes, share ideas with newsgroups, and work remotely and offline. Starting with the next chapter, you'll learn how to organize your schedule and manage your time, contacts, and tasks.

PART III

Scheduling Your Time and Tasks

Scheduling Appointments

You use the Calendar folder to arrange appointments, meetings, and events. A *meeting* is an appointment to which you invite others using Microsoft Outlook. Appointments and meetings have specific beginning and end times. In contrast, an *event* is an all-day affair to which you might or might not invite others. All three kinds of calendar items can be one-time occasions or can recur at regular intervals (daily, weekly, monthly, or yearly).

In this chapter, you'll learn how to work with the calendar and how to set up and change appointments and events. *You'll learn about meetings, and how to conduct online meetings, in Chapter 11, "Scheduling Meetings."*

Viewing the Calendar Folder

? SEE ALSO

To set or change your work hours, see "Calendar Work Week," on page 74. For other Calendar options, see "Calendar Options," on page 75.

Figure 10-1 shows a typical view of the Calendar folder. You can view the calendar in a number of ways, and you can adjust the window to suit your work habits and aesthetics. First, however, let's briefly review the various parts of the Calendar window.

Time Bar

The Time Bar shows the hours of the day in half-hour increments, with working hours shown in a lighter color than nonworking hours. To see a time that's out of view, use the scroll bar located along the right side of the Appointments pane.

Appointments and other calendar items, such as meetings, are shown in their appropriate time slots. Icons will appear indicating whether an entry is a group meeting, whether it is a one-time or a recurring event, whether it is private, and whether you've set a reminder for it. Outlook displays as much information about the appointment as fits. To see more details, just position the mouse pointer on the appointment for a moment to see a message box with the subject, location, and duration of the appointment. When an appointment or meeting is scheduled for a time not displayed, you'll see a yellow rectangle on the Time Bar that contains an ellipsis with a small arrow indicating which direction you need to scroll the appointments in order to bring it into view.

FIGURE 10-1.
The Calendar folder window.

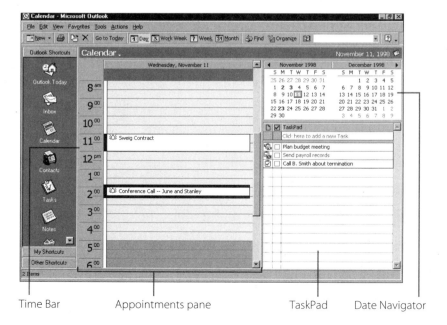

Time Bar   Appointments pane   TaskPad   Date Navigator

Reminder for the appointment

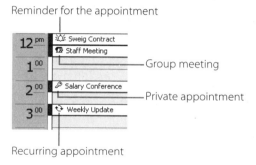

Group meeting

Private appointment

Recurring appointment

You can change the time interval of the Time Bar to one that's convenient for you—the intervals can be as long as 60 minutes or as short as 5 minutes. To change the time increment, take these steps:

1 Right-click anywhere on the Time Bar.

2 At the bottom of the shortcut menu that appears, click the time span you want to use.

 NOTE

If you conduct business in two time zones, you can display appointment times simultaneously in both. *To display a second time zone, see "Time Zone," on page 76.*

Date Navigator

SEE ALSO

For information about how to work with the Date Navigator, see "Using the Date Navigator," on page 307.

Use the Date Navigator to see appointments on other dates, even months and years in advance. To display appointments for a certain date, just click the date in the Date Navigator. You can also scroll the Date Navigator to jump months ahead or back. Dates that contain appointments are shown in bold, today's date has a red box around it, and dates that are currently visible in the Calendar window are highlighted in the Date Navigator.

TaskPad

The TaskPad shows a summary of the items in Outlook's Tasks folder. Icons to the left of each task indicate one-time, recurring, or assigned tasks. Typically, the TaskPad shows your currently active tasks, including those that are overdue (shown in red instead of black) and tasks without a due date.

III

Scheduling Your
Time and Tasks

SEE ALSO

For information about working with tasks, see Chapter 12, "Managing Your Tasks."

When you click the Complete box (the check box in the second column), Outlook draws a line through the task indicating that the task has been performed. Outlook removes the completed task from the TaskPad when the due date passes.

Setting the Number of Days Displayed

SEE ALSO

To learn about other views available in the Calendar, see "Viewing the Calendar in Other Ways," on page 332.

Outlook lets you display the calendar in several views. In the default Day/Week/Month view, you can choose between four time spans: one day, one workweek, one week, and one month. Set the time span by clicking one of these four buttons on the Standard toolbar:

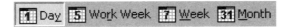

TIP

When you select dates on the Date Navigator, your selection affects how many days and which days appear in the Appointments pane. *For details, see "Selecting Days," on page 330.*

To display your calendar in Work Week view, click the Work Week button on the Standard toolbar. In Work Week view, you see the workdays for the calendar week. The default workdays are Monday through Friday, but you can change the days by clicking the Calendar Options button on the Preferences tab of the Options dialog box. *See "Setting Calendar Options," on page 74.* If you set the workweek from Monday through Saturday, for example, the Work Week view displays six days. No matter how many days you assign to a workweek, however, the Work Week button on the Standard toolbar will still display the number 5.

To display your calendar in Week view, click the Week button on the Standard toolbar. In Week view, you see one full week of your calendar. Each day is shown in a box without the Time Bar, as shown in Figure 10-2. Depending on the resolution of your display and on how you've arranged the Calendar window, you might see the starting and ending times for appointments, as well as their characteristics (private, recurring), subjects, and place.

Finally, to display your calendar in Month view, click the Month button on the Standard toolbar to see an entire month of your calendar, just like a traditional printed calendar. Again, depending on your display resolution and window arrangement, entries for your appointments in

FIGURE 10-2.
Week view.

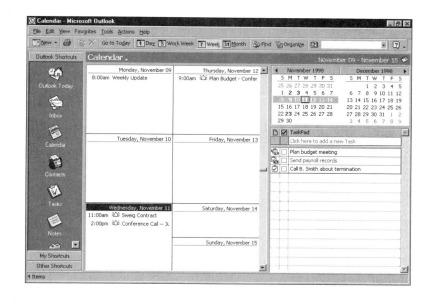

Month view might show the starting time and as much of the subject as fits on one line of the date box.

Changing the Date

You can use Outlook's Find command to find specific appointments, events, and meetings. For details, see "Searching Folder Contents," on page 470.

Much of your calendar work will focus on "today," and by default, the current day appears in the Calendar when you start Outlook. Setting appointments and scheduling meetings, however, involves dates in the future, and you may also want to see dates in the past to review previous activities. Use the Date Navigator or the Go To command on the View menu to display other dates in the calendar.

Using the Date Navigator

Depending on the size of the Outlook window, the resolution of your monitor, and the relative size of the Date Navigator pane, you can see one or more months at a time in the Date Navigator. See Figure 10-3, on the following page, for an example.

The Date Navigator does not appear when you select the Month view. To display the Date Navigator in Month view, place the mouse pointer on the right edge of the window until it becomes a double vertical line with horizontal arrows, and then drag the mouse to the left.

FIGURE 10-3.
The Date Navigator
displaying four
months.

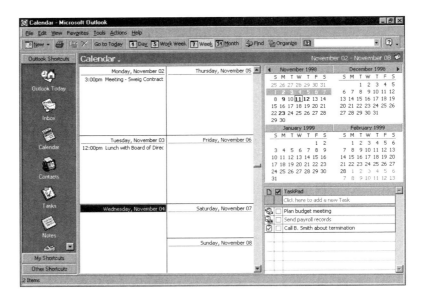

To jump to another date, use one of the following methods:

■ If the date is visible in the Date Navigator, click the date.

■ If the date is not in view in the Date Navigator, click the left
arrow in the top band of the Date Navigator to move back one
month or click the right arrow to move forward one month. Even
if two or more months are visible in the Date Navigator, clicking
the arrows scrolls only one month at a time.

■ Click and hold the name of any month in the Date Navigator
to open a list containing the three months before and the
three months after the month you've clicked. Then drag the
mouse pointer to the month you want to view and release
the mouse button:

After you have selected a new month and jumped to it, you can repeat this method to move three months before or after the newly displayed month.

> When you click a month label and open the list of months, you can drag the mouse pointer to the top or bottom border of the list to scroll through an even larger list of months. You must hold the tip of the mouse pointer arrow exactly on the top or bottom border line to scroll.

Using the Go To Date Command

For dates that are further away than a few months, you'll probably want to use the Go To Date command. To jump to any date, follow these steps:

1 Choose Go To from the View menu and click Go To Date to see the dialog box shown in Figure 10-4, on the following page. You can also right-click any empty area on the Appointments pane, and then choose Go To Date from the shortcut menu, or you can press Ctrl+G at any time.

2 Type the date you want to jump to, or open the list and choose the date from the calendar that appears.

3 Click OK.

In the Date box of the Go To dialog box, you can type the date you want in any standard date format—for instance, to jump to October 13, 1999, you can type *10-13-99, 10/13/99, Oct-13-99,* or *October 13, 1999.* You should note the following points about typing dates:

■ If you type a two-digit year number in the range 70–99, Outlook assumes that you mean 1970–1999. For the numbers 00–69, Outlook uses 2000–2069. To avoid possible errors, type all four digits of the year.

■ If you want a year that's not within the century from 1970 to 2069, you *must* type the entire year number. The earliest date you can type in the Date box is April 1, 1601. The latest date you can type in the Date box is August 31, 4500. That range should just about cover it for your use of this version of Outlook.

■ After you select or enter the date you want to see in the Go To Date dialog box, you can use the Show In list to choose to view the date in Day, Week, Work Week, or Month view.

III

Scheduling Your
Time and Tasks

FIGURE 10-4.
The Go To Date
dialog box.

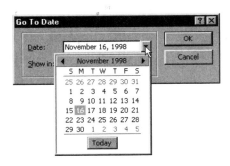

 **TIP**

After you type a date in the Date box of the Go To Date dialog box, click the down
arrow beside the date to see the month calendar for the date you've typed.

Jumping Back to Today

When you've moved to a past or future date, you'll often want to
jump back to today's date. You can do this quickly in any of the following ways:

- If you're in the Day/Week/Month view of the calendar, click the
  Go To Today button on the Standard toolbar. This button is available whether you're viewing a day, workweek, week, or month
  time span.

- Click today's date in the Date Navigator (it is outlined to make it
  easy to find).

- Right-click an empty area of the Appointments pane, and then
  choose Go To Today from the shortcut menu.

- Point to Go To on the View menu and click Go To Today.

Setting Up an Appointment

Once you display the date of the appointment, you're ready to set it
up. You can schedule an appointment quickly by typing it in the
appropriate spot in the Appointments pane or in more detail in a separate window. Let's look at the quick method first.

Quickly Setting Up an Appointment

To quickly set up an appointment without worrying about the finer
points, take these steps:

1 Go to the date for the appointment.

2 Point to the starting time on the Time Bar and drag down to the ending time. (You can also click the ending time and drag up to the starting time.) You can drag directly on the Time Bar or in the Appointments pane to its right.

3 Type a name for the appointment.

4 Press Enter or click outside the appointment box.

The appointment now appears on your calendar, as shown here:

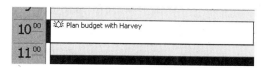

To change any of the information you typed, just click in the appointment, and then edit the information as you would any other text. You'll soon learn how to add more details about the appointment and how to change its time or date.

If you see an icon of a bell, it means that you'll be reminded about the appointment before its start time. *To learn more about reminders, see "Setting a Reminder" on page 313.*

Setting Appointment Details

The Appointments pane doesn't give you much room to enter details about an appointment. When you need to attach documents or enter information such as the meeting location and notes, create or modify the appointment in its own window, as described below.

If you already created the appointment in the Appointments pane, double-click it to open it. (This does not work if you are editing text within the appointment. In this case, click outside the appointment and then double-click the one you want to open.) You can also use either of these techniques:

- Right-click the appointment (when you are not editing text within it) and choose Open from the shortcut menu.

- Click the appointment and press Ctrl+O.

- Click the appointment, point to Open on the File menu, and choose Selected Items.

III

Scheduling Your
Time and Tasks

To schedule a new appointment in its own window, move to its date and then use one of the following methods:

- Click the New Appointment button on the Standard toolbar.
- Choose New Appointment from the Actions menu.
- Press Ctrl+N.
- Right-click an empty area in the Appointments pane, and then choose New Appointment from the shortcut menu.
- Point to New on the File menu, and then choose Appointment from the submenu.

In response to any of the above actions, Outlook opens a window similar to the one shown in Figure 10-5. Enter the necessary information in the window, including the subject, location, and start and ending dates and times. You can either type the dates and times or click the down arrows to choose them from the calendars that appear:

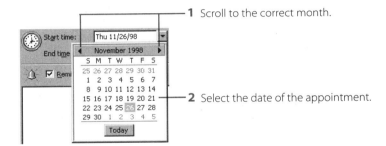

1 Scroll to the correct month.

2 Select the date of the appointment.

Select a time in half-hour increments by clicking the down arrow next to the times, or type an exact time in the list box.

Creating an Appointment from a Different Folder

If you're working in an Outlook folder other than the Calendar folder, you can set up a new appointment by using one of the following methods. Later you can change the item as necessary.

- Click the down arrow at the right side of the New button on the Standard toolbar, and then choose Appointment from the menu.
- Point to New on the File menu, and then choose Appointment from the submenu.
- Press Ctrl+Shift+A.

FIGURE 10-5.
The appointment
window.

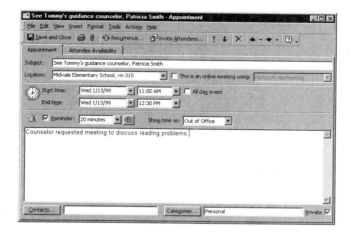

 TIP

> While you can specify the date and time when you start a new appointment
> window, it's quicker to drag over the appointment time on the Time Bar before
> opening the appointment window. The date and time selected will appear auto-
> matically in the appointment window.

 NOTE

> If you use the Attendee Availability tab of the window or the Invite Attendees
> button to invite others to an appointment, Outlook treats the appointment as a
> meeting. *You'll learn about meetings in Chapter 11, "Scheduling Meetings."*

Setting a Reminder

 SEE ALSO

You can change the
default reminder time
for all of your calendar
items; see "Reminder
Options," on page 102.

If you want to be reminded before the scheduled start time of your
appointment, select the Reminder check box. Outlook is initially set up
to remind you of a calendar item 15 minutes before the appointment's
start time. In many cases the 15-minute warning is sufficient, but you
might want to be reminded sooner, later, or not at all. To change the
reminder time, use this technique:

1 Select the Reminder check box in the appointment window.

2 Click the down arrow at the right end of the Reminder box, and
select a new reminder time from the list. You can also type the
reminder time you want directly in the Reminder box.

Categorizing Appointments

 SEE ALSO

For more information about categories, see "Working with Categories," on page 549.

Categories let you group appointments, meetings, tasks, and other Outlook items according to their purpose, such as personal or business. You can then use the categories to organize and view your activities. For example, you might assign all appointments about a specific project to a unique category. When you need to review your activities about the project, you can have Outlook display all appointments assigned to that category. You can even assign an Outlook item to more than one category if it relates to multiple projects or classifications.

To assign an appointment to a category, use the Categories button in the appointment window. (You can also type a category name in the text box to the right of the Categories button.) In the Categories dialog box that appears, shown opposite, select the check boxes for the categories to which you want to assign the item and then click OK.

TIP

To quickly assign a category to an appointment, right-click the appointment in the Appointments pane, and click Categories on the shortcut menu.

Changing the Reminder Sound

When the reminder is triggered, you'll hear a pleasant tone from your computer speaker. You can change the sound that is played for the reminder by designating another sound file with the .wav extension (called a *wave* file). You can find all sorts of interesting wave files on the Internet, or you can record your own using the Sound Recorder application that comes with Microsoft Windows.

To change the sound file, or to turn off the sound entirely, open the appointment and click the speaker icon in the appointment window (the Reminder check box must be selected to enable the speaker button).

When the Reminder Sound dialog box appears, clear the Play This Sound check box if you don't want to hear a reminder sound. If you do want to hear a sound, type in the name of the sound file to be played or use the Browse button to find a file. The sound you choose will only be used for the current appointment. Click OK to close the dialog box.

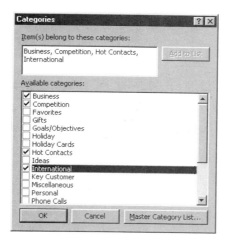

Linking Appointments with Contacts

In addition to categories, appointments and other Outlook items such as tasks can be associated with one or more contacts listed in the Contacts folder. You can then quickly list all of your Outlook activities that relate to the contact by opening the Activities page of the contact's listing.

To associate an appointment with a contact, open the appointment and click the Contacts button. In the dialog box that appears, shown in Figure 10-6, on the following page, click the contact's name and then click OK or Apply. To associate multiple contacts at one time, hold down the Ctrl key while you click their names.

Associating a contact with an appointment does not send the person an invitation or treat the appointment as a meeting. *You'll learn about meetings in Chapter 11, "Scheduling Meetings," and about contacts in Chapter 13, "Organizing Your Contacts."*

Describing Your Availability

For information about planning meetings and checking availability, see "Planning a Meeting," on page 337.

Other Outlook users in your company might be able to access your schedule to see if you are free to attend a meeting. When you schedule an appointment, that time period is designated as "busy" so your schedule shows that you are unavailable. There might be times, however, when you don't want to lock out that time period, just in case a meeting is being planned. That's where the Show Time As feature comes into play.

Scheduling Your
Time and Tasks

FIGURE 10-6.
The Select Contacts
dialog box.

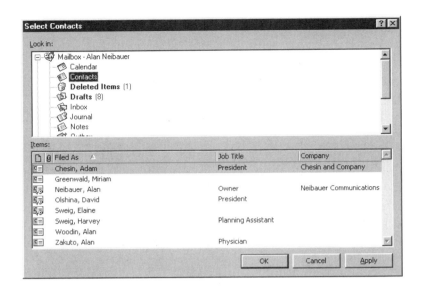

FIGURE 10-6.
The Select Contacts
dialog box.

Open an appointment and select one of these options from the Show
Time As list box:

- **Free.** Even though you have an appointment scheduled, you
  might want to be available for an important meeting—your
  appointment can be moved or canceled.

Categorizing Appointments with the Organize Button

The Organize button on the Standard toolbar provides some shortcuts for working with calendar items. You can use Organize, for example, to create categories
and to assign calendar items to a category. *You'll learn how to create, delete, and
manage categories in Chapter 20, "Organizing Folder Items."* To quickly assign a
calendar item to a category using Organize, however, follow these steps:

1 Open the Calendar folder.

2 Select one or more calendar items you want to assign to a category.

3 Click Organize on the Standard toolbar.

4 Click Using Categories.

5 You can either use the list next to the Add button to add the calendar
items to an existing category or type a new category in the box below
and click Create.

- **Tentative.** Sometimes you pencil in an appointment, either because you're not sure it will happen or because you want to be available for other engagements that might be more important.

- **Busy.** You have an appointment schedule that cannot be changed.

- **Out Of Office.** If you're going to be away from the office for an appointment, you might want to make it clear to anyone planning a meeting that you can't be reached.

 TIP

To quickly change the availability setting, right-click the appointment in the Appointments page, point to Show Time As, and choose Free, Tentative, Busy, or Out Of Office.

In the Appointments pane, the color line to the left of the appointment and the border that surrounds the appointment when it is selected indicate the availability. Busy is dark blue, Free is white, Tentative is light blue, and Out Of Office is purple.

Adding Notes and Attachments to an Appointment

In the box at the bottom of the appointment window, you can type any text that you want to keep with the appointment details. This box works the same as the message area in an e-mail message, and you can attach files, messages, and any other Microsoft Windows or Microsoft Office objects. For example, if your appointment is to discuss a certain project, you can type notes and include attachments that relate to that project. You can then quickly review the notes and the attached documents from within Outlook.

You can attach a file to an appointment by dragging or by using the Insert File button. Arrange the Outlook and appointment windows so you can see the Windows desktop, and then locate the file using My Computer or Windows Explorer. Drag the document you want to attach to the text area of the message window. As an alternative to dragging, click the Insert File button (the paper clip icon) on the appointment's toolbar and select the file from the dialog box that appears.

To attach an Outlook item to the appointment, such as an e-mail message from the Inbox, choose the item from the Insert menu.

You can also include an attachment by embedding it as an object. This means that another Windows or Microsoft Office document is enclosed

? SEE ALSO

For more information about attachments, see "Sending Files as Attachments," on page 158, and "Attaching Messages," on page 161.

within the appointment itself. You can create a new file and attach it to the appointment or attach an existing file. To create and embed a new object, follow these steps:

1 Click in the message area, and then choose Object from the Insert menu to open the dialog box shown in Figure 10-7.

2 Select the Create New option.

3 In the Object Type list, choose the type of object you want to create.

4 Click OK.

5 In the window that appears, create the object as you usually do in the application associated with the object. Figure 10-8, for example, shows a bitmap image object window. Use the application's toolbars and menus to create the object.

6 When you've finished creating the object, save and close it by clicking inside the message area, but outside the object area.

To insert an existing object into the appointment follow these steps instead:

1 Click in the message area and choose Object from the Insert menu.

2 Select the Create From File option.

3 Click the Browse button to find the file, or type the path and file-name in the File box.

4 Select the Link check box to create a link to the file.

5 If you want to display the file as an icon, select the Display As Icon check box.

6 Click OK.

FIGURE 10-7.

The Insert Object dialog box.

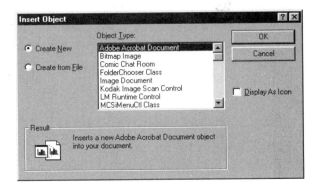

FIGURE 10-8.
Creating a bitmap object within the appointment window's message area.

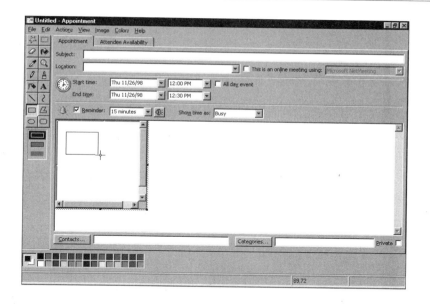

If you enter text directly in the message area, you can format it using the buttons on the Formatting toolbar. (To display this toolbar, point to Toolbars on the View menu and choose Formatting from the submenu.) You can choose such attributes as font, font size, font style, color, alignment, indentation, and bullets or numbering.

Keeping Items Private

 SEE ALSO

For information about granting permissions and assigning delegates, see "Using the Delegates Tab," on page 90.

When you give others permission to view your Calendar folder, or when you assign a delegate who can perform actions such as responding to meeting requests on your behalf, these people can see the details of your appointments. If you have an appointment that you want to keep private, select the Private check box in the appointment's window.

TIP

You can also turn the Private setting on or off by right-clicking the item in the Appointments pane and then choosing Private from the shortcut menu.

Saving the Appointment

When you're done adding or editing the details of your appointment, you have to save it. To save your information click the Save And Close button. This saves the appointment and closes its window, returning to

III

Scheduling Your Time and Tasks

the Calendar window. You can also choose Save from the File menu to save the information without closing its window.

> Be sure to save the appointment again if you later open and change any of its details.

To close the appointment without saving it, or any changes you've made, click the Close box in the upper-right corner of the window, or select Close from the File menu. If you made any changes to the appointment since you last saved it, you'll be asked if you want to save it at this time.

Creating Recurring Items

A recurring appointment is one that will be repeated at some regular interval. After filling out the information in the appointment window, click the Recurrence button on the appointment window's Standard toolbar, or choose Recurrence from its Actions menu to open the Appointment Recurrence dialog box, shown in Figure 10-9.

> To specify a recurring pattern when you first create an appointment, select New Recurring Appointment from the Actions menu.

You follow these steps to set a recurring appointment:

1 If necessary, adjust the start, end, and duration of the appointment in the Appointment Time section of the dialog box.

FIGURE 10-9.
The Appointment Recurrence dialog box.

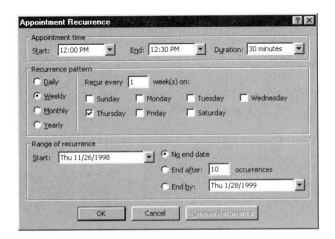

2 Select a recurrence pattern.

3 Set the start date and end date, as needed.

4 Click OK to close the Appointment Recurrence dialog box and any changes you have made—such as new meeting times or a new recurrence pattern—appear in the appointment window, which you can now save and close.

The following sections take a closer look at two parts of the Appointment Recurrence dialog box: the Recurrence Pattern area and the Range Of Recurrence area.

 NOTE

If you open an item already set up as recurring, you'll see the Open Recurring Item dialog box or the Open Recurring Item message from the Office Assistant before the item itself opens. Choose Open This Occurrence if only one appointment needs to be rescheduled, or choose Open The Series if you want to change the scheduling of all the recurring appointments.

If you open a single occurrence of a recurring series of items, you can change the location, subject, or reminder time for that occurrence in the calendar item window. You can also change the start or end time for that occurrence (but not for the series).

If you want to change the subject, location, or reminder for the entire series from the appointment window for a particular occurrence, choose Edit Series from the Actions menu. Doing so opens a separate calendar item window that pertains to the entire series.

If you want to change the actual recurrence schedule for the entire series, click the Recurrence button instead.

Recurrence Pattern

The recurrence pattern you select in the Appointment Recurrence dialog box tells Outlook how to set up your calendar for each engagement in the recurring series. Each recurrence pattern—Daily, Weekly, Monthly, and Yearly—has its own set of options, which appears to the right of the list of patterns. Select a recurrence pattern as follows:

Daily. When an engagement recurs every day or recurs with a specific number of days between occurrences, you should select the Daily recurrence pattern. Select this recurrence pattern if you have an engagement that recurs every 30 days, for example. You can set the appointment to occur every weekday, or you can specify a certain number of days between engagements by typing a number in the Every __ Day(s) box—from 1 (daily, including weekends) to 999 (about 2 years and 9 months).

Weekly. Select the Weekly recurrence pattern when an engagement recurs on a specific day of the week or recurs with a specific number of weeks between occurrences. Type in a number from 1 to 99 to set the number of weeks between engagements. You must also specify the day (or days) of the week.

Linking Objects and Displaying Them as Icons

Anytime you include a very large file in a message, consider displaying it as an icon. An icon takes up less space in the message window, and usually it's easier for people reading the message to view a large file in the application used to create it.

Also, depending on your version of Microsoft Exchange Server and its configuration on your network, there might be a limit on message size. If you're sending a large file, it's better to link it, which reduces message size considerably. Remember that a linked file must reside on a disk and in a folder to which the recipient has read access. In addition, the recipient needs to have the same program you used to create the object or another program that reads the same file format to be able to read the contents of the linked file.

Monthly. When an engagement recurs monthly on the same day or recurs with a specific number of months between occurrences, the Monthly recurrence pattern is your best choice.

When your engagement recurs on a specific date each month (or every so many months), select the first option on the right side of the Recurrence Pattern area. In the first box, type a number to set the specific date of the month. If the number you type for the date is greater than 28 (or 29 in leap years), Outlook notifies you that for months with fewer days than you specified, the engagement is set for the last day of the month. In the second box, type the number of months between engagements—from 1 month through 99 months.

When your engagement recurs in a specific monthly pattern but not necessarily on the same day of the month, select the second option on the right side of the Recurrence Pattern area, which specifies a relative day. For example, some organizations hold a meeting on the second Tuesday of each month. From month to month, the actual date changes—March 9 and April 13 are second Tuesdays in 1999, for instance. After you select this option, do the following:

1 Select the occurrence of the day during the month—first, second, third, fourth, or last.

2 Select the day pattern. In addition to the named days of the week, you can select Day, Weekday, or Weekend Day.

3 Set the number of months between engagements—from 1 month to 99 months (8 years and 3 months).

Yearly. Select the Yearly recurrence pattern when an engagement recurs annually on the same day every year.

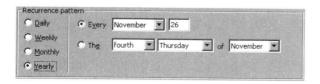

Select the first option on the right side of the Recurrence Pattern area when your engagement recurs on the same date each year. Choose a month from the drop-down list, and type in a number to set the specific date. Outlook will not let you select a date that doesn't occur in a given month, for instance April 31 or February 29 in a non-leap year.

Select the second option on the right side of the Recurrence Pattern area, which specifies a relative day, when your engagement recurs in a specific pattern but not necessarily on the same date each time. If, for example, your club holds its annual party each year on the second Tuesday of December, the actual date was December 8 in 1998—but it will be December 14 in 1999. After you select this option, follow these steps:

1 Select the occurrence of the day during the month—first, second, third, fourth, or last.

2 Select the day pattern—Day, Weekday, Weekend Day, or the named days of the week.

3 Select the month.

Range of Recurrence

When you create a series of recurring engagements, Outlook doesn't set an ending date for the series. That's fine for recurring engagements that you expect to continue for many years or for those times when you don't know if a series is ever going to end. Sometimes there is an end in sight, for example, if you signed up for a workshop that lasts for six weeks. In such a case, you will want to set the end of the series.

In the Range Of Recurrence area of the Appointment Recurrence dialog box, you have three choices for ending a series: No End Date, End After, and End By. The No End Date option is self-explanatory. Use one of the other options under the following circumstances:

End After.   If you know the number of engagements in the series, select the End After option and type the number in the box. (Setting the number of occurrences to 1 is the same as setting up a one-time engagement.) If your recurring engagements add up to more than 999, you will need to set an End By date instead.

End By.   If you know the date of the last engagement in the series, select the End By option. The End By box initially shows a date that matches 10 occurrences in the End After box (the default value). In the End By box, you can type a date, or you can click the down arrow to display a calendar from which you can select the end date.

TIP

If you set an End After number, Outlook sets the End By date to match the number of occurrences. You might not see this change until after you close the Appointment Recurrence dialog box and then reopen it. You can force Outlook to display the change, however, by setting the End After number and then clicking the End By option. You can then select either option to get the same result. Note, however, that this doesn't work in reverse—if you select a date in the End By box, Outlook does not change the number of occurrences. You cannot set a date beyond 999 occurrences.

Adjusting Appointment Properties

? SEE ALSO

For information about the AutoArchive feature, see Chapter 18, "Archiving Folder Items."

Each appointment can be customized using a Properties dialog box. To display the Properties dialog box, shown in Figure 10-10, open the appointment and then choose Properties from the File menu.

The contents of the Properties dialog box might vary depending on the type of calendar item, but the following options are typically included:

- **Importance.** Select the level of importance: High, Normal, Low.

- **Sensitivity.** Select the level of sensitivity: Normal, Personal, Private, or Confidential.

- **Do Not AutoArchive This Item.** Select this check box if you don't want this calendar item to be archived when the folder is automatically archived.

FIGURE 10-10.
The Properties dialog box for an appointment.

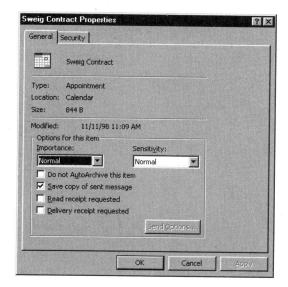

III

Scheduling Your
Time and Tasks

- **Save Copy Of Sent Message.** Select this check box to save a copy of the message.

- **Read Receipt Requested.** Select this check box to get a receipt when your item is read (or at least opened) by the recipient.

- **Delivery Receipt Requested.** Select this check box to get a receipt when the message reaches its destination.

If you've enabled security features in Outlook, such as encryption or digital signatures, you will also see a Security tab on the Properties dialog box. Use this tab to control the security for individual messages, and to change the default security setting.

Changing Times

After you set up an appointment, you might need to change its beginning or ending times. To change the times, open the appointment, and then select the new time in either the Start Time box or the End Time box (or both). If the new time is other than on the hour or half-hour, select the nearest time and then edit the minutes. For example, if the new time is 11:45, select 11:30 and then edit 30 to 45.

If you change the starting time of the appointment, the ending time will be adjusted automatically to keep the duration of the appointment constant. If this isn't what you want, adjust the ending time after you've adjusted the starting time. Notice that the times displayed in the End Time list box also show the duration of the appointment. This makes it easy to select a specific ending time or to select the duration of the meeting and let Outlook figure out what ending time that will be.

Instead of opening the appointment and setting the start time and end time, you can change the time by dragging the appointment in the Appointments pane, as follows:

- To change the appointment's starting time, drag its top border up for an earlier time or down for a later time. The bottom border stays put, which means that you are also lengthening or shortening the appointment period.

- To change the appointment's ending time, drag its bottom border up for an earlier time or down for a later time. The top border stays put, which means that you are also shortening or lengthening the appointment period.

- To change the appointment's time without changing its length, point inside the item and drag, or drag the left or right border of the item. Drag up for an earlier time or down for a later time. Both the top and bottom borders move together.

■ To move an appointment to another day, first make sure the new date is visible in the Date Navigator, and then drag the item from the Appointments pane and drop it on the new date in the Date Navigator. It will drop to the same time as it occupied on the original day. You can then go to that date and modify the time of the appointment as just described.

When you drag a calendar item, the box moves in increments reflecting the time span you have set for the time slots. *If you want to change these increments, see "Time Bar," on page 304.*

Deleting an Appointment

When you need to delete an appointment first click it in the Appointments pane to select it. Then use one of the following methods to cancel (delete) the item:

■ Click the Delete button on the Standard toolbar.

■ Press Ctrl+D.

■ Choose Delete from the Edit menu.

■ Right-click the appointment, and then choose Delete from the shortcut menu.

■ If the appointment is open, click the Delete button on the appointment window's Standard toolbar. For a meeting, you can also choose Cancel Meeting from the Actions menu.

Outlook moves deleted calendar items to the Deleted Items folder.

If you delete an appointment that is part of a series, you see the message shown at the left. (The Confirm Delete dialog box appears instead if you have turned off the Office Assistant.)

Choose whether you want to delete the entire series or just the selected occurrence, and then click OK.

If you open the series of a recurring item and delete the series, you won't see the Confirm Delete message.

Copying an Appointment

If you need to set up an appointment that is similar to an existing one, you can copy the original item rather than starting over. You can either drag the item to another date or use the Copy and Paste commands on the Edit menu.

Copying a calendar item using the mouse is similar to moving it, except that you hold down the Ctrl key when you drag the item from the Appointments pane to the new date on the Date Navigator. Remember to set the Date Navigator to show the new date before you start dragging the calendar item.

The steps for copying a calendar item using the Copy and Paste commands are as follows:

1 Locate the calendar item, and click its left border.

2 Choose Copy from the Edit menu (or press Ctrl+C).

3 Go to the date where you want to set up the new calendar item.

4 Click the slot in the Appointments pane for the beginning time of the new calendar item.

5 Choose Paste from the Edit menu (or press Ctrl+V).

6 Fine-tune the copy of the calendar item as necessary to fit the new circumstances.

Dealing with a Reminder

As you've learned, Outlook helps you remember your scheduled engagements by displaying a reminder on the date and at the time you set for the reminder. Here's how the reminder appears in the Office

Assistant (if the Office Assistant is turned off, a dialog box reminder will appear instead):

To close the reminder message so it does not appear again, click Dismiss This Reminder.

If you want to be reminded again, select one of the predefined time intervals from the list, and then click Remind Me Again In. Your choices range from five minutes to one week. If you postpone the reminder past the start time of the calendar item, the next reminder message displays the word *Overdue* in its title bar. If you need to reschedule the actual calendar item rather than the reminder, or want to see the details of the appointment, click the Open This Item button.

Scheduling All-Day Events

An event is an activity for which you set aside one or more entire days. An event might be an all-day conference, a special day off that you want to block out on your schedule, or a reminder about a birthday or anniversary.

To create an event, choose New All Day Event from the Actions menu. The event window looks just like an appointment window but the All Day Event check box is selected and you can only enter the starting and ending dates, not times.

Complete the information, just as you learned for an appointment, including scheduling recurrences, entering and formatting text, including attachments, setting reminders, and marking the event as private. Because an event is scheduled for the whole day, not a specific time, it appears above your appointments, just under the date heading as shown here:

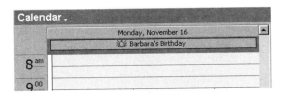

If you invite others to an event, it is called an Invited Event and it is treated like a meeting. You'll learn more about invited events and meetings in the next chapter.

Selecting Days

You might want to check on appointments for a set of selected days. When you select days in the Appointments pane or in the Date Navigator, only the schedule for those days appears. You can select a range of consecutive days in the Appointments pane, and you can select a range of consecutive days or scattered days in the Date Navigator.

Selecting Days in the Appointments Pane

To select a range of consecutive days in the Appointments pane take these steps:

1 Select Work Week view, Week view, or Month view so you can see more than one day at a time.

2 Move to the week or month where you want to select days.

3 Use one of these methods to select the days you want:

- Drag over the days you want to select.

- Click the first date of the range, hold down the Shift key, and then click the last date of the range. You can select as many visible days as you like this way, including all the visible days in the Appointments pane.

Selecting Days in the Date Navigator

You can select consecutive days or scattered days in the Date Navigator. When you select days in the Date Navigator, Outlook changes the Appointments pane to display the days you selected. In this way, you can display ranges and numbers of days that differ from what the Day, Week, and Month views show.

To select a range of consecutive days in the Date Navigator, follow these steps:

1 Adjust the Date Navigator pane to show the months in which you want to select days.

2 Use one of these methods to select the days you want:

- Drag over the days you want to select. You can select as many as eight consecutive days or as many as six consecutive weeks this way. After you select the ninth day, the selection expands to selecting weeks at a time.

- Click at the left end of a week to select that week. (The mouse pointer must appear as a diagonal arrow pointing toward the upper right.) Drag down along the left end of weeks to select as many as six weeks.

- Click the first date of the range, hold down the Shift key, and then click the last date of the range. You can select as many as 14 days this way.

To select scattered days in the Date Navigator, follow these steps:

1 Adjust the Date Navigator to show the months in which you want to select days.

2 Click one of the days you want to select.

3 Hold down the Ctrl key while you click the other days you want to select. You can select as many as 14 days this way.

Adjusting the Calendar Display

Because the Calendar shows the Appointments pane, the Date Navigator, and the TaskPad, the amount of space for each area is limited, especially if you work in an Outlook window that isn't maximized.

When you need to view or work in one of the areas and require a more expanded view of its contents, you can adjust its borders to give it a larger portion of the Calendar window. (You can also hide the TaskPad and the Date Navigator, but you can't hide the Appointments pane.)

Between each of the areas in the Calendar window is a border that you can drag to adjust the size of the panes. When you position the mouse pointer on one of these borders, the pointer arrow changes to a double line with two arrows (pointing either up and down or left and right).

- Drag the vertical border separating the Appointments pane from the Date Navigator and the TaskPad to the left or right to change the space given to the appointments.

- Drag the horizontal border between the Date Navigator and the TaskPad up or down to change the relative heights of these two panes.

- Drag the vertical border between the Time Bar and the Outlook Bar to change the size of the Outlook Bar, which also changes the width of the other panes.

Viewing the Calendar in Other Ways

You can also set up views to look at your appointments and meetings in various ways. For information, see Chapter 21, "Setting Up Views." For information about grouping, sorting, filtering, and adding custom fields, see Chapter 20, "Organizing Folder Items."

The Day/Week/Month view of the Calendar is the default view and is the view you'll probably use most often. In this view, you normally have the Date Navigator and the TaskPad available. Day/Week/Month view is not, however, the only view that Outlook provides. To switch views, point to Current View on the View menu and then choose the view you want from the submenu. In Day/Week/Month View With AutoPreview, for example, you'll see up to the first 256 characters of the appointment details without having to open the item.

The remaining views are table views. This means that your calendar information is arranged into rows and columns. Each appointment or meeting is in its own row, with columns for each detail, such as the subject and time. You'll usually need to scroll horizontally to see all the columns. The table views also enable you to edit information directly in the Calendar window without opening each appointment. Find the row of the appointment you want to edit, click in the column you want to edit, and then change the information. Figure 10-11, for example, shows the Active Appointments view.

In this and other table views, information is grouped together by some common element. In this case, calendar items are grouped by

FIGURE 10-11.

Active Appointments view.

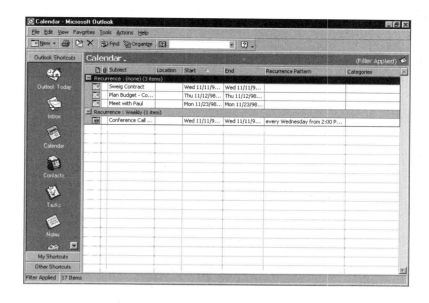

recurrence status—nonrecurring, daily, weekly, monthly, yearly, and any other recurrence pattern an appointment might have.

The gray headings show the group name and the number of items within the group—the number of appointments, for example, that are not recurring or that recur weekly. A plus sign next to the group name means that its items are not displayed. Click the plus sign to see the items within the group. When the items are displayed, you'll see a minus sign—click it to hide the items so that only the group heading appears.

Here's a summary of the table views.

- **Active Appointments View** lists of all your active appointments and meetings—that is, future appointments and meetings—grouped by their recurring status.

- **Events View** lists all events (including annual events) that you've added to your calendar, separated into two groups: nonrecurring and yearly recurrence.

- **Annual Events View** lists only the annual events on your calendar.

- **Recurring Appointments View** lists only recurring appointments and meetings, grouped by recurrence status—daily, weekly, monthly, yearly, and so on. The difference between this view and Active Appointments view is that Recurring Appointments view does not show one-time appointments and meetings.

III

Scheduling Your
Time and Tasks

■ **By Category View** lists calendar items grouped by their assigned category.

In this chapter, you learned how to schedule appointments and events, and how to use the Calendar folder. When you want to invite others to an appointment by sending them an e-mail invitation, you create a meeting. You'll learn how to create meetings, and even how to conduct meetings online, in Chapter 11, "Scheduling Meetings."

Using Organize to Change Views

In addition to using the View menu to determine how the Calendar is displayed, you can use the Organize command. When the Calendar window is displayed, click the Organize button on the toolbar or choose Organize from the Tools menu.

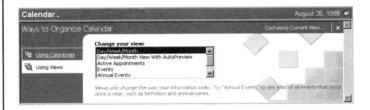

Click Using Views, and then select the view you want to use. You can also point to Current View on the View menu and choose Customize Current View to modify the objects and appearance of the view. *See Chapter 21, "Setting Up Views," for more information on customizing views.*

CHAPTER 11

Scheduling Meetings

In this chapter, you'll learn all about meetings. A meeting is simply an appointment to which you invite others via Microsoft Outlook. You'll also learn how to plan and conduct an online meeting using Microsoft NetMeeting. With NetMeeting, and the proper computer equipment, you can exchange written messages with others in real time, speak with them, and even see them over either the Internet or your local area network.

Setting Up a Meeting

A meeting is an activity to which you invite other persons through Outlook. If the invitees have e-mail addresses, Outlook automatically sends each person an e-mail notification about the meeting and checks the schedules of those who also use Outlook. It then keeps track of their responses so you know who will be attending.

> **NOTE**
>
> To use Internet mail to invite others so they can schedule the meeting and respond, their e-mail address must be set to use Microsoft Outlook rich text format. *See "Adding an Address," on page 117, for more information.*

You can create a meeting in three ways:

- Use the New Meeting Request command on the Actions menu to first specify the details of the meeting and who is invited and then to check the invitees' schedules if desired.

- Use the Plan A Meeting command on the Actions menu to first specify the time of the meeting, who is invited, to check the invitees' schedules, and then complete the details.

- Create an appointment, and then use the Invite Attendees button or Attendee Availability tab to invite others. When you do, Outlook changes the item from an appointment to a meeting.

> **NOTE**
>
> You can also invite persons to an all-day event. In the event window, click the Invite Attendees button or use the Attendee Availability tab. Outlook will check the invitees' availability and send invitations just as it does for a meeting.

Use the New Meeting Request command, or convert an appointment to a meeting, when you know that the time you select is convenient for all those you are inviting—you know they'll be there. You specify the date and time of the meeting, its subject and location, and then use the Attendee Availability tab to specify who is invited and to check their schedules.

Use the Plan A Meeting command when you want to find a time that fits the schedules of those you are inviting. You specify the date and time of the meeting, select the invitees, and check their schedules before completing the other details.

The end result of these techniques is really the same; it's just the order of steps that varies.

Planning a Meeting

To plan a meeting, take these steps:

1 Drag over the Time Bar to select the time for the meeting.

2 Choose Plan A Meeting from the Actions menu to display the Plan A Meeting dialog box.

3 Click the Invite Others button. You'll see the Select Attendees And Resources dialog box shown here.

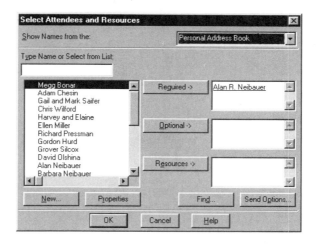

4 Open the Show Names list and select the address list containing the name of an invitee.

5 Select the invitee's name from the list, or select a distribution list to invite a group.

6 Click Required or Optional, based on the importance of each person's attendance. Use the Resources button to add meeting rooms, transportation, meals, equipment, or other materials that need to be available at the meeting.

7 Click OK to return to the Plan A Meeting dialog box. Outlook will check the schedule of other users on the network for their free/busy time. The Plan A Meeting dialog box now shows the schedules of those you invited, as shown in Figure 11-1, on the next page.

III

Scheduling Your
Time and Tasks

FIGURE 11-1.
The Plan A Meeting dialog box showing attendee availability.

These bars show when attendees are not available. —

Drag to change the starting time.
Drag to change the ending time.

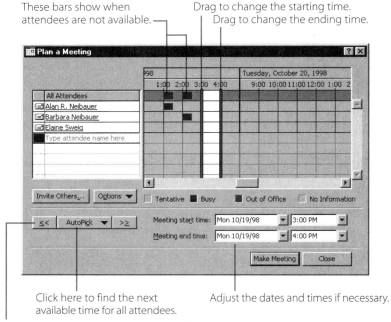

Click here to find the next available time for all attendees.

Click here to find an earlier time.

Adjust the dates and times if necessary.

 NOTE

When you select a distribution list in the Select Attendees And Resources dialog box, its name appears preceded by a plus sign. If you do not want to invite certain persons from the list, or want to check their individual schedules, click the plus sign and then click OK to the message that appears. Outlook replaces the distribution list name with individual listings for each of the group's members. You can't collapse a list once you expand it, so you'll need to start over if you want to return to treating the entire distribution list as one attendee.

8 Now review the schedules for attendees. Horizontal bars indicate when invitees are busy. The top dark-gray line labeled All Attendees shows the consolidated schedules of all the invitees—a bar on this line means that at least one invitee is busy for that time period. Individual lines appear next to each busy invitee's name. You can adjust the time of the meeting by dragging the vertical bars that mark the start and end times or by entering new dates and times in the Meeting Start Time and Meeting End Time boxes. You can also click AutoPick or its arrow buttons to look for an earlier or later time when all recipients are available. Click and hold the mouse on the AutoPick button and choose from the menu shown below to specify which schedules are checked when you use AutoPick.

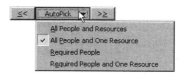

The term *One Resource* means that Outlook 2000 will find a common time when all the invitees are available and *one* of the resources you've picked, such as a meeting room, is available. For example, you usually don't want Outlook to find a time when six potential conference rooms and six invitees are available—instead, you want to know when the six invitees can meet in any *one* of the six potential conference rooms.

9 Click Make Meeting when you've selected all of the invitees and chosen a time to see the window shown in Figure 11-2.

10 Complete the other details of the meeting just as you learned for appointments in Chapter 10, "Scheduling Appointments," including setting a reminder, creating recurring events, applying categories, designating the item as private, and attaching items such as agendas and background materials.

11 If you want to check meeting details again, click the Attendee Availability tab in the Meeting window. This tab displays the information you set up in the Plan A Meeting dialog box. On this

FIGURE 11-2.
The Meeting window before invitations have been sent to invitees.

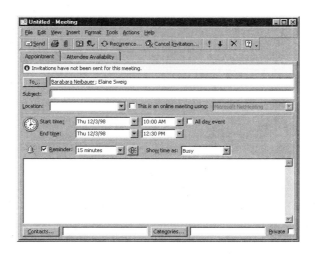

tab, you can review and change the details of the meeting, review the schedules of the invited attendees, adjust the display of the schedule, and invite other attendees if necessary.

12 When you've finished reviewing the meeting details in the meeting window, click the Send button. Outlook then sends messages to the people and resources you invited.

Including but Not Inviting Others

Sometimes you want to include in a meeting people you've already invited or who don't have e-mail addresses. You can list them as invitees to let others know that they will be at the meeting but not send them an invitation.

To not send an invitation, click the envelope icon to the left of the person's name in the Plan A Meeting dialog box or the Attendee Availability tab to see a menu like this, and choose Don't Send Meeting To This Attendee.

Inviting Resources to Your Meeting

Meeting resources include conference rooms, audio/visual equipment, and other equipment or material you need for a meeting. You might want to include a resource in the list of meeting invitees so that the equipment will be reserved and available to you. If your server administrator has set up rooms and equipment in the global address list, you can "invite" the resource to a meeting by choosing it as you would an invited guest. When you invite a resource to a meeting, a message is delivered to the inbox for the resource, which is usually handled by a staff person.

If you are in charge of monitoring the inbox for a resource, you can set options for processing meeting requests automatically. Choose Options from the Tools menu, click the Calendar Options button on the Preferences tab, and then click the Resource Scheduling button. You can set options so that Outlook will automatically accept meeting requests and process cancellations, decline conflicting meeting requests, and decline recurring meeting requests. If you are using your server mailbox folders, rather than personal folders, you can also assign permissions so that others can access your Calendar folder to schedule the resource when you are offline. *For more information, see "Resource Scheduling," on page 78.*

Updating Free/Busy Time

If you are using Outlook with Microsoft Exchange Server, you can store your schedule information on the server. Anyone who is planning a meeting can then use this information to ensure that all the attendees are free at the scheduled date and time. In fact, when you add people to the list of invitees for a meeting or event, Outlook automatically retrieves their free/busy information from the server.

You control when your free/busy time is sent to the server. To specify how often the information is uploaded to the server and how much information is sent, choose Options from the Tools menu, and then click the Preferences tab. Click the Calendar Options button, and then click the Free/Busy Options button. You can set how often your free/busy information is updated to the server and how many months of information are recorded.

The Internet Only setup of Outlook lets you store and update free/busy time over the Internet, but you'll need an Internet address where the information can be saved, such as a page on a Web site or a corporate intranet. Your colleagues or clients can store this URL as part of the address book entry they have for you so that the location is checked automatically for your availability. Internet Only users can update their free/busy time manually by choosing Send/Receive from the Tools menu and clicking Update Free/Busy Time.

Requesting a Meeting

When you use the New Meeting Request command on the Actions menu to create a meeting, you'll see the meeting window shown in Figure 11-2, on page 339. To invite others, click the To button to open

III

Scheduling Your
Time and Tasks

Handling a Meeting Request When You're Working Remotely

You can request meetings and respond to meeting requests you receive while you're working offsite—either working offline or working through a remote connection to your e-mail server. This is possible because meeting requests are sent as e-mail messages.

Before you can deal with meeting requests offline, you must take these steps:

1 Download the offline address book. *For information about how to do this, see "Downloading the Offline Address Book," on page 279.*

2 Be sure that you're using Outlook for your scheduling. If you set up Outlook to use Microsoft Schedule+ 95 as your primary calendar, you won't be able to request or plan meetings. *For more about this setup, see "Use Microsoft Schedule+ As My Primary Calendar," on page 76.*

3 If you're working remotely in a time zone different from that of your office, you might want to display an additional time zone on the Calendar window's Time Bar. *For details, see "Time Zone," on page 76.*

---

the Select Attendees And Resources dialog box. Choose those you want to attend and then click OK.

To specify a recurring meeting before specifying meeting details, select New Recurring Meeting from the Actions menu instead of New Meeting Request.

Next, enter the details about the meeting, its place and time, and click the Attendee Availability tab to check the schedules of those you invited.

If you already scheduled an appointment, you can convert it into a meeting. Open the appointment and click the Invite Attendees button on the toolbar to display the To box. This converts the appointment window into a meeting window.

Creating a Meeting from a Different Folder

If you're working in an Outlook folder other than the Calendar folder, you can set up a new meeting by using one of the following methods. Later you can change the item as necessary.

■ Click the down arrow at the right side of the New button on the Standard toolbar, and then choose Meeting Request from the menu.

- Point to New on the File menu, and then choose Meeting Request from the submenu.

- Press Ctrl+Shift+Q for a meeting request.

You can also drag other Outlook items to the Calendar folder icon on the Outlook Bar to create appointments. For example, if you are working in the Contacts folder, you can select a contact card and drag it to the Calendar folder icon. Outlook opens a meeting window addressed to the contact. Modify the meeting information—subject, location, start time, and end time—and then send the meeting request.

Changing a Meeting

You can change the details of a meeting just as you can an appointment. Double-click the meeting in the Appointments pane (when the meeting is not already selected) to open it, and then make your changes accordingly.

If you want to invite additional attendees and resources, click the To button on the Appointment tab. You can also click the Attendee Availability tab and then click the Invite Others button. Then in the Select Attendees And Resources dialog box, select the people and resources you want to invite, and click OK. If you want to remove a name from an invitation list, select the name on the Attendee Availability tab, and then press the Delete key.

When you're done, click the Send Update button to send a message to attendees informing them of the new time or other change.

> **NOTE**
>
> If you change the specifics of a meeting and close it before clicking Send Update, Outlook displays a dialog box in which you can choose to send the updated notice to the invitees.

Dragging a Calendar Item to Change Its Time

Instead of opening a meeting and setting the start time and end time, you can drag the starting and ending times as you learned to do when changing appointment times in Chapter 10, "Scheduling Appointments." If you change the start or end time for a meeting by dragging, Outlook displays a message asking whether you want to update the meeting attendees about the change in time, which is a good thing to do if you haven't notified them in some other way. Click Yes to send a message to attendees alerting them of the change. Outlook opens the calendar

III

**Scheduling Your
Time and Tasks**

item, which displays the new time. Click the Send Update button to send a message to the meeting attendees.

Dragging Invitation Times

In the Plan A Meeting dialog box and on the Attendee Availability tab in the meeting window, two vertical bars on the time grid show the start time (the green bar) and end time (the red bar) of the meeting you are planning. You can drag these bars to change the start and end times. When you do, the start and end times also change in the time boxes at the bottom of the dialog box.

 TIP

You can also select a new time using the AutoPick feature.

Canceling Invitations

If you delete a meeting from the Calendar window, Outlook displays a dialog box in which you can choose to send a cancellation notice to the invitees or to delete the item without sending a notification.

If you have not yet sent the invitations, you can cancel a meeting using the Cancel Invitation button on the Standard toolbar or by choosing Cancel Invitation from the Actions menu. This changes the meeting to an appointment.

If you later change your mind and decide to issue the invitations after all, choose Invite Attendees from the Actions menu. Outlook uses the original invitation list on the Attendee Availability tab in the calendar item window.

Receiving and Responding to a Meeting Request

Meeting Request

When someone invites you to a meeting or an event, you receive an e-mail message with the meeting request icon next to it. To properly respond to such messages, you should open the message in its own window, rather than using the preview pane, as shown in Figure 11-3.

 **NOTE**

In order to process the meeting request, you must receive it using Outlook. The meeting request format is not compatible with Outlook Express.

If you click Accept, Tentative, or Decline, Outlook asks whether you want to send your response and whether you want to add comments to it (if the Office Assistant is turned on, you will see the same message in a balloon):

If the meeting conflicts with something already on your calendar, you'll see a notice to that affect above the sender's name in the message window. In any case, before responding to the invitation, you may want to check your schedule. If you click the Calendar button on the message window's Standard toolbar, a separate calendar window appears with the item shown at the proposed date and time. If there is already something at that time, the two items will appears side by side in the

FIGURE 11-3.

A message window showing a meeting request.

Click here to accept the invitation.
Click here if you might attend.
Click here if you can't attend.
Click here to view the meeting on your calendar.
Click Forward to send the invitation to someone else.
Click here to delete the invitation without responding.

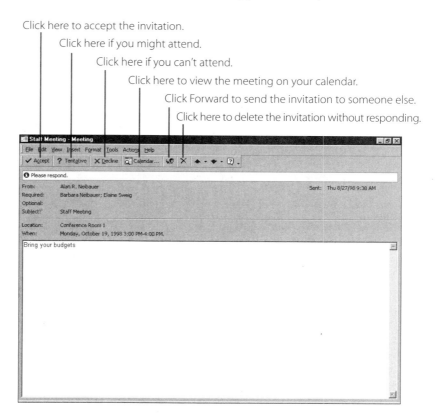

III

Scheduling Your
Time and Tasks

Appointment Pane. In this calendar window, you can review the details of the meeting and any conflicting items to determine how you want to respond. Close the calendar window to return to the meeting request window and click the appropriate button on the Standard toolbar to accept, tentatively accept, decline, or forward the invitation. You can also choose to delete the invitation, which doesn't send back any response.

Checking Attendees

If you organized the meeting, you'll receive e-mail messages when invitees accept or decline the invitation. The Subject column of your Inbox's message list shows the general response of Accepted, Tentative, or Declined. You can also look at the meeting request icon next to each message header to see if it shows a check mark (accepted), a question mark (tentative), or an *X* (declined). Open the messages to see if they contain more detailed responses.

For a summary of responses, and to check availability, open the meeting in the Calendar. A note on the Appointment tab summarizes the responses:

For more details, click the Attendee Availability tab. You can select one of two options to determine how you view the information—Show Attendee Availability and Show Attendee Status.

If you select Show Attendee Availability, you'll see who is invited and their free/busy time, as shown in Figure 11-4. If you select Show Attendee Status, the tab shows the responses you've received so far to your meeting request, as shown in Figure 11-5. Both tabs allow you to invite additional persons by clicking the Invite Others button at the bottom of the tab.

If you are an invited participant to the meeting, you can also open the meeting item to check the availability of other participants. When you select Show Attendee Status, you'll see who is invited and who is a required or an optional participant. Select Show Attendee Availability to check the free/busy time of guests. Once you accept an invitation, your time will appear as busy on the tab. Other invitees' times will not appear as busy until their free/busy time has been updated to the server—by default, every 15 minutes.

FIGURE 11-4.
The Attendee Availability tab showing availability.

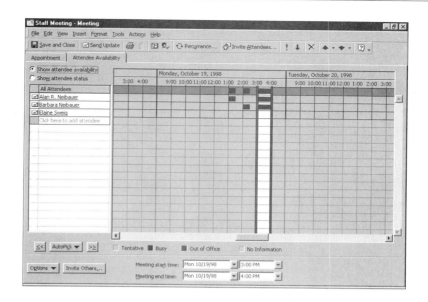

Conducting Online Meetings

Do you ever get tired of going into the office or traveling out of town for a meeting? With Outlook and a program called Microsoft NetMeeting that comes with it, you might not have to leave your home or go into the office. You can participate in meetings from wherever your computer is located: at home, on the road at a convention or on vacation, or even in your car if you have the proper hardware. You can

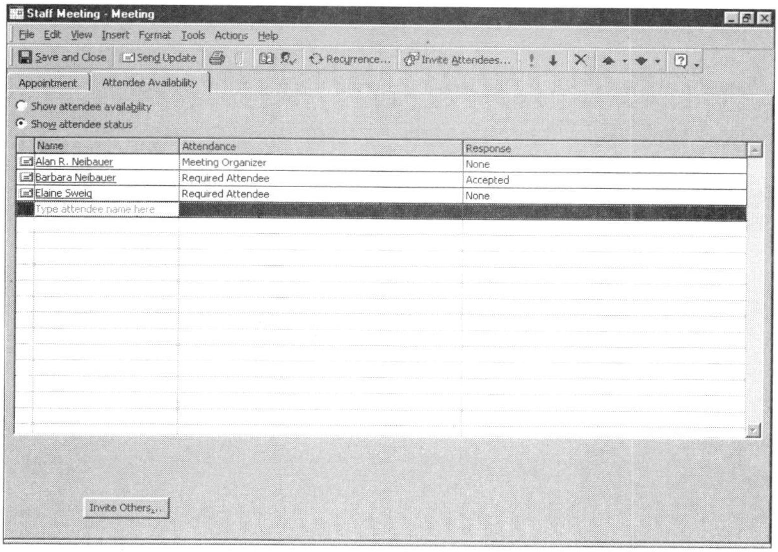

FIGURE 11-5.
The Attendee Availability tab showing status.

III

Scheduling Your Time and Tasks

also use NetMeeting to chat online with friends, business associates, or even strangers! In addition, NetMeeting is a perfect tool to conduct meetings with others on your network.

 NOTE

> For more information about the operation and features of NetMeeting, refer to the NetMeeting online Help.

With NetMeeting and the proper hardware, you can:

- Talk and listen to others live over the Internet or your network

- See other meeting participants who have a digital video camera installed on their system

- Share programs and work together over the Internet or your network

- Draw and annotate on screen, interactively

If you do not have a sound-equipped computer, you can type and receive written notes from others in the meeting.

You can use NetMeeting in conjunction with Outlook to plan and conduct meetings and to make Internet calls. An Internet call connects you with another person who is also running NetMeeting to hold a conversation. In addition, you can use NetMeeting as a separate program to make Internet calls and join online chats and conversations.

All of this is made possible by directory servers provided by Microsoft and other companies. The directory server is the link between you and others running NetMeeting, and it channels audio, video, typed chat, shared programs, and a Whiteboard between users.

Setting Up NetMeeting Conferences

A NetMeeting conference is simply a meeting conducted over the Internet through a common directory server. To set up a NetMeeting conference, follow these steps:

1 Open the Calendar folder.

2 Choose New Meeting Request from the Actions menu.

3 In the meeting window, select the This Is An Online Meeting Using check box and select Microsoft NetMeeting in the next list box. Outlook expands the meeting window to include the online meeting options shown in Figure 11-6.

4 Select or enter the invitees as you would for any other meeting.

To invite a person to an online meeting, NetMeeting information must be included in the person's Contacts folder. *To learn how to enter NetMeeting information, see "Details Tab," on page 409.*

5 Enter the specifics of the meeting.

6 Choose the server you want to use to conduct the meeting from the Directory Server list.

7 Enter your (or the meeting organizer's) e-mail address.

8 Select the Automatically Start NetMeeting With Reminder check box to start NetMeeting 15 minutes before the meeting time.

9 Enter the name of a Microsoft Office document, or use the Browse button to select it, if you want the document available to all meeting participants. You could specify a Word file containing the meeting agenda and an Excel spreadsheet, for example.

FIGURE 11-6.
A meeting window showing options for an online meeting.

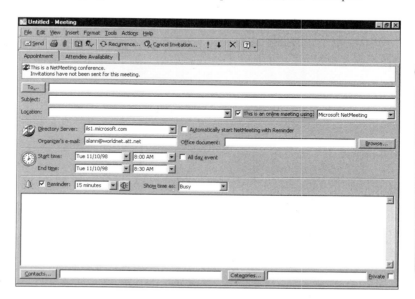

III

Scheduling Your
Time and Tasks

To convert an existing appointment or meeting to an online meeting, open the item and select the This Is An Online Meeting Using check box.

Starting a Meeting

If you set the meeting to start automatically, Outlook will start NetMeeting 15 minutes before the meeting time and connect you to the chosen directory server over the Internet. For the participants who accepted the meeting, their copy of Outlook will also start NetMeeting and dial into the same server 15 minutes before the scheduled meeting time. You can also set up NetMeeting to connect across a network.

If you want to start the meeting manually, open the meeting window from the Calendar and click the Start Meeting Now button on the Standard toolbar. Outlook will start NetMeeting immediately and look for the invitees on the selected server.

Joining a Meeting in Progress

If you are not the meeting organizer or you miss the online meeting call, you can join the meeting in progress by following these steps:

1 Open the online meeting item in the Calendar.

2 Click Join Meeting.

Setting Up NetMeeting

The first time you run NetMeeting, you'll have to set it up on your system. Rather than wait until your first actual online meeting, you can set up NetMeeting beforehand using either of these techniques:

- Point to Go To on the View menu, point to Internet Call on the Go To menu, and then choose Internet Call from the submenu.

- Point to Go To on the View menu, point to Internet Call on the Go To menu, and then choose From Address Book on the submenu. Choose the person you want to call, and then click OK.

- If you installed NetMeeting as a separate application, click Start on the taskbar, point to Programs, and then click Microsoft NetMeeting. The program might also be listed in the submenu that appears when you point to Internet Explorer.

A series of dialog boxes begins in which you set up NetMeeting. The steps you see might vary slightly from the following description,

depending on your system's configuration. Respond appropriately to
each box described below and then click Next to move to the next one.

1 The first dialog box simply explains some of the features available
in NetMeeting. Click Next.

2 If you see a dialog box telling you that you must enable sharing
in NetMeeting in order to share applications during a NetMeeting
call, make a note to enable the setting when NetMeeting appears.

3 In the next dialog box, choose whether you want to log on to a
server whenever NetMeeting starts, and choose the server to use
by default. If you plan to use NetMeeting over your local area
network instead of the Internet, choose not to log on to the
server. Click Next to continue.

4 On the next screen enter your name, e-mail address, your city,
state, and country, and a brief comment about yourself that will
appear on screen to identify you to other NetMeeting users. Click
Next to continue.

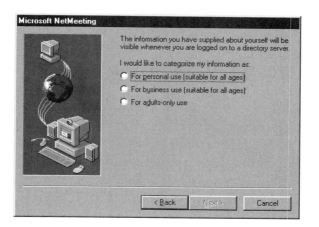

5 Specify the category of information that you plan to communicate
over the Internet, and then click Next.

6 Select the speed of your connection. The options are 14400 bps
modem, 28800 bps or faster modem, ISDN, and Local Area Network. Click Next.

7 If you have a video capture board or other video capability installed on your computer, you'll see a dialog box that asks you to confirm its use. Click Next to continue.

8 Next you might see a dialog box that asks you to select the devices that will record and play back sound on your system. Generally your sound card performs both functions. On some configurations this step can be skipped. After selecting the devices, click Next.

9 The next screen merely informs you that the Audio Tuning Wizard is about to help you tune your audio settings, and it instructs you to close all other programs that play or record sound. Click Next.

NOTE

Once you start NetMeeting, you can change all of your setup options, and fine-tune Internet calling, audio, and video settings by choosing Options on the NetMeeting Tools menu.

10 Click here to listen to sample audio.

11 Adjust the slider bar to a comfortable listening level.

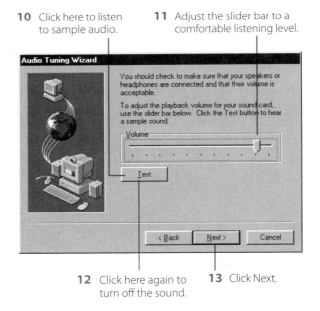

12 Click here again to turn off the sound.

13 Click Next.

14 Read this sentence, speaking clearly and distinctly into your microphone.

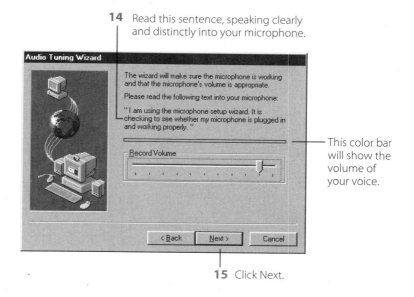

This color bar will show the volume of your voice.

15 Click Next.

16 Click Finish when the Audio Tuning Wizard reports that you have tuned your settings.

When you click Finish, NetMeeting starts and connects to the directory server you chose earlier. Depending on your connection and configuration, you might need to click Connect if the Dial-Up Connection box appears, or you might need to start your Dial-Up Connection manually and connect. The NetMeeting window appears as it attempts to connect to the server, as shown in Figure 11-7, on the following page.

> **NOTE**
>
> To log on to the directory server manually, choose Log On from the Call menu. Choose Log Off when you're ready to disconnect from the server and stop placing or accepting calls.

Using NetMeeting

When you place an online call, either for a meeting or for just a one-on-one chat, NetMeeting connects to the directory server, checks that your invitee is online, and then asks the invitee whether he or she wants to accept your call.

FIGURE 11-7.
The NetMeeting
window.

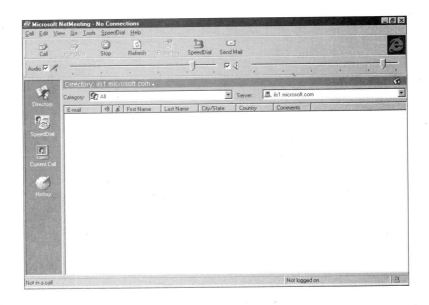

 **TIP**

If you do not want to be bothered with calls, choose Do Not Disturb from the Call menu.

If the person chooses to ignore the call, you'll be asked whether you want to leave a message.

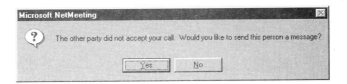

If you choose Yes, a message window appears and you can write and send a message, attach a file, and so on.

NOTE

NetMeeting might also display a message reporting that the person you called is currently in a meeting and cannot accept your call, or it might report that the person is in a meeting and ask whether you would like to join.

When your call is accepted, the person's name is displayed in the Current Call folder of NetMeeting, as shown in Figure 11-8, and you can start communicating. If the window does not appear, click Current Call in the NetMeeting folder list.

You can only speak to and view on screen one person at a time. If there are more than two participants in the meeting, click the Switch button on the NetMeeting window toolbar and choose the person with whom you want to communicate.

When you're running NetMeeting, you can click Microsoft NetMeeting in the System Tray, the area at the right of the Windows taskbar, to display the following buttons. You'll learn how to use these features later in this chapter.

To end the meeting, click the Hang Up button on the toolbar, or choose Log Off from the Call menu.

FIGURE 11-8.
Conducting a call in NetMeeting.

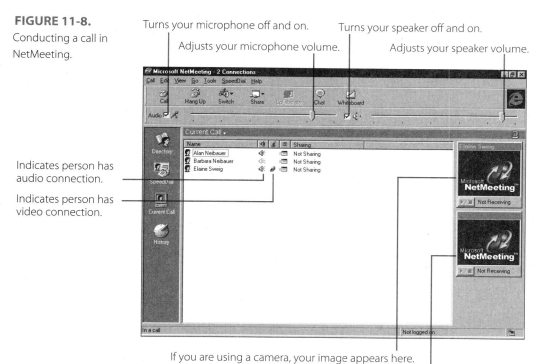

Chatting

Even with the proper equipment, the audio quality of a NetMeeting call might be poor, depending on the speed of your modem and the traffic on the directory server. You may want to open a chat window and write messages to the other members of the meeting instead. Follow these steps:

> **NOTE**
>
> You can talk (speak) and chat (write) at the same time.

1 Click Chat on the NetMeeting toolbar, or choose Chat from the Tools menu to open the chat window, shown in Figure 11-9. When the meeting originator opens the chat window, it also opens on the other participants' screens.

2 Read the chat messages as they appear in the large text box.

3 In the Send To list, choose to send your messages to everyone in the group or just to a specific participant in the list.

4 Type your message in the Message box and press Enter to transmit it.

Using the Whiteboard

Sometimes you need to discuss something online that you can't easily express in words. Suppose, for example, that you want the participants in the meeting to review a drawing. You'd like to give each participant the opportunity to comment on the drawing or even make changes to it as the meeting progresses. Or suppose you're conducting an online

FIGURE 11-9.

The Chat feature of NetMeeting.

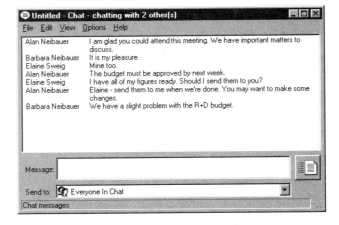

training session and want to write out important points that you would use a flipchart for if this were an in-person meeting. In these instances you can use the Whiteboard.

The Whiteboard is a drawing window that you can display and share with all participants in the meeting. Whatever you draw on the Whiteboard appears on the Whiteboards of all meeting participants. If you permit it, other meeting participants can add to your drawing using their Whiteboards. See Figure 11-10 for an example.

To use the Whiteboard, follow these steps:

1 Click Whiteboard on the NetMeeting toolbar, choose Whiteboard from the Tools menu, or press Ctrl+W.

2 Draw on the Whiteboard.

Use the tools on the Whiteboard tool palette, shown in Figure 11-11, on the following page, to create drawings. The same features are also available on the Tools menu. Use these tools as follows:

■ **Selector.** Use this tool to click or drag over objects you want to select. Drag the selected object to move it on the screen, or choose Delete, Copy, or Cut from the Edit menu.

FIGURE 11-10.
The Whiteboard feature of NetMeeting.

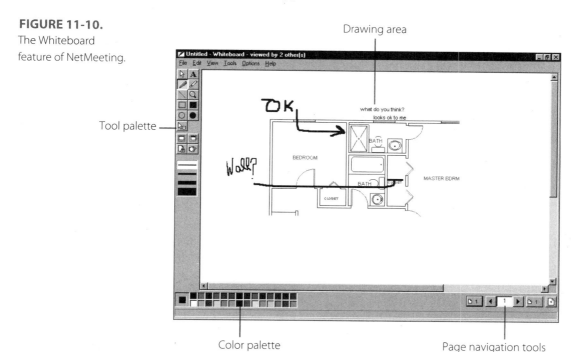

III

Scheduling Your
Time and Tasks

FIGURE 11-11.
The Whiteboard tool palette.

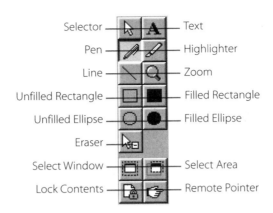

■ **Text.** Use this tool to type in the Whiteboard. Choose a color from the color palette, or click the Font Options button that appears when using the tool to change the font, font size, and font style. You can also use the Colors and Font commands on the Options menu.

■ **Pen.** Use this tool to draw freehand on the screen by dragging the mouse.

Use the Bring To Front and Send To Back commands on the Edit menu to layer overlapping objects in relation to each other.

■ **Highlighter.** Choose a line width and a color, and then use this tool to drag over the area you want to highlight.

■ **Line.** Use this tool to draw straight lines by dragging the mouse from one point to the next. Select a line width from the choices shown below, and choose a color from the palette. You can also use the Colors and Line Width commands on the Options menu.

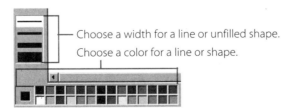

Choose a width for a line or unfilled shape.
Choose a color for a line or shape.

■ **Zoom.** Use this tool to toggle between normal and enlarged views. You can also use the Zoom command on the View menu.

- **Rectangle.** Use the rectangle tools to draw rectangles on the screen, choosing a line width and color from the palette. Choose Unfilled Rectangle to draw just a border; use Filled Rectangle to draw a solid rectangle of the selected color.

- **Ellipse.** Use the ellipse tools to draw filled and unfilled circles, choosing a line width and color from the palette.

- **Eraser.** Use this tool to erase objects by clicking them, or use it to drag a rectangle over an area and all objects even partially within the area will be completely removed.

- **Select Window.** This tool works similarly to the Windows clipboard. Click any window on your screen to copy the contents onto the Whiteboard; you can click even a partially obscured window. The Whiteboard will reopen with the window inserted as a graphic. You cannot open a file, other than a saved Whiteboard file, directly in the Whiteboard window.

- **Select Area.** Use this tool to drag a rectangle over the area of the screen you want to copy to the Whiteboard.

Using NetMeeting on a Network

You can use NetMeeting to conduct online meetings over your network as well as the Internet. To place a call to another network computer, choose New Call from the Call menu to see this dialog box:

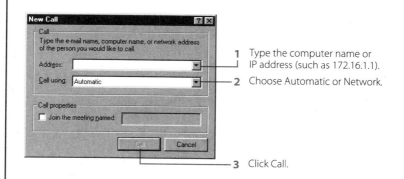

1 Type the computer name or IP address (such as 172.16.1.1).

2 Choose Automatic or Network.

3 Click Call.

The call will be placed to the other network user running NetMeeting, and you can now conduct your meeting and use all of the NetMeeting features discussed in this chapter—including audio, video, chat, Whiteboard, sharing, and collaborating.

III

**Scheduling Your
Time and Tasks**

- **Lock Contents.** Select this tool to prevent others from changing the Whiteboard contents. Deselect it to allow others to change the Whiteboard.

- **Remote Pointer.** Select this tool to display a pointer and move it to the area of the Whiteboard you want others to look at. Click again to turn it off.

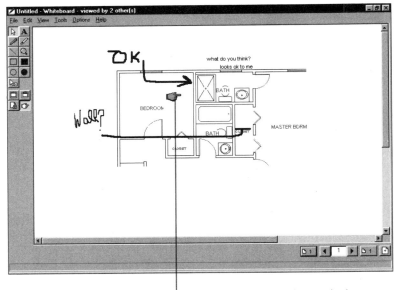

Drag the remote pointer to show others where to look.

Adding and Changing Whiteboard Pages

If you were conducting an in-person meeting, you might use a flip chart to draw images and highlight important points. When one page gets full, you just fold it over and start with a fresh sheet. You can use the Whiteboard in the same way, changing pages as needed.

Use these buttons to move from page to page:

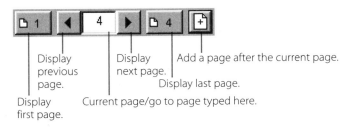

You can also add a new page before or after the current page using one of these techniques:

■ Choose Insert Page Before from the Edit menu to insert a page before the current page.

■ Choose Insert Page After from the Edit menu to insert a page after the current page.

Choose Clear Page from the Edit menu to erase the current page, or choose Delete Page from the Edit menu to delete the page. This will delete the participants' page as well.

You can also work with pages using the Page Sorter command on the Edit menu to display a dialog box showing thumbnail sketches of the pages like this:

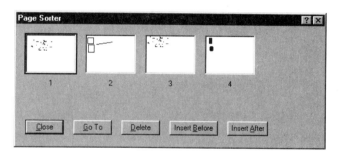

To change the order of a page, drag its thumbnail to a new position. Use the Insert Before and Insert After buttons to add new pages before or after the selected page, and use Delete to remove the selected page. Click the Go To button to go to the selected page in the Whiteboard and close the Page Sorter.

Normally, everyone in the meeting can see the same page that you have displayed on your screen. If you want to change pages without letting everyone see what you are doing, deselect Synchronize on the Tools menu.

Saving and Printing the Whiteboard

When your meeting is over, there is no need to lose the contents of your Whiteboard. While the Whiteboard is still displayed, each participant in the meeting can choose Print from the File menu to print a copy of the Whiteboard or Save from the File menu to save it. Whiteboards are saved in a special format, with the .wht extension;

III

Scheduling Your
Time and Tasks

these files can later be reopened in the Whiteboard by choosing Open from the File menu.

> If you close the Whiteboard before saving the contents, NetMeeting will ask if you want to save it at that time. Closing your own Whiteboard does not close those of the other participants, who can continue to draw on theirs. If you open the Whiteboard again, NetMeeting will locate and display the Whiteboards of the other participants.

Sharing and Collaborating

In addition to sharing a drawing on the Whiteboard, you may want participants to share a program as well. This is especially true if your meeting is aimed at training or user support and you want to help participants use a program. You may also want users to interact with another program, even Outlook itself. That is the purpose of sharing and collaborating.

- When you *share* a program with others, the meeting participants can see the program, but they cannot interact with it. The person sharing the program is called the *owner* and has control over who can work with it.

- When you *collaborate* with others on a program, the meeting participants can also work with the program.

Sharing a Program

To share a program, follow these steps:

1 Start the program you want to share, and then switch back to NetMeeting.

2 Click Current Call to open the Current Call folder.

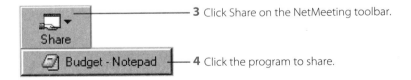

3 Click Share on the NetMeeting toolbar.

4 Click the program to share.

5 Click OK to confirm if another message appears.

You can also choose Share Application from the Tools menu. Other meeting participants will now be able to see exactly what you are doing with the shared program.

Collaborating

After you've shared a program, if you want your meeting participants to be able to use it, click the Collaborate button on the NetMeeting toolbar or choose Start Collaborating from the Tools menu.

To work with the program, the meeting participant must double-click the program or click the Collaborate button on his or her own screen, and then click in the program window to begin using it. This transfers control of the program to the participant, and you are no longer allowed to use your pointer on screen.

Press Esc to stop any participant who is currently working with the shared program and regain control over the program and your cursor, or click your mouse button. You can then click the Collaborate button to prevent others from using the program further. Click the Share button and then click each shared program to remove it from others' screens.

WARNING

If you share a window that shows your disks and folders, such as My Computer or Windows Explorer, every program in the folder will be visible during the meeting. If you then choose to Collaborate with your participants, they can freely open, edit, and even delete files, folders, and even entire disks on your system!

Sending and Receiving Files

While you are in a meeting, you can send files to other participants and receive files from them.

Point to File Transfer on the Tools menu, and then choose one of these commands:

- **Send File.** This command lets you select the file to send.

- **Cancel Send.** This command stops the file transfer in progress.

- **Cancel Receive.** This command stops the receiving of the incoming file.

- **Open Received Files Folder.** This command opens a folder containing files received during meetings.

III

Scheduling Your
Time and Tasks

After you send a file, a message appears reporting that the file has been transferred successfully. When you receive a file from someone else you'll see a dialog box similar to that shown here with options to close the dialog box, open the file, or delete the file.

Using NetMeeting Directories

When you conduct an online meeting, you connect to persons for whom you have NetMeeting information in their listing in your address book. You can also use NetMeeting as a separate application to contact other persons who are logged on to the same server by following these steps:

1 Start NetMeeting and click the Directory button to display a directory of those logged on to the server, as shown in Figure 11-12.

2 Open the Category list and choose a category of user, such as Personal or Business.

3 To log on to a different server, select it from the Server list.

4 Double-click the person's listing in the directory to place the call.

NetMeeting will place the call and ask the person to accept or decline your call. If the person accepts, the Current Call folder appears and you can use all of NetMeeting's features to communicate.

To send an e-mail message to a person in the directory, select his or her name, and then choose New Mail Message from the Call menu.

Speed Dialing

When you place a call or when someone calls you, the other person's NetMeeting information is added to your SpeedDial list. The list is

FIGURE 11-12.
Directory of persons logged on.

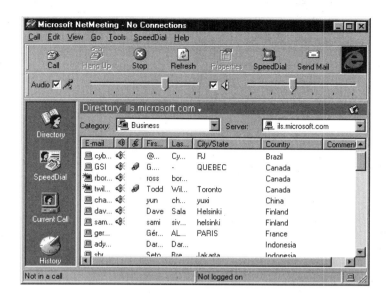

updated each time you start NetMeeting so you can quickly see who is currently available online. You can then call someone by following these steps:

1 Click the SpeedDial button on the NetMeeting Standard toolbar.

2 Find the person you want to call in the SpeedDial list and double-click the entry.

NetMeeting Etiquette

Treat the NetMeeting directory as you would a telephone book. Some people enjoy being called by strangers because they like experimenting with NetMeeting or just chatting with people from other parts of the world. Others do not appreciate calls from strangers.

Before placing a NetMeeting call, read the brief note in the Comments column of the directory window. It might indicate that the person wants to hear from anyone or only wants calls from friends, business associates, males, females, or whatever. For the full text of the comment, right-click the listing and choose Properties from the shortcut menu.

If you place a call and get a response that it was declined, don't try again. If you really have to reach the person, send an e-mail message. E-mail addresses are listed in the first column in the directory window or in the Properties dialog box.

III

Scheduling Your Time and Tasks

To add a person to the SpeedDial list manually, follow these steps:

1 Choose Add SpeedDial from the SpeedDial menu to open the Add SpeedDial dialog box:

2 Enter the person's e-mail or network address.

3 Choose to use a directory server or network for the call.

4 Select an action to take using the address.

5 Click OK.

As connections to the Internet continue to get faster and technology continues to improve, conducting meetings online will become increasingly practical and we'll be able to have more contact with less cost in travel and time, whether for business or pleasure.

In these past two chapters, you learned how to use Microsoft Outlook's calendar to schedule appointments, meetings, and events. By maintaining schedules on your network server, or on a Web site if you use the Internet Only installation, Outlook can automatically schedule meetings to avoid conflicts. In the the next chapter, you'll learn how to manage your tasks and how to assign tasks to others.

Managing Your Tasks

We all have tasks to perform, and it's a lot easier to keep track of them with a task list. You could stick notes on your refrigerator door, list them on a notepad on your desk, or let Microsoft Outlook organize your tasks for you. With Outlook's Tasks folder, you are reminded which tasks have to be done, which are overdue, and which you've already completed. You can even assign tasks to other Outlook users and keep track of their progress.

A typical Tasks folder is shown in Figure 12-1, on the next page.

FIGURE 12-1.
Icons that appear in
the Tasks pane.

Task you assigned
to another person

Task assigned to you

Recurring task

One-time task

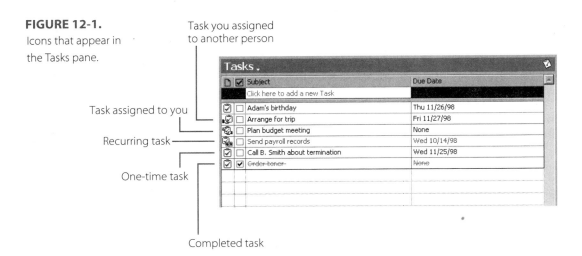

Completed task

Setting Up a Task

When you set up a task, you specify its subject and an optional description, along with the starting date, due date, priority, status, recurrence, and ownership. As with an appointment or meeting, a task can be a one-time event or an event that recurs at some regular interval. Ownership designates who actually performs the task—you or someone you assign the task to.

When you need to set up a new task, open the Tasks folder and use one of the following methods:

- Click the New Task button at the left end of the Standard toolbar.

- Choose New Task from the Actions menu.

- Point to New on the File menu, and then choose Task from the submenu.

- Press Ctrl+N from within the Tasks folder, or Ctrl+Shift+K from anywhere in Outlook.

- Double-click in the top row of the task list (which reads Click Here To Add A New Task).

Outlook opens a task window, with the Task tab shown, as in Figure 12-2, on page 370. Here you name the task, set due dates, assign a priority, and set up various other features that will help you accomplish

Other Ways of Looking at Tasks

You will probably work with tasks mostly from the Tasks folder. However, you can also perform some functions with tasks using the TaskPad and Outlook Today.

The TaskPad is available from the Calendar folder and is linked to your entries in the Tasks folder. It displays active tasks and tasks completed for the date shown on the calendar. You can open a task from the TaskPad and edit its details, just as you can by opening it in the Tasks folder. You can also create a new task in the TaskPad, and you can customize the task information that is displayed in the TaskPad. *For more information, see "Using the TaskPad," on page 392.*

You can also review active tasks from the Outlook Today window. It displays all active tasks, each with a check box for you to mark when the task is completed. Overdue tasks appear in red to draw your attention.

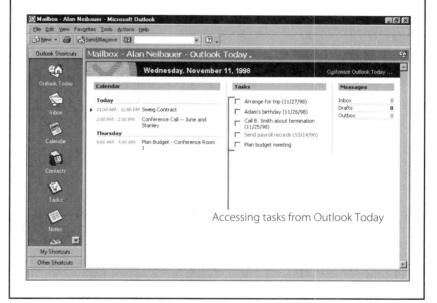

Accessing tasks from Outlook Today

the task. Most of the settings are similar to those for appointments and meetings:

- Enter text or attach objects in the large box to add details about the nature of the task.

- Select the Private check box when you don't want others to see the task.

FIGURE 12-2.
The Task tab of a new task window.

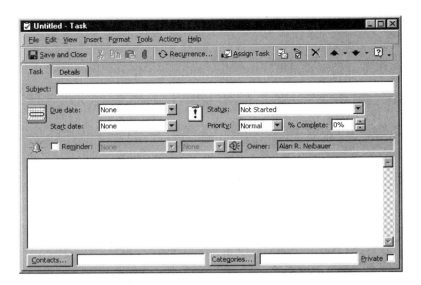

- Use the Categories button (or the Organize button in the Tasks folder) to specify one or more categories for the task if you want to be able to sort your tasks this way.

- Set a visual and audible reminder to appear on screen if you want one.

- Designate a recurrence pattern if applicable.

- Associate the task with a contact if others are involved.

After you enter information for a task, click the Save And Close button to add the task to your task list. If you want to close the window without saving the information you've entered, click the Close button in the upper right corner of the window (or choose Close from the File menu), and then click No when Outlook asks whether you want to save your changes.

Quickly Setting Up a Task

SEE ALSO

In the Contacts folder, you can set up a new task to be performed by a contact. For details, see "Assigning a Task to a Contact," on page 422.

When you need to set up a task quickly without worrying about the fine points of the settings, you can simply open the Tasks folder and do the following:

1 Click the top row of the task list (which reads Click Here To Add A New Task).

2 Type the subject of the task.

3 If applicable, click in the Due Date column and type a due date for the task, and then press Enter.

4 Continue adding tasks by repeating steps 2 and 3. When you are finished, press the Down arrow key or click the mouse outside the new task box to deactivate it.

Later, if you want to add more information about a task or make any other changes, open the task by double-clicking it, make your additions or changes, and then click the Save And Close button.

> To select a due date from a calendar rather than type the date, click the Due Date box and then click the down arrow that appears. Select a date from the calendar that Outlook displays. You can move around the calendar as you would the Date Navigator. *See "Using the Date Navigator," on page 307.*

Setting Up a Recurring Task

When a task has to be repeated at some regular interval, create a recurring task by assigning a recurrence pattern to the task. This is very similar to the process of setting up a recurring appointment, as discussed in Chapter 11, "Scheduling Meetings." Open an existing task or create a new one, and then click the Recurrence button on the Standard toolbar or choose Recurrence from the Actions menu.

> If you want to establish a recurrence pattern for a task that you assign to someone else, you must set up the recurrence when you create the task. You can't add recurrence or change the recurrence pattern after you send a task request. *For more details about task requests, see "Sending a Task Request," on page 376.*

In the Task Recurrence dialog box, shown in Figure 12-3, on the following page, you can set the intervals at which the task should recur and designate the start and end dates for the series of recurring tasks. You can also change a recurring task to a one-time task by clicking Remove Recurrence.

The recurrence pattern tells Outlook when each occurrence in the series of tasks is active and due. When you complete one occurrence of the task, Outlook creates the next occurrence based on the recurrence pattern you set and adds the next occurrence to your task list. The recurrence pattern options for tasks are nearly the same as those in the Appointment Recurrence dialog box. *See "Recurrence Pattern," on page 321, for details about how to set these options.*

III

Scheduling Your Time and Tasks

FIGURE 12-3.

The Task Recurrence dialog box.

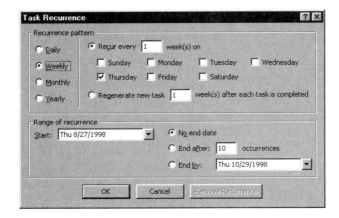

The one difference between setting recurrence patterns for a task and for an appointment or meeting is the Regenerate New Task option in the Task Recurrence dialog box. This option is valuable when a task must recur a specified number of days (or weeks, months, or years) after the previous completion of the task rather than at a specific interval. For example, you could set up the recurring task of changing your security password every 60 days. If, for one reason or another, you change your password in fewer than 60 days, you'd want to be reminded 60 days later to change it again. If you have turned on the Regenerate New Task option, Outlook creates a new occurrence of the task, resetting the due date to 60 days after the date you mark the previous occurrence of the task completed. This feature also works for tasks you complete later than planned—for example, if you visit the dentist every six months for a cleaning but don't go for eight months on one occasion, the next task will be assigned in another six months rather than four months.

When you click OK in the Task Recurrence dialog box, you return to the task window. If you have set up a recurrence pattern, the colored band at the top of the Task tab now displays information about the intervals at which the task will recur. Notice also that if you have changed the recurring task's start date in the Task Recurrence dialog box, Outlook changes the due date in the task window (and in the task list) accordingly.

> If you open a recurring task and change the due date or start date for the task in the task window, Outlook displays a message telling you that this action will change the date for only one occurrence of the task and that to change all future occurrences you need to click Cancel and open the Task Recurrence dialog box. If you click OK in the message box to accept the changes you've made to the single occurrence of the task, Outlook lists that occurrence of the task as well as the next regularly scheduled occurrence. The Task tab for the task you've changed will indicate the effective date when the task returns to its normal schedule.

Skipping a Task in a Series

When a recurring task comes due, you might find that you don't need to perform the task this time, although you will need to do so for future due dates. When you want to skip one occurrence of a recurring task, open the task and choose Skip Occurrence from the Actions menu. Outlook resets the due date to the next occurrence of the recurring task.

You cannot undo skipping an occurrence, so if you skip an occurrence in error, you need to reset the start date on the Task tab.

> The Skip Occurrence command is not available for recurring tasks you've set up with the Regenerate New Task option in the Task Recurrence dialog box. Instead, open the task and change its due date to the next date you want for the task. The Regenerate New Task setting will still create a new task each time you complete the current one.

Prioritizing Tasks

Most tasks that you perform are routine, at least within the context of your daily chores. From time to time, however, you'll have very important tasks that require your immediate attention. You may have other tasks that are less important than your routine tasks that can be deferred or delayed without serious consequences.

When you create a new task in the task list, Outlook assigns it an importance level (or priority) of Normal. If you create a new task using the task window, you can enter the importance level directly in the Priority box. Your choices are Normal, High, and Low. You can change the importance level of a task at any time, by using one of these methods:

- Open the task and select the level of importance in the Priority box on the Task tab.

III

Scheduling Your
Time and Tasks

■ Open the task and choose Properties from the File menu. Select the level of importance in the Importance box.

■ If the Priority column is visible in the task list (the column with an exclamation mark as its label), click the Priority box for the task you want to change. Then select Low, Normal, or High from the list that appears. (The Priority column appears in all views of the Tasks folder window except Simple List view and Task Timeline view. *To change the view, see "Viewing Your Tasks," on page 389.* You can also customize any view to show the columns you are interested in.)

In the Tasks folder window, a red exclamation mark in the Priority column indicates a task with a High importance level. A blue downward-pointing arrow indicates a task with Low importance. The Priority column is blank for a task with a Normal level of importance.

Creating a Task from a Calendar Item (and Vice Versa)

If you have set up an appointment, meeting, or event on your Outlook calendar that also involves a task, you can easily use the item to create the task. You can either drag the item from the Calendar window to the Tasks folder or copy the item to the Tasks folder.

To drag the item, follow these steps:

1 Open the Calendar folder.

2 Locate the item you want to create a task for.

3 Drag the item from the Appointments pane and drop it on the Tasks folder in the Outlook Bar. The task window then appears with the calendar information inserted.

4 If appropriate, change the task information.

5 Click Save And Close.

To copy the calendar item instead, select the calendar item in the Calendar, and then choose Copy To Folder from the Edit menu. In the Copy Items dialog box that appears, select the Tasks folder, and then click OK to display the task in the task window.

You can also create an appointment or meeting from a task. This is useful when you want to schedule time to work on or complete the task. The process is similar to the one just described: either drag the task from the task window to the Calendar folder on the Outlook Bar, or use the copy to folder method.

Setting a Task Reminder

With appointments and meetings, you can only set a reminder to appear so many minutes before the event. For a task, you can set both the date and time for the reminder. If your task does not have a due date, Outlook does not automatically set up a reminder. When you create a new task with a due date, Outlook sets up a reminder for 8:00 AM on the date the task is due. You can add or change the reminder time from within the task window.

NOTE

> If you inadvertently set the task reminder for a time that has already passed, Outlook displays a message telling you that the time has passed and that a reminder won't be set. If that's all right with you, click OK to dispense with the reminder. To reset the reminder time, click No. Outlook returns you to the task window, where you can set a new reminder time.

Adjusting Other Task Properties

SEE ALSO

For information about using AutoArchive, see "Using the AutoArchive Feature," on page 506.

In each task window, you can set additional properties for the task by choosing Properties from the File menu to open the Properties dialog box. Figure 12-4 shows the options and information for a new task. When setting up a new task, you can adjust such items as the priority and sensitivity of the task and whether it is included in AutoArchiving. Other options pertain to task requests you send to someone else, including options to have a receipt sent to you when your request is

FIGURE 12-4.
The Properties dialog box for a new task.

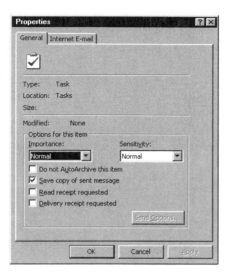

delivered to the recipient or when the recipient reads (or at least opens) the request. Certain properties are not available after a task is first created, and the Properties dialog box changes accordingly. For instance, the sensitivity level cannot be changed after your task is entered on your task list or sent as a task request, and you can't request a receipt after the task has been set up.

Use the Internet E-mail tab of the dialog box to set properties for sending task requests over the Internet.

Sending a Task Request

You might have a task that you want to assign to someone else to perform. You can set up a task and send an e-mail message to someone else, who can either accept the task, decline to perform it, or pass it on again to someone else.

> To send a task request over the Internet, the recipient's e-mail address must be set to use Microsoft Outlook rich text format. *See "Adding an Address," on page 117, for more information.*

When you send a task request and it is accepted, the ownership of the task passes to the person who accepted it. At that point, you can receive updates to track the progress of the task, but you can no longer make any changes to the task record.

Once a task is assigned, Outlook keeps track of who owns the task and when it gets updated. Updated means that the percentage of the task that is completed is recorded on the task record. When the task owner updates the task, Outlook updates the task in the folders of anyone else who is keeping a record of the task. (A task can appear on task lists of several people because the person you assign a task to might assign that task to someone else. *For information, see "Passing Along a Task Request," on page 381.*) When the task has been completed, Outlook sends a status report to those who assigned the task and who requested a status report. The person performing the task can see the names of people who will receive updates and status reports about the task by viewing the Update List box on the Details tab in the task window.

If you assign the same task to two or more people, you will not receive automatic updates as the task progresses. To keep your finger on the pulse of an assigned task, divide the task into smaller parts and send each part to an individual assignee. That way, you'll receive updates on each segment of the task.

To assign a task to someone else, follow these steps:

1 Open the Tasks folder, and create a task request in one of the following ways:

- Click the small arrow to the right of the New Task button on the Standard toolbar, and choose Task Request from the menu.

- Choose New Task Request from the Actions menu.

- Point to New on the File menu, and then choose Task Request from the submenu.

- Press Ctrl+Shift+U.

- Create a new task, and then, in the task window, click Assign Task on the Standard toolbar or choose Assign Task on the Action menu.

2 Outlook displays a task request window, as shown in Figure 12-5, on the next page. Fill out as much of the information on the tabs as you need to—you can set a due date and a start date, prioritize the task, add notes, and so on. Selecting the Keep An Updated Copy Of This Task On My Task List check box retains a copy of this task on your task list so that you receive periodic status

Creating a New Task Anywhere in Outlook

If you're working in an Outlook folder other than the Tasks folder and need to set up a new task, use one of the following methods to create the task. Later you can fine-tune or change it as necessary.

- Click the small arrow on the Standard toolbar's New button (at the far left), and then choose Task or Task Request from the menu.

- Point to New on the File menu, and then choose Task or Task Request from the submenu.

- Press Ctrl+Shift+K for a new task or press Ctrl+Shift+U for a new task request.

III

Scheduling Your
Time and Tasks

FIGURE 12-5.
A task window for assigning a task.

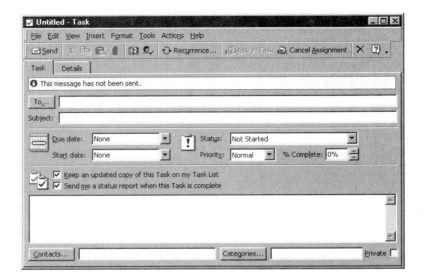

reports. Selecting the Send Me A Status Report When This Task Is Complete check box provides you with a status report when the assignee marks the task completed.

3 In the To box, type the name of the person or persons to whom you're assigning the task, or click the To button and choose the names from the Select Task Recipient dialog box (a variation of the Address Book dialog box you use for e-mail messages).

4 Click the Send button in the task request window to send the task request to the person or persons you've assigned to the task.

After you send a task request, you can't change the names of the assignees unless one of them declines the task.

Receiving and Responding to a Task Request

When you receive a task request, you can accept or decline it, or you can attempt to assign it to someone else. When you accept a task, it appears on your task list. When you decline a task assignment, it is returned to the sender and reappears on the sender's task list. You can also delete the task request message, but this doesn't give the sender any information on the status of his or her request.

In order to process the task request, you must receive it using Outlook. The task request format is not compatible with Outlook Express.

Reassigning a Task

Suppose you've assigned a task to someone and that someone has accepted the task, but now you change your mind about who should complete the assignment. In such a case, you can create an unassigned copy of the task and assign the copy to someone else. To do this, you must have selected the Keep An Updated Copy Of This Task On My Task List check box on the Task tab of the original task request (otherwise, you won't even see the task in your task list after it's been accepted).

When you create an unassigned copy of a task, everyone who formerly received task updates or status reports will not receive them for the reassigned task. The original task you assigned stays on the task list of the person you assigned it to, but an updated copy of the original task will not appear on your task list. If you or anyone else who was assigned the original task requested a status report for that task, you and the people who requested it will receive the status report when the owner of the original task marks the task complete.

To create an unassigned copy of a task and reassign the task, take the following steps. Remember, you must have selected the Keep An Updated Copy Of This Task On My Task List check box in the original task request you sent.

1 In your task list, open your copy of the task you want to reassign.

2 Click the Details tab.

3 On the Details tab, click the Create Unassigned Copy button and then click OK. Outlook makes a copy of the task and displays it in the task window.

4 In the task window, choose Assign Task from the Actions menu.

5 In the To box, enter the name of the person you now want to assign the task to, and then click Send.

III

Scheduling Your
Time and Tasks

When you receive a task request, it appears as a message in your Inbox. Open the message to see the request like the one shown on the Task tab in the illustration below:

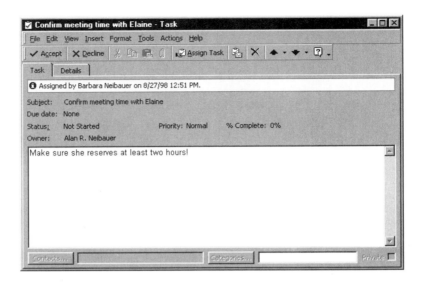

After you've clicked the Accept or Decline button, Outlook displays a message asking whether you want to edit your response or send your reply without a response. If you choose not to edit your response, Outlook sends the message without displaying any further windows. If you choose to edit the response, Outlook provides a typical message window with a colored band showing your response. Your response also appears in the Subject box when the task request is returned. Type any message you want to include, and, when your response is ready, click the Send button. Once you respond to the request, the message is removed from your inbox.

If you decide to assign the task request to someone else and click the Assign Task button, Outlook displays a task request window that you can use to forward the task request along. *See "Passing Along a Task Request," on the next page.*

Accepting a Task

When you accept a task request, you take over ownership of the task. You can then make any changes to the task setup that suits the circumstances. You'll probably want (or be required) to send status reports to the person who assigned the task to you. In some cases, Outlook sends a status report automatically; in other cases, you must prepare and send the report yourself. *For more information, see "Sending a Status Report," on page 386.*

Declining a Task

When you click the Decline button for a task request, you can send your response with or without comment. Outlook returns the ownership of the task to the sender.

If you are the person who assigned the declined task, you receive a message telling you that the person to whom you assigned the task has declined to accept it. You then have four choices:

- Close the message window. The task stays on your task list and shows an assigned task icon, but when you open it, you see that the task was declined.

- Click Return To Task List in the message window and perform the task yourself.

- Click Assign Task in the message window and reassign the task to someone else when the task window opens.

- Find the task in your task list and delete it. Outlook does not ask you to confirm the deletion.

Passing Along a Task Request

If you receive a task request but don't want to perform the task yourself, you can pass along the request to another person who might be able to carry out the task. To do so, simply assign the task to another person. The recipient is then in the same boat you were in when you received the task request. If the recipient accepts the task, you're off the hook; the task ownership passes to the recipient. You and the person who originally sent the task request will receive status reports about the task.

> **NOTE**
>
> Do *not* forward a task request using the Forward button in your message window unless you're only keeping someone else informed about your workload. Forwarding the task request message (rather than assigning the task to another person) means that you cannot use Outlook's task management features.

You have two ways to attempt to reassign a task:

- When you open the task request message, click the Assign Task button on the Standard toolbar, or choose Assign Task from the

III

Scheduling Your
Time and Tasks

Actions menu. Follow the steps listed in "Sending a Task Request," on page 376, to assign the task. With this method, you don't actually accept the task. You're likely to use this method when you know right away that you need to assign the task to someone else.

■ You can accept the task and then assign it to someone else later. Use this method when you've accepted a task and later realize you cannot complete it.

Deleting a Task Request

For more about deleting tasks, see "Canceling a Task," on page 388.

If you attempt to delete a task request message instead of answering it, a dialog box (or the Office Assistant balloon) opens with these four choices:

■ **Decline And Delete.** Send a reply declining the request and then delete the task request.

■ **Mark Complete And Delete.** Mark the task completed and then delete the task request.

■ **Delete.** Delete the request without a response (this is impolite and should be avoided).

■ **Cancel.** Close the dialog box and return to the message to take another action.

Working with Tasks

Outlook's task features can help you develop efficiency and accountability in your work and your projects. As due dates approach, you can receive timely reminders. You can track the progress of a task during the course of a project. You can record certain additional information about a task—mileage, billing information, contacts, and company names—to help with wrapping up a task. You can send or receive periodic status reports. And, you can keep a list of completed tasks.

Receiving a Reminder

As the due date for a task approaches, Outlook displays a reminder on the date and at the time you set:

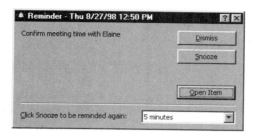

Click the Dismiss button to cancel any further reminders. If you need to change the due date for the task, or if the circumstances have changed and should be reflected in the task setup, click the Open Item button to open the task window, where you can make necessary adjustments.

If you want Outlook to remind you of the task again, you can postpone the reminder by selecting one of the delay times in the list at the bottom of the message box. The list contains choices ranging from five minutes to a week. After you select a delay time, click the Snooze button. Remember that this merely determines when the reminder will reappear, it doesn't change the due date for the task.

If you postpone the reminder until after the task's due date and time (not a very useful thing to do), Outlook will display the Reminder message box again at the time you set, with the word *Overdue* in the title bar.

> **NOTE**
>
> The Reminder message box is the only place where you can assign a Snooze time to a reminder. You can change the time the initial reminder will appear in the task window.

Tracking the Progress of a Task

The task window provides three indicators to help you track the progress of a task: Status, Percent Complete (% Complete), and Actual Work.

III

Scheduling Your
Time and Tasks

Status

The status of each task is displayed on the Task tab. Here you can record the current status of a task by selecting one of these choices from the list:

- **Not Started.** Outlook assigns this description to all new tasks.

- **In Progress.** Select this option after you've started a task. If you set the Percent Complete box to a number other than 0, Outlook sets the Status box to In Progress (except when the current status is set to Waiting On Someone Else or Deferred—see below).

- **Completed.** Select this option when you've finished the task. When you mark a task completed in one of the other ways available to you, Outlook also sets the Status box to Completed.

- **Waiting On Someone Else.** If your task requires that someone else complete a prerequisite task before you can continue work on yours, select this option.

- **Deferred.** Select this option when you defer a task until a later time.

Percent Complete

 **SEE ALSO**

For additional ways to mark a task completed, see "Marking Tasks Completed," on page 387.

In the Percent Complete box on the Task tab, you can type any percentage from 0 to 100 to indicate how much of the task you've completed, or you can click the arrows to select a preset value of 0%, 25%, 50%, 75%, or 100%.

Note the following points about the Percent Complete box:

- When you set the percentage to any number other than 0 or 100, Outlook changes the Status box setting from Not Started to In Progress. (If the Status box is set to Waiting On Someone Else or Deferred, changing the Percent Complete box doesn't change the Status box setting.)

- If you set the percentage to 100%, Outlook changes the Status box setting to Completed. Likewise, if you set the Status box to Completed, Outlook sets the Percent Complete box to 100%.

- If you reduce the percentage in the Percent Complete box to 0%, Outlook changes the Status box setting from In Progress to Not Started. (If the Status box is set to Waiting On Someone Else or Deferred, changing the Percent Complete box doesn't change the Status box setting.)

- If you reduce the percentage in the Percent Complete box below 100%, Outlook changes the Status box setting from Completed to In Progress, Waiting On Someone Else, or Deferred, depending on what the Status box setting was before the task was set to 100% completed.

Setting Up a Task Estimate

SEE ALSO

For more information about the Details tab, see "Recording Other Task Information," on page 388.

On the Details tab in the task window, shown in Figure 12-6, you can record your estimate of the number of hours that it will take to complete the task. You might want to use this number to estimate the cost and billing for a task or to later compare it to the actual hours worked.

To set a time estimate for a task, simply click the Details tab in the task window and type the estimated number of hours in the Total Work box. Outlook converts the number of hours you type to days or weeks. The conversion is based on the number of hours per day and hours per week that you set in Outlook's Options dialog box (choose Options from the Tools menu, select the Other tab, and then click the Advanced Options button).

NOTE

> The number of hours you enter in the Total Work box does not set the due date on the Task tab. You must adjust the due date yourself if you want it to correspond to the start date plus the estimated work time.

In the Actual Work box on the tab you can record the number of hours that a task has taken so far. You can use this number to estimate the

FIGURE 12-6.
The Details tab of a task window.

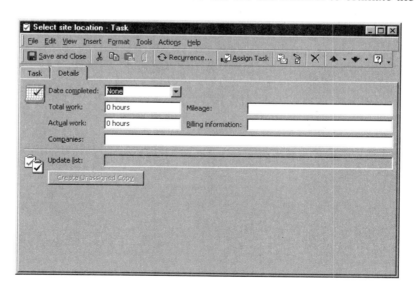

percentage of a task that has been completed. You can also use it to check the accuracy of your early estimates, by comparing it to the figure you entered in the Total Work box when you set up the task.

When you type the number of hours worked so far in the Actual Work box, Outlook also converts that number to days or weeks based on the number of work hours per day and per week that you set as your standard in Outlook's Options dialog box.

> The number in the Actual Work box is not connected to the settings in the Status box or the Percent Complete box on the Task tab. You have to set the values in those boxes manually if you want them to reflect the Actual Work values.

Sending a Status Report

Whether you're working on a task that you set up yourself or a task that someone assigned to you, you might need to send periodic status reports. Sending a status report is a pretty simple matter.

To send a status report, follow these steps:

1 Open the task whose status you're going to report.

2 Update the status of the task, ensuring that the information in the Subject, Priority, Due Date, Status, Percent Complete, Total Work, and Actual Work boxes of the task window is accurate. Outlook will add this information to the text of the status report message.

3 Choose Send Status Report from the Actions menu.

4 You'll see a message window like the one shown here. Outlook has already supplied the status information and has filled in the information in the message header boxes.

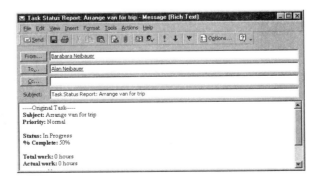

5 Add any message you want to the status report.

6 Click Send.

If you have been assigned and have accepted a one-time (nonrecurring) task, Outlook automatically creates and sends a status report to the person who assigned the task when you mark the task completed.

> ⭐ **TIP**
>
> To prevent Outlook from automatically sending a status report at the completion of an assigned task, clear the Send Status Reports When Assigned Tasks Are Completed check box. To reach this check box, choose Options from the Tools menu, click Advanced Options on the Other tab, and then click Advanced Tasks.

Marking Tasks Completed

When you've finished a task, you'll want to cross it off your task list by marking it completed. Marking a task completed draws a line through the task in the task list, removes the task from your list of active tasks, sets up the next task (in a recurring series), shuts off reminders for the task, and (for assigned tasks) sends a status report to the person who assigned the task to you.

To mark a task completed, use any of the following methods:

- In the task window, choose Mark Complete from the Actions menu.

- Select Completed in the Status box on the Task tab of the task window.

- Set the Percent Complete box on the Task tab of the task window to 100%.

- Set the Date Completed box on the Details tab of the task window to today or a date before today. Type the date, or click the arrow beside the box to select a date from the calendar. (This method is especially useful if you actually finished the task earlier than the date on which you mark it complete. If you use another method to mark it complete on the later day, Outlook inserts the current date in the Date Completed box. In this case, you'll want to reset the completion date to the actual date you finished the task.)

- Click the Complete box in the TaskPad of the Calendar folder when it's in Day/Week/Month view. *See "Using the TaskPad," on page 392.*

■ Click the Completed box for the task in the Outlook Today window.

As you'll learn later in this chapter, Outlook gives you numerous ways to set up and view the task list in the Tasks folder window. *See "Viewing Your Tasks," on the next page.* In certain views, you can use these additional methods of marking a task completed:

■ If you have selected Simple List view, click the Complete column in the Tasks folder window (the one that shows a check mark in the column heading).

■ If you have selected a view that displays the Status column in the Tasks folder window, click the task's entry in that column and select Completed from the list that appears.

■ If you have selected a view that displays the Percent Complete column in the Tasks folder window, set the task's entry in that column to 100%.

■ If you have selected a view that displays the Date Completed column in the Tasks folder window, set the entry in that column to today's date or to an earlier date.

Recording Other Task Information

In addition to task status and particulars, you might want to record other information about a task, such as mileage, billing information, contact names, or client and company names. You can record this information on the Details tab of the task window, shown in Figure 12-6, on page 385.

? SEE ALSO

For information about the Total Work and Actual Work boxes on the Details tab, see "Setting Up a Task Estimate," on page 385.

On the Details tab, you can record valuable information that can help you perform your ongoing work, evaluate your efforts on this task, and plan for future tasks. For instance, you can type the number of miles you've logged for this task in the Mileage box. In the Billing Information box, enter any particulars about billing for this project. Type the names of the companies for whom you are performing the task in the Companies box.

Canceling a Task

When you want to cancel a task, locate it in the Tasks folder window and select the task. Then use one of the following methods to delete it:

■ Click the Delete button on the Standard toolbar.

■ Press Ctrl+D.

- Choose Delete from the Edit menu.

- Right-click the task item, and then choose Delete from the short-cut menu.

- Open the task, and then click the Delete button on the Standard toolbar.

Outlook moves deleted tasks to the Deleted Items folder.

If you delete a recurring task, you'll see a dialog box asking whether you want to delete just the current task or the entire series. If you're not sure or if you want to postpone the deletion, click the Cancel button.

Viewing Your Tasks

Outlook provides several ways to view your tasks. Initially, Outlook displays the Tasks folder window in Simple List view. To select a different view, point to Current View on the View menu, and then choose a view from the submenu.

All of Outlook's built-in views for the Tasks folder (except the Task Timeline view) are table views. A table view displays task information in columns and rows: each task is displayed on its own row, and the type and number of columns vary with the particular view you select. In two of the table views (By Category and By Person Responsible), the rows of tasks are also grouped. The Task Timeline view shows tasks graphically along a calendar, similar to the Gantt-chart style popular in project management software. *You can find instructions for changing the format of both a table view and a timeline view in "Formatting Views," on page 578.*

SEE ALSO

You can also change the task view using the Organize button on the Standard toolbar. For information on viewing tasks on the TaskPad in the Calendar folder, see "Selecting a TaskPad View," on page 394.

In addition to Outlook's built-in views for tasks, you can set up your own views to look at folder contents in various ways. *For information about views, see Chapter 21, "Setting Up Views." For details about grouping, sorting, and filtering items in a folder, see Chapter 20, "Organizing Folder Items."*

Here is a summary of the task views:

- **Simple List view.** Shows all the tasks in your Tasks folder in a table that has four columns: the Icon column (in which different icons indicate the type of task—one-time, recurring, or assigned), the Complete column (in which a check mark indicates a completed task), the Subject column, and the Due Date column.

III

Scheduling Your
Time and Tasks

- **Detailed List view.** This is similar to the Simple List view in design, but it displays eight columns: Icon, Priority, Attachment, Subject, Status, Due Date, Percent Complete, and Categories.

- **Active Tasks view.** Displays the same eight columns as Detailed List view but filters the tasks to show you only those that are active. Completed tasks are not displayed.

- **Next Seven Days view.** Also displays the same eight columns as Detailed List view but filters your tasks to show only those with due dates occurring within the next seven days.

- **Overdue Tasks view.** Also displays the same eight columns as Detailed List view but filters your tasks to show only those that are overdue. All completed tasks as well as tasks that are not overdue as of today are hidden.

- **By Category view.** Groups tasks by category with the same eight columns as Detailed List view, as shown below. The tasks are then grouped by category, with headers showing each category you've used. If you assign a task to more than one category, Outlook lists that task in each of the assigned category groups.

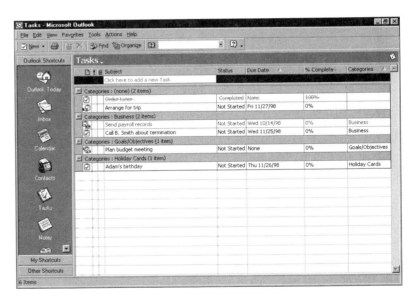

- **Assignment view.** Shows only those tasks that you have assigned to someone else (tasks for which you sent a task request). The assigned tasks appear in a table with seven columns: Icon, Priority, Attachment, Subject, Owner (the person to whom you sent the task request), Due Date, and Status. Tasks are listed if the recipient of your task request has accepted the task or has not yet replied to your request.

■ **By Person Responsible view.** Displays all the tasks in your Tasks folder grouped according to who owns the tasks (you and those to whom you've assigned tasks). If you assigned a task to more than one person, the task appears in the group for each owner. This view shows tasks in a table with eight columns: Icon, Priority, Attachment, Subject, Requested By (for tasks that were assigned to you), Owner, Due Date, and Status. Headers indicating the name of each owner separate the groups.

■ **Completed Tasks view.** Displays only those tasks that you have completed. This view's table contains seven columns: Icon, Priority, Attachment, Subject, Due Date, Date Completed, and Categories.

■ **Task Timeline view.** Arranges all the tasks in your Tasks folder on a timeline that shows the dates in a band across the top of the window. Tasks are listed below the dates. A timeline bar delineates the date range for each task.

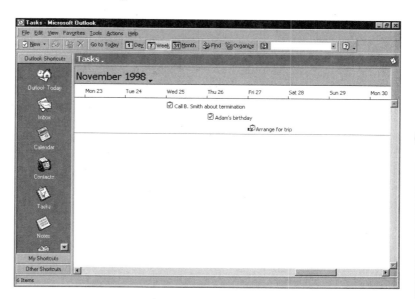

When you are using Task Timeline view, the three time-scale buttons on the Standard toolbar work as follows:

- **Day.** Click this button to see tasks for a single date, listed by the hour.

- **Week.** Click this button to see tasks for a single week, listed by the day.

- **Month.** Click this button to see tasks for a month, listed by the day of the year. When you're viewing tasks for a month, you see only task icons, not the subjects of the tasks. Place the mouse pointer on a task icon or on the bar marking the duration of the task to quickly display the task's subject.

After you use Outlook for a while, you'll have task entries so far away from today's date that you can't easily or quickly scroll to them in Task Timeline view. When you want to jump to a date far away from today's date, you have two choices: click the small arrow beside the month name or point to Go To on the View menu and choose Go To Date.

To jump to a date within the current year, click the small arrow beside the month name in the Tasks folder window, and use the calendar that appears. You can select any date in the currently displayed month or click the Today button. To select a different month, use the left and right arrows on either side of the month name or click the month name in the calendar and select the month from the list that appears.

To jump to any date, you can use the Go To Date command on the View menu in the Tasks folder window. *For detailed information about how to do this, see "Using the Go To Date Command," on page 309.*

Using the TaskPad

The TaskPad provides an informative view of your tasks integrated into the Calendar Window. On the TaskPad in the Calendar folder, you see a summary of your tasks, as shown in the figure on the facing page.

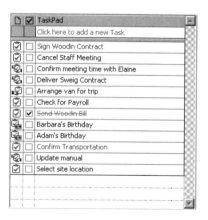

Typically, the TaskPad shows your currently active tasks, including tasks that are overdue (shown in red instead of black) and tasks without a specific due date. When you click the Complete box (the check box in the second column), Outlook draws a line through the task. When you've marked a task as completed and the due date passes, Outlook removes the completed task from the TaskPad.

Instead of switching to the Tasks folder to set up a new task, you can quickly add a new task to the TaskPad. To do so, follow these steps:

1 Click where it says Click Here To Add A New Task.

 TIP

Right-click in this area to open a new task window, assign a task, or change the TaskPad view or settings.

2 Type the subject of the task, and then press Enter.

The new task still has no due date. To set or change the properties of the task, you have to edit it. To edit a task on the TaskPad, double-click the task name, make your changes in the task window, and then click the Save And Close button in the task window. *For more information about task properties, see "Setting Up a Task," on page 368.*

TIP

Right-click a task in the TaskPad for a shortcut menu of options, including Assign Task, Mark Complete, and Send Status Report.

Hiding and Restoring the TaskPad

If you want to use the space the TaskPad occupies for either the Appointments pane or the Date Navigator, you can hide the TaskPad. To do so, perform one of the following actions:

- Drag the left border of the TaskPad to the right.

- Drag the bottom border of the Date Navigator down.

After you've hidden the TaskPad, you might want to see it again. Take the action that fits the circumstances in your Calendar window:

- If the Time Bar and Appointments pane occupy the full window, place the mouse pointer on the right window border, and then drag the border to the left toward the center of the window.

- If the Date Navigator covers the TaskPad, place the mouse pointer on the bottom border of the Date Navigator, just above the status bar, and then drag the border upward toward the middle of the Date Navigator.

Adjusting the TaskPad

The TaskPad typically lists your active tasks. Overdue tasks appear in red. You can change the view of your tasks, and you can also change the formatting and arrangement of TaskPad columns.

Selecting a TaskPad View

For more ways to view tasks, see "Viewing Your Tasks," on page 389.

When you point to TaskPad View on the View menu, you can select a view of the TaskPad from a submenu. Some of the views you can choose are similar to the views you have in the Tasks folder itself, but they have been modified to suit the TaskPad, where you have limited space and where you're more likely to be concerned about current tasks than tasks that are long past or far in the future.

- **All Tasks view.** Lists every task you have set up (for all days), including completed tasks, which have a line drawn through them. If you have many task items, you will have to spend a lot of time scrolling through the list to find what you need. If the TaskPad pane is small and you have many tasks, you may find this view quite useless.

- **Today's Tasks view.** This is the default for the TaskPad. In this view, the TaskPad list contains only the tasks that are active for today (including overdue tasks). For the TaskPad and the Appointments pane, *today* means the date indicated by your computer clock.

- **Active Tasks For Selected Days view.** Shows the tasks just for the days selected in the Appointments pane or in the Date Navigator. If you are planning a business trip, for example, seeing the tasks for the days you'll be away might help you determine what preparations you need to make before you leave.

- **Tasks For Next Seven Days view.** Displays the tasks with a due date that falls during the next seven days, including today. (If you have the Include Tasks With No Due Date check box selected, the list also includes tasks without a due date. To exclude these tasks so that the list contains only tasks with a due date during the next seven days, see the next section, "Including Tasks with No Due Date.") To determine the seven days included in this view, Outlook counts from today's date as indicated by your computer clock.

- **Overdue Tasks view.** Lists tasks that have not been completed by their due date. (When you choose this view, you'll probably want to exclude tasks without a due date. For details, see the next section, "Including Tasks with No Due Date.")

- **Tasks Completed On Selected Days view.** Displays tasks that you completed on the days selected in the Appointments pane or in the Date Navigator.

Including Tasks with No Due Date

In all the available TaskPad views, the list can either display or hide tasks without a due date. Initially, the TaskPad includes these tasks in its list of task items. To exclude tasks without a due date, simply point to TaskPad View on the View menu and click Include Tasks With No Due Date on the submenu to deselect this option. If you decide later that you would like to display tasks without a due date again, repeat this procedure to select the option.

Setting Up Parts of the TaskPad

🕐 **SEE ALSO**

For information about all the commands on this shortcut menu see Chapter 20, "Organizing Folder Items." For information about formatting columns, see "Using the Format Columns Command," on page 548. For information about the Customize Current View command, see "Modifying a View," on page 577.

You can also set up your TaskPad to show additional or different columns or to group tasks. You can sort tasks, and you can format the view you use for the TaskPad. To change TaskPad settings, right-click a TaskPad column label to display this shortcut menu:

Keeping track of your tasks is a critical step in managing your time. Review the status of your tasks, and those you assign to others, frequently to be sure you do not miss important deadlines. When you are part of a workgroup, using Microsoft Outlook to manage tasks can help you accomplish projects of all types and sizes. In the next section of this book, you'll learn how to use Outlook to keep track of your contacts and activities.

PART IV

Keeping Track of People and Things

Organizing Your Contacts

I n Chapter 4, "Using Address Books," you learned how to use the Address Book in Microsoft Outlook to store information about people you want to send e-mail to. When you need to store more detailed information about business associates, colleagues, and friends, use the special features of the Outlook Contacts folder. The Contacts folder can be accessed as a list in the Address Book, and the information can also be linked to all the features of Outlook, such as task assignment, meeting requests, digitally signed and encrypted mail, distribution lists, and electronic faxes. A typical Contacts folder might look something like the one shown in Figure 13-1, on the next page.

FIGURE 13-1.
The Contacts folder
window.

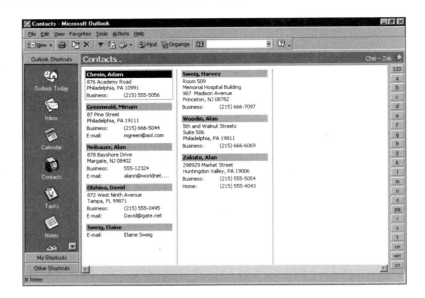

 **TIP**

You can set up the Address Book—which you use for sending messages in Outlook and for addressing letters and envelopes in Microsoft Word—to include the entries in your Contacts folder as one of your address lists. *For details, see the sidebar "Why Isn't the Show This Folder Check Box Available?" on page 538.*

Setting Up Contacts

Display the Contacts folder by clicking Contacts on the Outlook Bar. To add a new entry to your contact list, use one of the following methods:

- Click the New Contact button on the toolbar.

- Choose New Contact from the Actions menu.

- Point to New on the File menu, and then choose Contact from the submenu.

- Press Ctrl+N from the Contacts folder or Ctrl+Shift+C from anywhere in Outlook.

Outlook opens a contact window, in which you enter information for the new contact. Each of the five tabs in this window has a specific function, as explained in the following sections.

When you're finished entering information, click the Save And Close button to close the contact window and add the new entry to your contact list. Notice, however, that the contact window also contains the Save And New button.

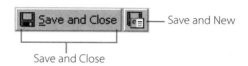

Save and New

Save and Close

 **TIP**

> You don't have to open the Contacts folder to locate contact information. From any Outlook folder, click in the Find A Contact box on the right side of the toolbar, type the contact's name—or a part of it—and press Enter.

When you want to add several new contacts, click the Save And New button, which appears to the right of Save And Close. This button saves the information you've just entered, adds the new entry to your contact list, and displays a new contact window, ready for you to enter information for another new contact.

You can also save an entry and add another contact who works for the same company. Choose New Contact From Same Company from the Actions menu to open a new window with the same company name, business address, business phone, and business fax. Enter the new person's name, title, and other information, and then save it or start a new contact as desired.

To review or change the information for a contact, double-click the contact's listing in the Contacts folder to reopen the window. If you add or change information, however, you must click Save And Close or Save And New again.

 If you create a contact with the same name or e-mail address as an existing one, Outlook 2000 displays the Duplicate Contact Detected dialog box, shown on the following page.

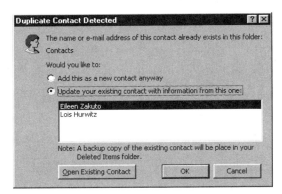

This dialog box lists the current contacts that contain matching items. You can choose to add the contact anyway or to update an existing entry with the new information you've just entered. Updating means merging the new information into the existing contact. Fields without new information retain the information from the old entry. After updating, the original contact is moved to the Deleted Items folder.

Now let's look at the information you can enter on the five tabs of the contact window.

General Tab

On the General tab of the contact window, shown in Figure 13-2, you enter the name, address, phone numbers, and other basic information for the contact.

FIGURE 13-2.
The General tab of the contact window.

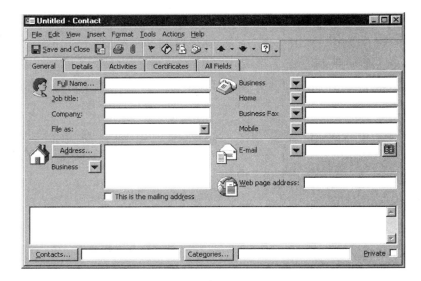

IV

Keeping Track of
People and Things

⭐ **TIP**

> If you are running Windows at a low resolution, such as 640x480, be sure to maximize the contact window when you use the General or Detail tabs. You won't see any scroll bars, but if the window isn't maximized or sized large enough, you won't see the full contents of some of the boxes.

Full Name

Type the contact's full name in this box—first, middle, and last, along with a title, such as Ms., or a suffix, such as Jr. Outlook recognizes the distinct parts of the name and saves the information appropriately. Notice that the name you enter in the Full Name box appears by default in the File As box as well.

If you enter only part of a name (for example, *Billy*) or if you manage to confuse Outlook with an unusual mix of names and punctuation (for example, *Fred, Smith, Mr., Jr.*) and then move elsewhere on the form, Outlook displays the Check Full Name dialog box with its best guess of how to record the name. Use this dialog box to enter the other parts of the contact's name or to reassign the parts of the name to the correct fields—*Title, First, Middle, Last,* and *Suffix*—so that the name will be handled correctly in the future. You can display this dialog box any time to help you enter a name by clicking the Full Name button on the General tab.

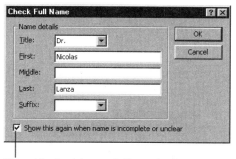

Clear this check box only if you don't
want Outlook to display this dialog box
when you enter an incomplete name.

File As

In the File As box, you can select or type the name that should appear as the title of the contact card. Outlook uses the entry in this box to sort the cards in the Contacts folder. *See "Sorting Contacts," on page 428.*

> ### Adding a New Contact from a Different Folder
>
> If you are working in an Outlook folder other than the Contacts folder, you can add a new contact using one of the following methods:
>
> - Click the down arrow beside the New button on the Standard toolbar, and then choose Contact from the menu.
> - Point to New on the File menu, and choose Contact from the submenu.
> - Press Ctrl+Shift+C.

Assuming that you have entered the contact's name and company name, clicking the down arrow next to the File As box displays the information in all of these combinations:

> Last name, First name
>
> First name Last name
>
> Company name
>
> Last name, First name (Company name)
>
> Company name (Last name, First name)

If you don't fill in a company name, for example, the list includes only the first two options. You can also type in a different title for the contact card if none of these selections is quite right, or if you want to control how the name is sorted in the contact list.

Address

You can enter three different addresses for each contact—Business, Home, and Other. Click the down arrow below the Address button, select the type of address you want to enter, and then type the address in the Address box. Press the Enter key at the end of each line. To enter another address for this contact, use the down arrow to select a different address type, and then type the address in the now-blank Address box.

You have to designate one of the addresses as the contact's mailing address. Choose the address from the list to display it, and then select the This Is The Mailing Address check box. (If you've entered only one address for a contact, Outlook automatically considers it the mailing address.)

As with the parts of a name, Outlook recognizes the individual parts of the address—street, city, and so on. If you enter only part of an address or an address Outlook doesn't understand, when you move elsewhere in the dialog box Outlook displays the Check Address dialog box, which you can use to complete or correct the address entry. You can also open this dialog box by clicking the Address button. Do this to verify that Outlook has recognized the address correctly, to enter the contact's address part by part, or to add one or two elements to the address, such as just the country.

Phone

You can record up to four phone numbers for any one contact. Outlook includes four preset labels (Business, Home, Business Fax, and Mobile), but if any of these don't suit your needs, click the down arrow next to the phone number and select a different description from the list that appears. The phone description list provides nineteen possibilities, such as Car, Callback, ISDN, Home Fax, Assistant, and Radio. Once you select a label, it is displayed next to that phone number entry.

Outlook is pretty good at recognizing a number's area code and phone number no matter how you enter it. When you move out of the phone field, Outlook formats the number as it thinks correct. When entering phone numbers for international calls, however, it's a good idea to type a plus sign before the country code part of the number and to use spaces or punctuation as shown here: +*country code (area code) local number*—for example, +01 (201) 555-1212.

If you don't enter a complete telephone number or one that Outlook understands, when you move elsewhere in the dialog box, Outlook will display the Check Phone Number dialog box. Choose the country or region, if needed to enter the proper country code, and then complete the area code and number as necessary. If you want to check the number yourself or enter the number directly in the Check Phone Number dialog box, just double-click the phone number box and the dialog box opens.

Mapping a Contact's Address

While Outlook makes it easy to communicate with contacts over your server and the Internet, you might still have to get out of the office and visit a contact from time to time. When you do have to make a site visit to a new contact, it would certainly help if you had a map of his or her location. That's easy with Outlook.

To display and print a map of an address, open the contact item, and then choose Display Map Of Address from the Actions menu. You can also click the Display Map Of Address button (the yellow road sign) on the Standard toolbar.

Outlook launches your Web browser, connects to the Microsoft Expedia Maps service, and maps the address, as shown in Figure 13-3. Expedia Maps are part of a more comprehensive travel service that can even provide point-to-point driving instructions and travel agency services, as well as links to local weather, news, events, restaurants, and places to visit. For more information on using Expedia, refer to the Expedia home page.

NOTE

Outlook does not recognize letters in a phone number. You can, however, include notes after the phone number—for example, an extension for the contact.

E-mail

You can enter up to three e-mail addresses for your contact. If you want to enter only one e-mail address, simply type it in the empty box. To enter additional e-mail addresses, click the down arrow to select a designation for the address (E-mail 2, E-mail 3), and then type the e-mail address.

If you want to retrieve an e-mail address from one of your address lists, click the Address Book button to the right of the box. Select the address list from the Show Names list (you can't use the Outlook Address Book as a source for an e-mail address), select the contact's name, and then click OK.

When you move elsewhere in the window, Outlook underlines the e-mail address, indicating it is a clickable object.

Web Page Address

In this box, type the URL for a contact's site on the World Wide Web. Outlook uses this information when you want to visit the Web page. *See "Connecting to a Contact's Web Page," on page 421.*

FIGURE 13-3.
Retrieving a map of
a contact's location.

Choose the
correct address,
if more than
one is shown.

Click here to
look up another
address.

Click a location
on the map to
center it in
the window.

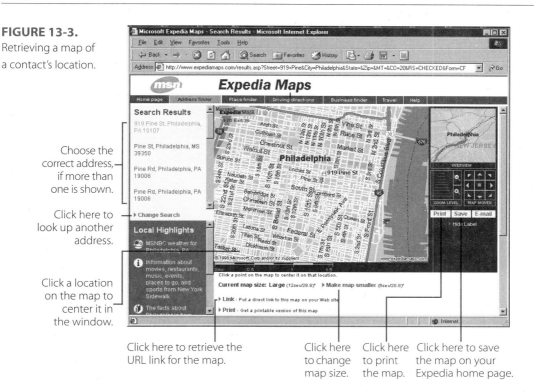

Click here to retrieve the
URL link for the map.

Click here
to change
map size.

Click here
to print
the map.

Click here to save
the map on your
Expedia home page.

Notes

In the large unlabeled box near the bottom of the contact window, you
can type any text, comments, or notes about the contact. Also, if you
have entered dates for the contact's birthday and anniversary on the
Details tab of the contact window (see "Details Tab," on page 409),
you'll see small calendar icons here representing the dates (you must
click Save And Close and then reopen the contact window for the icons
to appear). When you double-click one of these icons, Outlook opens
the Recurring Event window, where you can designate the birthday or
anniversary as an event on your calendar. Click the Save And Close
button in that window to add the event to your Outlook calendar.
(Later, when you set up a birthday party or an anniversary dinner, you
can change the calendar item to a specific appointment.

Contacts

You can link a contact with one or more other contacts in the folder,
just as you can link an appointment, meeting, or task to a contact. Use
this feature to associate contacts who work for the same company or

who are involved in the same project. Click the Contacts button, and then choose the contacts from the dialog box that appears.

Categories

You can assign a contact to any number of categories. Make up your own categories by typing them in the box, or click the Categories button to select from Outlook's list of categories. You can have Outlook display your contact list grouped according to the categories you've specified. *For details, see "By Category View," on page 427.*

Private

When you give others permission to view your Contacts folder, or when you assign a delegate who can perform actions on your behalf that involve using your Contacts folder, you might prefer that these people not have access to all your contact information. If you want to prevent a contact listing from being visible to others, select the Private option. *For more information about assigning delegates, see "Using the Delegates Tab," on page 90.*

Sending Meeting and Task Requests to Contacts over the Internet

You don't have to do anything special to send meeting and task requests to contacts over your Microsoft Exchange Server. When you click Send in the item window, the request is transmitted and can be picked up by the recipient to be accepted or declined.

To send meeting requests, task requests, and voting buttons to a contact over the Internet, you must send the mail in Rich Text Format. To set up this capability for one or more of the contacts in your Contacts folder, follow these steps:

1 Open or create the contact entry.

2 Type the recipient's e-mail address in the E-mail box on the General tab, or retrieve it by clicking the Address Book button to the right of the box.

3 Press the Tab key or click elsewhere in the window to have Outlook read and underline the e-mail address you've entered.

4 Double-click the e-mail address to open the contact's Properties dialog box.

5 In the E-mail Properties dialog box, select the check box labeled Always Send To This Recipient In Microsoft Outlook Rich-Text Format.

6 Click OK.

The recipient must receive the mail in Outlook in order for meeting requests, task requests, and voting buttons to work.

Details Tab

To add more information about the contact, fill out the Details tab of the Contact dialog box, shown in Figure 13-4.

For birthday and anniversary information, you can either type a date in the appropriate box or click the down arrow to display a calendar from which you can select a date. Birthdays and anniversaries are then inserted as annual recurring items in your calendar, and shortcuts to the calendar appear as icons in the notes section of the General tab (save, close, and reopen the contact window to update the notes box).

In the Online NetMeeting Settings section, enter the directory server where you will log on to conduct meetings and the contact's e-mail address or online name. Click Call Now to place an Internet call to the contact using NetMeeting.

Activities Tab

On the Activities tab of the contact window, you can view all of the items that you linked with this contact and all journal entries for the activities you perform with or for the contact. You'll see, for example, all e-mail messages you sent to or received from this contact, even messages still in your Outbox and ones you deleted that are still in the Deleted Items folder. You'll also see all meetings to which the contact was invited and all tasks assigned to the contact.

FIGURE 13-4.
The Details tab of the
contact window.

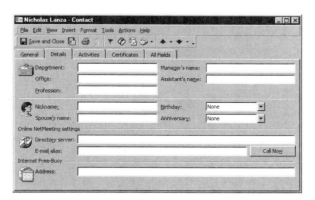

SEE ALSO

For information about recording activities for contacts, see "Setting Journal Options," on page 79. For information about Outlook's journal feature, see Chapter 14, "Keeping a Journal."

When you click the Activities tab, Outlook takes a moment to scan all its folders looking for items linked to that contact, and then lists them as shown in Figure 13-5. You can double-click an item in the list to open it.

Use the Show list to choose what items are displayed. The options are All Items, Contacts, E-mail, Journal, Notes, and Upcoming Tasks/Appointments.

Certificates Tab

On the Certificates tab of the contact window, you can view the digital IDs that you have on record for sending encrypted mail to the contact. You can display properties for the ID and you can choose a default certificate to use.

All Fields Tab

The General tab and the Details tab provide a number of fields that you can use to record information about a contact. However, Outlook includes many other fields related to contacts that you might find useful. You'll find these fields on the All Fields tab in the contact window, shown in Figure 13-6. You can use these fields to set up each contact entry to fit the contact and the type of information you want to maintain about the contact.

From the Select From list choose All Contact Fields to see every field of information that you can add for a contact, or choose another type of

FIGURE 13-5.
The Activities tab of the contact window.

Select the types of activities you want to see.

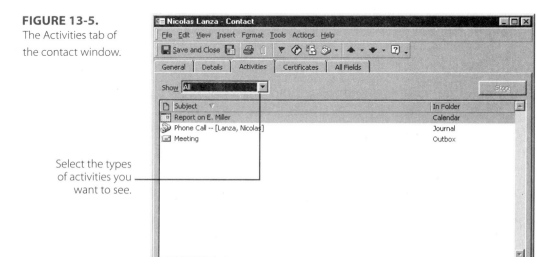

FIGURE 13-6.
The All Fields tab of the contact window.

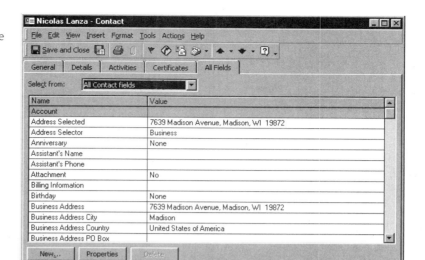

field to display a subset of fields. You can then add or change information for individual fields, even those not shown on other tabs.

If you find that among all the contact fields provided by Outlook, you still can't find the field you need, you can use the New button on the All

---

Linking Objects to Contacts

You know that you can associate an appointment, meeting, and task to a contact by clicking the Contacts button in the item's window. The item will then be listed on the contact's Activities tab.

You can also associate any document on your disk or any existing Outlook item with a contact without opening it. This is especially useful when you want to associate an e-mail message with a contact who was not the sender or a recipient of the message.

To associate an existing Outlook item with a contact, select or open the contact's listing, point to Link on the Action menu, and choose Items. In the dialog box that appears, choose the Outlook folder containing the item and then the item itself, and then click OK. The item is added to the contact's Activities tab.

To associate a non-Outlook file with a contact, point to Link on the Action menu and choose File. In the Choose A File dialog box, choose the file and then click OK. A journal entry window appears, with the file attached to it. You can add more information if you want. Then click Save And Close. The item is added to the contact's Activities tab list as a journal item.

Double-click any of the items in the list to open the corresponding Outlook item or file.

Creating a Contacts Distribution List

In Chapter 4, "Using Address Books," you learned how to create a distribution list to store the names of a related group of contacts as one entry. When you want to send an e-mail message to all members of the group, you select the group name from the Contacts list in the Address Book.

You can also create and manage a distribution list from within the Contacts folder. To create a list, choose New Distribution List from the Actions menu.

When the Distribution List dialog box opens, create the list as you learned in Chapter 4. When done, click the Save And Close button, and the item appears in the Contacts list with only the name of the group displayed, as shown here:

To add or delete members from a list, double-click it in the Contacts folder to reopen the Distribution List dialog box and make your changes.

Fields tab to create your own field. *For information about using custom fields in Outlook, see "Working with Custom Fields," on page 563.*

Removing a Contact

To remove a contact from your list, select the contact and click the Delete button on the Standard toolbar or choose Delete from the Edit menu. Outlook immediately moves the deleted contact entry to the Deleted Items folder.

Working with Your Contacts Folder

The Contacts folder is more than a convenient place to keep a record of names and addresses. Outlook uses the information in the contact entries to help you carry out activities with your contacts, such as the following:

- Dialing a contact's telephone number
- Sending an e-mail message to a contact
- Sending a printed letter to a contact
- Connecting to a contact's World Wide Web page
- Setting up a meeting with a contact

- Setting up a task that you need to perform for a contact

- Using Mail Merge to merge an e-mail, letter, or fax with more than one contact

From the Contacts folder, you can also assign a contact to a category with the Using Categories option in the Organize pane. Click the Organize button on the Standard toolbar in the Contacts folder window, and then choose Using Categories if it isn't already selected. Select the contact in the bottom pane, choose a category from the top list, click Add or type a new category in the Create A New Category box, and then click Create.

Phoning a Contact

If you have a modem set up, you can use your computer to dial any of the telephone numbers listed in any of Outlook's folders. The Contacts folder offers an especially rich variety of ways to dial phone numbers from Outlook.

To start an Internet call, select or open the contact item in the Contacts folder, and then choose Call Using NetMeeting from the Actions menu. *See Chapter 11, "Scheduling Meetings," for more information on NetMeeting.*

When you use Outlook to make a phone call, you must do so from the New Call dialog box, whether or not you already have a phone number listed for the contact. To open this dialog box, take one of the following actions:

- Click the Dial button (the telephone icon) on the Standard toolbar.

- Right-click the contact's name in the Contacts folder, and choose Call Contact from the shortcut menu.

- In the Contacts folder, or from an individual's open contact window, point to Call Contact on the Actions menu, and then choose New Call from the submenu.

- If the currently selected contact is the one you want to call, point to Call Contact on the Actions menu, and then click the phone number, which appears on the submenu. Alternatively, click the small down arrow on the AutoDialer button and select the number from the list.

- In any Outlook folder, press Ctrl+Shift+D.

After you take any of these actions, Outlook opens the New Call dialog box, shown in Figure 13-7. If the action you took involved a specific phone number—for example, you right-clicked a contact's card containing a phone number before you chose Auto-Dialer or you selected a number from the Call Contact submenu of the Actions menu—the New Call dialog box displays the phone number and the contact's name. Otherwise, the dialog box is empty, allowing you to type in the contact's name and the telephone number that you want Outlook to dial. This is handy if you don't yet have an entry recorded in your address books or Contacts folder for the person you want to call.

To place a telephone call from the New Call dialog box, follow these steps:

1 If the name of the person you want to call doesn't already appear in the Contact box, you can type it there. (Note, however, that including the name is optional.)

2 If the Number box is empty, type the phone number. If the box already contains a phone number but the contact has several numbers recorded in your address books or Contacts folder, click the down arrow next to the Number box and select the appropriate phone number.

3 To record a journal entry for the call, select the check box labeled Create New Journal Entry When Starting New Call. *(See "Recording a Call in a Journal Entry" on page 417.)*

4 Click the Start Call button to have Outlook dial the number.

5 Pick up your telephone receiver.

6 When you've finished your conversation, or if the line is busy or not answered, click the End Call button in the New Call dialog box, and then click the Close button.

FIGURE 13-7.
The New Call
dialog box.

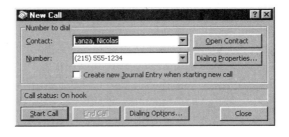

TIP

If the name (or part of a name) that you type in the Contact box of the New Call dialog box is already recorded in one of your address books or in your Contacts folder, Outlook completes the name and fills in the contact's first phone number for you when you move the insertion point to the Number box. Click the down arrow next to the Number list to choose an alternate phone number.

? SEE ALSO

For information about setting up dialing properties, see "Setting Dialing Options," on page 183, and "Setting Up Calling Card Dialing," on page 297.

Notice the Open Contact button in the New Call dialog box. When this button is available, you can click it to review or change contact information in the contact window. You can also click the Dialing Properties button to display the My Locations tab of the Dialing Properties dialog box and review or change information about the location you're dialing from, about how you dial from this location, or about your calling card.

Speed Dialing

Many modern telephones provide a memory system that allows you to store several telephone numbers that you call frequently. You can assign each number to a specific button and then call the number simply by pressing the button. In Outlook, you can store a great many frequently called numbers by using the Speed Dial feature.

To set up or change speed dial entries, you need to open the Dialing Options dialog box shown in Figure 13-8. The most common way to find this dialog box is to open the New Call dialog box, as explained in the preceding section, and click the Dialing Options button.

FIGURE 13-8.
The Dialing Options dialog box.

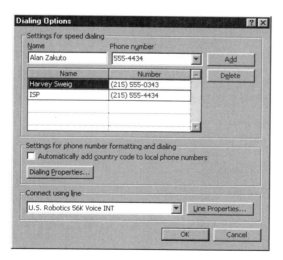

To set up or change a speed dial entry, take these steps in the Dialing Options dialog box:

1 Type the contact's name or another designation for the phone number, and press the Tab key.

2 If the correct phone number doesn't automatically appear, type or select it.

3 Click Add.

4 Repeat steps 1 to 3 for each contact you want to register a speed dial number for.

5 Click OK when you're finished.

In step 1 above, if you type a name or part of a name that Outlook recognizes from one of your address books or your Contacts folder, Outlook automatically displays the corresponding phone number for you in step 2. You can, of course, modify the results of the automatic completion. If the name you type has more than one telephone number (for example, a voice number or two and a fax number), you can select from the Number list the one you want to set up for speed dialing. If you want to set up more than one number for a person, make several speed dialing entries with slightly different contact names, such as *Bob's Home* and *Bob's Office*.

At any time, you can return to the Dialing Options dialog box to change a speed dial name or number. To change the name or number, simply click it, edit the entry, and click OK.

When you want to speed dial a number, use either of these techniques:

■ Click the small arrow next to the AutoDialer button on the Standard toolbar, point to Speed Dial, and click the number.

■ Choose Call Contact from the Actions menu, point to Speed Dial, and click the number to call.

Redialing

Outlook keeps a list of recent phone numbers you've dialed from within Outlook. When you want to redial a number you've called recently, take these steps:

1 Choose Call Contact from the Actions menu, or click the down arrow next to the AutoDialer button on the Standard toolbar.

2 Point to Redial and then click the number you want to redial on the submenu.

3 When the New Call dialog box appears, click the Start Call button or press Enter.

Recording a Call in a Journal Entry

Although Outlook can keep an automatic record of some of your activities with your contacts, it does not include an option for automatically keeping track of phone calls. The New Call dialog box, however, does give you an option for recording telephone calls and for keeping notes of your conversation during the call.

In the New Call dialog box (see Figure 13-7, on page 414), select the check box labeled Create New Journal Entry When Starting New Call. Then, when you click the Start Call button, a journal entry window appears, as shown below. The contact's name appears in the Contacts box, and the call is added to the contact's Activity tab listing.

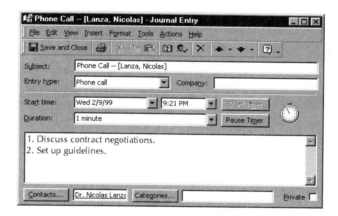

As Outlook dials the number, the window remains on your screen, and the timer immediately begins to time the call. If you don't want to time the call, click the Pause Timer button to stop the timing. (To resume timing, click Start Timer.) During the call, you can type notes, reminders, comments, and so on in the text area at the bottom of the dialog box. At the end of the call, click the Save And Close button to save the record of the call in your Journal folder.

Sending an E-mail Message to a Contact

Here's an easy way to quickly set up and send a message to a contact. Start by using either of the techniques on the following page.

■ Right-click the contact's name in the Contacts folder, and choose New Message To Contact from the shortcut menu.

■ Click the contact's entry in your Contacts folder, or open the item, and choose New Message To Contact from the Actions menu.

NOTE

The contact item must contain a valid e-mail address.

Each of these techniques opens a new message window and addresses the message to your contact. Complete the message and send it as you learned in Chapter 5, "Sending and Receiving Messages."

TIP

Here's an even easier way to send a message to a contact. Drag the contact's listing in the Contacts folder and drop it on the Inbox icon on the Outlook Bar, compose the message in the window that appears, and then click Send.

Sending a Letter to a Contact

Occasionally, you might need to print out a letter to send to a contact by snail mail (through the postal service), overnight mail, or fax. You can easily set up and print a letter from an entry in your Contacts folder.

NOTE

To create a letter from your Contacts folder, you must have Microsoft Word 97 or later installed on your computer.

When you select the contact's entry in your Contacts folder, and choose New Letter To Contact from the Actions menu, Outlook calls on Microsoft Word. Word starts up, and Word's Letter Wizard opens. You can then work through the Letter Wizard to create the letter, and you can print both the letter and an envelope in Word. When you've finished, exit Word if you don't need it for other purposes.

TIP

If you have a fax service installed in your profile, you can send a fax to the contact by choosing New Fax Message from the Actions menu.

Using Mail Merge with Contacts

If you have an e-mail message, letter, or fax you want to send to more than one contact, you could send it using a distribution list. The message you send, however, will be the same for each contact. When you want to personalize each copy of the message, perform a mail merge.

This feature lets you create a merge document in Microsoft Word using the address information from contacts that you select in the Contacts folder. You can also use the mail merge feature to address envelopes or print labels.

When you want to send a personalized message to a number of contacts, follow these steps:

1 Open the Contacts folder.

2 Select the contacts you want to send the message to. To select more than one contact entry, hold down the Ctrl key as you click each entry in the Contacts folder. To select several consecutive entries, click the first entry, and then hold down the Shift key while you click the last one. To select all the contacts, choose Select All from the Edit menu or press Ctrl+A. (If you select all the contacts, you can then hold down the Ctrl key and deselect those you don't want to include.) You can also create a custom view or filter that selects just those contacts. *You'll learn about views and filters in Chapter 21, "Setting Up Views."*

3 Choose Mail Merge from the Tools menu to display the Mail Merge Contacts dialog box, shown in Figure 13-9, on the following page.

4 In the Contacts section, select All Contacts In Current View or Only Selected Contacts (if you've manually selected several contacts).

5 Select the New Document option in the Document File section to create a new Word merge document, or select the Existing Document option to use an existing merge document. If you select the Existing Document option, click Browse and choose the document in the dialog box that appears.

6 From the Document Type list in the Merge Options section, choose the type of Microsoft Word document to create:

- **Form letters.** Create a separate document for each contact.

- **Mailing labels.** Make labels for each contact.

- **Envelopes.** Print envelopes for each contact.

- **Catalog.** Place all of the information in one document.

7 From the Merge To list, choose the destination for the documents.

- **New Document.** Create new documents in Word.

FIGURE 13-9.

The Mail Merge
Contacts dialog box.

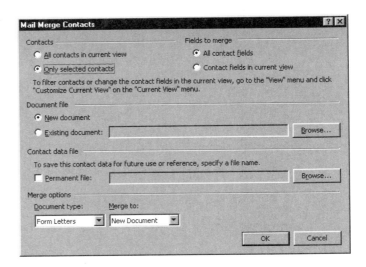

- **Printer.** Print individual documents in Word.

- **E-mail.** Send each document via the Internet as an e-mail message.

- **Fax.** Send each document via your fax modem to the recipients' fax numbers.

8 In the Fields To Merge area, make all the Contacts fields available to the mail merge or only the fields in the current Contacts folder view.
If you want to use this set of contacts again, select the Permanent File check box in the Contact Data File section, and then provide a filename.

9 Click OK. Outlook opens Microsoft Word and starts a blank mail merge document or opens the existing one you chose.

10 Create or edit the document in Word, using Word's Insert Merge Field button to insert codes where you want contact information to appear. Notice that when you click the Insert Merge Field button, the Outlook fields you included are displayed to make it easy for you to pick each type of information you want to use in your letters. A typical merge document might appear as shown in Figure 13-10.

11 When you have completed the document, click the Start Mail Merge button on Word's Mail Merge toolbar and then click the Merge button in the Merge dialog box that appears.

FIGURE 13-10.

A merge document in Word.

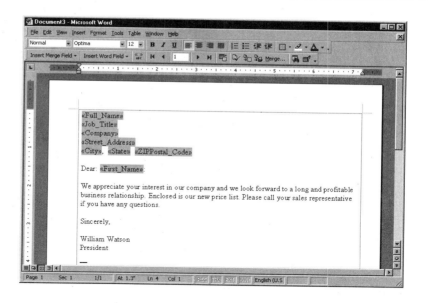

Connecting to a Contact's Web Page

If you entered a contact's World Wide Web page address (URL) in the contact window, you can use that URL to quickly connect to the contact's Web page. To do so, switch to your Contacts folder, and then use one of the following methods:

- Open the contact's entry and choose Explore Web Page from the Actions menu.

- Open the contact's entry and press Ctrl+Shift+X.

Setting Up an Appointment or Meeting with a Contact

When you need to set up an appointment or meeting with a contact, you can do so from the contact's entry in your Contacts folder. Simply open your Contacts folder, select the contact or open it, and take one of the following actions:

- Drag the contact's listing from the Contacts folder and drop it on the Calendar folder icon on the Outlook Bar to create a meeting. (If you prefer to make an appointment, after the meeting window opens, click the Cancel Invitation button, and the meeting will be converted to an appointment, with the selected contact linked in the Contacts text box at the bottom of the appointment window.)

- Choose New Meeting Request To Contact from the Actions menu.

- Choose New Appointment With Contact to create an appointment linked to the contact.

Outlook opens the appointment or meeting window for you to complete the details.

Assigning a Task to a Contact

When you have a task you want to have one of your contacts perform, you can use the contact's entry in your Contacts folder as the starting point for setting up the task. Use either of these methods:

- Drag the contact's listing in the Contacts folder to the Task folder on the Outlook Bar.

- Select or open the contact's listing, and then choose New Task For Contact from the Actions menu.

Outlook opens a task window, like the one shown here:

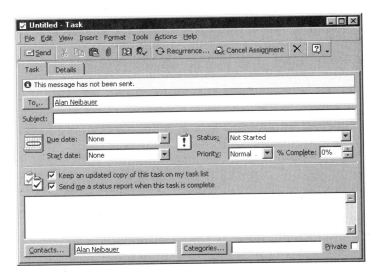

? SEE ALSO

For complete information about setting up tasks and working with them, see Chapter 12, "Managing Your Tasks."

Outlook fills in the To box on the Task tab with the contact's e-mail address and fills in the Contacts box with the contact's name. You can fill in the subject of the task and as much other information as you need, on both the Task and Details tabs. When you've finished, click the Send button to send the task request to the contact.

Sending Contact Information to Others

People change positions—as a result of promotions, retirements, resignations, or lateral moves. When you change your position within your organization, you might need to turn over at least some of your contacts to your replacement. It's easy to do this in Outlook: you simply forward the contacts.

You can forward the contact information as either an Outlook contact window so it contains the same information as it has in your Contacts folder, or as a *vCard*. The vCard standard does not contain some Outlook information, such as birthday and anniversary dates, and does not contain an Activities tab, but it is compatible with the many programs that observe the vCard standard, such as Lotus Organizer, Netscape Communicator, and Sidekick 98.

To send contact information to someone else, take these steps:

1 Open the Contacts folder, and select or open the contact entry you want to send. To select more than one contact entry, hold down the Ctrl key as you click each entry in the Contacts folder. To select several consecutive entries, click the first entry, and then hold down the Shift key while you click the last one. To select all the contacts, choose Select All from the Edit menu or press Ctrl+A. (If you select all the contacts, you can then hold down the Ctrl key and deselect those you don't want to include.)

2 Choose Forward or Forward As vCard from the Actions menu. Outlook opens a message window that contains an icon representing each contact. The shape of the icon depends on the format you've chosen:

Alan Neibauer — Outlook contact item

Alan Neibauer.vcf — vCard

3 Fill in the To box.

4 Type any message you want to send with the contact information.

5 Click Send.

When the recipient receives the message with the contact icons, he or she can select the contact icon in the message area and drag it to the Contacts folder icon on the Outlook Bar to add the contact information to the contact list.

The recipient can also double-click the icon to open either an Outlook contact window or the vCard.

Flagging Contacts for Follow Up

Sometimes you need to remember to perform some action regarding a contact. You might want to remind yourself to make a call, set up a meeting, send a letter or e-mail message, or perform some other follow-up. Rather than write the reminder down on a scrap of paper, you can add a follow-up flag directly to the contact's item.

Use these steps to set a follow-up flag:

1 Select the contact in the Contacts folder or open it.

2 Choose Flag For Follow Up from the Actions menu, click the red Flag For Follow Up button on the Standard toolbar, or press Ctrl+Shift+G. The Flag For Follow Up dialog box appears as shown here:

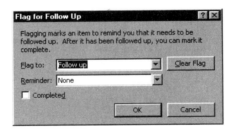

3 Choose the action you want to perform from the Flag To list. Choices include Follow-Up, Call, Arrangé Meeting, Send E-mail, and Send Letter.

4 Select a date for the reminder from the Reminder list box.

5 Click OK.

A note about the follow-up flag appears with the contact's listing in the Contacts folder, as shown here, and a reminder will appear if you have set one.

If you open the contact, you'll also see a colored banner that runs across the top of the General tab and lists the flag information. To remove the flag, redisplay the Flag For Follow Up dialog box, and click Clear Flag. To mark the follow-up as completed, redisplay the Flag For Follow Up dialog box and turn on the Completed option. This leaves the flag on the contact item and displays the date and time the follow-up was completed. To remove the flag completely, right-click the contact and choose Clear Flag from the menu that appears.

Viewing Your Contacts

Outlook gives you seven standard ways of viewing your contacts. To switch from one view to another, point to Current View on the View menu, and then choose the view you want from the submenu.

TIP

You can quickly change views with the Using Views option in the Organize pane. Click the Organize button on the Standard toolbar in the Contacts folder window, choose Using Views, and select a view from the list that appears.

Using Card Views

SEE ALSO

You can set up custom views for looking at folder contents; for information, see Chapter 21, "Setting Up Views." You can also group, sort, filter, and add custom fields to folder items; for details, see Chapter 20, "Organizing Folder Items."

In two views of the Contacts folder—Address Cards view and Detailed Address Cards view—Outlook displays the contact information in a "card" format, almost as if you were looking at rotary file cards laid out on a desk.

- **Address Cards view.** Displays your contacts as small cards that contain some of the basic information from the General tab of the contact window, such as the contact's name, address, phone numbers, and e-mail address. Figure 13-1, on page 400, shows the Address Card view.

- **Detailed Address Cards view.** Shows larger cards containing more fields of data. You'll see fewer of them on the screen than you would in Address Cards view, as shown in Figure 13-11, on the following page.

In both views the cards are arranged alphabetically by the first word in the card title. You can move to a specific alphabetical section of your contact list by clicking the corresponding alphabetical tab along the right side of the folder window, just as you might use tabs to thumb to various sections of a paper address book.

FIGURE 13-11.
Detailed Address
Card view.

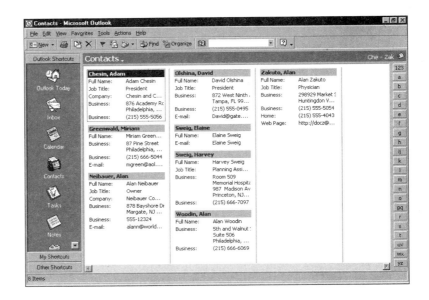

If some items on a contact card are incompletely displayed and end with an ellipsis (…), you can widen the column of cards to see the complete information. When you place the mouse pointer on the vertical line dividing the columns of cards, the pointer becomes a two-headed arrow. Drag the line to widen the card until you can see all the information you need.

If you left a box blank on the General tab of the contact window when you entered information about the contact, Address Cards view and Detailed Address Cards view do not initially display that field. If you want to see all the fields that a contact card can display in these two views, select the Show Empty Fields check box in the Format Card View dialog box. *For details, see "Card Views," on page 585.*

Using Table Views

SEE ALSO

You can change the format of a view. For details about formatting table views, see "Formatting Views," on page 578.

The two card views of the Contacts folder display your contact list intuitively and attractively, but the cards take up a lot of space in the window. To see more contacts at one time, and to sort the list in different ways, switch to one of these table views: Phone List, By Category, By Company, By Location, or By Follow Up Flag.

These views display your contact information in a table arrangement with rows and columns, such as the Phone List view shown in Figure 13-12. The names are listed down the left side of the screen, and various pieces of information (depending on the view) appear in columns to the right. You'll usually need to scroll horizontally to see all the columns. The table views also enable you to enter a new contact directly in the Contacts folder without opening a new contact window. Click the top line of the table just under the column headings and enter new contact information.

The By Category, By Company, By Location, or By Follow Up Flag views group contacts accordingly. To group contacts by their company, for example, choose the By Company View. You can collapse and expand the groups as you learned to do for calendar items. *See "Viewing the Calendar in Other Ways," on page 332.*

Here's a summary of the table views.

- **Phone List view.** Includes columns with the Full Name, Company, File As (the title of a contact card), and numerous telephone and fax numbers. You'll also find a Categories column listing the categories to which you've assigned the contact and a Journal column, where a check mark indicates that you've chosen to record interactions with this contact in your Journal folder.

- **By Category view.** Groups contacts by category. If you assign a contact to more than one category, Outlook lists that contact in each category.

- **By Company view.** Lists contacts grouped by company name. This way, you can quickly find the contact you need for a particular company. Contacts without a company affiliation are listed first.

FIGURE 13-12.
Phone List view of the Contacts folder.

Click here
to add a
new contact.

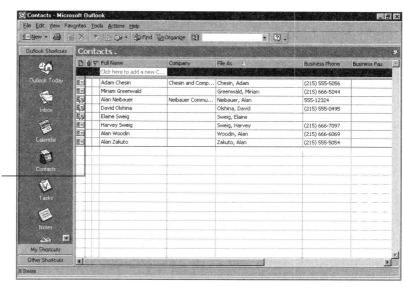

■ **By Location view.** Groups by country. Those with no country specified are listed first.

■ **By Follow Up Flag view.** Organizes contacts by flags, so items that are flagged are easy to identify. They are in three groups: Normal (no flag), Completed (gray flag), and Flagged (red flag). The red flag indicates that the activity is not marked as completed.

Understanding Icons in Contacts Folder Views

In the various table views of your Contacts folder, you'll see several icons that act as column headings or provide information about a contact. Use this graphic as a guide to the meaning of each:

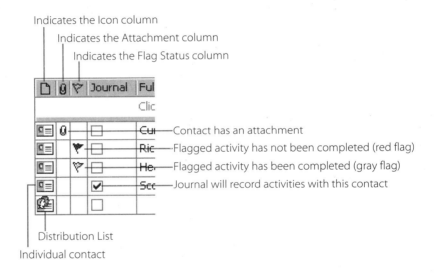

Indicates the Icon column
Indicates the Attachment column
Indicates the Flag Status column

Contact has an attachment
Flagged activity has not been completed (red flag)
Flagged activity has been completed (gray flag)
Journal will record activities with this contact

Distribution List
Individual contact

 NOTE

To change the status of a flag in a table view, click the flag box for the contact you want to change and choose Normal, Completed, or Flagged from the menu that appears. Click outside the flag box to have Outlook update the sort order.

Sorting Contacts

 SEE ALSO

For details about sorting in table views, see "Sorting," on page 555.

By default, Outlook sorts contacts alphabetically by the File As entry. In table views, you can sort the list by clicking a column heading. In the card views, you can change the way a particular contact appears by setting the File As option in the contact window. To do so, open each contact and select or type a new entry in the File As text box. To change the default order for all contacts, choose Options from the Tools menu, and click Contact Options on the Preference tab to see the dialog box shown here. Choose the default order for displaying names in the Full Name field and the File As field. This will only affect new names you add after changing the setting.

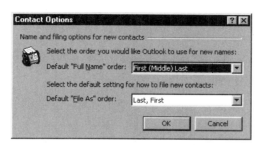

As you learned in this chapter, the Contacts folder is much more than a place to store e-mail addresses and phone numbers. Contacts can be associated with other Outlook items, such as appointments, they can be assigned tasks, and they can be used as the data source for a mail merge in Microsoft Word. If you use the Contacts folder to store information about clients, each Outlook activity for the client can be logged into the journal and displayed in the Contact window activities page to aid in preparing reports and invoices. In the next chapter, you'll learn more about the Journal folder and keeping track of your Outlook and Microsoft Office activities.

Keeping a Journal

Remembering everything you've done during a day can be difficult. You probably remember the big events pretty easily, but can you honestly remember every e-mail message you sent, every appointment you made, every person you contacted? Would you remember them tomorrow? Next week? Next month?

You could scan through your Microsoft Outlook folders to review your activities. But that means going through the Sent Messages folder to see your e-mail messages, the Tasks folder to see your tasks, and so on. And that won't show you the Word documents and Excel worksheets that you worked on.

Fortunately, you can keep a record of all of your Microsoft Office activities in the Outlook Journal folder—e-mail messages, task and meeting requests and responses, and interactions with contacts. The journal identifies each action and records the date and time you performed it. You can also set Outlook to record a journal entry each time you create, open, close, or save a file in an Office application. Outlook creates a shortcut to the Office file in the journal entry, even if Outlook isn't running.

You can have Outlook automatically record activities in the journal, and you can add journal entries yourself manually. Add your own entries, for example, for activities that you've already performed and for activities that Outlook cannot record automatically. You can even add entries that act as shortcuts to files on your hard disk or to files on another computer on your network so that you can open those files from your Journal folder. The Journal folder is located in the My Shortcuts group.

 The Journal folder displays a timeline showing each document you worked on and each call, meeting or other Outlook activity for which you created a journal entry, as shown in Figure 14-1.

FIGURE 14-1.
The Journal folder.

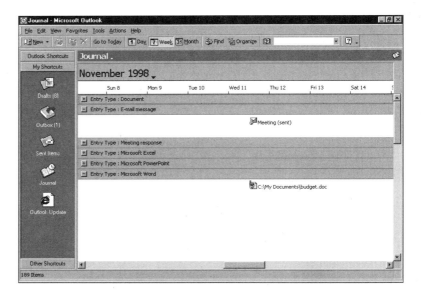

Setting Up the Journal

Before using the Journal folder, you should do the following:

- Choose which Outlook activities are recorded.

- Choose the contacts for whom Outlook activities are recorded.

- Choose the Microsoft Office programs for which activities are recorded.

To set up the journal, follow these steps:

1 Choose Options from the Outlook Tools menu, click the Preferences tab, and then click Journal Options to open the dialog box shown in Figure 14-2.

FIGURE 14-2.
The Journal Options
dialog box.

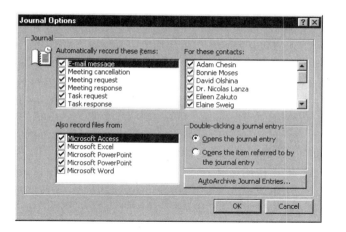

IV

Keeping Track of
People and Things

2 In the For These Contacts list, select the check boxes for the contacts for whom you want Outlook to record activities.

3 In the Automatically Record These Items list, select the check boxes for the Outlook activities you want to record.

4 In the Also Record Files From list, clear the check boxes for the applications whose file activities you do *not* want Outlook to record.

5 In the Double-Clicking A Journal Entry section, select what should happen when you double-click a journal entry.

6 Click OK.

The For These Contacts list in the Journal Options dialog box includes only the names listed in your Contacts folder. If you haven't set up any contact entries, this list is empty. If a name you want to select is not listed, click OK to close the Journal Options dialog box, add the new contact to the Contacts folder, and then reopen the Journal Options dialog box, where the name now appears in the list.

For details about double-clicking a journal entry and specific settings in the Journal Options dialog box, see "Choosing What to Open," on page 438. You'll also see a button called AutoArchive Journal Entries in the Journal Options dialog box. For information about the AutoArchive feature, see Chapter 18, "Archiving Folder Items."

Adding Entries to Your Journal

The Journal Options dialog box lets you record entries for Microsoft Office 97 and later, e-mail messages, task and meeting requests, and task and meeting responses. To record journal entries for other Outlook activities (such as appointments, notes, and phone calls), for Office files and documents that you haven't opened, or for files and documents you create with programs that aren't part of Office, you have to add the journal entries manually. You will also have to manually create journal entries for contacts whose check boxes you did not select in the Journal Options dialog box.

Manually Adding a New Journal Entry

To add a new journal entry manually, you need to open the Journal folder and then open a new journal entry window using any of the following techniques:

- Choose New Journal Entry from the Actions menu.
- Point to New on the File menu, and then choose Journal Entry from the submenu.
- Click the New Journal button on the Standard toolbar.
- Press Ctrl+N.

When the journal entry window appears, as shown in Figure 14-3, follow these steps:

1 If you want to include the time you are about to spend creating this entry as part of the time spent on the activity, click Start Timer.

2 Type a subject line.

3 Select a type of activity from the Entry Type list.

4 Type the contact's name or click the Contacts button and select the name.

5 Enter the company name, if appropriate.

6 Add any comments, notes, attached files, or other information.

7 Enter or select categories, as needed.

8 Select the Private check box, if needed.

FIGURE 14-3.
A journal entry window.

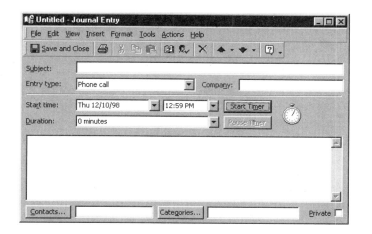

9 If you started the timer, click Pause Timer to stop it.

10 When you are finished, click Save And Close.

> You can also assign a journal entry to a category with the Using Categories option in the Organize pane. Click the Organize button on the Standard toolbar, and then choose Using Categories, if it's not already selected. Select the entry in the Journal folder, choose an existing category in the Add Entries list, and click the Add button, or type in a new category in the Create A New Category box and click the Create button.

When you add a journal entry manually, Outlook does not create a related Outlook item. For example, suppose you manually add a journal entry to record a phone call. You decide that you want to assign yourself a task based on the phone call. To create the task, copy the journal item to the Tasks folder, so Outlook opens a new task window for the item, where you can set up the task and add it to your task list. *For more information, see "Moving and Copying Folder Items," on page 456.*

Using the Timer

A journal entry's timer gives you a record of how much time you spend on activities such as completing a task, making a phone call, or meeting with a contact. To use the timer, simply open the journal entry window, and click the Start Timer button. As you work, leave the journal entry window open. (Minimize the window if you need to see more of the screen.) You can pause the timer if a phone call or a visit that isn't related to the matter at hand interrupts you.

Adding a New Journal Entry from a Different Folder

If you're working in an Outlook folder other than the Journal folder when you need to set up a new journal entry, use one of these methods to open the journal entry window:

- Click the down arrow beside the New button on the Standard toolbar, and then choose Journal Entry from the menu.

- Point to New on the File menu, and then choose Journal Entry from the submenu.

- Press Ctrl+Shift+J.

When you finish the activity, click the Save And Close button in the journal entry window. Outlook stops the timer for you.

Adding Existing Outlook Items to Your Journal

When you've worked on a task, held a meeting, or sent e-mail to a contact, for example, and have not recorded a journal entry for the activity, you might want to add an entry afterward. Here's how to add a journal entry for an existing Outlook item:

1 Open the Outlook folder containing the item for which you want to add a journal entry.

2 Select the item.

3 Drag the selected item and drop it onto the Journal folder icon on the Outlook Bar.

4 Outlook opens a journal entry window for the item. You can add or change information for the entry as needed. Outlook sets the entry type based on the type of item you added. For example, if you add a contact to your journal, Outlook sets the entry type to Phone Call. If necessary, you can select a more accurate description from the Entry Type list.

5 When you've made your adjustments to the journal entry, click Save And Close.

TIP

When you add an existing Outlook item to your journal, Outlook adds a shortcut to the original item in the text and attachments box at the bottom of the journal entry window. The icon used for the shortcut (a contact card, a small calendar, a task checklist, or an envelope, for example) represents the type of the original Outlook activity or document. If you double-click the shortcut, Outlook opens the window in which you set up the item—the contact window, the calendar item window, the task window, or the message window, for instance—allowing you to review details about the item or make any necessary changes.

Adding Existing Documents to Your Journal

You've probably already created documents and files in other programs that you might want to add to your Journal folder. Adding existing files and documents to your journal allows you to organize a list of entries that all relate to a single project or task. Also, a journal entry makes it possible for you to open the file or document from Outlook rather than searching with other tools—such as Windows Explorer or My Computer.

To create a journal entry for an existing file or document created in another program, take these steps:

1 Click Other Shortcuts in the Outlook Bar.

2 Click My Computer in the Other Shortcuts group.

3 Open the folder containing the file or document you want to add as a journal entry, and select the file or document.

4 Open the group on the Outlook bar that contains the Journal shortcut.

5 Drag the selected item and drop it onto the Journal folder icon on the Outlook Bar.

6 Outlook now opens a journal entry window for the file or document. A shortcut icon for the file or document appears in the message area of the window, and the name of the file or document appears in the Subject box. You can change the entry name or the entry type and add other information that you want to record with the journal entry.

7 Click the Save And Close button.

Opening and Changing Journal Entries

To open a journal entry to view or edit its details, perform one of the following actions in the Journal folder:

- Right-click the entry, and then select Open from the shortcut menu.

- Double-click the entry.

- Select the entry, and then choose Open from the File menu.

- Select the entry, and then press Ctrl+O.

You can review, add, or change information. If you make additions or changes, be sure to click the Save And Close button when you want to close the window.

Choosing What to Open

By default, Outlook opens the journal entry window when you double-click an entry in the Journal folder or use any of the other methods described previously to open a journal item. But, if you prefer, you can change this behavior and instead have Outlook open the item referred to by the journal entry, such as a calendar item for a meeting or a task window for a task.

 NOTE

> This setting affects not only the double-click action but also all other ways in which you can open a journal item.

As you saw in Figure 14-2, on page 433, the Journal Options dialog box contains a section labeled Double-Clicking A Journal Entry. If you want to open the journal entry window when you double-click an entry in the Journal folder, select the Opens The Journal Entry check box. If you'd rather open the item associated with the journal entry when you double-click the entry, select the check box labeled Opens The Item Referred To By The Journal Entry. If the journal entry relates to an Office file, Outlook will open the associated application and the file. For example, if the entry relates to an Excel worksheet, double-clicking the entry will both start Excel and open the worksheet from that entry.

Regardless of how you set the Double-Clicking A Journal Entry option, you can always choose which item to open—the journal entry or the related item. If you set the double-click action to open the related item rather than the journal entry, you can open the journal entry by right-clicking it and choosing Open Journal Entry from the shortcut menu. If there is no related item for a particular entry (if it's a simple journal entry), double-clicking opens the journal entry, regardless of the setting in the Journal Options dialog box.

If you set the double-click action to open the journal entry, you can open the related item using either of these techniques:

- Right-click the journal entry, and choose Open Item Referred To from the shortcut menu.

- Open the journal entry, and double-click the shortcut for the associated item, which appears in the text and attachments area at the bottom of the journal entry window.

Removing a Journal Entry

SEE ALSO

You can archive journal entries before deleting them. For details, see Chapter 18, "Archiving Folder Items."

When you no longer want or need a journal entry, you can remove it from your Journal folder. To remove a journal entry, simply open the Journal folder, select the entry you want to remove, and click the Delete button on the Standard toolbar. Deleting a journal entry does not affect any associated file, document, or Outlook item.

When you delete a journal entry, Outlook moves the entry to the Deleted Items folder. To permanently delete the journal entry from Outlook, you have to empty the Deleted Items folder by choosing Empty "Deleted Items" Folder from the Tools menu.

Viewing Journal Entries

SEE ALSO

For details about grouping journal entries as well as specifying sorting procedures, setting up special filters, and adding custom fields, see Chapter 20, "Organizing Folder Items."

Outlook provides several ways to view a listing of your journal entries. To switch to a different view, point to Current View on the View menu, and then choose the view you want from the submenu. *For details about formatting views or setting up custom views, see Chapter 21, "Setting Up Views."*

The first time you look into your Journal folder, you'll see journal entries listed in By Type view, as shown previously in Figure 14-1, on page 432. When you've used Outlook for a while, your journal entries might range over a long period of time, and you won't be able to scroll to them easily or quickly. You can use one of the following techniques to quickly jump to another date:

- To jump to a date far away from today's date, you can either click the down arrow beside the month name or point to Go To on the View menu and choose Go To Date.

TIP

You can also click the Organize button on the Standard toolbar in the Journal folder, choose Using Views in the Organize pane, and then select a view from the list that appears.

 **SEE ALSO**

For information about timeline views, see "Timeline Views," on page 581.

■ To jump to a date within a few months of the current date, click the down arrow beside the month name in the Journal folder window, and select the date from the calendar that appears.

■ To jump to any date, point to Go To on the View menu and choose Go To Date in the Journal folder window (or press Ctrl+G). *For more information about using the Go To Date dialog box, see "Using the Go To Date Command," on page 309.*

 TIP

In By Type view, By Contact view, and By Category view, you can click the Day, Week, or Month buttons on the Standard toolbar to set the time span displayed on the screen. Click Day, for example, to display a single day on the screen with the timeline divided into hours.

Here's a summary of the other Journal folder views:

■ **By Contact view.** Groups journal entries by the contact as shown in the following illustration. If you assign more than one contact to a journal entry, Outlook lists that journal entry under each contact name.

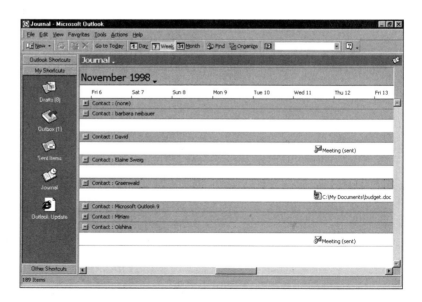

■ **By Category view.** Lists entries by category. If you assign a journal entry to more than one category, Outlook lists that entry in each category. There will also be a group for entries that have no category assigned to them.

SEE ALSO

For details about changing the columns you see in Entry List view, see "Setting Up Columns," on page 544. You can group your journal entries by some of the columns you set up in Entry List view; for details, see "Grouping," on page 551.

■ **Entry List view.** Shows journal entries in a table arrangement, with columns for the following items: icons for entry types, attachments, descriptions of the entry types, subjects, start dates and times, times spent so far on the journal entries (duration), contact names for each entry, and categories to which each entry has been assigned. The next illustration shows a typical Journal folder displayed in Entry List view. Click the column heading for the column you want to use to sort the journal entries. The first click sorts either alphabetically (A–Z) or newest to oldest. A second click sorts either reverse alphabetically (Z–A) or oldest to newest. You can sort the list of journal entries by attachment (with or without), type, subject, start date and time, or duration. You cannot sort journal entries by category or by contact in Entry List view. To sort your journal entries by category or contact, choose By Category view or By Contact view.

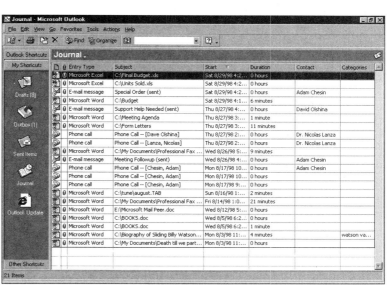

■ **Last Seven Days view.** Displays your journal entries for the past seven days only, in a table arrangement similar to Entry List view. You can sort these entries in all the same ways you can sort in Entry List view.

■ **Phone Calls view.** Displays only those journal entries for phone calls you made from the Contacts folder and journal entries you've created yourself by adding a contact to your journal. You can sort these entries in all the same ways you can sort in Entry List view.

While you can view items in the Inbox, Calendar, and Tasks folders in a variety of ways, the Journal lets you see your overall activities at a glance. By adding a record of other Office 2000 documents, you'll get a clear picture of your efforts and progress. Appointments, meetings, tasks, and journal entries are rather formal Outlook items that involve completing a form. When you just want to record a quick informal message or reminder use the Notes folder, the electronic equivalent to stick-on notes. You'll learn about the Notes folder in the next chapter.

Making Notes

Taking notes, posting notes, sticking notes on everything—from writing notes to classmates in school, notes to ourselves, and notes to family and roommates, to taking notes in meetings—jotting down points that we want to remember or communicate to others seems to be one of the major jobs we do just about every day.

Microsoft Outlook comes with a folder for notes—a place where you can type notes and keep track of them. You can even print your notes (explained in Chapter 17, "Printing Folder Items"), and you can forward a note to anyone with an e-mail address.

Adding a Note

To create a new note, open the Notes folder, and use one of the following methods:

- Click the New Note button on the Standard toolbar.
- Point to New on the File menu, and then choose Note from the submenu.
- Press Ctrl+N.
- Double-click an empty space in the Notes folder window.

When you use any one of these methods, Outlook opens a note window, shown here:

Leave the note open
or click here to close it.

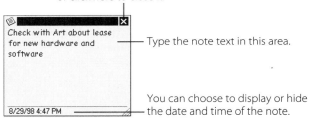

Type the note text in this area.

You can choose to display or hide
the date and time of the note.

Once you have a note open, you can also create a new note by clicking the icon in the upper-left corner of the note window and choosing New Note from the menu shown here:

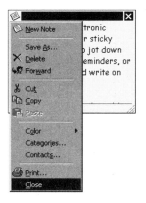

If you're working in an Outlook folder other than the Notes folder when you need to create a note, use one of the following methods:

- Click the down arrow beside the New button on the Standard toolbar, and then choose Note from the menu.

- Point to New on the File menu, and then choose Note from the submenu.

- Press Ctrl+Shift+N.

After you finish a note and click the Close button, Outlook displays the note text and a note icon in your Notes folder window.

Working with Notes

 SEE ALSO

For details about printing options, see Chapter 17, "Printing Folder Items."

You can edit the text of a note, change the note's color, assign the note to various categories, forward the note to someone else, and copy or move the note to another folder. You can also adjust the default settings for all your notes, changing the default color, size, font, and time and date display.

Editing Note Text

When you want to change the text of a note, simply open the Notes folder, and double-click the note you want to edit. Then type your text changes, and click the Close button.

You can also open a note for editing in any of the following ways:

- Right-click the note, and choose Open from the shortcut menu.

- Select the note, and choose Open from the File menu.

- Select the note, and press Ctrl+O.

Giving a Note Some (Other) Color

By default, Outlook's notes have a yellow background and a yellow icon. But you can easily change a note's color to one of four other colors: blue, green, pink, or white. (You can also change the default note color, as explained in "Changing Default Note Settings," on page 447.) Keeping notes of different colors is a handy way to organize your notes. You might make personal notes one color and notes related to your job another color.

Here's how to change the color of a note:

1 Open the Notes folder, and select the note you want to color differently.

2 Right-click the note, point to Color on the shortcut menu, and then choose the new color from the submenu.

 TIP

> If you have a note open, you can click the icon in the upper left corner of the note window, point to Color on the menu, and then choose the new color from the submenu.

Assigning a Note to a Category

SEE ALSO

For more information about using categories with Outlook items, see "Working with Categories," on page 549.

As with other Outlook items, such as e-mail messages, meetings, or tasks, you can organize notes by assigning them to one or more categories. To assign a note to a category, open the note and click the icon in the upper left corner of the note window. Then choose Categories from the menu. (You can also right-click the note in the Notes folder window and choose Categories from the shortcut menu.) Select one or more of Outlook's built-in categories or enter categories of your own.

Assigning a Note to a Contact

You can also associate a note with one or more contacts who are involved with the note's topic. When you do this, the note will be listed on the Activities tab of each contact's properties dialog box, enabling you to quickly find the matters in which each contact is involved. To add contacts to a note, open the note, click the icon in the upper left corner of the note, and choose Contacts. In the Contacts For Note dialog box, type the name of each contact or click the Contacts button to select each contact from the Select Contacts dialog box.

Sending a Note to Someone Else

If you want someone else to benefit from your careful note taking, you can send the note to another user in one of two ways. You can send the text of the note as a message, or you can include the note as an attachment to a message.

■ To send the text of the note as the text of the message, drag the note from the Notes folder to the Inbox folder on the Outlook Bar.

■ To send a note to someone else as an attachment, right-click the note icon and choose Forward; or, open the note, click the icon in the upper left corner of the note window, and then choose Forward from the menu.

In the message window that Outlook displays, type the name of the recipient to whom you want to forward the note, or click the To button to select a name. If you dragged only one note or selected only one note to forward, the Subject line will show the note text. If you selected more than one note to forward, the Subject line will be blank. Add any text you want to send with the note(s). When you're ready to send the message with the note(s) attached, click the Send button on the Standard toolbar.

Copying or Moving a Note to Another Folder

? SEE ALSO

For more details about moving items from one folder to another, see "Moving a Folder Item," on page 457.

You can move a note to another folder the same way you move any Outlook item. You can drag a note and drop it on a folder icon on the Outlook Bar to move the note to another folder. For example, if you want to use a note to create a task, open the Notes folder window, select the note you want to use to set up the task, and drag it to the Tasks icon on the Outlook Bar. Outlook opens a task window, which you can use to enter more details about the task.

Changing Default Note Settings

Outlook's default is a medium-size yellow note. (The note icons are also yellow.) If you want to change the default color, size, or font for your notes, choose Options from the Tools menu, click the Preferences tab of the Options dialog box, and then click Note Options to display the Notes Options dialog box:

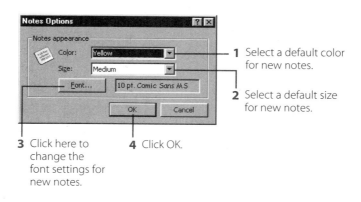

1 Select a default color for new notes.

2 Select a default size for new notes.

3 Click here to change the font settings for new notes.

4 Click OK.

> Changes you make to the default note settings affect only new notes. The existing notes will retain their original appearance.

Date and Time Stamping Notes

If you want, you can have Outlook display the date and time that a note was created at the bottom of the note. To turn this setting off or on, choose Options from the Tools menu, click the Other tab, and click Advanced Options. In the Advanced Options dialog box, select or clear the check box labeled When Viewing Notes, Show Time And Date.

> Clearing the Show Date And Time check box simply omits the date and time from the note window; Outlook still records the date and time you created the note and displays this information in a column in certain views.

Viewing Your Notes

The views available for the Notes folder include views based on displaying icons as well as views that use a list format. When you first begin to work in your Notes folder, you'll see the window in Icons view, which is the default setting.

To switch to a different view of your Notes folder, use one of the following methods:

- Point to Current View on the View menu, and then choose the view you want from the submenu.

- Click the Organize button on the Standard toolbar to display the Organize pane, click Using Views, and choose a view from the list.

> You can also resize a note. To do so, point to a corner or border of the note so the mouse pointer appears as a two-headed arrow and then drag. Drag outward to make the note larger; drag inward to make it smaller. The direction of the arrow indicates how the note will be changed. The lower right corner has a larger area to grab if you want to change both the height and width of the note at the same time.

SEE ALSO

You can set up custom views for looking at your notes. For information, see Chapter 21, "Setting Up Views." To set up special filters and sorting procedures for your notes, see "Filtering," on page 557, and "Sorting," on page 555.

Icons View

Icons view displays your notes with an icon and the note text. In Icons view, you can choose how to display the icons: as large icons, as small icons, or as an icon list.

To select one of these icon displays, click one of the three icon buttons on the Standard toolbar, as shown here:

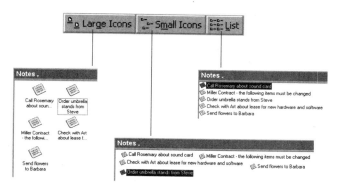

If you click the Large Icons button or the Small Icons button, Outlook gives you several ways to arrange the icons in the Notes folder window. The easiest way to arrange a few notes is to simply drag the icons where you want them to appear in the window. (If you display the icons as a list, however, you can't arrange the icons in the window.)

If you want to align notes automatically in relation to each other, use the Format Icon View dialog box as follows:

1 Open the Notes folder, point to Current View on the View menu, and then choose Icons.

2 Point again to Current View on the View menu, and then choose Customize Current View. Outlook opens the View Summary dialog box.

3 Click the Other Settings button in the dialog box to display the Format Icon View dialog box shown in Figure 15-1, on the following page.

4 Select the view type. The buttons in the View Type section have the same effect as similarly named buttons on the Standard toolbar.

5 Select an option in the Icon Placement section and preview the results in the box to the right. Choose from the four options on the next page.

- **Do Not Arrange.** Lets you drag the icons to any spot in the Notes folder window, giving you the freedom to arrange the icons yourself.

- **Line Up Icons.** Arranges the icons according to a preset grid in the Notes folder window but leaves them close to their original positions. It does not close up gaps between icons.

- **AutoArrange.** Lines up the icons in rows and columns, closing any gaps.

- **Sort And AutoArrange.** Sorts the icons alphabetically by the first word of the note and then lines up the icons in rows and columns, closing any gaps.

6 Click OK.

FIGURE 15-1.
The Format Icon View dialog box.

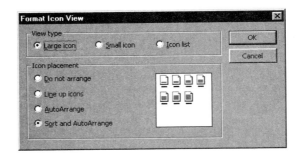

Other Note Views

In addition to Icons view, you can display notes in these views:

To learn other ways to sort notes, see "Sorting," on page 555. For details about changing the columns in Notes List view, see "Setting Up Columns," on page 544. You can group your notes by some of the columns you set up in Notes List view; for details, see "Grouping," on page 552.

- **Notes List view.** Shows your notes with more detailed information in a multiline table format, with columns for icons, subjects, creation dates and times, and categories, as in Figure 15-2. The text of each note is indented under its subject heading.

  Notes List view initially sorts notes alphabetically by subject. To sort the notes differently in this view, click the column heading for the column you want to use to sort the notes. The first click sorts alphabetically or newest to oldest. A second click sorts reverse alphabetically or oldest to newest.

- **Last Seven Days view.** Looks identical to the Notes List view but only displays notes created in the past seven days.

- **By Category view.** Lists notes by category. A single note can appear in as many categories as you have assigned it to.

FIGURE 15-2.
Notes List view.

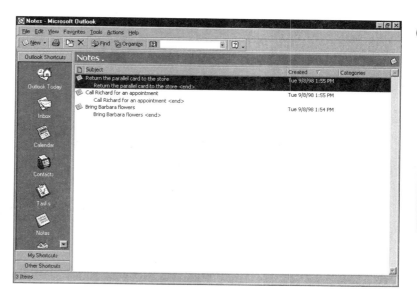

To assign a note to an additional category in By Category view, drag that note's icon to the new category. The note then appears in both categories.

■ **By Color view.** Organizes notes by their color. Choose this view if you use different colors for different types of notes.

To change a note's color, drag that note's icon to the section that lists the new color. The note then appears with the new color.

Notes are handy to have around and can cut down on the clutter around your desk. Use notes not only as reminders to yourself, but as places to store information before you have time to add it to a message or other Outlook item. Starting with the next chapter, you will learn how to manage folders, organize and print items within folders, and create custom views.

PART V

Bending Folders to Your Will

Managing Folder Contents

To get the most from Microsoft Outlook 2000, you need to manage folder contents and clean up the loose ends that inevitably arise from managing your mail, appointments, contacts, tasks, and notes—in short, your life. Can't you just hear your parents (or spouse) telling you, "Straighten up your room—it's a pigsty"? Well, this chapter describes the tools you need to straighten up the messes in your Outlook folders. (Your room is your own business.)

Moving and Copying Folder Items

You can move or copy folder items to any other Outlook folder or to any folder on your system. Outlook generously provides several ways to move and copy folder items. Use whichever method you find convenient.

When you move or copy an item to a folder of another type (such as moving a task to the Inbox or a message to any non–e-mail folder), Outlook opens a new item window for that folder. When you move or copy an item to the Journal folder, the item appears as an attachment in the journal entry window. In all other folders, the moved item appears as text in the new item window. Figure 16-1, for example, shows how a meeting appears when moved to the Inbox. The details of the meeting become the text of the message. You can change any of the information in the new item window and fill in the rest before clicking the Save And Close button.

 **TIP**

Drag a contact to the Inbox to send a message, to the Calendar to set up an appointment, or to the Tasks folder to assign a task. The name of the contact will automatically appear in the To text box as the recipient of the message, appointment notice, or task assignment.

FIGURE 16-1.
A meeting moved to
the Inbox.

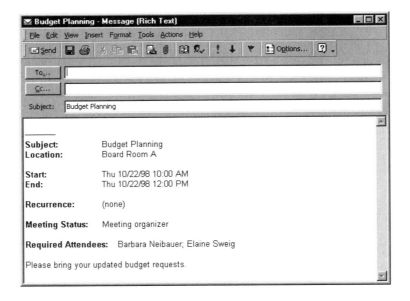

Moving a Folder Item

You can move a folder item either while it's open or while it's closed. The easiest way to move a folder item, however, is when it is closed. Just drag the item to the folder where you want to place it, using the following steps.

> When you drag an item to a folder of a different type, Outlook actually copies rather than moves the item.

1 Open the folder containing the item you want to move.

2 Click the item you want to move. Hold down the Ctrl key if you want to select multiple items, or use the Shift key to select a series of consecutive items.

3 If necessary, scroll the Outlook Bar, or choose another group on the Outlook Bar, to see the icon for the folder where you want to place the item.

4 Drag the item from the open folder to the folder on the Outlook Bar.

> If the Folder List is displayed, you can also drag the item to the destination folder on the list.

You can also move an item by selecting a destination folder from a dialog box. To move the item without opening it first, follow these steps:

1 Open the folder containing the item you want to move.

2 Click the item you want to move. You can select and move more than one item at the same time.

Move To
Folder

3 Click the Move To Folder button on the Standard toolbar to see a list of folders as well as the Move To Folder command.

4 Select the destination folder, if it is listed, or click Move To Folder to display additional choices.

The Move Items dialog box lists additional folders, as shown in Figure 16-2, on the next page. Depending on the type of item you're moving, you can open this dialog box using one of the following techniques:

■ Click the Move To Folder button on the Standard toolbar, and choose Move To Folder from the menu.

■ Press Ctrl+Shift+V.

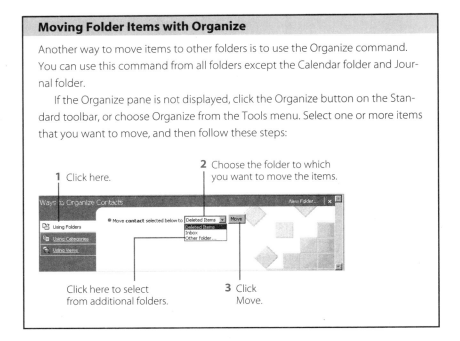

Moving Folder Items with Organize

Another way to move items to other folders is to use the Organize command. You can use this command from all folders except the Calendar folder and Journal folder.

If the Organize pane is not displayed, click the Organize button on the Standard toolbar, or choose Organize from the Tools menu. Select one or more items that you want to move, and then follow these steps:

1 Click here.

2 Choose the folder to which you want to move the items.

Click here to select from additional folders.

3 Click Move.

- If you've selected the item in a folder window, choose Move To Folder from the Edit menu.

- Right-click an e-mail item in the folder window, and choose Move To Folder from the shortcut menu.

- If you've opened an item (except for a note) in its own window, choose Move To Folder from the File menu.

Once you've opened the Move Items dialog box, follow the steps on the next page to move the selected item or items.

FIGURE 16-2.

The Move Items dialog box.

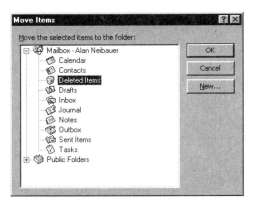

1 Select the destination folder. If necessary click the plus sign to expand subfolders.

2 Click OK.

If you want to move items to a new folder, select an existing folder where you want to add the new subfolder, and then click New. In the Create New Folder dialog box that appears, type a name for the new folder, and then click OK.

Copying a Folder Item

You can copy a folder item either while it's open or while it's closed. If the item is closed and displayed in the folder window, hold down the Ctrl key while you drag the item to the destination folder on the Outlook Bar or in the Folder List. You do not have to hold down the Ctrl key to copy an item to a folder of a different type.

> You actually do not have to hold down the Ctrl key the entire time you are dragging an item. Just make sure the Ctrl key is pressed down when you release the mouse button. When you press the Ctrl key, a small plus sign will appear next to the mouse pointer indicating that you are making a copy of the item rather than moving it.

To copy the item by using a dialog box instead of dragging, follow these steps:

1 Open the folder containing the item, and select the item or open it. You can select more then one item in a folder window.

2 Choose Copy To Folder to see the Copy Items dialog box. Copy To Folder appears on the Edit menu when you're viewing a folder and on the File menu when you have opened an item. The dialog box is identical to the Move Items dialog box shown in Figure 16-2, except for the title.

3 Select the destination folder.

4 Click OK (or double-click the destination folder).

Bending Folders to Your Will

V

Copying a Folder Item to an Office Application

You can copy messages, contact information, or notes to other Microsoft Office applications in one of two ways: you can copy the folder item as an embedded object, or you can add the text of the item to a document in the application.

> In this chapter, references to Microsoft Office always refer to Office 97 and later versions.

To copy a folder item to an Office application as an object, follow these steps:

1 Select the folder item you want to copy.

2 Start the Office application to which you want to copy the folder item, and create or open the document to which you'll copy the item.

3 Arrange the Outlook window and the Office document window on your screen so you can see both at the same time.

4 Drag the folder item into the document window.

The item is displayed as an icon in the document. You can double-click the icon to see the folder item. If you want to copy the text of the folder item into the Office document, take these steps:

1 Select the folder item you want to copy.

2 Choose Save As from the File menu in Outlook to open the Save As dialog box.

3 Open the Save As Type list. For all items other than e-mail, choose Rich Text Format; for e-mail items choose HTML.

4 Type or edit the filename in the File Name box.

5 Click Save.

6 Switch to or open the Office application, and then choose Open from the File menu in that application to open the file for the folder item. Open the file that you saved. You'll see the text in the

appropriate format for the Office application. Figure 16-3 is an example of a Rich Text Format journal entry opened in Microsoft Word.

7 Edit and save the Office document or just close it if you don't want to make any changes.

FIGURE 16-3.

A journal item opened in Word.

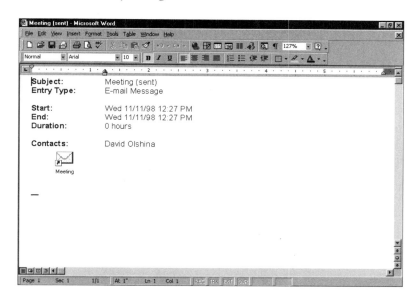

Posting Your Ideas in a Folder

Another way to add new information to a folder—especially to a public folder shared by members of a group—is to post a notice or a response to a previous posting. Many public folders are designed for posting information that is of interest to specific groups of people. These folders are different from e-mail folders because they're designed for public rather than private use. Although you can compose new postings in e-mail folders and in public folders, posting in an e-mail folder is less common. You cannot compose new postings or post replies in file system folders.

To post a new notice in an e-mail or public folder, follow these steps:

1 Open the e-mail or public folder where you want to add a new posting.

2 If you open a public folder, click the New Post In This Folder button on the Standard toolbar to open a message window as shown on the next page. For public folders as well as all e-mail folders (Inbox, Outbox, Drafts, and Sent Items), you can also press

Ctrl+Shift+S, or click the down arrow beside the New button on the Standard toolbar, and select Post In This Folder from the menu.

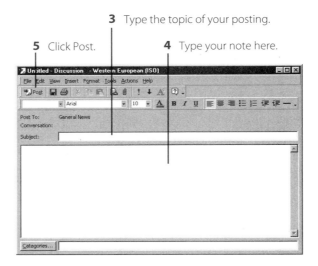

3 Type the topic of your posting.

5 Click Post.   **4** Type your note here.

After you click the Post button, Outlook adds the notice to the folder, marking it with the icon shown at the left.

To reply to a posted notice, first double-click it to open a discussion window containing the notice (the word *Discussion* appears in the title bar). Click the Post Reply button to open a window in which you can type your reply. Notice the header shows the topic of discussion in the Conversation field. You can repeat this field in the Subject field, or enter a unique subject line for just your reply. To view the messages in a discussion folder arranged by the conversation topic, point to Current View on the View menu and choose By Conversation Topic.

If you are reading the message in the preview pane and want to post a reply without opening the item, do this:

1 Right-click the item in the message list and choose Post Reply To Folder from the shortcut menu.

2 Type your reply in the message window.

3 Edit the original item text, if you like, but it is considered bad etiquette to change someone else's message.

4 Click Post.

Adding Files to a Folder

In addition to moving an Outlook item to another folder, you can copy files from your disk to an Outlook item. For example, you might want to attach a Word document or an Excel worksheet to a journal entry or task.

To put a file from your file system into an Outlook folder, follow these steps:

1 Open the Other Shortcuts group on the Outlook Bar, and then choose My Computer.

2 Locate the disk, folder, and then the file to be attached using the Folder List (if open) or the item list.

3 Select the file.

4 Now return to the Outlook Bar and open the group that contains your destination folder. If necessary, scroll so that the folder is visible. (Don't click the folder.)

5 Drag the selected file to the Outlook folder on the Outlook Bar and drop the file when the small plus sign appears. Outlook creates an item that is appropriate for the folder. In the example shown in Figure 16-4, a shortcut to the file has been placed in a journal entry window, opened for your review.

6 Make any changes you want to the information in the item window. You can add text in the message area where the file shortcut appears, if you want.

FIGURE 16-4.

A file item attached to a journal entry.

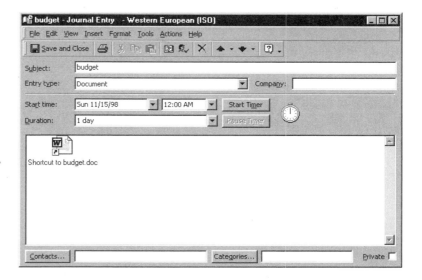

7 For all items other than e-mail messages, click Save And Close. For e-mail messages, click the Send button if you want to send the shortcut now, or click the Save button and then close the message if you don't want to send a message but do want to keep the item in an e-mail folder.

The new folder item contains a shortcut to the file.

As an alternative to dragging a file to the Outlook folder, you can use the File command on the Insert menu as follows:

1 Open the Outlook folder in which you want to place the file.

2 Create a new item in the Outlook folder, such as a new task, calendar item, or e-mail message.

3 In the item window, choose File from the Insert menu (or click the Insert File button on the Standard toolbar) to see the Insert File dialog box shown in Figure 16-5.

4 Switch to the disk and folder that contains the file.

5 Select the file.

6 Select the method of inserting the file by clicking the down arrow of the Insert button (if available) at the bottom of the dialog box. Depending on the file type, you may see one or more of these options:

- **Insert** adds the file using the default for the Outlook item and the file type.

- **Insert As Text** inserts the file as standard text. Typically, you'll select this option when you want to insert plain (unformatted) text files in order to send the file in a message across the Internet. This option makes sense only for simple text files. Art files and files containing formatted text appear as gibberish if sent this way.

- **Insert As Attachment** inserts a complete copy of the data from the file, represented as an icon. Select this option if you will need to readily access the file from the folder item. This option lets you send any format of file, which a recipient can open if he or she has a program that reads the same file format. Because the entire file is stored as part of the folder item, you should select the Shortcut option instead if the file is extremely large.

- **Insert As Shortcut** inserts a pointer to the original file, represented as a shortcut icon. Select this option to include a reference to the location of a large file. Note, however, that anyone else whom you want to view the file must have direct or network access to the disk, folder, and file, including permission to access it. For the Shortcut option, it's a good idea to store the file on a network server or in a public folder to which others who must view the file have access.

7 Click OK.

8 Fill in the folder item window with the information you want. You might, for example, want to enter a description of the file on the Subject line.

9 If you are working in an e-mail folder, click the Save button, and then click the Close button in the folder item window (click Send to transmit the file). For other folder item types, click the Save And Close button.

Whether you copied a file to an Outlook folder as an attachment or as a shortcut in step 6 above, you can easily view the contents of the file. In the folder window, right-click the folder item, and choose View Attachments from the shortcut menu. Then select the attachment name from the submenu.

If you open the item, you can use any of these methods in the folder item window to view the file:

■ Double-click an attachment or shortcut icon.

FIGURE 16-5.

The Insert File dialog box.

Bending Folders to Your Will

- Right-click an attachment or shortcut icon, and choose Open from the shortcut menu.

- Right-click an attachment or shortcut icon, and choose Quick View from the shortcut menu. (Microsoft Windows Quick View must be installed on your computer for this method to work.)

Adding Items to the Favorites Folder

The Favorites folder contains shortcuts to items, documents, and other folders that you use frequently.

 In all Office 2000 applications, the Favorites folder is accessible in the Save As dialog box, just as it is in the Insert File dialog box shown in Figure 16-5, on the previous page. To add an item to Favorites, select the item in Outlook, choose Save As from the File menu in the folder item window, and then click Favorites in the list of folders on the left of the dialog box. Type a name for the item, and then click Save.

You can also add items to the Favorites folder in these ways:

- You can drag folder items to the Favorites folder in the Other Shortcuts group of the Outlook Bar.

- You can add icons to the Favorites toolbar on the Office shortcut bar.

- You can add the address of a World Wide Web page (a URL) to the Favorites list in Microsoft Internet Explorer.

> If you add an item to your Favorites folder (either in Outlook or in the Favorites folder inside the Windows folder), to the Favorites list in Microsoft Internet Explorer, or to the Favorites toolbar of the Office shortcut bar, the new favorite automatically appears in all of these places.

Making Web Pages Available Offline

In Microsoft Internet Explorer, you can add World Wide Web sites to your Favorites folder. With Internet Explorer 4.0 and later, you can also choose to make some Web pages available offline, also referred to as *subscribing* to a site. The Web pages you select are made available for offline use by downloading and storing them on your computer.

Web pages stored offline are most valuable when they're reasonably up to date. You can update, or *synchronize,* your pages whenever you want, and you can also have Internet Explorer update each offline Web page automatically, according to a schedule you can specify for each page. This means that Internet Explorer will periodically check the site to determine whether it has changed since you last viewed it, and download any new information.

Here's how to add a Web site to your Favorites folder, make it available offline, and keep it updated:

1 Start Microsoft Internet Explorer.

2 Locate the Web page (URL) you want to add to your Favorites folder.

3 Choose Add To Favorites from the Favorites menu to see the dialog box shown here:

4 In the Name box, edit the name as you want it to appear in the Favorites list.

5 If you want to save the shortcut in a folder other than Favorites, or in a subfolder of the Favorites folder, click the Create In button and then choose the folder from the list that appears.

6 If you only want to add the Web site to your Favorites list, click OK to finish. But to make the Web page available when you're not online, select the Make Available Offline check box instead of clicking OK and then complete the remaining steps.

7 Click Customize.

8 The Offline Favorite Wizard opens and displays an introductory screen. If you don't want to see this screen each time you subscribe to a site, select the check box at the bottom of the screen. Click Next.

9 If you want to also make available offline any pages that are stored as links on the Web site, choose Yes. To save disk space and synchronization time, choose No.

V

Bending Folders to Your Will

10 Click Next to see this page of the wizard:

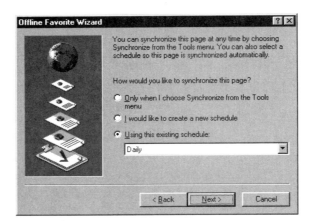

11 Choose to synchronize manually from the Tools menu to create a new schedule for automatic synchronization or to use an existing schedule for automatic synchronization. Then click Next.

12 If you chose to create a new schedule, use the next page of the wizard to designate the number of days between synchronization, the time to synchronize, and a name for the schedule, and then click Next.

13 The final Wizard lets you enter your username and password if the site requires one for you to log on. Click Finish to complete the wizard.

14 Click OK to close the Add Favorite dialog box.

If you selected the Make Available Offline check box, Internet Explorer will download the latest version of the Web page to your computer. If your e-mail account is set up to dial as needed, Internet Explorer will dial your ISP if you are not currently online. Otherwise, go online before attempting to synchronize your offline pages.

After they are downloaded, your offline Web pages will be available at any time, from the Favorites folder in Outlook's Other Shortcuts group on the Outlook Bar, in the Favorites menu of all Office 2000 applications, and from the Favorites menu of the Microsoft Windows Start menu.

If you want to make a site available offline that is already listed in your Favorites, right-click the item, and then choose Make Available Offline from the shortcut menu to start the Offline Synchronization Wizard. Complete the wizard as just described.

Synchronizing Web Pages Manually

If you did not choose to automatically synchronize your Web sites, you have to do so manually. You can synchronize the items from within Outlook, Internet Explorer, or any open folder in the Windows 98 desktop.

To update a single offline Web page, find the page in your Favorites folder, right-click it, and then choose Synchronize. From within Outlook, open Favorites from the Other Shortcuts group on the Outlook Bar.

NOTE

> The Synchronize command won't appear if the page hasn't been set for offline use. In this case, click Make Available Offline, and then set up the page for offline use as described earlier.

To synchronize all your offline folders from within Outlook, including Outlook folders and Web sites, point to Synchronize on the Tools menu, and then choose All Folders.

Changing Synchronization Settings

You can also change synchronization schedules, remove a site from synchronization, or update selected multiple sites from within Internet Explorer. Choose Synchronize from Internet Explorer's Tools menu to open the dialog box shown in Figure 16-6.

To synchronize selected sites, select the check boxes for the sites you want to synchronize, and then click Synchronize.

FIGURE 16-6.
The Items To Synchronize dialog box.

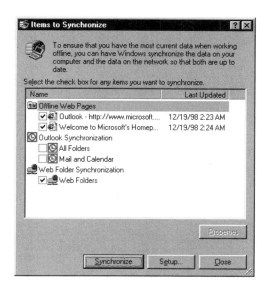

V

Bending Folders to Your Will

To change your general synchronization settings, such as your network adapter and synchronization tasks, click the Setup button in the Items To Synchronize dialog box.

To change synchronization settings for a specific site, select the site in the Name list, click the Properties button, and then perform one or more of these actions:

■ Clear the Make This Page Available Offline check box on the Web Document tab if you no longer want to store the page offline.

■ To change the update schedule, click the Schedule tab, and then choose to synchronize the page manually or on an automatic schedule you specify here.

■ To select how many links to download with the page, to limit how much hard disk space is used for storing the site, to receive an e-mail message when the site has changed, and to limit which elements of a Web site are stored on your hard disk, set the relevant options on the Download tab, shown here:

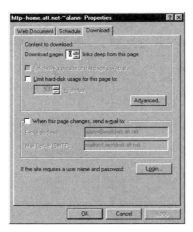

Searching Folder Contents

Outlook provides two ways to help locate items in a folder. You can use the Find command to search just for words or phrases in folder items, or you can use Advanced Find to specify what is searched and to look for specific values within items.

Performing a Simple Search

When you want to locate all folder items that contain a certain word or phrase, follow these steps:

1 Click the Find button on the Standard toolbar, or choose Find from the Tools menu.

2 Type a word or phrase to search for.

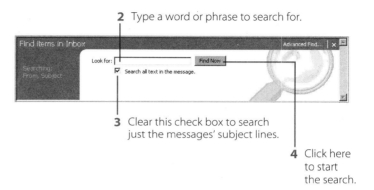

3 Clear this check box to search just the messages' subject lines.

4 Click here to start the search.

Outlook displays, in list form, all of the folder items containing the text that you entered. To look for something else, enter another search phrase and click Find Now.

 NOTE

> If you see a Web Folders item in the Items To Synchronize dialog box, it refers to network folders you subscribe to using the Web Folders feature from My Computer.

Conducting an Advanced Search

To conduct a more sophisticated search for items in a folder, you need to use the Advanced Find dialog box, shown in Figure 16-7, on the next page. Open this dialog box using any one of these methods:

- Choose Advanced Find from the Tools menu. This command is only available in Outlook folders, not disk folders.

- Right-click the folder you want to search, and choose Advanced Find from the shortcut menu. From some folders, the command might appear as Find, but it still opens the Advanced Find dialog box.

- Click Find on the Standard toolbar, and then click Advanced Find.

- Press Ctrl+Shift+F.

FIGURE 16-7.

The Advanced Find dialog box.

Specify the type of folder item here...

...and the tab name, and its contents, change accordingly.

To stop a long search, click Stop.

To clear all search criteria, click New Search.

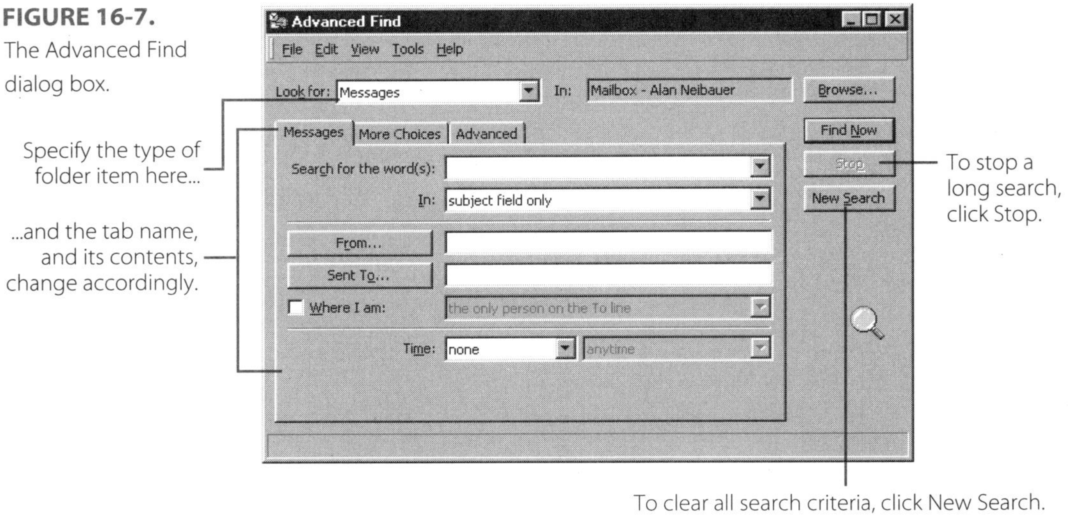

The entry in the Look For box of the Advanced Find dialog box shows the type of item for the open folder, such as messages for the Inbox folder or journal entries for the Journal folder. To search for a different type of item, select another type from the list. The In box (beside the Look For box) shows the default folder in which Outlook searches for the items.

The first of the three tabs in the Advanced Find dialog box corresponds to the type of folder item you're looking for. As you change the setting in the Look For box, this tab also changes—for example, from the Messages tab to the Journal Entries tab. Although the tabs for different types of folder items vary somewhat, you set them up in similar ways. For instance, on the Messages tab, shown in Figure 16-7, you specify search criteria as follows:

- In the Search For The Word(s) box, type a word or phrase that appears in all the messages you're searching for. (If you want to choose words you used in past searches, you can select them from the list box, where Outlook stores them, by clicking the small down arrow.)

- In the In box, tell Outlook whether to look for the word or phrase only in the Subject line of messages (the subject field), in both the Subject line and the body of messages, or in other text fields.

The term *field* simply refers to a location that shows data or to an empty box that you can fill in with details about an item.

To narrow the search even further, you can also set up the following optional criteria:

- Specify messages that were received from or sent to certain people. Type the names of these people in the appropriate boxes, or click the From button or the Sent To button to display the Select Names dialog box, where you can choose names from your address books.

- Tell Outlook to search for messages in which you are the only addressee, messages in which you are the addressee along with others, or messages for which you received copies. To do this, click the Where I Am check box and select from the adjoining list.

- Specify a time. By selecting options in both the Time boxes, you can narrow the search to messages that were, for instance, received or sent within a certain time frame.

When you've set as many search criteria as you need, click the Find Now button to begin the search. The Advanced Find dialog box expands to display the items that match your criteria. If none of the folder items shown fits your needs, click the New Search button and set up different criteria.

When you change your selection in the Look For box after a search, Outlook notifies you that the previous search will be cleared. If you want to start a fresh search, click OK. If you want to keep the previous search, click Cancel.

The next several sections take a closer look at some of the features of the Advanced Find dialog box.

You can open any found item directly from the Advanced Find dialog box by double-clicking the item.

Look For Box

As mentioned earlier, the setting in the Look For box of the Advanced Find dialog box determines where Outlook searches for the items you're seeking and adjusts the first tab of the dialog box to match. The In box next to the Look For box indicates the folder in which Outlook will

V

Bending Folders to Your Will

search for the folder items you've specified. Table 16-1 summarizes how the setting in the Look For box determines which folder is searched by default and the first tab you see in the Advanced Find dialog box.

Browse Button

If you need to expand your search beyond the folder indicated in the In box, you can specify additional folders that Outlook should search. You can't type directly in the In box, but you can click the Browse button to open the Select Folder(s) dialog box:

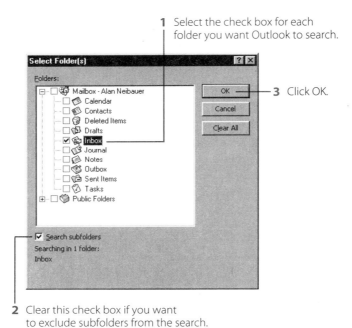

1 Select the check box for each folder you want Outlook to search.

3 Click OK.

2 Clear this check box if you want to exclude subfolders from the search.

After you click OK in the Select Folder(s) dialog box, Outlook adds the folder names you selected to the In box and includes those folders in the search.

> If you select Files in the Look For box and then click the Browse button, you'll see a Select Folder(s) dialog box that contains a list of all the folders in your file system rather than a list of folders in Outlook.

Files Tab

If you're searching for a file with the Advanced Find dialog box, you'll notice that the tab Outlook displays when you select Files in the Look

TABLE 16-1. Effects of Settings in the Look For Box

Choosing This Setting in the Look For Box	Shows This Default Folder in the In Box to Be Searched	And Displays This Tab for Setting Up the Search
Any Type Of Outlook Item	Personal folders or server mailbox	Any Items
Appointments And Meetings	Calendar	Appointments And Meetings
Contacts	Contacts	Contacts
Files	My Documents	Files
Files (Outlook/ Exchange)	Inbox	Files
Journal Entries	Journal	Journal Entries
Messages	Inbox	Messages
Notes	Notes	Notes
Tasks	Tasks	Tasks

For box is a little different from the tabs displayed for other items. In particular, the Named box on the Files tab lets you enter either a filename or a file specification.

To enter a filename, type the complete filename and filename extension. For a file specification, use one of these methods:

- Type an asterisk (*) to include all filenames or extensions—for example, type *.pst to include all files that have the .pst filename extension.

- Type word*.* to find all files of any type (any extension) whose filenames start with word.

- Type one or more question marks (?) to include files regardless of the character(s) at those locations. For example, type fig??-01.?if to include all filenames that start with fig, end with –01, and whose extensions end with if.

If you've looked for files before by typing a filename or a file specification in the Named box, you can retrieve these entries by clicking the down arrow next to the Named box.

If you want to search for all the files of a certain type—for example, all Microsoft Excel workbooks—choose the file type from the Of Type box.

NOTE

When you type a filename or a file specification in the Named box on the Files tab, Outlook's search ignores the selection in the Of Type box.

More Choices Tab and Advanced Tab

The other two tabs in the Advanced Find dialog box, More Choices and Advanced, offer still more options for structuring your search. These two tabs are the same as the More Choices tab and the Advanced tab in the Filter dialog box, discussed in Chapter 20, "Organizing Folder Items." *For information about setting up these tabs, see "Setting Up the More Choices Tab," on page 559, and "Setting Up Advanced Criteria," on page 561.* The next section also provides an example of using the Advanced tab.

Searching for Items by Fields on a Form

When you're looking for specific folder items, you might consider searching for the individual fields that appear on the various types of forms. As you'll learn in Chapter 22, "Designing and Using Forms," a form is a window that you use or create to display, enter, or edit information. To use a field as a search criterion, you have to first select the form that contains the field. Here's how:

1 Choose Advanced Find from the Tools menu to display the Advanced Find dialog box.

2 In the Look For box, select the type of folder item you want to find, or select Any Type Of Outlook Item to include all item types in the search.

3 If the folder you want to search does not appear in the In box to the right, or if you want to search more than one folder, click Browse to select from a list. In the Select Folder(s) dialog box, select the check boxes next to the folders you want to search, and clear the check boxes next to the folders you don't want to search. Click OK.

4 Click the Advanced tab in the Advanced Find dialog box.

5 Click the Field button to display the list of fields.

6 Click Forms on the list to see the dialog box shown in Figure 16-8.

7 Click the down arrow to open the forms list, and then select the forms library you want to use. If you select Application Forms, you'll see a list of Outlook's built-in forms, which you've been using to create and display e-mail and other Outlook items.

FIGURE 16-8.

The Select Enterprise
Forms For This Folder
dialog box.

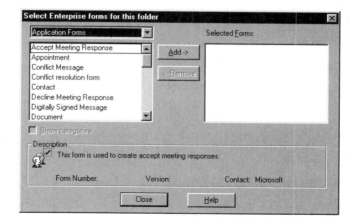

8 In the left-hand box, click the form containing the field that you want to use in the search criteria.

9 Click Add to place the selected form in the Selected Forms right-hand box.

10 Click Close.

11 In the Advanced Find dialog box, click the Field button again to display the list, and point to the name of the form you selected. On the submenu, click the specific field you want to use in the search criteria. Outlook displays the name of the field in the box under the Field button.

12 In the Condition box, you can select a condition to use with the field to set up a specific search criterion.

13 If the condition you select requires a value in order to make sense, Outlook activates the Value box, in which you can enter a value to complete the criterion.

14 Click the Add To List button and your query is added to the Find Items That Match These Criteria box.

15 To use additional fields from the selected form as search criteria, repeat steps 11 through 14.

16 Click the Find Now button to conduct the search with the new criteria.

NOTE

When setting search criteria, if you select more than one search criterion, Outlook finds only the items that meet *all* the search criteria. However, if you enter several criteria that search the same field, Outlook finds items that meet any one (or more) of the multiple criteria you entered. For instance, if you define one criterion to search the subject field for the word *Budget* and enter a second criterion to search the subject field for *Board meeting,* items that contain either or both of these terms will be listed.

Opening Documents or Starting Programs from Outlook

Because you can show any disk folder on the Outlook Bar and, more important, because you can display the Folder List, which can show all the folders on all the disks connected to your computer, it's relatively easy to open any document or start any program from within Outlook.

All you need to do is switch to the Other Shortcuts group on the Outlook Bar and open the folder that contains the document you want to open or the program you want to start. (If the folder does not have an icon on the Outlook Bar, display the Folder List, and click the icon for the folder there.) Then simply double-click the icon for the document or program file.

What's a Forms Library?

A forms library is where Outlook stores published forms. If you have a custom form that you've designed and you want to share it with others, you publish it in one of the three types of forms libraries: a personal forms library, a folder forms library, or an organizational forms library. *Forms libraries are discussed in detail in Chapter 22, "Designing and Using Forms."*

Forwarding Folder Items

You can send any Outlook folder item to someone else—you just forward the item. Here's how to send a folder item to someone else:

1 Open the folder, and select the folder item you want to send to someone else. (To select more than one item, hold down the Ctrl key as you click each item. To select several consecutive folder items, click the first item, and then hold down the Shift key while you click the last item. To select all the folder items, choose Select All from the Edit menu or press Ctrl+A.)

SEE ALSO

You can also set up Outlook to automatically send new messages to another person or to any other folder, which is especially useful when you're out of the office. For details, see "Organizing Messages," on page 51.

2 Choose Forward from the Actions menu. In e-mail folders you can also click the Forward button on the Standard toolbar. A message window appears. If you're forwarding an e-mail message, its contents appears in the message area. Other Outlook items are sent as attachments.

3 Fill in the To box.

4 Type any message you want to send with the item.

5 Click Send.

Removing Items from a Folder

Clutter, clutter, clutter! What a mess! You'll find that you receive many messages that you don't need and don't want to keep. Just as you can quickly dump unwanted postal deliveries in the recycling bin; you can dump folder items in the Deleted Items folder.

To delete an Outlook item, simply select the item in the folder window or open the item, and then click the Delete button on the Standard toolbar. As an alternative, you can move the folder item to the Deleted Items folder. *See "Moving a Folder Item," on page 457.*

If you delete a file from your disk folders, it's just as if you deleted it using Windows Explorer—it's moved to the Recycle Bin.

Retrieving Deleted Items

How many times have you thrown something away by accident? If you delete an Outlook item and then change your mind, you can easily recover it. Just move the item from the Deleted Items folder back to its original, or some other, location. *See "Moving a Folder Item," on page 457.* However, you must retrieve the folder item *before* you empty the Deleted Items folder. After you empty that folder, the folder item is gone for good. Your only recourse then is to have someone send you a copy of the folder item, restore it from a backup copy, or, as the final resort, re-create it.

If you've deleted a file from one of your disk folders, you can recover it by accessing the Recycle Bin from the Windows Start menu before Windows permanently empties it from the Bin.

V

Bending Folders to Your Will

Purging Deleted Items

When you are certain you no longer need the Outlook items you deleted, you can empty the Deleted Items folder. Just remember: deleting items from the Deleted Items folder wipes them out forever.

You can set up Outlook to automatically purge your Deleted Items folder when you quit an Outlook session. To do this, choose Options from the Tools menu, click the Other tab, select the Empty The Deleted Items Folder Upon Exiting check box, and then click OK. Rather than automatically purge deleted messages, however, you may want the extra safety of purging them manually. Here are ways to remove items from the Deleted Items folder:

- To completely empty the Deleted Items folder, choose Empty "Deleted Items" Folder from the Tools menu. When Outlook asks whether you want to permanently delete all the items and subfolders in this folder, click Yes.

- When you want to purge only certain folder items and folders from the Deleted Items folder, open the Deleted Items folder and select the items and folders you want to delete. Click the Delete button on the Standard toolbar, choose Delete from the File menu, or press Ctrl+D. When Outlook asks whether you want to permanently delete the selected items, click Yes.

If you are using your mailbox folders as the delivery point over Microsoft Exchange Server, your network administrator might have set your mailbox to retain purged files for a number of days. If this is the case, you can recover purged files by choosing Recover Deleted Items from the Tools menu.

Viewing Other Shortcuts

For more information about folders in the Other Shortcuts group on the Outlook Bar, see "Exploring the Other Shortcuts Group," on page 33.

You can use the miscellaneous group of folders labeled Other Shortcuts on the Outlook Bar to view files and folders throughout your file system. The My Computer folder, for instance, displays the same icons you see in the My Computer window on your desktop. By clicking one of these icons, you can see a list of all the folders on a disk drive. The My Documents folder, which might also be part of the Other Shortcuts group, contains documents that you've saved with Microsoft Office applications. Outlook provides a number of options for viewing the files in these folders. Switch to a different view of the folder by pointing to Current View on the View menu, and then choose one of the following views from the submenu.

⑦ SEE ALSO

You can set up custom views for looking at your files; for information, see Chapter 21, "Setting Up Views." You can also group your files, specify sorting procedures, set up special filters, and add custom fields to file properties; for details, see Chapter 20, "Organizing Folder Items."

■ **Icons view.** In this view, disk drives, folders, and files are displayed with an icon and their name. When you select Icons view, Outlook adds three buttons to the Standard toolbar: Large Icons, Small Icons, and List. Clicking these buttons varies the Icons view, displaying either large or small icons or an icon list. You can also decide how to arrange the file icons in the window.

■ **Details view.** This view provides more information about your files, similar to Details view in a My Computer or a Windows Explorer window. You see your files listed with columns for icons, filename, author, type, size, date and time of the last modification, and keywords.

■ **By Author view.** In this view, your files are grouped by author, making it easier to find files created by a specific person.

■ **By File Type view.** In this view, files are grouped by their file type, making it easier to find files created by a specific program.

■ **Document Timeline view.** In this view, your files are arranged on a timeline that shows the dates in a band across the top of the window. Document Timeline view resembles the Journal window.

■ **Programs view.** This is the standard view you see the first time you look at the files in one of the folders in the Other Shortcuts group. Programs view is a filter that permits only program files (a file that starts an application, for example) and folders to appear in a files folder window.

⑦ SEE ALSO

For details about changing the columns in Details view, see "Setting Up Columns," on page 544. You can group your files by some of the columns you set up in Details view; for details, see "Grouping," on page 552. For more information on arranging icons, see "Icons View," on page 449.

Files shown in Details view are initially sorted alphabetically by filename. To arrange the files a different way in Details view, click the column heading for the column you want to use to rearrange the files. The first click sorts alphabetically, smallest to largest, or newest to oldest. A second click sorts reverse alphabetically, largest to smallest, or oldest to newest.

You can also change Document Timeline view in the following ways:

■ Click the Day button on the Standard toolbar to see documents for a single date, listed by the time.

■ Click the Week button on the Standard toolbar to see documents for a single week, listed by the day of the week.

■ Click the Month button on the Standard toolbar to see documents for a month, listed by the date.

V

Bending Folders to Your Will

When you have files so far away from today's date that you can't scroll to them quickly in Document Timeline view, you can to jump to a date in one of three ways:

- Click the down arrow beside the month name in the files folder window, and use the calendar that appears.

- Point to Go To on the View menu and choose Go To Date. *For details about how to use this command, see "Using the Go To Date Command," on page 309.*

- Click the Go To Today button on the Standard toolbar, or point to Go To on the View menu and choose Go To Today, to display the current date in the timeline.

Folders are an important component of Outlook because they help you organize your messages, other Outlook items, and disk folders. The folders in the Other Shortcuts group on the Outlook Bar give you access to your own disk as well as your entire network. You can use the Outlook Bar to work with Windows folders and files without having to return to the Windows desktop. In the next chapter, you will learn how to print Outlook items.

Printing Folder Items

Printing a copy of an item from a Microsoft Outlook folder is straightforward. If you want to use Outlook's standard print style, it's simply a matter of selecting an item and clicking a button on the toolbar. But if the standard print style doesn't meet your needs, you can select a different print style—Outlook offers several built-in styles for various folders. You can also print a view of an entire folder rather than an individual item, and you can adjust the printing options for either items or views. And if you can't find a built-in print style that suits your purposes, you can modify one of the built-in styles or even create your own.

Printing with Outlook's Standard Style

Outlook comes with a default print style for each Outlook folder and for each view of that folder. To print folder items using the standard print style, follow these steps:

1 Select the folder item or items that you want to print. (To select more than one item, hold down the Ctrl key as you click each item. To select several consecutive items, click the first item and then hold down the Shift key while you click the last item you want to select. To select all the items in a folder, choose Select All from the Edit menu or press Ctrl+A.)

Print

2 Click the Print button on the Standard toolbar.

You can preview the printed copy before you actually print it. Select the folder item, and choose Print Preview from the File menu. *See "Previewing Printing," on page 490.*

Changing Printing Settings

If you're not pleased with the default print settings used when you click the Print button on the toolbar, you can change the settings before you print. To set print options, open the Print dialog box in one of the following ways:

■ Choose Print from the File menu.

■ Point to Page Setup on the File menu, and then choose a style (or define a new style and then choose it). Then click the Print button in the Page Setup dialog box.

■ Choose Print Preview from the File menu, and then click the Print button on the Print Preview toolbar. *See "Previewing Printing," on page 490.*

Figure 17-1 shows the Print dialog box. Use this dialog box to set the following print options:

■ **Printer Name.** If necessary, select a different printer.

■ **Properties.** If necessary, click this button to adjust the global settings for the selected printer driver for this and all other Windows-based applications.

FIGURE 17-1.

The Print dialog box.

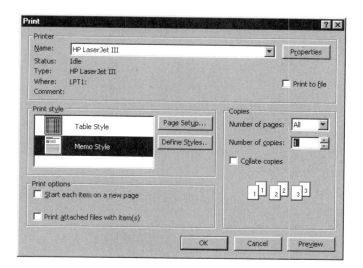

- **Print To File.** Select this check box to send the job to a file instead of the printer. If you don't have the selected printer connected to your system, you can take the file to another computer and copy the file to the printer.

- **Print Style.** Select one of the available print styles, or click Define Styles to create your own print style.

- **Number of Pages.** Select which pages to print (All, Even, or Odd).

- **Number of Copies.** Set the number of copies you want to print.

- **Collate Copies.** If you are printing multiple copies of more than one page, you can select this check box to print complete sets of the job. If you clear this check box, printing might be faster, but all your page 1s will print first, and then your page 2s, and so forth. You will have to collate them into sets manually.

- **Print Options; Print Range.** This section's name and contents vary with the type of items selected, such as whether to start each item on a new page, whether to print attachments, which items or rows to print, and which dates to include from the Calendar.

- **Preview.** Click this button to see a preview of the printed page on your screen.

Choosing Alternate Print Styles

Outlook comes to you with certain print styles that are set up for each view in each folder, as listed in Table 17-1. The print styles available for the current folder and view appear in the Print dialog box and on the Page Setup submenu on the File menu.

If you want to use another print style, follow these steps:

1 Open the folder that contains the folder items you want to print.

2 Use the Current View command on the View menu to change the view setting if necessary. If you want to print one or more individual folder items, select the item or items.

3 Choose Print from the File menu to open the Print dialog box.

4 Select the print style you want to use.

5 Click OK to print.

As an alternative, you can also point to Page Setup on the File menu, choose the style from the submenu that appears, and then click Print in the Page Setup dialog box. You'll learn more about using the Page Setup dialog box later in this chapter.

Table 17-1 shows the print styles available for printing various views of the Outlook folders, either all of the entries shown in the view or a selection of them. Once you open and choose to print any individual Outlook item, the Memo style is the only built-in print style available.

TABLE 17-1.   Built-In Print Styles, by Folder and View

Folder	View	Folder Print Style
Inbox	Message Timeline	Memo*
	All other views	Table, Memo
Calendar	Day/Week/Month, Day/Week/Month with AutoPreview	Daily, Weekly, Monthly, Tri-Fold, Calendar Details, Memo
	All other views	Table, Memo

(continued)

TABLE 17-1.   *continued*

Folder	View	Folder Print Style
Contacts	Address Cards, Detailed Address Cards	Card, Small Booklet, Medium Booklet, Phone Directory, Memo
	All other views	Table, Memo
Tasks	Task Timeline	Memo*
	All other views	Table, Memo
Journal	By Type, By Contact, By Category	Memo*
	Entry List, Last Seven Days, Phone Calls	Table, Memo
Notes	Icons	Memo*
	All other views	Table, Memo

*When a view displays a timeline or icons, you cannot print the view itself. Instead, select individual items and print them using the Memo print style, or select another view capable of printing multiple items.

Here's a brief description of what Outlook's built-in print styles do by default:

Memo.   Prints one or more selected folder items in a standard memo format. It is also the only built-in print style for individual items you open. For instance, a printout of an appointment on your calendar might look like this:

Subject: Lunch with Mark
Start: Thursday 3/18/99 12:30 PM
End: Thursday 3/18/99 2:00 PM
Recurrence: (none)

Table.   Prints either selected folder items or all the items in the current view. The information appears in a table format with the items in rows with the same column headings that are shown in the current view.

Daily.   Prints your calendar for the selected day, 7AM to 7PM, and includes the TaskPad and a Notes section.

Weekly. Prints your weekly calendar on one page. This style does not include the TaskPad or a Notes section.

Monthly. Prints your monthly calendar on one page. Like Weekly style, this style does not include the TaskPad or a Notes section.

Tri-Fold. Prints your daily calendar, weekly calendar, and TaskPad in three equal sections, using landscape orientation.

Card. Prints either selected contact cards or all the cards in the current view of your Contacts folder. Contact cards appear in alphabetical order, marked by letter tabs, from top to bottom on the page in two columns. Outlook prints two blank cards at the end.

Small Booklet. Prints either selected contact cards or all the cards in the current view of your Contacts folder. This style is designed for printing on both sides of a sheet of paper, with eight pages per sheet. You can cut, fold, and assemble the pages to form a booklet.

Medium Booklet. Prints either selected contact cards or all the cards in the current view of your Contacts folder. This style is designed for printing on both sides of a sheet of paper, with four pages per sheet. You can cut, fold, and assemble the pages to form a booklet.

Phone Directory. Prints names and telephone numbers for all your contacts or for selected contacts. The list is in alphabetical order, marked by letter tabs. Other contact information is omitted.

Setting the Print Range or Options

The settings area below the Print Style section of the Print dialog box is labeled either Print Options or Print Range, based on the selected style. Table 17-2 lists the print styles and the options available for each style.

 When you print your calendar in the Daily, Weekly, Monthly, Tri-Fold, or Calendar Details print styles, you can also choose not to print the details of private appointments.

⭐ **TIP**

Most of the time, you'll want to select All in the Number Of Pages box in the Print dialog box to print all the pages of folder items. But when you need to collate the pages in a special way, you can select Odd or Even to print only the odd-numbered or even-numbered pages. *For information about printing odd-numbered and even-numbered pages to form a booklet, see the sidebar "Printing and Assembling a Booklet," on page 491.*

TABLE 17-2.   Print Range Options

Print Style	Print Range Options	Description
Memo	Start Each Item On A New Page	Select this check box to print each folder item on a separate page.
	Print Attached Files With Item(s)	Select this check box to print the contents of attachments with the text of each folder item.
Table	All Rows	Select this check box to print all items in a folder view.
	Only Selected Rows	Select this check box to print only the folder items you selected before opening the Print dialog box.
Daily, Weekly, Monthly, Tri-Fold, Calendar Details	Start	Select or type the earliest date of the items you want to print.
	End	Select or type the latest date of the items you want to print.
	Hide Details Of Private Appointments	Select this check box if you don't want to print the details of any appointments marked as Private.
Phone Directory, Card, Small Booklet, Medium Booklet	All Items	Select this check box to print all items in a folder view.
	Only Selected Items	Select this check box to print only the folder items you selected before opening the Print dialog box.

V

Bending Folders to Your Will

Previewing Printing

Before you print an item or a view, you can preview it to see what it will look like on paper. Print Preview uses the settings for the currently selected print style in the Print and Page Setup dialog boxes. To preview a selected item or a view before printing, take one of the following actions:

- Choose Print Preview from the File menu.

- Point to Page Setup on the File menu, choose the print style you want to preview, and then click the Preview button in the Page Setup dialog box.

- Choose Print from the File menu, and then click the Preview button in the Print dialog box.

Figure 17-2 shows a preview of a calendar printout and the Print Preview toolbar.

Print Preview displays a full-page layout of the items to be printed, reducing the size of the folder item text in order to display an entire page on screen at one time. It's an extremely useful feature when you want to check how the various print styles look on the page, how columns line up, whether the print style needs adjustment, and so on.

If you don't like what you see in Print Preview, you can click the Page Setup button on the Print Preview toolbar to open the Page Setup

FIGURE 17-2.
The Print Preview window.

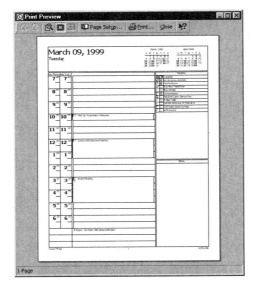

Printing and Assembling a Booklet

The booklet print styles are designed so that you can print pages on both sides of a sheet of paper and then cut and staple the pages to create a booklet. (In Outlook, *paper* refers to a physical sheet of paper. *Page* refers to the area of the paper that is actually printed.) The layout and page numbering for the booklet are arranged automatically by Outlook.

You can print a booklet on either a duplex printer (a printer that can print on both sides of the paper) or a printer that prints on only one side of the paper at a time. When using a duplex printer, be sure it is set up for duplex printing.

1 Click the Properties button in the Print dialog box to open the Properties dialog box for your duplex printer.

2 Select the Flip option you prefer. (Note that None is the default and is for one-sided printing only.)

3 If you are using a printer that prints on only one side of the paper at a time, print even-numbered pages first (by selecting Even in the Number Of Pages box in the Print dialog box).

4 Finally, load the printed pages into the printer again so that their blank sides will be printed on, starting with the lowest-numbered page first (usually Page 1), and then select Odd to print the odd-numbered pages. Make sure you have additional blank sheets in the printer, in case there is an extra odd-numbered page at the end.

Before printing, verify your paper settings on the Page setup dialog box.

1 Click the Page Setup button, and then click the Paper tab when the Page Setup dialog box opens.

2 Set Paper Type to the size of the paper in your printer, and then select the Page Size to the right. Page Size lets you print one page on each sheet of paper or 2, 4, or 8 pages per sheet of paper if you select 1/2 Sheet Booklet, 1/4 Sheet Booklet, or 1/8 Sheet Booklet. You can also select the orientation of the pages.

3 Click Print Preview to check settings, and then click OK to start printing.

After the booklet's pages are printed, if necessary cut the paper into the number of sections you specified. For example, if you specified a 1/8 Sheet Booklet, cut the paper into four sections. Each section will show two pages on each side of the sheet. Stack the sheets of paper in the order of the page numbering, and fold along a ruler or straight edge. You can then staple the sheets of paper together into a booklet.

dialog box. You can then adjust the current print style as explained in "Modifying a Print Style," below, returning to Print Preview whenever you want to check the results of your changes. Or, if you decide to try a different print style, you can click the Print button either on the Print Preview toolbar or in the Page Setup dialog box to open the Print dialog box and select a new style.

If you need to see the text in actual size while you are in Print Preview, click the page (the pointer will show a magnifying glass with a plus sign). To switch the view back to full page, click again inside the page area (now the pointer shows a minus sign). To see multiple pages, move the pointer outside the page area (another minus sign appears) and click again. You can also switch between viewing sizes by using the Actual Size, One Page, and Multiple Pages toolbar buttons.

When you're ready to print, click the Print button on the Print Preview toolbar, and then click OK in the Print dialog box.

Modifying a Print Style

You can make a number of changes to a print style, including changes to its format, to its standard paper settings, and to the information included in headers or footers.

> **⊘ NOTE**
>
> If you decide to modify a built-in print style for all print jobs, the changes will affect that print style in all folders and views where you can use it. For example, if you change the Table style to print with a landscape orientation instead of portrait, all printing you do using this style will be in landscape. If you change a built-in print style, you can return it to its original settings. *See "Resetting a Print Style," on page 501.*

To change the print style, you have to open the Page Setup dialog box. You can do this using any of these techniques:

- Point to Page Setup on the File menu, and choose the print style you want to use from the submenu. (The submenu lists the available built-in styles as well as any print styles you have created that apply to the view. *See "Creating a Print Style," on page 502.*)

- Choose Print on the File menu, choose the print style you want to change, and then click the Page Setup button.

■ Point to Page Setup on the File menu, and choose Define Print Styles. In the dialog box that appears, choose the style you want to change and then click the Edit button. To avoid changing an existing style, click the copy button instead.

Now you can review and change any of the settings shown in the Page Setup dialog box (described in more detail in the next three sections) to customize the print style.

You can also use the Print Preview feature in this process. As you make your changes in the Page Setup dialog box, you can click the Print Preview button at any time to see how your adjustments affect the printed page. If you're dissatisfied with the results, click the Page Setup button on the Print Preview toolbar to return to the Page Setup dialog box so that you can continue refining the print style.

When you're satisfied with what you see in Print Preview (and if you don't want to change another print style), click the Close button on the Print Preview toolbar to return to Outlook, or click the Print button on the same toolbar to open the Print dialog box, where you can begin printing as soon as you click OK.

Changing Format Tab Settings

The Format tab of the Page Setup dialog box always provides a small preview picture of the print style. For all print styles, you can change the fonts used in headings and in the body of the folder items, and you have the option of printing with or without gray shading. Figure 17-3, on the next page, shows the Format tab for the Table print style; the tab for the Memo style is very similar.

Format Tab Settings for Printing Calendars

The Format tab for the Calendar Details print style is similar to the tab shown in Figure 17-3, on the following page, except the Options section contains these additional settings:

■ **Start A New Page Each.** This option lets you choose to start a new page for each day, week, or month.

■ **Print Attachments.** This option lets you choose whether or not to print attachments with the calendar item.

You can also change the format of the Daily, Weekly, Monthly, and Tri-Fold print styles, which are used to print calendar items. Again, you can use different fonts for date headings and for appointments, and you

FIGURE 17-3.
The Format tab for the
Table print style.

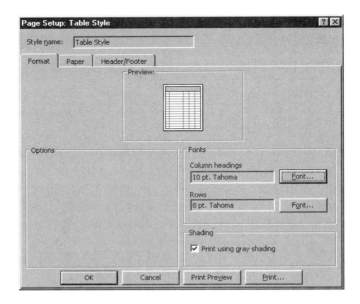

can print with or without gray shading. But the Options area gives you
some additional layout choices, as shown here for the Daily style:

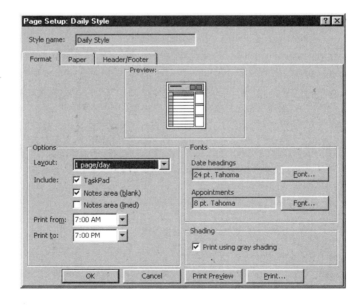

In the Layout box for the Daily print style, you can tell Outlook to print
the day's calendar on two pages rather than one, giving you more room
to add information about your appointments and meetings. You can
choose to include or omit the TaskPad (which is lined) and the Notes

section (which is lined or unlined), and you can specify the range of time to be printed for the day (in the Print From and Print To boxes).

The Format tabs for the Weekly and Monthly print styles are similar to the Daily print style, with the following variations:

- The Format tab for the Weekly print style offers the same options you find for the Daily print style. (In this case, of course, you choose whether to use one or two pages to print a week rather than a day.) In addition, this tab contains two Arrange options: click Top To Bottom to have Outlook arrange the seven days down two columns on the page (omitting hour markers), or click Left To Right to have Outlook set up seven columns across the page, one for each day, including hour markers. (If you choose Top To Bottom, Outlook turns off the Print From and Print To boxes—there's no need to specify a range of hours when the hour markers are omitted.)

- The Format tab for the Monthly print style provides the Layout option, which prints a month on one page or two, and the Include options to print the TaskPad and the Notes section, but it omits the Arrange options and the Print From and Print To boxes. You can also choose not to print weekends and to print exactly one month on each page.

The Format tab for the Tri-Fold print style is a little different. It contains only three options: Left Section, Middle Section, and Right Section. For each section (fold) of a tri-fold printing, you can specify one of the following items to print in that section:

- Daily calendar
- Weekly calendar
- Monthly calendar
- TaskPad
- Notes (blank)
- Notes (lined)

V

Bending Folders to Your Will

Format Tab Settings for Printing Contacts

The Format tabs for the Card, Small Booklet, and Medium Booklet print styles, used for printing contact items, are identical, and the Options area contains these choices:

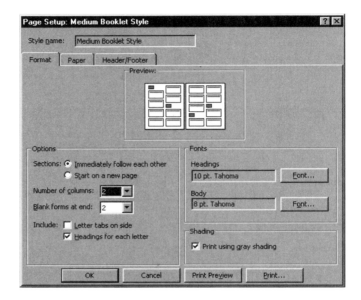

- **Sections** refers to the alphabetical sections of your contact list. You can print alphabetical sections one after another in continuous columns, or you can begin the entries for each letter of the alphabet on a new page.

- **Number Of Columns** lets you specify the number of columns per page.

- **Blank Forms At End** lets you tell Outlook to include blank contact cards (forms) at the end of the printing—these are useful when you're out of the office and need to handwrite contact information to be entered later into your contact list in Outlook.

- **Include** lets you include or omit headings for each alphabetical section as well as letter tabs on the side of the page. When you include letter tabs, they appear on the right side of the page in a shaded column, as shown in Figure 17-4. Notice how the color of the tabs indicates which contacts are on each page so that you can use the tabs to quickly find the information you need.

Finally, the Format tab for the Phone Directory print style is fairly simple. You can specify the number of columns to print, and you can

FIGURE 17-4.
Letter tabs indicate which contacts appear on each page.

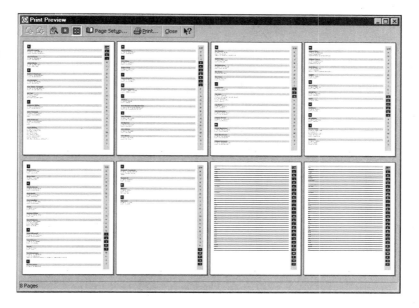

include or omit headings for each alphabetical section and letter tabs on the side of the page.

Changing Paper Tab Settings

The various print styles have their own paper settings—paper size (or type), page size, orientation, paper source (the tray(s) in your printer), and margins. You can adjust these settings on the Paper tab of the Page Setup dialog box, shown in Figure 17-5, on the following page.

Setting Paper Type and Page Size

The Paper tab displays the same information for all print styles. You can select a paper size or enter dimensions for a custom page, choose the appropriate paper feed, and set the page margins and the orientation. In the Size box of the Page section, you set the area each formatted Outlook page occupies on each sheet of paper. For example, you can choose to print your calendar on standard letter-sized paper in 1/2 Sheet Booklet size.

When printing Outlook items and views, it's important to understand how Outlook distinguishes between paper and page. In Outlook, *paper* and *paper type* refer to the physical sheet of paper you put in the printer. *Page* refers to the area of that sheet of paper that each formatted Outlook *page* will be printed on. You can print several of these *pages* on a single sheet of *paper*. For example, in the Small Booklet

FIGURE 17-5.

The Paper tab for the Memo print style.

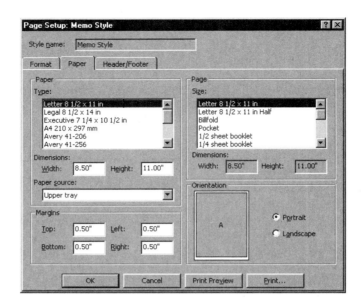

print style, you can select 1/8 Sheet Booklet and print eight pages of a booklet on each side of a single sheet of paper.

Each print style starts with a default paper type and page size, which you can modify. When you select a paper type, the list of page sizes available for use with that paper type is displayed in the Page Size list. Settings for paper type and page size in the Page Setup dialog box take precedence over any paper settings you select in the Properties dialog box for your printer (which you open by clicking the Properties button in the Print dialog box). Settings you make in the Orientation area of the Paper tab apply to pages, not to paper type.

Let's say you want to use the Daily print style to print four days worth of calendar items. By default, Outlook prints the items for each day on a separate sheet of 8.5-by-11-inch paper. If you want to have all four days appear on one sheet of paper, select Billfold from the Size list on the Paper tab, or select the Half setting to put two pages on each side of one sheet of paper.

Setting a Custom Paper Size

You can set up any custom paper size you want. To specify a custom paper size, simply select Custom in the Paper Type list, and then set the width and height of the paper in the Dimensions boxes in the Paper Type section.

> **NOTE**
>
> If you change the width or height of a listed paper type in the Dimensions boxes, Outlook automatically selects Custom in the Paper Type list.

When you set up a custom paper size, the Page Size list includes the appropriate page size choices for that paper size. Outlook also adds Custom and Custom Half as the first two items in the Page Size list.

Setting Margins

When you change the margin settings, you're changing the width and height of the blank space at the borders of the page. Keep margins small unless you like lots of blank space around the printed information. The larger the margins, the more cramped the information appears because it must fit into a smaller space. You'll often need to print on more sheets of paper if you use large margins.

Outlook's default margins are .50 inches for the top, bottom, left, and right borders of the page. You can click the Print Preview button in the Page Setup dialog box to see the effect of changes you make to the margins.

Changing Header and Footer Settings

The process of setting up headers and footers is the same for all print styles. The Header/Footer tab of the Page Setup dialog box provides six boxes in which you can insert the text and fields that you want Outlook to print in headers and footers, as shown in Figure 17-6, on the next page. For some print styles, Outlook presets parts of the header or footer, but you can change any section of the header or footer as you like.

You can use text only, fields only, or a combination of text and fields in your headers and footers. Placing information in the left, center, and right boxes of the Header and Footer sections controls how the information is displayed on the printed page—if you enter text only in the center header box, for instance, Outlook prints a centered header on each page. Text entered in the left boxes is aligned on the left margin of each page, and text in the right boxes is aligned on the right margin. For the footer set up in Figure 17-6, on the next page, Outlook will print the user's name on the left, the page number in the center, and the date of printing on the right.

 **NOTE**

The term *field* refers to a location that shows data or to an empty box that you (or Outlook) can fill in with information.

To insert a field into a header or footer, click in the boxes where you want to insert a field, and then click one of the field buttons on the Header/Footer tab, which are labeled in Figure 17-6.

Outlook displays an inserted field as words inside square brackets: *[Page #]*, for example. (You can type the field in the header or footer box instead of clicking a button if you type it in this format.) During printing, Outlook replaces the field with the proper information—the page number, the date of printing, and so on.

You can type any text in any of the header and footer areas. The text might be some special information about the printed items, such as the date range of appointments, meetings, or tasks. You might want to type the word *Page* before the Page Number field. Or you might type the word *of* between a Page Number field and a Total Pages field and then type the word *pages* after the Total Pages field—this way, on each page Outlook prints a header or footer such as *5 of 10 pages*.

FIGURE 17-6.
The Header/Footer tab of the Page Setup dialog box.

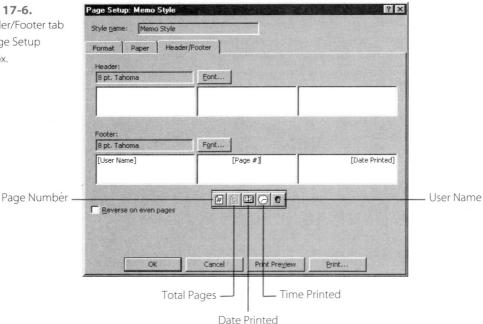

If you want the same headers and footers to print on every page, leave the Reverse On Even Pages check box cleared. But if you're printing on both sides of the paper or if you're going to photocopy single-sided printed pages back to back to assemble a booklet, you might want to have Outlook always print the text you place in the left-most box of the header or footer on the inside edge of all pages, and the text you place in the right box on the outside edge of all pages. This would, for instance, allow page numbers placed in the right box to appear on the outside edge of each of two facing pages (both odd and even pages), as you see in this book. To do this, select the Reverse On Even Pages check box.

Resetting a Print Style

After you make changes to a built-in print style, you might want to restore the original settings. To reset a built-in print style, follow these steps:

1 Point to Page Setup on the File menu, and choose Define Print Styles from the submenu to open the dialog box shown in Figure 17-7.

2 Select the print style you want to reset.

3 Click Reset.

4 When Outlook asks you to confirm resetting the print style, click OK.

5 Repeat steps 2 through 4 for each built-in style you want to reset.

6 When you've finished, click the Close button in the Define Print Styles dialog box.

FIGURE 17-7.

The Define Print Styles dialog box.

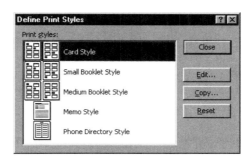

NOTE

> You can't reset a print style that you have created. You can only modify it or delete it.

Creating a Print Style

What if you want to modify a print style but only want it to apply to certain print jobs? Rather than changing a built-in print style, which will affect the printing of all folder items for which you use the style, you can create a print style of your own. Start by first making a copy of a built-in print style (or a copy of a print style you've already created). This method gives you several advantages. First, you start from an existing batch of settings, which means that you need to modify only the specific settings that you want to change rather than having to set all the options yourself. Second, in any instance in which the print style you copied applies, your custom style also appears on the Page Setup submenu (after you exit and restart Outlook) and in the Print dialog box for easy selection. You don't have to recreate your special print style for every view or folder.

Here's how to create a print style:

1 Point to Page Setup on the File menu, and choose Define Print Styles from the submenu to see the Define Print Styles dialog box, shown on the previous page in Figure 17-7. As an alternative, you can choose Print from the File menu, select the print style in the Print Style list, and then click the Define Styles button.

2 In the Define Print Styles dialog box, select the print style you want to copy.

3 Click Copy to see the Page Setup dialog box.

4 In the Style Name text box, type a name for your custom style to replace the *Copy Of...* text.

5 Change any settings on the three tabs in the Page Setup dialog box. *For details, see "Changing Format Tab Settings," on page 493, "Changing Paper Tab Settings," on page 497, and "Changing Headers and Footer Settings," on page 499.*

6 Click OK in the Page Setup dialog box.

7 Click the Close button in the Define Print Styles dialog box.

You can also use the Print Preview feature in this process. As you make your changes (step 5), you can click the Print Preview button at any time to see how your style will appear on the printed page. If you're dissatisfied with the results, click the Page Setup button on the Print Preview toolbar to return to the Page Setup dialog box and continue creating the print style.

Deleting a Print Style

If you no longer want or need a print style that you created, you can delete it. To do so, take these steps:

1 Point to Page Setup on the File menu, and choose Define Print Styles from the submenu. As an alternative, you can choose Print from the File menu, select the print style in the Print Style list, and then click the Define Styles button.

2 In the Define Print Styles dialog box, select the print style you want to delete, and then click the Delete button.

3 When Outlook asks you to confirm that you want to delete the print style, click OK. Repeat steps 2 and 3 for each custom style that you want to delete.

4 When you've finished, click the Close button in the Define Print Styles dialog box.

By taking advantage of Outlook's extensive printing features, you can format and organize the information you usually access on screen to produce an attractive printed form suitable for traveling, sharing, or producing reports. Your printouts can also serve as a backup reference in case you delete an item by mistake. For even better insurance against losing important information, however, you can archive Outlook data for safekeeping, as you will learn how to do in the next chapter.

V

Bending Folders to Your Will

Archiving Folder Items

A s you use Microsoft Outlook, your folders can eventually become cluttered with items that you no longer need on a day-to-day basis—tasks that were long since completed, e-mail messages about a project that has been canceled, appointments from the past, and so on. You can, of course, simply delete these items if you're sure that you'll never need them again. But if the items might be important in the future—perhaps that canceled project comes back to life, for instance—you can put them into storage.

Outlook lets you transfer old items to an archive (storage) file on your hard disk, removing them from your current folders. If you need the items in the future, you can retrieve them from the archive file. You can archive folder items in two ways:

■ Let AutoArchive automatically archive folder items of specified ages on a regular basis.

■ Archive folder items manually as the need arises.

When you archive Outlook folder items, your existing folder structure is maintained in the archive file. For example, if you choose to archive the items in a subfolder, the main folder is also created in the archive file, but the items in the main folder are not necessarily archived. Even if folders are emptied during archiving, Outlook leaves the folders in place. To remove an empty folder, right-click the folder name in the Folder List, and choose Delete from the shortcut menu.

Using the AutoArchive Feature

Outlook might be initially set up to automatically archive old items in folders you've specified every 14 days. Outlook lets you know when it's preparing to run the AutoArchive feature and gives you a chance to cancel it. Every 14 days when you start Outlook, you'll see the following prompt shortly after startup:

You can vary the 14-day time span, and you can specify additional folders to be archived. You can also change the definition of an "old" (expired) item, and you can use AutoArchive for both archiving and deleting. To set up automatic archiving the way you like, you first need to review or adjust the AutoArchive settings on the Other tab of the Options dialog box. Then you need to set the AutoArchive properties for each folder that you want Outlook to archive.

While AutoArchive is running, you'll see an animated icon on the right side of the status bar. Right-click the icon if you want to see details of the archiving process or to cancel archiving.

Setting General AutoArchive Options

As you might recall from Chapter 3, "Setting Outlook Options," the Options dialog box contains tabs whose settings govern Outlook's default behavior in various areas. To review or change Outlook's default AutoArchive settings, follow these steps:

1 Choose Options from the Tools menu, select the Other tab, and then click the AutoArchive button to display the dialog box shown in Figure 18-1.

2 Select the AutoArchive Every __ Days check box to turn on AutoArchive. If you want to turn off AutoArchive, clear the check box and then click OK to close the dialog box. Otherwise, set the interval of days between archiving and then continue with step 3.

3 Clear the Prompt Before AutoArchive check box if you want automatic archiving to proceed without asking your approval.

4 Clear the Delete Expired Items When AutoArchiving check box if you don't want expired e-mail items to be deleted.

5 If the name of the archive file is incorrect, enter it in the Default Archive File text box or click Browse to locate it.

6 Click OK.

TIP

AutoArchive runs only when you start up Outlook. *If you want to archive items in the middle of an Outlook session, see "Archiving Folder Items Manually," on page 511.*

FIGURE 18-1.
The AutoArchive dialog box.

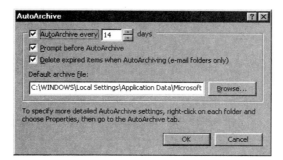

V

Bending Folders to Your Will

When the Delete Expired Items When AutoArchiving check box is selected, Outlook moves expired e-mail messages to the Deleted Items folder rather than adding them to the archive file. Clear this check box to prevent deletion of the items. Also, when AutoArchive runs, items in the Deleted Items folder are not moved to the archive file. Instead they are deleted.

> The location of the Archive.pst file depends on how your system is set up. Make a note of the location shown in the AutoArchive dialog box for future reference.

Outlook's default archive file is named Archive.pst. The .pst filename extension indicates a personal folders file, which Outlook uses for archiving. You can create more than one archive file. For example, you can create a separate archive file for each of your folders, and you can manually select and archive groups of items that relate to a particular project.

> The settings in the AutoArchive dialog box affect both automatic archiving and manual archiving (explained in "Archiving Folder Items Manually," on page 511).

Setting a Folder's AutoArchive Properties

Once AutoArchive is turned on and the settings adjusted (if necessary) on the AutoArchive tab of the Options dialog box, you need to specify which folders Outlook should automatically archive. By default, the

---

Archiving vs. Exporting Outlook Folder Items

When thinking about archiving Outlook folder items, it's helpful to keep in mind some differences between archiving items and exporting items. You can only archive Outlook items by using a personal folder file (a file with a .pst extension), but you can export Outlook items to many file types, such as text. Although Outlook can archive all types of Outlook items, other files (such as an attached Microsoft Excel spreadsheet or Microsoft Word document) are only archived if they are stored in an e-mail folder. A file not stored in an e-mail folder cannot be archived.

When you archive, the original items are copied to the archive file and then removed from the folder that is currently open. When you export, the original items are copied to the export file but are not removed from the current folder.

AutoArchive feature is turned on for the Calendar, Journal, Tasks, Sent Items, and Deleted Items folders. To turn on automatic archiving for the Inbox folder, the Notes folder, or any folder that you have created (or to turn it off for the default folders), you need to change the folder's properties, as explained here:

1 Right-click a folder icon on the Outlook Bar, and choose Properties from the shortcut menu. If the folder you want does not appear on the Outlook Bar, choose it from the Folder List instead.

Display the Folder List by selecting Folder List from the View menu.

2 In the Properties dialog box, click the AutoArchive tab.

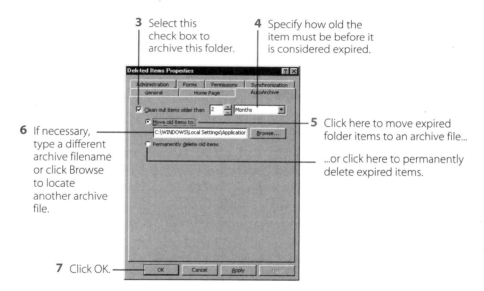

3 Select this check box to archive this folder.

4 Specify how old the item must be before it is considered expired.

6 If necessary, type a different archive filename or click Browse to locate another archive file.

5 Click here to move expired folder items to an archive file...

...or click here to permanently delete expired items.

7 Click OK.

Your AutoArchive choices take effect the next time Outlook automatically archives the folder's items or when you archive them manually. You'll need to repeat this procedure for each folder that you want to set up for automatic archiving.

The Clean Out Items Older Than option defines the number of days, weeks, or months that Outlook should use to consider an item expired. If you enter 60 days, for example, Outlook will consider items expired:

- An e-mail message will expire 60 days after the most recent date it was sent, received, or modified.

■ An appointment or meeting will expire 60 days after the date of the appointment or meeting or 60 days after the date the item was created or last modified.

■ A task will expire 60 days after the date it was marked completed or 60 days after the date it was created or last modified.

■ A note will expire 60 days after the date it was created or last modified.

■ A journal entry will expire 60 days after the date it was created or last modified.

 NOTE

Outlook does not archive items from the Contacts folder. Task items from the Tasks folder (both your own tasks and tasks that you have assigned to someone else) are not archived unless they have been marked completed.

Preventing the Automatic Archiving of a Folder Item

Somewhere, in at least one Outlook folder, you're likely to have an item that you don't want Outlook to archive. Maybe it's an item that you want to keep as a reminder. Or perhaps you've set up AutoArchive to permanently delete expired items from the folder, but you don't want to lose this one particular item. In such cases, you can designate the item as "Do Not AutoArchive."

To prevent a single folder item from being archived (or deleted by AutoArchive), take these steps:

1 Open the item.

2 Choose Properties from the File menu, and click the General tab in the Properties dialog box. The dialog box you see depends on the type of item you opened.

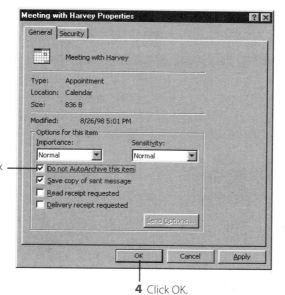

3 Select this check box to exclude the item from AutoArchiving.

4 Click OK.

You must repeat this procedure for each folder item you want to designate as "Do Not AutoArchive." If a folder contains a number of items that you do not want to archive automatically, consider turning off AutoArchive for that *folder* and then manually archive the other individual items.

> You can always archive a folder item manually, even if you've designated it as "Do Not AutoArchive." This designation simply prevents AutoArchive from taking any automatic action with the folder item.

Archiving Folder Items Manually

Even though you set up AutoArchive to archive folder items on a regular basis, you still might want to archive items manually from time to time. Perhaps you've finished a project and want to archive the related items sooner than the next scheduled AutoArchive. Maybe you've turned off AutoArchive for a certain folder but nevertheless want to archive a few items from that folder. Or maybe you're finally ready to archive an item that has previously been designated as "Do Not AutoArchive."

To archive folder items manually, follow these steps:

1 Choose Archive from Outlook's File menu to open the Archive dialog box.

2 If you select the first option in the dialog box, Archive All Folders According To Their AutoArchive Settings, the rest of the options become unavailable and you should just click OK to begin the archive process immediately.

If you select the second option, Archive This Folder And All Subfolders, proceed to step 3.

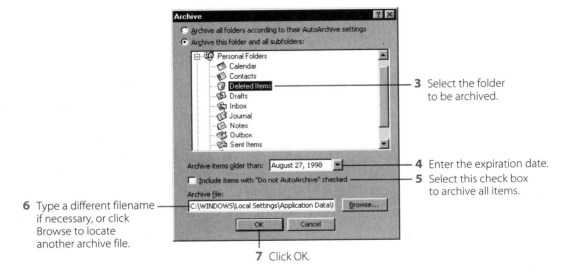

3 Select the folder to be archived.

4 Enter the expiration date.

5 Select this check box to archive all items.

6 Type a different filename if necessary, or click Browse to locate another archive file.

7 Click OK.

You must repeat this procedure for each folder that you want to archive manually.

To type a date in the Archive Items Older Than box, you can use any standard date format: 10-13-99, 10/13/99, Oct-13-99, October 13, 1999, and so on. Alternatively, you can click the down arrow beside the date to display a calendar from which you can select the date.

Retrieving Archived Folder Items

The main reason you archive your old items rather than delete them is so you can retrieve them later if you need to. You can retrieve items from an archive file by opening the archive file, by adding the archive file to your user profile, or by importing the archive file.

To open the archive file (or any file with the .pst extension) point to Open on the File menu, click Personal Folders File, and then choose the file in the dialog box that appears. You'll probably have to navigate to the folder containing the file. Once you open the folder, you can drag the items you want to restore from the Archive folder to one of your current folders.

To retrieve items from an archive file by importing the file, choose Import And Export from the File menu to start the Import And Export Wizard. On the wizard's first page, select Import From Another Program or File, and then click the Next button. On the next wizard page, select Personal Folder File (.pst), and then click the Next button. From there, you can follow the instructions in the Import And Export Wizard. Outlook moves the archived items back into your current folders.

Archiving provides a convenient way to trim your folders of older information that you do not need to refer to often but that you may need at a later date. If you choose not to archive automatically at some regular interval, you should develop a pattern of manually archiving based on how full your folders become. In the next chapter, you will learn how to manage your folders in other ways.

V

Bending Folders to Your Will

Managing Folders

Microsoft Outlook stores all items in folders, and it can display the folders and files on any disk that's connected to your computer. In Chapter 16, "Managing Folder Contents," you learned how to manage the contents of folders. But to make Outlook work more effectively and efficiently, you also need to be able to manage the folders themselves. That's what this chapter describes.

Opening a Folder

Outlook gives you several ways to open a folder. As you know, icons for most Outlook folders appear on one of the three groups on the Outlook Bar, so opening a folder from the Outlook Bar is a quick and convenient option. To open a folder that appears on the Outlook Bar, click the group label that contains the folder you want to open, and then click the folder icon. If necessary, click the small up or down arrow on the Outlook Bar to scroll to the folder you want.

In addition to the Outlook Bar, you can use the Folder List or the Go to Folder command on the View menu to open folders.

Opening a Folder from the Folder List

If you need to use a folder that's not listed on the Outlook Bar, you can open the folder from the Folder List. In Chapter 2, "Discovering Outlook," you learned how to open the Folder List. In fact, you learned that you can keep the Folder List displayed on the screen until you close it manually, or you can have it close automatically after you select a folder. Either way, once the Folder List is open, click the folder you want to open.

If you open a folder from the Other Shortcut group that is a shortcut to a folder on your computer, the Folder List displays file folders instead of Outlook folders. This list looks just like the lists you see in My Computer or Windows Explorer.

Opening a Folder from the View Menu

The Go To command on the View menu displays a list of the Outlook Today, Inbox, Drafts, Calendar, Contacts, and Tasks folders, as well as the Folder command for opening any folder. To open a folder listed on the Go To menu, point to Go To on the View menu, and then choose the folder name on the submenu. To open a folder that does not appear on the submenu listed on the Go To menu, do the following:

1 Point to Go To on the View menu and choose Folder from the menu that appears. (You have to expand the Go To menu to choose this option.)

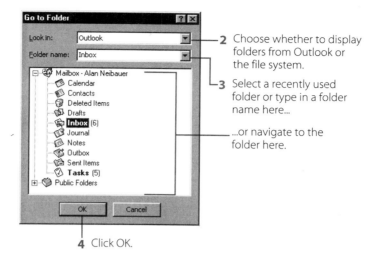

2 Choose whether to display folders from Outlook or the file system.

3 Select a recently used folder or type in a folder name here...

...or navigate to the folder here.

4 Click OK.

Opening a Folder in a Separate Window

If you want to see the contents of two folders at the same time, you can open the second folder in a separate window. This arrangement enables you to switch from one folder to another quickly.

To open a folder in a separate window, right-click the folder, either on the Outlook Bar or in the Folder List, and then choose Open In New Window from the shortcut menu.

Outlook displays a new Outlook window with the selected folder open. You can set up this Outlook window in all the same ways you set up the first Outlook window. Of course, having a separate window gives you the opportunity to set up each window differently.

Creating a Folder

Creating a new folder is a pretty simple task. You can add a new folder inside any existing folder or subfolder.

To create a new folder, follow these steps:

1 Choose Folder from the File menu, and then choose New Folder from the submenu, as shown in the graphic on the next page.

V

Bending Folders to Your Will

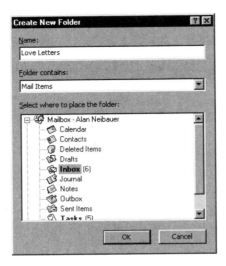

2 Type a name for the new folder.

3 Choose the type of Outlook item the folder will contain.

4 Select the folder where the new folder will reside.

5 Click OK.

Most of the folder management commands on the Folder submenu can also be accessed from the Folder List. Right-click the folder, and then choose the appropriate command from the shortcut menu that appears.

Copying a Folder

If you have a folder that might prove to be useful in more than one location, you can make a copy of it as a subfolder of another folder (rather than move it). For example, you might copy a server folder to your personal folders. You can even create a new folder in which to place the copy during copying.

The easiest way to copy a folder is by using the Folder List. In the Folder List, click the folder that you want to make a copy of. Hold down the Ctrl key and drag the folder to the one in which you want to place the copy, and then release the mouse button.

You can also copy a folder using a dialog box by following these steps:

1 Open the folder you want to copy.

2 Point to Folder on the File menu, and then choose Copy from the submenu. Alternatively, you can right-click the folder in the Folder List (not on the Outlook Bar) and then choose Copy from the shortcut menu.

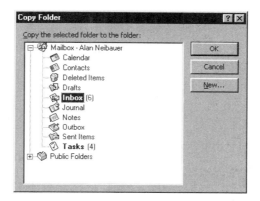

3 Select the folder in which the copy will reside, or click New to copy it to a new folder. If you click New you will have to name the new folder and place it in another existing folder using the Create New Folder dialog box that appears.

4 Click OK.

Copying a Folder Design

You can sometimes put a lot of effort into designing a folder—setting up views, grouping items, adding filters, sorting, designing forms, and granting permissions. After you set up the design of a folder, you might want to apply the same design to another folder. Rather than going through a laborious setup procedure for each folder, you can simply copy a folder design from one folder to another. Here's how:

1 Open the Folder List, and select the folder *to which* you will be copying the design of another folder.

2 Choose Folder from the File menu, and then choose Copy Folder Design from the submenu.

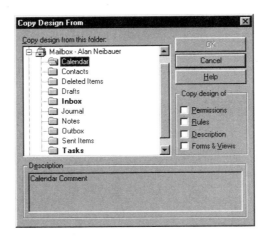

3 Select the folder whose design you want to copy.

4 Select the check box for each design element you want to copy.

5 Click OK.

After you copy a folder design, you can adjust it further to suit your needs. *For information about folder design, see Chapter 20, "Organizing Folder Items."*

Moving a Folder

Sometimes you may want to move a folder to another location rather than copy it. You can move a folder into another folder in several ways. The easiest way is by dragging. Simply display the Folder List and expand it as needed so that both folders are visible. Then drag the folder you want to move to the folder where it will be stored (the destination folder).

You can move only the folders that you have created. You can't move the standard (built-in) Outlook folders or server or personal folders. Unless you have permission from the system administrator, Microsoft Exchange won't let you move a folder to the Public Folders folder.

Alternatively, instead of dragging the folder, you can choose Folder from the File menu, and then choose Move from the submenu. Or you can right-click the folder in the Folder List, and then choose Move from the shortcut menu. Either action displays the Move Folder dialog box, similar to the Copy Folder dialog box shown on page 519. Select the destination folder or click New to move the folder into a new folder that you name and create. Click OK to complete the move.

Renaming a Folder

If you didn't get the name right when you created a folder, you can change it. To rename a folder that you created, follow these steps:

1 Select the folder you want to rename.

2 Choose Folder from the File menu, and then choose Rename from the submenu. (The Rename command shows the name of the open folder.) If the Folder List is not displayed, you'll see the Rename dialog box.

3 In the Rename dialog box, type the new folder name.

4 Click OK.

You can quickly rename a folder in the Folder List by clicking it once to select it, and then clicking the selection a second time. You can then type a new name directly over the current name. Press Enter to finish.

If you choose the Rename command while the Folder List is displayed, Outlook highlights the folder name in the Folder List, allowing you to rename the folder simply by typing the new name and pressing the Enter key.

You can rename only the folders that you have created. You can't rename the standard Outlook folders (although you can rename the shortcuts to these folders—the folder icons—on the Outlook Bar). Renaming a folder does not change the name of the corresponding folder icon on the Outlook Bar. *To change the name of a folder icon on the Outlook Bar (whether the icon represents a standard Outlook folder or a folder that you created and renamed), see "Renaming an Icon on the Outlook Bar," on page 39.*

Removing a Folder

Outlook gives you no warning that deleting a folder also deletes all items and subfolders in the folder. So, if you want to keep any of a folder's subfolders or items, move them before you delete the folder. *See "Moving and Copying Folder Items," on page 456, and "Moving a Folder," on page 520.*

When you delete a folder, Outlook moves the folder and its contents to the Deleted Items folder. From there, you can retrieve the folder and its contents if you change your mind, or you can permanently delete them. To retrieve (undelete) a folder, move it to some other folder. To completely delete folders and their contents from Outlook, you must also delete them from the Deleted Items folder. *See "Purging Deleted Items," on page 480.*

Outlook gives you a number of ways to delete a folder:

- Select the folder in the Folder List, and then click the Delete button on the Standard toolbar or press the Delete key.

- Right-click the folder, and then choose Delete from the shortcut menu.

- Select the folder in the Folder List, choose Folder from the File menu, and then choose Delete from the submenu.

- Drag the folder to the Deleted Items folder.

> **NOTE**
>
> You can delete only the folders that you have created. You can't delete the standard Outlook folders. If the folder you delete has an icon on the Outlook Bar, deleting the folder does not remove the corresponding folder icon from the Outlook Bar. *To remove the folder icon from the Outlook Bar, see the directions in "Removing an Icon from the Outlook Bar," on page 38.*

Working with Public Folders

A public folder is similar to other Outlook folders or disk folders, in that it can contain any type of folder item—a message, an appointment, a contact, a task, a journal entry, a note, a posting, a file, or a form. The purpose of public folders is to allow wide access to folder items that are interesting to everyone in an organization or to a particular group within an organization—for example, a project team or a specific department. Public folders can also be used to organize information by subject matter, which gives people interested in the subject a handy place to browse.

In most public folders, you can read items and add your own items, but you cannot delete items other than those you added. Some public folders are even more restricted—you might be able to see and read the items but be unable to add any items to the folder. In some cases, the public folder is not available to you at all. The difference has to do with permissions. *See the sidebar "Do You Have Permission?" on the next page.* To open a public folder and read its folder items, you must have permission to do so. You must also have permission to add items to a public folder before you can create items. In most cases, public folders grant such permission to anyone who has access to them.

Opening Public Folders

Public folders are contained in the folder labeled Public Folders on your e-mail server, so to view the list of public folders, you must be connected directly to your server. You can't view public folders while you're working offline unless you set up public folder favorites and set your system to work offline. *See "Using Public Folder Favorites," on page 525.*

To open a public folder, take these steps:

1 Choose Folder List from the View menu, if the Folder List is not already displayed.

2 In the Folder List, expand the list of subfolders by clicking the plus sign beside Public Folders. The first level of public folders contains only two folders: Favorites and All Public Folders.

3 To see the list of public folders, click the plus sign next to All Public Folders.

Each folder can contain folder items and subfolders. You'll know that a folder has subfolders if you see a plus sign next to its name in the Folder List. To see the subfolders, click the plus sign. Click any additional plus signs to expand the subfolders.

You treat items in public folders the same way you treat mail messages, except that you probably won't be able to delete or move the folder items—unless you meet at least one of the following criteria:

■ You have administrative privileges

■ You are the owner of the folder

■ You put the item in the folder yourself

You can, however, copy a folder item to your Outlook folders and disk folders, and you can save any folder item as a file on a disk.

Creating a Public Folder

If you are connected to your server, you can create public folders yourself. The folder will then be available to everyone on your network, unless you assign specific permissions.

To create a public folder, follow these steps:

1 Choose Folder List from the View menu, if the Folder List is not already displayed.

2 In the Folder List, expand the list of subfolders by clicking the plus sign beside Public Folders. The first level of public folders contains only two folders: Favorites and All Public Folders.

3 Click All Public Folders.

4 Choose Folder from the File menu, and then choose New Folder from the submenu to see the Create New Folder dialog box shown on page 518. All Public Folders will be highlighted in the dialog box as the designation folder for your new folder.

Do You Have Permission?

Some public folders are open and available to all Outlook users on your system. Other public folders are limited to people who have a special affiliation with the folder, such as members of a project team or group with a common interest.

In general, if you can open the folder, you'll be able to read its contents. If you don't have permission to use a folder, you can't open it. If you don't have permission to post an item to a folder, you'll either see an error message when you try to post the item, or the commands you need to post a message will be unavailable.

You can check your permissions for a public folder by opening the Properties dialog box for the folder. To display this dialog box, right-click the folder in the Folder list and choose Properties from the shortcut menu, or click the folder, choose Folder from the File menu, and then choose Properties from the submenu.

If you do not already have "owner" permissions for the folder, which some folders provide to all users by default, click the Summary tab (read the next paragraph if you see a Permissions tab instead) in the Properties dialog box, and review your permissions. After you review the level of your permissions, you can discuss any changes you want to make with your network administrator.

If you created the public folder, or have been assigned "owner" permissions, click the Permissions tab that appears on the Properties dialog box. Here you can grant or change permissions for other users. *For more information about folder permissions, see "Permissions Tab," on page 534.*

5 In the Name text box, type a name for the new folder.

6 Click OK.

Using Public Folder Favorites

Public folders can contain a wide variety of information about topics that fit within a general category. To help you make some sense of it all, your server administrator is likely to also set up several levels of subfolders.

For example, if your e-mail system includes a public folder for Internet newsgroups, the folder probably contains a subfolder for each newsgroup area. Many newsgroups have a large number of subareas. When you want to check the latest postings to a specific folder, you might have to click (and scroll) many times to get there. Instead, you can set up shortcuts to your favorite public folders.

Outlook provides two tools to help you navigate through public folders—the Other Shortcuts group on the Outlook Bar and the Public Folders Favorites folder. Each tool has its own purpose:

- Setting up a shortcut on the Outlook Bar gives you quick access to a favorite public folder. *For details, see "Using the Outlook Bar," on page 29.*

SEE ALSO

For information about synchronizing folders, see "Synchronizing Folders," on page 283.

- You can drag a folder from the All Public Folders collection of public folders to the Favorites folder (listed within the Public Folders folder). Once there, you can quickly click each folder to work with the contents of the folder online as well as offline. *For details about setting up a favorite folder for offline work, see "Setting Up an Offline Folder File," on page 277.* Of course, when you're working offline, the information in a favorite public folder will be only as current as your last synchronization with the public folder to which it's linked. You can also use a shortcut in the Public Folders Favorites folder to quickly open the related public folder: open the Folder List, open the Public Folders Favorites folder, and then open the shortcut.

NOTE

Do not confuse the Public Folders Favorites folder with the Favorites folder on your hard disk. The Public Folders Favorites folder contains shortcuts only to public folders. The Favorites folder on your hard disk contains shortcuts to folders, files, and disks connected to your computer, as well as to Web sites that you added to favorites using Microsoft Internet Explorer.

V

Bending Folders to Your Will

Following a Public Folder Conversation

In Chapter 8, "Communicating with Newsgroups," you learned how to work with newsgroup messages and threads in Outlook Express. Public folders are much like newsgroups, with various levels of messages and replies. To organize public folder messages into threads, follow these steps:

1 Choose Current View from the View menu, and then choose By Conversation Topic from the submenu.

2 Locate the thread (topic) that you want to follow, and then click the plus sign to expand the thread.

3 Double-click the first item in the thread to read it.

4 Click the Next Item button on the Standard toolbar in the item window to see the next item in the thread.

5 When you've read the entire thread, click the Next Item button. If the next thread is expanded, Outlook opens the first item in that thread. If that thread is not expanded, Outlook closes the item window. If you have read as much as you need before you reach the end of the thread, click the Close box in the upper right corner of the item window.

 TIP

> **Moving Quickly Through Messages**
> To read messages in the preview pane, select the first message you want to read and repeatedly click the Spacebar to scroll through the message and then move automatically to the next message. If this feature isn't enabled, you can turn it on as follows: Open the Options dialog box by choosing Options from the Tools menu, click the Other tab, click the Preview Pane button, and then select the check box for Single Key Reading Using Space Bar.

Sending Messages to a Public Folder

In Chapter 16, "Managing Folder Contents," you learned how to post and reply to messages in public folders. If your profile is set up so personal addresses go into the Personal Address Book, you can also send a message to a public folder via e-mail. (This setting is on the Addressing tab of the Services dialog box you use to create or modify your profile.) You add the public folder to your address book so you can send a message directly to the folder. Here's how:

1 In the Folder List, right-click the public folder, and choose Properties from the shortcut menu. You can also open the public

folder, choose Folder in the File menu, and then choose Properties from the submenu.

2 In the Properties dialog box, click the Summary tab (if you do not have owner permissions) or the Administration tab (if you do have owner permissions).

3 Click the Personal Address Book button to add the folder address.

4 Click OK.

Opening Exchange Folders

If you are connected to Microsoft Exchange Server, you can also open another user's Calendar, Contacts, Inbox, Journal, Notes, or Tasks folders as follows:

1 Choose Open from the File menu, and choose Other User's Folder from the submenu to display the following dialog box.

2 Type the user's name or click Name to select it from the dialog box that appears.

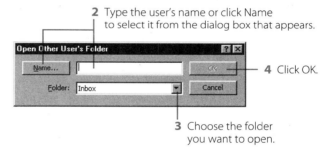

4 Click OK.

3 Choose the folder you want to open.

Outlook displays the folder in a separate window. You can then add appointments, tasks, and other items. Messages you send from the user's Inbox, however, will be sent under your own name. Appointments and tasks that you assign to others will be under your name but listed as "on behalf of" the user whose folder you opened.

If you want to add another user's Mailbox folder to your own Folder List, choose Services from the Tools menu, select Microsoft Exchange Server, and click Properties. Then click the Advanced tab, and click the Add button in the Mailboxes section. Select each user whose Mailbox you want to add to your own, and then click OK to close each dialog box.

V

Bending Folders to Your Will

Working with Personal Folders

You can use a personal folder to store related items, hold archived information, or just to organize files for quick reference and retrieval. However, personal folders must first be set up as part of your profile, as described in "Storing Information Locally," on page 12. You can then use the personal folders as your delivery point for all Outlook items or use them just to store specific messages and items that you do not want to store on your server folders.

You open a personal folder, and move items in and out of it, as you would any other folder by using the Folder List. To open a personal folder, just display the Folder List, expand the Personal Folders list, and click the name of the folder you want to open. If the personal folders file you open has been assigned a password, Outlook displays the Personal Folders Password dialog box. (You assign a password to a personal folder when you create the folder as part of your profile, as explained in "Storing Information Locally," on page 12). Enter the password for the personal folders file, and then click OK. You can also open a personal folder even if it is not listed in the Folder List. Removing a personal folder from the profile, for example, does not delete it from your disk. So if you remove a folder from the profile, you can still open it by following these steps:

1 Choose Open from the File menu.

2 Choose Personal Folders File (.pst) from the submenu.

3 In the Open Personal Folders dialog box, navigate to the location where the folder is stored.

4 Select the folder.

5 Click OK.

Sharing Folders over the Internet

Public folders let you share information over your Microsoft Exchange network. Net Folders, a separate component of Outlook, lets you share folders over the Internet.

To use Net Folders, you must have installed the Net Folders component using the Add/Remove Components feature of the Office setup program. You then designate a folder to be shared and the individuals with whom you want to share the folder. The information in the shared folder will be downloaded to the persons sharing it and updated at regular intervals.

> You cannot share public folders stored on Microsoft Exchange Server, but you can share Outlook folders and personal folders.

Here's how to set up folders for sharing over the Internet, once the Net Folders component is installed:

1 Click the folder you want to share, either on the Outlook Bar or in the Folder List.

2 Point to Share on the File menu, and choose This Folder. The Share command is only available when the Net Folders component is installed.

3 The introductory screen of the Net Folders Wizard appears. Click Next to move to the page shown in Figure 19-1. The wizard lists all persons who already have permission to share your net folders.

4 Click Add to add additional persons to the list. Outlook opens the Add Entries To Subscriber Database dialog box.

5 Select the people whom you want to share your folder. Hold down the Ctrl key to select more than one person.

6 Click the To button to copy the selected names into the right list box.

7 Click OK to return to the Net Folder Wizard.

FIGURE 19-1.
The Net Folder Wizard showing the list of people with permissions to share your net folders.

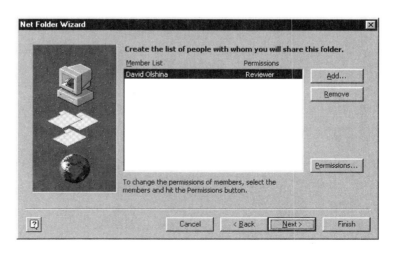

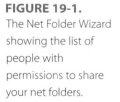

8 In the member list, select each name and click Permissions to display the dialog box shown in Figure 19-2.

9 Select the level of sharing you want to allow.

10 Click OK to return to the Net Folder Wizard.

11 Click Next.

12 In the page that appears, type a descriptive name for the folder and then click Next.

13 Click Finish and then OK in the next two dialog boxes.

FIGURE 19-2.
The Net Folder Sharing
Permissions dialog box.

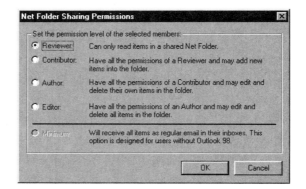

All new members will now be sent e-mail messages inviting them to share your folder. (If necessary, click Send And Receive to send the messages over the Internet.) They will receive an e-mail message like the one shown in Figure 19-3.

The recipient can click Accept to send an acceptance message and to receive the folder, or Decline to send a rejection message. The recipients can also change the name for the shared folder on their systems.

Dealing with Folder Properties

You can set the properties for each folder in Outlook and for public folders for which you have appropriate permission. Each folder has its own unique properties as well as certain properties that are common to all folders.

FIGURE 19-3.
E-mail invitation to accept sharing of a net folder.

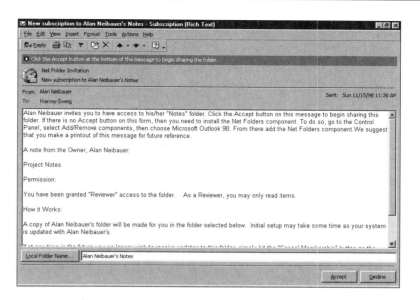

 **NOTE**

To set all the properties of a folder, you must have administrative permissions for the folder. Even so, in some cases, you can't set certain properties because they don't apply to the folder. In almost all cases, it is best to set folder properties while you're working online. You can, however, set folder properties for personal folders while you are working offline.

All Outlook folders (except the Contacts folder) have the same five tabs in the Properties dialog box: General, AutoArchive, Administration, Forms, and Home Page. Server folders have two additional tabs: Permissions and Synchronization. The Properties dialog box of the Contacts folder has a unique tab, Outlook Address Book, instead of the AutoArchive tab. When you create an Outlook folder or copy an Outlook folder, the new folder has the same properties—and therefore the same tabs—as the folder on which it is based. Disk folders have a different set of tabs; see "Disk Folders," on page 538.

The general steps for changing the properties of a folder are as follows:

1 Right-click the folder on the Outlook Bar or in the Folder List, and choose Properties from the submenu.

2 Change the property settings on any or all of the tabs.

3 Click OK to close the Properties dialog box.

The following sections illustrate and describe the General, Administration, Permissions, and Outlook Address Book tabs of the Properties dialog box. The remaining tabs are discussed in other sections of this book, as indicated here:

- For details about the AutoArchive tab, see "Setting a Folder's AutoArchive Properties," on page 508.

- For information about the options on the Forms tab, see "Copying Forms Between Folders," on page 629.

- For details about synchronizing folders and using the Synchronization tab, see "Working Remotely with Public Folders," on page 280.

- For details about displaying Web sites with a folder, see "Displaying Web Sites," on page 34.

General Tab

The General Tab of the Properties dialog box, shown in Figure 19-4, contains information such as the folder name and its description. You cannot change the names of Outlook's standard folders, nor can you change the name or description of a public folder without having the proper permissions. For a custom folder that you created, however, you can select the folder's name in the box at the top of the tab and type a new one in its place. In the Description text box, you can type or edit the description of any folder, custom or standard.

The When Posting To This Folder, Use list offers the options Post and Forms. Select Post to use the default Outlook form for posting items in this folder—that is, to use a message form for the Inbox folder, an appointment form for the Calendar folder, and so on. When you select Forms, you can choose a custom form in this folder. *For information, see "Opening a Custom Form," on page 628.*

If some members of your organization use the Microsoft Exchange client instead of Outlook, select the Automatically Generate Microsoft Exchange Views check box so that they can use the views that are set up for this folder. Typically, you'll set this check box for a public folder or a folder you share with others who use the Microsoft Exchange client. You'll also want to select it if you switch between the Microsoft Exchange client and Outlook.

FIGURE 19-4.
The General tab of the Properties dialog box for a folder.

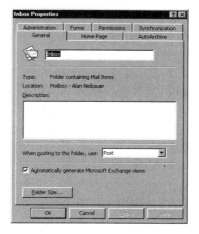

Administration Tab

The Administration tab, shown in Figure 19-5, on the following page, is used primarily with public folders. For Outlook folders and for public folders for which you do not have administrative permission, most of the options on this tab are unavailable. If you do have administrative permissions for a folder, you can use this tab to set which view of a folder is used when it is first opened, what happens when you drag and drop an item into the folder, and who can access the folder.

The Initial View On Folder list includes all the built-in views for the folder plus any views you have created for it.

The button called Add Folder Address To Personal Address Book (which can also appear on the Summary tab for public folders, depending on your level of permission) lets you add this folder to your personal address book. *For information, see "Sending Messages to a Public Folder," on page 526.*

Use the Folder Assistant button to set up rules for dealing with the items sent to this folder. The Folder Assistant is similar to the Rules Wizard. (*For information about using the Rules Wizard to set up rules for folder items, see "Managing Your Mail with the Rules Wizard," on page 51.* You can easily apply the information in that section to setting up the rules you want to use with the Folder Assistant.) You can use the Folder Assistant to set up rules for acting on items sent by or to a particular person, items about a certain subject, or items that contain a particular word or group of words in the body of the message. You can return items to the sender, delete items, reply to items, or forward items.

V

Bending Folders to Your Will

FIGURE 19-5.

The Administration tab of the Properties dialog box for a folder.

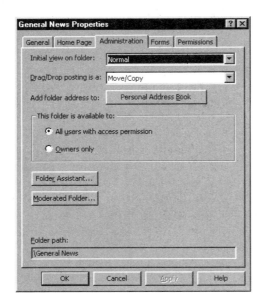

Use the Moderated Folder button to automatically send newly posted messages to an individual for review before being posted in the folder for public viewing. The person you assign as the moderator can send a response to the sender and then actually post the message to the folder. This button is active only for public folders for which you have administrative permissions.

Permissions Tab

The Properties dialog box for server folders and for public folders for which you have appropriate permissions contains a Permission tab, as shown in Figure 19-6. On this tab, you give others permission to open the folders that you want them to see or use.

 SEE ALSO

If you have delegates who work in your Outlook folders on your behalf, you can set up delegate permissions on the Delegates tab of the Options dialog box. For details, see "Using the Delegates Tab," on page 90.

The Permissions tab for Microsoft Mail shared folders on a peer-to-peer network lets you assign read, write, and delete permission to other users on the network.

A server folder is simply a folder in your Mailbox that you access from the server—Outlook automatically sets up the folders in your Mailbox on the server. If you are working from a personal folder file (.pst) on your hard disk, you are not accessing the folders from the server, but rather from your own hard disk.

FIGURE 19-6.

The Permissions tab of the Properties dialog box for a server folder.

On this tab, you can compile a list of names of the people who have permission to use the folder. Each name is assigned a role, and each role has specific privileges attached to it. Users' names and roles appear in the upper box. You can remove an existing user by selecting the name and clicking the Remove button.

Use the Permissions tab to select, customize, and later modify the permissions for use of the folder. For example, someone who has an Author role can create folder items, read folder items, and edit or delete his or her own folder items but cannot create a subfolder and cannot edit or delete items created by other people. Table 19-1, on the next page, lists the roles and their respective privileges. (The role None is not listed because this role grants no permissions or privileges other than the folder being visible in the Folder List or on the Outlook Bar.

When you create a folder in your mailbox, the default role listed is None (no privileges). When you create a public folder, the default role listed is Author.

To add a name, click the Add button. Outlook displays the Add Users dialog box, in which you can type or select the name or names you want to add. When you click the Add button in this dialog box and then click OK, Outlook adds the names to the list on the Permissions tab, assigning each the default role (None or Author).

To assign or change the role for a person in the list, select the name, and then select a role from the drop-down list in the Roles box.

Instead of assigning one of the predefined roles to a name, you can assign privileges one by one to that person by setting individual options in the tab's Permissions area. If the resulting combination of privileges is the same as one of the predefined roles, Outlook assigns that role to the person (the role name in the Roles list box will change automatically). If the combination of privileges is different from all of the predefined roles, Outlook assigns Custom as the role. (You won't see a Custom role listed in the Roles box; it appears only when you change an assigned role in a way that doesn't match any of the predefined roles.)

TABLE 19-1.   Roles and the Permissions They Grant

	Author	Non-editing Author	Contributor	Editor	Owner	Publishing Author	Publishing Editor	Reviewer
Create Items	✔	✔	✔	✔	✔	✔	✔	
Read Items	✔	✔		✔	✔	✔	✔	✔
Create Subfolders					✔	✔	✔	
Folder Owner					✔			
Folder Contact					✔			
Folder Visible	✔	✔	✔	✔	✔	✔	✔	✔
Edit Items	Own	None	None	All	All	Own	All	None
Delete Items	Own	Own	None	All	All	Own	All	None

TIP

You can change the default role from None to, say, Author or Contributor. But remember that the default role applies to everyone who uses your Microsoft Exchange Server network. If you want to limit access to your folder to only those people you specify on the Permissions tab, leave the default role set to None. If you want, you can set the default permissions so that not even the folder is visible, by clearing the Folder Visible check box.

Outlook Address Book Tab

The Properties dialog box for the Contacts folder contains the Outlook Address Book tab instead of the AutoArchive tab. This tab is shown in Figure 19-7.

Selecting the check box labeled Show This Folder As An E-mail Address Book adds your Contacts folder items to the Outlook Address Book, giving you access to the names, addresses, fax numbers, e-mail addresses, and URLs of the people you list as contacts. You can then use your contacts list to send messages and faxes, place telephone calls, write letters, and connect to the Web pages of your contacts, even while you're working in another Microsoft Office program.

Although you can't change the name of the Contacts folder itself, you can change the name that appears in your Outlook Address Book. For example, if you want your Contacts list to be called "Buddies" in the Outlook Address Book, type *Buddies* in the Name Of The Address Book box in the Contacts Properties dialog box.

FIGURE 19-7.
The Outlook Address Book tab of the Contacts Properties dialog box.

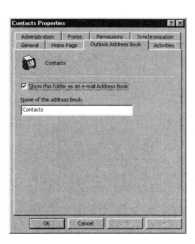

 Bending Folders to Your Will

---

Why Isn't the Show This Folder Check Box Available?

The check box labeled Show This Folder As An E-mail Address Book won't be available on the Outlook Address Book tab of the Contacts Properties dialog box if you have enabled Microsoft Schedule+ as you primary calendar. *See "Use Microsoft Schedule+ As My Primary Calendar," on page 76.* To use your Contacts folder as an e-mail address book, you must choose Options from the Tools menu, click Calendar Options on the Preferences tab, and then clear the Use Microsoft Schedule+ As My Primary Calendar check box in the Calendar Options dialog box. You must then exit and log off Outlook and restart Outlook for this change to take effect. Once you do this, the Show This Folder As An E-mail Address Book check box will be available, and you can select it to use your Contacts folder as an address book.

As an alternative way of setting up your Contacts folder as an address book, open the profile you use for Outlook and add Outlook Address Book as a service. This also replaces Schedule+ as your primary calendar and automatically adds your Contacts folder as an e-mail address book. *For information about adding a service to a profile, see "Modifying a Profile," on page 20.*

Disk Folders

Disk folders that you set up and view in Outlook have the same properties as they have in a My Computer window or a Windows Explorer window. The Properties dialog box for a disk folder contains two tabs: General and Sharing. Figure 19-8 shows the General tab, which provides a description of the folder and allows you to set the folder's attributes.

On the Sharing tab of the Properties dialog box for a disk folder, shown in Figure 19-9, you can specify whether the folder will be shared with other people. (A second type of Sharing tab is described next.) If you designate it as a shared folder, you can also specify how the folder will be shared.

To make the folder available to others, select the Shared As option. Then accept or change the share name for the folder. The share name is the name shown for the folder across the network. To help users make sure that they've found the correct folder, you can add a comment that identifies the folder more fully. You can also specify a password for read-only and full access.

Select the option in the Access Type section for the level of access you want others to have. You can choose to allow others to read only, or to read, write, create, and delete files. You can also set two passwords:

FIGURE 19-8.
The General tab of the Properties dialog box for a disk folder.

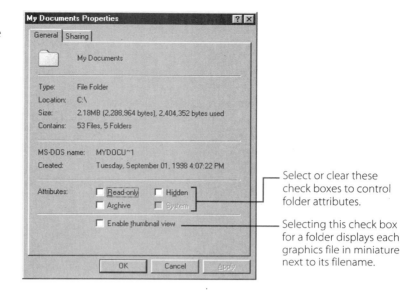

Select or clear these check boxes to control folder attributes.

Selecting this check box for a folder displays each graphics file in miniature next to its filename.

one for people to whom you want to grant read access and another for those you grant full access. By controlling how you distribute the passwords, you can have two levels of access to the same folder.

You can share a folder only if you have administrative control over it. You usually have this control over the folders on a disk that's part of your computer.

FIGURE 19-9.
The Sharing tab of the Properties dialog box for a disk folder when share-level access control is in effect.

You'll see the Sharing tab shown in Figure 19-9, on the previous page, if your system is set up to control access according to each device, such as your hard disk, printer, or a folder file. However, if your system is set up for user-level access control, you'll see the Sharing tab shown in Figure 19-10 instead. This Sharing tab lets you control access to each device, but it also lets you tailor the degree of access to each device according to settings you make for the users who access your system. You'll find the choice between share-level access control and user-level access control on the Access Control tab of the Network dialog box, which you access by opening the Windows Control Panel and opening the Network icon.

The rest of this chapter will show you how to set permissions if your system is set to user-level access control.

When your Sharing tab appears as in Figure 19-10, it is set by default to allow full access to everyone on the network, as represented by the user name The World. You can limit access to everyone by editing access rights for The World, or you can specify individual users or groups of users and their access rights. To change the level of access given to everyone, take these steps:

1 Select The World and click the Edit button to open the dialog box shown in Figure 19-11.

2 In the Change Access Rights dialog box, select from among three access levels: Read-Only Access Rights, Full Access Rights, and

FIGURE 19-10.

The Sharing tab of the Properties dialog box for a disk folder when user-level access control is in effect.

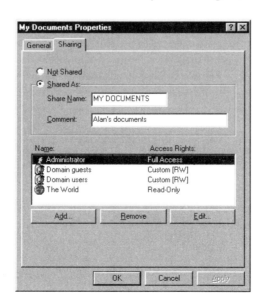

FIGURE 19-11.

The Change Access Rights dialog box.

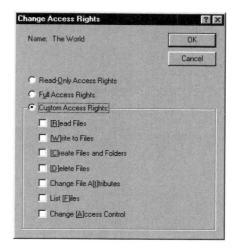

Custom Access Rights. If you select Custom Access Rights, you can then choose specific permissions.

3 Click OK.

It only makes sense to grant rights to individuals or groups if you have removed full access from The World. Everyone is a member of The World and would therefore automatically have complete access to the folder regardless of what other group or individual status you might give them. To limit access to the folder for specific users or groups of users, first select The World and do one of the following:

■ Assign a low level of access (such as Read-Only Access Rights) to The World, suitable for everyone who has access to the network, and then selectively assign greater access levels to specific individuals or groups.

■ Click the Remove button (on the Sharing tab) to remove The World, removing all access from the network except for those users you specifically add.

When you are ready to grant access rights to specific individuals and groups, follow these steps:

1 Click the Add button on the Sharing tab of the Properties dialog box to open the dialog box shown in Figure 19-12, on the following page.

2 Select a user or group from the list.

3 Click Read Only, Full Access, or Custom.

V

Bending Folders to Your Will

FIGURE 19-12.
The Add Users
dialog box.

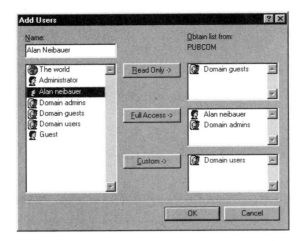

4 Repeat steps 2 and 3 for each user whose permissions you want
to configure.

5 Click OK.

Now that you've learned how to manage the folders that Outlook
accesses, the next chapter will show you how to organize the contents
of these folders.

CHAPTER 20

Organizing Folder Items

Organizing information so that it makes sense is an essential part of managing projects and tasks. As you've seen in previous chapters, Microsoft Outlook offers you numerous ways to view your folders and the information they contain. You can choose the view that best meets your needs, one that lets you focus on the most important information in the folder and makes that information clear, readily accessible, and easy to work with. Outlook provides a set of built-in views for each folder, drawn from the five general types of views: table, timeline, card, icon, and day/month/week.

Chapter 21, "Setting Up Views," explains how to modify Outlook's built-in views or even design your own views. To do so, however, you first need to understand the methods and techniques described in this chapter for setting up folders and displaying their contents. What you see in a folder depends on the combination of settings you select for columns, categories, grouping, sorting, filtering, and fields.

Setting Up Columns

Outlook's table views show items in rows and columns. Each item is in a row, with the fields for the items in columns. You can add or remove columns, and you can rearrange the order of the columns to suit your needs. You can also adjust the width of the columns to show more or less information or to fit more columns within the folder window.

Adding Columns from the Field Chooser

The Field Chooser is a window listing the fields that you can add to a table view. Outlook's fields are organized into groups, called field sets. When you use the Field Chooser, you first select the set that contains the type of field you want to add, and then drag the specific field into the table to the position where you want the column to appear. You can add fields from more than one set. After adding fields from one set, just choose another field set and drag any fields from it to the table.

> The term *field* refers to a location that stores data of the same type. By placing similar kinds of data in fields, you can find, sort, and process information quickly.

Here's how to add columns to a folder view using the Field Chooser:

1 Open a folder, and select a view that has columns (any table view).

2 Right-click the column headings, and choose Field Chooser from the shortcut menu.

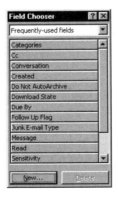

3 Click the down arrow at the top of the Field Chooser window to see a list of field sets.

SEE ALSO

You can also add a column during the sorting process; see "Sorting with the Sort Dialog Box," on page 556.

SEE ALSO

If you can't find an appropriate predefined field, you can create a custom field as explained in "Creating a Simple Custom Field," on page 564.

4 Select the field set that contains the type of field you want to add. When you select a field set, Outlook displays the fields contained in the set in the lower portion of the window.

5 Drag the field name from the Field Chooser into the folder window and position it in the column headings at the location where you want it to appear. (Outlook displays two red arrows to show you where the column will be inserted.) When you release the mouse button, Outlook adds the column to the folder view, with the field name as the new column heading. Outlook also removes the field name from the Field Chooser.

6 When you've added as many columns as you want, click the Close box in the upper-right corner of the Field Chooser window.

Removing Columns

If you no longer want a column to appear in a folder view, you can easily remove it from the screen, without actually deleting the information contained in the column. You can later reinsert the column from the Field Chooser to display the information again.

To delete a column, use either of these techniques:

- Drag the field name away from the column heading until you see a large black X appear over the field, and then release the mouse button.

- Right-click the heading of the column you want to remove, and then choose Remove This Column from the shortcut menu.

Rearranging Columns with the Mouse

When you want to quickly move a column to a new position, just drag its column heading to the new location. As you move the column heading between existing columns, you'll see two red arrows pointing to where the column will be inserted when you release the mouse button.

Using the Show Fields Dialog Box

The most general way to add, remove, and rearrange columns is by using the Show Fields dialog box. Begin by opening a folder and selecting a view that has columns, and then follow these steps:

1 Point to Current View on the View menu, and then choose Customize Current View from the submenu to open the dialog box

V

Bending Folders to Your Will

shown in Figure 20-1. You can also right-click the column headings and choose Customize Current View from the shortcut menu.

2 You'll learn more about the View Summary dialog box in Chapter 21, "Setting Up Views." For now, click the Fields button to display the Show Fields dialog box shown in Figure 20-2.

3 To add a field, select it in the Available Fields list and then click the Add button.

4 To remove a field, select it in the Show These Fields In This Order list and then click Remove.

5 To change the position of a field, select it, and then click the Move Up button to move the field toward the left; click Move Down to move the field to the right.

FIGURE 20-1.
The View Summary dialog box.

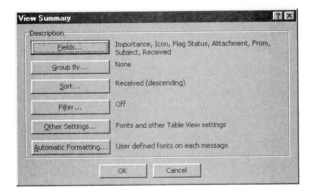

Changing Column Format

To customize the appearance of the table view, you can adjust the width of a column, alter the alignment of information within a column, and generally modify the format of a new column in a folder view.

Changing Column Width

To change the width of a column using the mouse, drag the right edge of the column heading to the right or left.

To have Outlook automatically size the column to best fit its contents, right-click the column heading and choose Best Fit from the shortcut menu. You can also double-click the right-hand border of a column to set the column width to best fit.

Setting column width with the Best Fit command is usually a temporary arrangement so that you can fully see a particular column's contents.

FIGURE 20-2.
The Show Fields
dialog box.

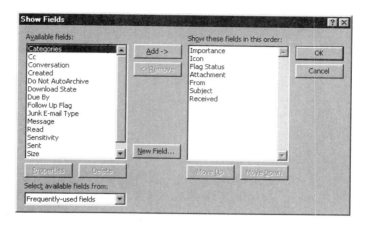

When Outlook sets a column width to best fit, it has to adjust the width
of other columns in the folder window. Some columns might even be
reduced to a single character's width, which makes them pretty useless.

The Date/Time Fields Dialog Box

In a timeline view, Outlook positions folder items according to the date in their
start and end fields, or for a message, the time the message was sent and the
time it was received. When you select Fields from the View Summary dialog box
when a timeline view is displayed, Outlook opens the Date/Time Fields dialog
box shown here:

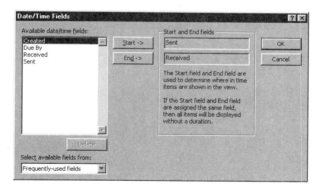

To add or delete fields, choose the field set from the Select Available Fields
From list at the bottom of the dialog box. In the Available Date/Time Fields list,
select the field that you want to use as the item start date, and click the Start
button. To change the field that Outlook uses to display each item's end date,
select a field from this list and click the End button.

V

Bending Folders to Your Will

In that case, you might want to remove a column or two or adjust the width of other columns, using the techniques described in this chapter.

Changing Column Alignment

By default, the contents of columns are left-aligned. To change column alignment, follow these steps:

1 Right-click the column heading.

2 Choose Alignment from the shortcut menu.

3 Choose the alignment you want (Align Left, Align Right, or Center) from the submenu.

Using the Format Columns Command

The Format Columns command lets you change the width, the alignment, the heading, and the format of the information for a single column from one dialog box.

To change the format of a column by using the Format Columns command, follow these steps:

1 Open the folder, and select a view that has columns.

2 Right-click the column headings, and choose Format Columns from the shortcut menu.

3 Select the field you want to format.

4 Select the format of the information.

5 You can type a column label instead of displaying the field name.

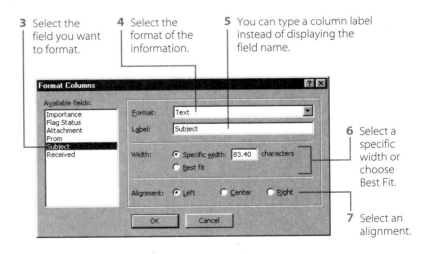

6 Select a specific width or choose Best Fit.

7 Select an alignment.

8 Repeat steps 3 through 7 for each field you want to format, and then click OK when you're finished.

NOTE

NOTE

> For some columns, you have only one choice in the Format list of the Format Columns dialog box. For other columns, Outlook provides several format choices. *You'll learn more about formats in "Creating a Simple Custom Field," on page 564.*

Working with Categories

Whether you think of your life as being organized into neat categories or not, you probably use categories to some extent for organizing various activities and records—shopping lists, reminders, house repairs, friends, pets, and so on. At work, you might have categories of folder items for various projects, personal business, daily tasks, customers, suppliers, orders, billing, and so on. Outlook provides a list of 20 built-in categories for folder items, and you can add your own categories as well.

To assign a folder item to one or more categories, follow these steps:

1 Open the folder, and select one or more items that you want to assign to a category.

2 Open the Categories dialog box, shown in Figure 20-3 on the following page, in one of the following ways:

- Choose Categories from the Edit menu.

- Right-click the folder item, and choose Categories from the shortcut menu.

- For individual calendar items and tasks, open the item and click the Categories button in the folder item window.

- For a single note, open the note, click the icon in the upper-left corner of the note window, and then choose Categories from the menu.

3 Assign an item to as many categories as you want, by selecting the check boxes of each chosen category.

4 Click OK.

To remove a folder item from a category, clear the check box for that category in step 3.

V

Bending Folders to Your Will

FIGURE 20-3.

The Categories dialog box.

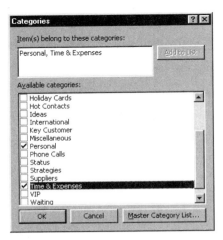

Adding Your Own Categories

The categories provided by Outlook might not satisfy all of your requirements. You might want to group items, for example, by a specific project or client. To get the most from this Outlook feature, create your own categories to add to the list using these steps:

1 Open a folder, and select an item that you'd like to assign to a new category.

2 Open the Categories dialog box in any of the ways described in the preceding section.

3 Type the new category name in the Item(s) Belong To These Categories box. If you are adding more than one category, separate the names with a comma.

4 Click Add To List. Outlook assigns the item to the new category and adds the new category to the list so that you can easily assign other folder items to this new category later.

5 Click OK.

Managing the Master Category List

The master category list contains Outlook's built-in list of categories as well as any categories that you've added. In the master category list, you can add categories, remove categories, and reset the category list to the original ones built into Outlook.

Organizing Categories with Organize

You can quickly assign a category to a calendar, contact, task, or journal item without opening it, and you can even create new categories directly from the folder window. Here's how:

1 Open the Calendar, Contacts, Tasks, or Journal folder.

2 Click the Organize button on the Standard toolbar.

3 Select the items that you want to assign to a category.

4 Click Using Categories.

5 Choose an existing category from the top list and click Add, or type in a new category in the lower box and click Create.

6 Specify as many categories as you want, and then click the Organize button again to close the Organize pane.

> **NOTE**

Deleting a category from the Master Category List dialog box doesn't remove the category from any items that have already been assigned to it.

To display the Master Category List dialog box, shown in Figure 20-4, open the Categories dialog box and then click the Master Category List button. Use the Add button to create a new category, the Delete button to remove a category, and the Reset button to restore all of the original categories.

FIGURE 20-4.
The Master Category List dialog box.

Grouping

Grouping is a way to organize folder items to more easily find and examine related items. You can use views such as By Category, By Company, or By Location to group folder items under headings that correspond to the various entries in the Category, Company, or Location field. For example, By Person Responsible groups tasks according to the person who is responsible for the task. If there is no built-in view that groups items the way you want, you can interactively create a custom view that groups by fields you select and drag into position in the folder window, as described next. Alternatively, you can use a dialog box approach to group up to four fields that you select. The dialog box method is described in "Grouping with the Group By Dialog Box," on page 554, and is most useful when you want to group items by one or more fields that are not displayed in the current window.

Grouping in the Folder Window

If the column heading you want to use for grouping is displayed on the screen, the quickest way to group items is directly from the folder window. Just right-click that column heading, and then choose Group By This Field from the shortcut menu. Outlook groups the items by the selected field, and then displays the field name in the Group By box above the column headings, as shown in Figure 20-5.

 NOTE

You can also display the Group By box first, and then drag a field to it. To do so, right-click a column heading and choose Group By Box from the shortcut menu.

FIGURE 20-5.

Grouping items using the Group By box.

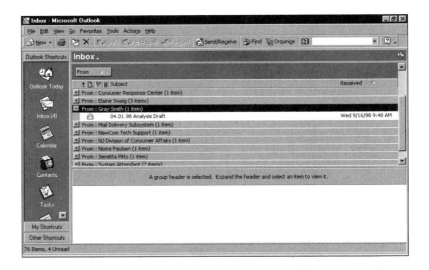

You can then add one or more subgroups to further organize the items. To add a subgroup, use either of these methods:

- Right-click the field, and choose Group By This Field from the shortcut menu.

- Drag the field heading to the Group By box.

When you use multiple levels of grouping, Outlook first groups the folder items by the first field you specified for the group. Then, within each one of those groups, Outlook creates a subgroup based on the second field, and so on. The fields will be indented in the Group By box to illustrate this order visually, as shown here. Items containing no information in the specified field are grouped first and labeled (None).

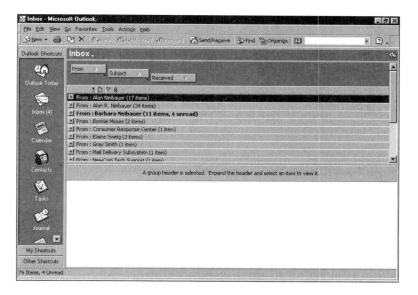

To change the order in which the fields are used for grouping, rearrange the fields within the Group By box. For example, to change a subgroup into the primary grouping field, drag it to the left of any other groups in the Group By box and then release the mouse.

When you no longer want to group by a field, drag it from the Group By box back to the column heading, or right-click the field name in the Group By box and choose Don't Group By This Field from the shortcut menu.

If you no longer want to display the Group By box, right-click a column heading and choose Group By Box from the shortcut menu, or click the Group By button on the Advanced toolbar. If this toolbar is not visible, point to Toolbars on the View menu and choose Advanced. You can click the Group By button again whenever you want to redisplay the Group By box. Closing the Group By box doesn't remove grouping from the folder view. To do that, you first must remove the fields from the Group By box.

Grouping with the Group By Dialog Box

As an alternative to dragging fields into the Group By box, you can group items using a dialog box. The Group By dialog box lets you select fields that aren't visible, group based on up to four fields, select the order of the fields, and choose how you want the groups expanded or collapsed.

To change the way items are grouped in an open folder, follow these steps:

1 Point to Current View on the View menu, and then choose Customize Current View from the submenu.

2 Click Group By in the View Summary dialog box to display the Group By dialog box.

3 In the Select Available Fields From list, select the field set containing the fields that you want to use for grouping.

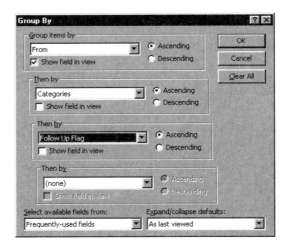

4 Start with the Group Items By list box and select the primary field to group by.

5 Select the Show Field In View check box if you want to display the field in the column heading as well as in the Group By box.

6 Choose Ascending or Descending for sorting the field items.

7 Repeat steps 3 through 6 to group by as many as three additional fields if you want. Note that you can change the field set in step 3 for any of the additional levels of grouping.

8 Select how you want the items displayed (As Last Viewed, All Expanded, or All Collapsed).

9 Click OK.

> To remove all the groupings from a folder view, open the Group By dialog box and click the Clear All button.

Sorting

You can sort folder items in any type of view except timeline and day/week/month views. Microsoft Outlook gives you two ways to sort folder items: with the mouse and with the Sort dialog box. You can sort by as many as four fields.

> Sorting lets you display items in the same order as grouping. Use sorting, however, when you just want an alphabetical or numeric listing, and do not need to organize items under group headings or collapse and expand specific groups.

Sorting with the Mouse

Sorting with the mouse is quick and convenient, but you can use this method only in a view with columns. You can sort items in either ascending or descending order. Ascending order is alphabetical, earlier time to later time, or lower number to higher number; descending order is the reverse.

- To sort items in ascending order, click the heading of the column you want to use to sort the items so it contains an up-pointing triangle.

- To sort items in descending order, click the column heading so it contains a down-pointing triangle.

- To sort items by more than one sorting field, click the column headings in reverse order—that is, begin by clicking the heading of the last column you want to sort by, and end by clicking the heading of the first column you want to sort by. For example, if you want to sort tasks first by subject, followed by priority, and then by the due date, click the Due Date heading first, then the Priority heading, and then the Subject heading.

Sorting with the Sort Dialog Box

The Sort dialog box gives you more options for sorting than you have using the mouse, such as sorting on a field that is not visible in the current view of the folder. You can also use the dialog box to sort in card and icon views in addition to table views.

To sort folder items using the Sort dialog box, follow these steps:

1 Open a folder, and select a table, card, or icon view.

2 Point to Current View on the View menu, and then choose Customize Current View from the submenu to display the View Summary dialog box.

3 Click the Sort button to display the Sort dialog box.

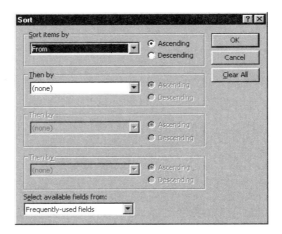

4 In the Select Available Fields From list at the bottom of the dialog box, select the field set containing the fields that you want to use for sorting. If you sort by more than one field, you can select the fields from more than one set.

5 Select the first sorting field in the Sort Items By list, and choose either Ascending or Descending order.

6 Use the Then By list boxes to select a second, third, and fourth sort level, as desired, and their sort order.

7 Click OK.

If you select a field for sorting that isn't displayed in the current view of the folder, Outlook asks whether you want to display that field. Click Yes to display the field for each item in the view. (If you are using a table view, for instance, this can be a handy way of adding a column to the view.) Click No to keep the current folder view, without displaying the additional field. Whichever choice you make, Outlook can sort items by the fields you choose, whether the fields are visible or not.

> If you select (None) as a sorting key in any box in the Sort dialog box, all the boxes below it automatically revert to (None), the same as if you click the Clear All button in the Sort dialog box. The sort order will remain in the order you last set.

Filtering

A filter lets you temporarily hide items that you are not interested in seeing. This limited view makes it easier to analyze certain folder items without interference from irrelevant items and the information they contain. When you remove the filter, you can see all the items again.

To set up and apply a filter for the current view, display the Filter dialog box, shown in Figure 20-6, by following these steps:

1 Open the folder.

2 Point to Current View on the View menu, and then choose Customize Current View from the submenu to display the View Summary dialog box.

3 Click the Filter button.

FIGURE 20-6.
The Filter dialog box for the Inbox folder showing the Messages tab.

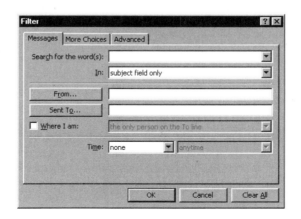

You can use all three of the tabs in this dialog box to set up criteria for a filter. As you might notice, the Filter dialog box resembles the Find dialog box, discussed in Chapter 16, "Managing Folder Contents." *See "Searching Folder Contents," on page 470, for more information.* The processes of setting up a search and setting up a filter are similar in many ways.

For example, you could use the Filter dialog box to just display all Inbox messages sent by Jane Doe pertaining to a networking project in which your organization is involved by following these steps:

1 Open your Inbox folder.

2 Open the Filter dialog box.

3 On the Messages tab of the Filter dialog box, type the word *networking* in the Search For The Word(s) box.

4 Select Subject Field And Message Body from the In list.

5 In the From box, type *Jane Doe.*

6 Click OK to close the Filter dialog box.

7 Click OK again to close the View Summary dialog box and apply the filter.

Your Inbox folder would now display only messages sent by Jane Doe that contain the word *networking* in either the Subject line or the body of the message. Notice that Outlook adds the words *Filter Applied* to the status bar (in the lower left corner of the folder window) and to the right of the folder window's title.

If you want to narrow your filter even further, you can set additional filter criteria on the Messages tab—specifying messages sent during a certain time range, for example—or on either of the two other tabs in the Filter dialog box. *See "Setting Up the More Choices Tab," on page 559, and "Setting Up Advanced Criteria," on page 561, for information about the second and third tabs.* A folder item must meet all of the criteria specified on all of the tabs in order to appear in the filtered view of the folder.

The first of the three tabs in the Filter dialog box varies according to the type of folder that is currently open. For instance, you'll see the Messages tab shown in Figure 20-6 if you are setting up a filter for a folder that contains message items. If you open a different type of folder to set up a filter, Outlook changes not only the name of the first tab in the Filter dialog box but also the options it contains. Table 20-1 describes the options available on this tab for each type of folder.

TIP

> You don't have to fill out all the tabs of the Filter dialog box. You can set conditions on any tabs you want and ignore those you don't need.

TABLE 20-1.   Options on the Filter Dialog Box's First Tab

Folder	First Tab Name	Available Filters
Inbox	Message	Search For The Word(s), In, From, Sent To, Where I Am, Time
Calendar	Appointments And Meetings	Search For The Word(s), In, Organized By, Attendees, Time
Contacts	Contacts	Search For The Word(s), In, E-mail, Time
Tasks	Tasks	Search For The Word(s), In, Status, From, Sent To, Time
Journal	Journal Entries	Search For The Word(s), In, Journal Entry Type, Contact, Time
Notes	Notes	Search For The Word(s), In, Time
Disk Files	Files	Named, Of Type, Search For The Word(s), In, Time

Setting Up the More Choices Tab

The More Choices tab of the Filter dialog box, shown in Figure 20-7, on the following page, is the same for most types of folders, except some options are unavailable for a few types, as noted in the following summary.

Here's a brief summary of the options on the More Choices tab and how to set them up as filter criteria:

Categories. When you use categories as filter criteria, Outlook displays folder items that have been assigned to the categories you list. Type the category names, separated by a comma, or click the Categories button to select category names in the Categories dialog box. (If you want to specify categories you used in a previous filter, select them from the list, where Outlook stores them.)

V

Bending Folders to Your Will

FIGURE 20-7.

The More Choices tab of the Filter dialog box.

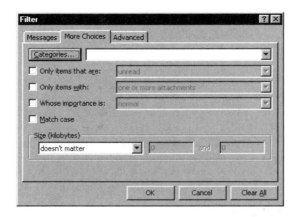

Only Items That Are. Select this check box, and then select either Read (for folder items that you have already read) or Unread (for folder items that you haven't yet read).

Only Items With. Select this check box, and then select One Or More Attachments (to filter for folder items that contain attachments) or No Attachments (to filter for items that have no attachments). This option is unavailable for the Notes folder.

Whose Importance Is. This option filters for folder items that have the specified level of importance: High, Normal, or Low. Select this check box, and then select a level from the list. This option is not available for folders that contain contact items, note items, or journal entries.

Match Case. Select this check box to display only those folder items whose capitalization exactly matches that of the characters you type in the Search For The Word(s) box on the first tab.

Size. You can use this option to restrict the filter to only those folder items whose size, in kilobytes, matches a specified size range. Select Doesn't Matter from the list if you don't want to filter for a particular size. If you select Equals (Approximately), Less Than, or Greater Than, Outlook activates the first box to the right, and you must enter a specific size value. If you select Between, Outlook activates both boxes to the right, and you must enter the upper and lower end of a size range.

When you set up a filter for a folder that contains disk files, the More Choices tab offers only three options: Match Case, Match All Word Forms, and Size. You can set up the Match Case and Size options exactly as you do for other types of folders. If you choose the Match All Word Forms option, you are in effect widening the scope of your filter criteria to include all files that contain variations of the words you typed in the Search For The Word(s) box on the first tab. For instance, if you've set up the word *write* as a filter criterion in the Search For The Word(s) box, choosing Match All Word Forms means that files containing the text *write, writes, wrote, written,* and so on will be displayed in the filtered view.

Setting Up Advanced Criteria

If you need to refine the filter for your folder view beyond the settings available on the first two tabs of the Filter dialog box, you can click the Advanced tab, shown in Figure 20-8. On this tab, you can select a field, specify a condition and a value for the field, and then have Outlook filter folder items according to this criteria. This tab is the same for all types of folders, including folders that contain disk files.

The following steps show you how to set up advanced criteria, using a simple example:

1 In the Filter dialog box, click the Advanced tab.

2 Click the Field button to open a menu of the available field sets.

3 Point to a field set to display a submenu containing all the specific fields on that list that are available for the open folder. As an example, let's say that you want to set up a filter for your Contacts folder that will display all contacts whose business address is in Seattle. In that case, you'd point to the Address Fields list.

4 Click the field you want to use—for this example, click Business Address City. Outlook adds the field name to the box under the Field button and activates the Condition box and the Value box.

FIGURE 20-8.

The Advanced tab of the Filter dialog box.

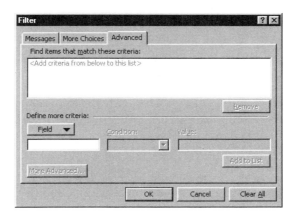

5 Choose a condition from the list in the Condition box. (The set of conditions available in this box depends on the specific field you selected.) For this example, choose Contains.

6 In the Value box, type a value—in this case, type *Seattle*. Outlook activates the Add To List button.

7 Click the Add To List button. Outlook adds the criterion to the Find Items That Match These Criteria box.

8 If you want to add additional criteria, repeat steps 2 through 7. (Remember that when you set up multiple criteria, a folder item must meet *all* the criteria in order to appear in the filtered view.) If you change your mind about including a criterion, select it in the Find Items That Match These Criteria box and click the Remove button.

You can enter multiple values in the Value box. For text fields, use the word *and*, an ampersand (*&*), or a blank space to filter items whose field contents match both values. For instance, to display messages that you've assigned to *both* the categories Key Customer and International, type *Key Customer and International* in the Value box. To display messages that you've assigned to *either* category, use the word *or*, a comma, or a semicolon. For date fields—used most often with the conditions On, On Or After, and On Or Before—you can use AutoDate to describe the value. For example, you can assign Birthday for the Field contents, On Or Before as the Condition, and for the value you can type *two days*. The Filter will show only those Contacts whose birthday is on or before today's date.

9 Click OK to close the Filter dialog box and click OK again to close the View Summary dialog box. The folder now appears with its contents filtered. For the example described here, your Contacts folder displays a filtered view of all contact entries whose Business Address City field contains the word *Seattle*.

10 Not all fields and conditions require a value (step 6). If a condition requires a value, Outlook activates the Value box and does not activate the Add To List button until you've entered the value.

Turning Off a Filter

To turn off a filter, take these steps:

1 Open the folder.

2 Point to Current View on the View menu, and then choose Customize Current View from the submenu to display the View Summary box.

3 Click the Filter button.

4 In the Filter dialog box, click the Clear All button.

5 Click OK in the two dialog boxes to return to the unfiltered folder.

Working with Custom Fields

Outlook lets you create your own fields when you cannot find a built-in field that serves your needs. Use the field to display information, to perform calculations, or to group items in the folder.

> When you create a custom field, it is only available to the folder in which you created it. The custom field name appears in the User-Defined Fields In Folder in the Sort, Filter (Advanced Fields), and Group By dialog boxes. Custom fields automatically appear in table views to which you add them; but, to display the new field in a built-in form, such as a message or appointment window, you have to customize the form to add the field to it, as covered in Chapter 22, "Designing and Using Forms."

You can create three kinds of custom fields: simple, combination, and formula.

■ Use a simple field to add a basic piece of information to folder items such as a column in a table view or a row on a card view. For example, you might add a field called Summary Report Submitted in your Tasks folder, to record the date you wrote and submitted a summary of a completed project. You then add this field as a column in Detailed List view or Completed Tasks view.

■ In a combination field, you can combine existing fields to appear in a single column or a single row in a folder. For example, you might create an Attendees field for your Calendar folder that combines the Optional Attendees and Required Attendees fields, if the distinction between optional and required attendance isn't important or practical in your organization. You could then display the Attendees column in, for instance, Active Appointments view or Recurring Appointments view.

■ With a formula field, you perform a calculation that involves the information contained in other fields. You might create a formula field for messages, for instance, that shows the number of days since each message was received and its importance icon with any due dates that might occur for the task associated with the message.

Each new custom field must be based on a specific data type—that is, the field must be able to contain the appropriate kind of data: text, numbers, dates, or other data. The basic steps for creating all three types of custom fields are the same, although combination and formula fields involve a few additional steps.

 NOTE

You can create custom fields only for table views and card views—not for timeline, day/week/month, note, or icon views.

Creating a Simple Custom Field

To create a simple custom field for a folder, follow these steps:

1 Open the folder for which you want to create a custom field.

2 Select a table view or a card view.

3 Point to Current View on the View menu, and then choose Customize Current View from the submenu to display the View Summary dialog box.

4 Click the Fields button.

5 In the Show Fields dialog box, click the New Field button.

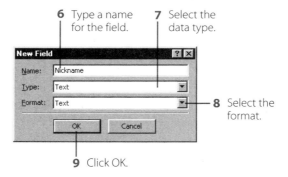

6 Type a name for the field. **7** Select the data type. **8** Select the format. **9** Click OK.

10 In the Show Fields dialog box, you can click the Move Up button to change the position of the field.

11 Click OK in the Show Fields dialog box, and then click OK in the View Summary dialog box.

TIP

> In the Contacts folder there is another way to create a new field. Double-click the item, click the All Fields tab in the item's window, and then click the New button.

When you create a custom field, you select a data type in the Type box of the New Field dialog box. The data type determines the kind of information you'll be storing in the field. Table 20-2, on page 567, lists the data types you can choose.

For each data type except combination and formula, you can also choose a format in which the information will appear. Table 20-3, on page 568, lists these standard formats.

TIP

> To quickly change a field's format from within the folder window, right-click a column heading and choose Format Columns from the shortcut menu. In the Available Fields box, select the field, and then select a format in the Format box.

Creating a Combination Field

You can combine simple fields (both built-in fields and custom fields) in a single column or row—the result is called a combination field. For example, you can create a column that combines the City and State fields in an address list to save space. *For more examples, see Table 20-4, on page 571.*

To create a combination field, follow these steps:

1 Open the New Field dialog box, as explained in "Creating a Simple Custom Field," on page 564 (steps 1 through 4).

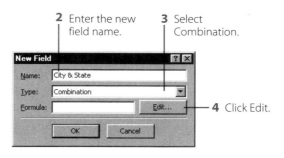

V

Bending Folders to Your Will

5 Click here to join fields together, or ....

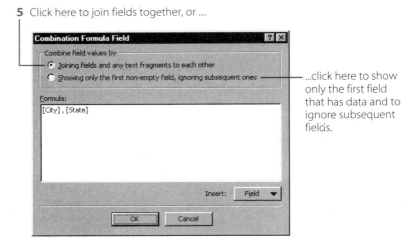

...click here to show only the first field that has data and to ignore subsequent fields.

6 Click the Field button, point to the field set containing the first field you want to combine, and then click the field. Repeat for each field you want to combine.

7 In the Formula text box you can type additional material around the fields. For instance, if you combine City and State, you could type a comma and a space after the City field and before the State field.

8 When you've inserted all the fields, click OK in the Combination Formula Field dialog box and again in the New Field dialog box.

9 In the Show Fields dialog box, you can click Move Up to move your new field up the list if you want to adjust the position in which the field will be displayed in the folder window.

10 Click OK in the Show Fields dialog box.

To add or change the information in a combination field, you must add or change the information in the simple fields that make up the combination. For example, if you create a combination field consisting of city and state names, you need to add or change the city name in the simple City field and the state name in the simple State field. You can't directly edit the information in a combination field. As with all new fields, you have to customize an existing form to add the combination field to it, as covered in Chapter 22, "Designing and Using Forms."

TABLE 20-2.   Data Types for Custom Fields

Data Type	Use For
Combination	Combinations of fields and text in a column (table view) or row (card view). You can show each field of the combination or show the first field containing data.
Currency	Numbers shown as currency; calculations of money amounts.
Date/Time	Dates and times.
Duration	Numbers. You can enter a duration using a standard format based on a 24-hour day or based on Work Time, the number of hours per day you work. (From the Other tab in the Options dialog box, click Advanced Options to set the length of your working day.) For example, if you have set 10 hours as a work day in the Advanced Options dialog box, entering 15 hours in the duration field shows as 1.5 days.
Formula	Calculations using data contained in any field. Use appropriate functions and operators to set up a formula.
Integer	Nondecimal numbers.
Keywords	User-defined fields that you can use to group and find related items, in much the same way you use the Categories field. If the text contains multiple values, you must separate them with commas. Each value can be grouped individually in a view.
Number	Numbers; mathematical calculations except those involving money amounts. (Use the Currency data type for money.)
Percent	Numbers as a percentage.
Text	Text or combinations of text and numbers (as many as 255 characters), such as addresses and phone numbers.
Yes/No	Data that can be only one of two values, such as Yes/No, True/False, or On/Off. (For example, the Do Not AutoArchive field uses a Yes/No data type.) A Yes/No field can also be displayed as an empty box or a box with a check mark.

Combination fields use the default format of the data type on which they are based. To display a data type with a custom format, you must create a formula field and use the Format function, as explained in the next section.

 NOTE

You cannot sort, group, or filter the contents of a combination field.

V

Bending Folders to Your Will

TABLE 20-3. Some Standard Formats for Data Types

Data Type	Standard Formats
Currency	$12,345.60 or ($12,345.60) $12,346 or ($12,346)
Date/Time	Monday, March 1, 1999 8:15 PM March 1, 1999 8:15 PM (plus 13 other formats)
Duration	12h or 12 hours (assumes a 24-hour day) 12h (Work Time) or 12 hours (Work Time) To set the length of your workday, click the Other tab in the Options dialog box, and then click the Advanced Options button.
Integer	1,234 Computer: -640 K; 2,300 K; 3,100,000 K Computer -640 K; 2.3 M; 3.1 G Computer -640 K; 2.3 MB; 3.1 GB
Keywords	Text
Number	All Digits: 1,234.567 or -1,234.567 Truncated: 1,235 or -1,235 1 Decimal: 1,234.6 or -1,234.6 2 Decimal: 1,234.57 or -1,234.57 Scientific: 1235E+03 or -1235E+03 Computer 64 K or 128 K or 65,536 K Computer: 64 K or 128 M or 1 G Computer 64 KB or 256 MB or 2 GB Raw: 12345.67 or -12345.67
Percent	All Digits: 65.4321% Rounded: 65% or -65% 1 Decimal: 64.4% or -64.4% 2 Decimal: 65.43% or -65.43%
Text	Text
Yes/No	Yes or No On or Off True or False Icon—Empty box or box with a check mark

Creating a Formula Field

You use a formula field to perform a calculation that involves the information contained in other fields. Formula fields combine functions, operators, and fields to perform the calculation. *To see some examples of formula fields, see Table 20-4, on page 571.*

To create a formula field, follow these steps:

1 Open the New Field dialog box, as explained in "Creating a Simple Custom Field," on page 564 (steps 1 through 4).

2 Enter a new name for the formula field in the Name box.

3 Select Formula in the Type box.

4 Click Edit to open the Formula Field box, as shown in Figure 20-9.

5 Insert the fields, functions, and operators needed to create the calculation.

- To insert a function, click the Function button, point to the category containing the function you want, and then click the function. The function appears in the Formula box with the names of any arguments it requires.

- To insert a field, click the Field button, point to the field set, and click the field. To insert a field inside a function argument, select the function argument in the Formula box and then choose the field. The field will be inserted in place of the argument you selected.

- Type any operators or literal information, such as text and numbers, that are needed to complete the calculation.

6 Click OK in the Formula Field dialog box, and then click OK in the New Field dialog box.

7 In the Show Fields dialog box, click the Move Up button if you want to adjust the position of the field in the list.

FIGURE 20-9.
The Formula Field
dialog box.

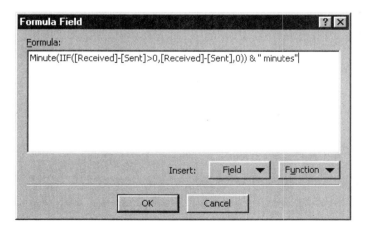

Bending Folders to Your Will

8 Click OK in the Show Fields dialog box.

If you need to add or change the information contained in a formula field, you must add or change the information in the simple fields that make up the formula. You can't directly edit the information in a formula field.

Formula fields are recalculated any time you change a view, such as when you change the width of a column.

 NOTE

> You cannot sort, group, or filter the contents of a formula field.

Examples of Formula and Combination Fields

Formula and combination fields can be a little tricky, but they can also be extremely useful. Table 20-4 offers a few examples of such custom fields, showing you what the formulas and combinations look like and providing some sample results for each field.

Changing a Custom Field

You can change the format, formula, or label of a custom field. But if you want to change a custom field's data type or field name, you'll have to delete the custom field and create a new one (see "Deleting a Custom Field," on page 572).

Here's how to change the format, label, or formula for a custom field:

1 Locate the field in a folder view and right-click the column heading.

2 Select Format Columns from the menu that appears.

3 With the custom field already selected and the formula displayed in the Formula box, click the button to its right labeled with an ellipsis (...) to modify the field's formula or combination.

4 When the Formula Field or the Combination Formula Field dialog box appears, modify the formula or create a new one, and then click OK. (For a combination field, you can't change the option of showing all fields or showing only the first field with data. To do that you'll just have to delete the field and start over.)

5 If you want to change the label that appears for the field in your folder view, type the new label in the Label box.

TABLE 20-4.   Examples of Formula and Combination Fields

For the Field to Show This:	Enter This Specification:	To Show This Result:
Formula Fields		
Number of days since an item was received	DateValue (Now())-DateValue ([Received]) & "Day(s)"	6 Day(s) (if 6 days have elapsed since the date the message was received)
Description of a meeting in your calendar	"This meeting occurs" & [Recurrence Pattern] & "in" & [Location]	This meeting occurs every day from 12:00 AM to 1:30 AM in room 10b
Amount charged for a phone call recorded in the Journal at $.75 a minute	IIF ([Entry Type] = "Phone call", Format ([Duration] *.75, "Currency"), "None")	$1.50 (if the duration of the call was 2 minutes)
Description of a message flag	IIF ([Flag Status] = "2" [Message Flag] & " " & [Due By],"")	Follow up 10/5/98 10:00:00 AM
Combination Fields		
The first phone number recorded for a contact, in order of appearance in the formula	[Business Phone] [Business Phone 2] [Home Phone] [Car Phone]	(555) 555-1234 (only the first phone field with an entry appears)
A description of a field combined with the field itself	Task Due: [Due Date]	Task Due: 10/5/98 10:00:00 AM

6 If you want to change the format of the field, such as its width or alignment, modify the appropriate settings in the Format Columns dialog box.

7 Click OK to close the Format Columns dialog box.

You can't edit Outlook's built-in fields.

Deleting a Custom Field

If you no longer have a use for a field you created, you might as well get rid of it. To delete a field you created, take these steps:

1 Point to Current View on the View menu, and then choose Customize Current View from the submenu to display the View Summary dialog box.

2 Click the Fields button.

3 If you're using the custom field, it will appear in the Show These Fields In This Order list. Move it to the Available Fields list by selecting it and clicking Remove.

4 Select the field name in the Available Fields list, and then click the Delete button.

5 When Outlook asks you to confirm the deletion, click OK.

6 Click OK in the Show Fields dialog box and then in the View Summary dialog box.

> **NOTE**
>
> You can't delete any of Outlook's built-in fields.

You'll find that for most purposes, Outlook's default folder organization is practical and convenient, displaying the fields most commonly needed. However, the capability to reorganize the way information is displayed, and to create your own fields, makes Outlook an even more powerful organizational tool.

CHAPTER 21

Setting Up Views

I n Chapter 20, "Organizing Folder Items," you learned how to set up columns and organize information in a folder. Sometimes, however, you want to make more extensive changes to the way information is displayed. Microsoft Outlook lets you customize the way its built-in views appear, and you can even create new views yourself. You can select the fields to be included, group and sort the information, and filter the view all in one operation. You can also modify the view, rename it, change its format, and even decide who can use the view and in which folders they can use it.

Defining a View

While Outlook provides a number of views for each type of folder, you may want to organize a folder in an entirely different way. Rather then make drastic changes to one of the built-in views, you can define a new view just for you.

When you define a view for a folder, you give the view a name, and you set up the fields, the sorting, the grouping, and the filtering you want to use.

To create your own view, follow these steps:

1 Open the folder in which you want to define a new view.

2 Point to Current View on the View menu, and then choose Define Views from the submenu to open the Define Views For dialog box, shown here:

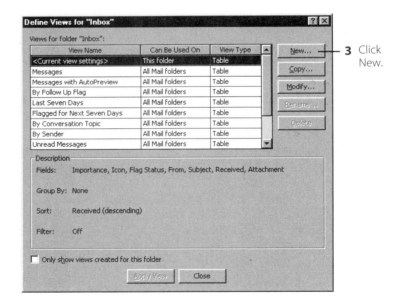

3 Click New.

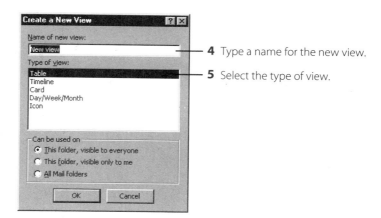

4 Type a name for the new view.

5 Select the type of view.

6 In the Can Be Used On area, select one of the three options to specify where the view can be used and who can use it:

- **This Folder, Visible To Everyone** makes the view available only in the folder in which you created it. Anyone who has permission to open the folder can choose to display the view from the Current View submenu.

- **This Folder, Visible Only To Me** makes the view available only in the folder in which you created it and does not allow other people to use the view.

- **All [Folder Type] Folders** makes the view available to all folders that are the same type as the folder in which you created the view. Anyone who has permission to open a folder of this type can use this view to organize items in a similar folder.

7 Click OK. Depending on the type of view you've chosen, Outlook displays the View Settings dialog box or the View Summary dialog box, shown in Figure 21-1, on the next page, which provides a complete description of the view as it currently exists.

8 Use the buttons in this dialog box to set up the elements of the new view. Some buttons might be unavailable, depending on the type of view you're defining. If the button is available, clicking Fields, Group By, Sort, or Filter takes you to a dialog box that should be familiar from Chapter 20, "Organizing Folder Items." The Other Settings button is discussed in "Formatting Views," on page 578. Clicking the Automatic Formatting button opens the

FIGURE 21-1.

The View Summary dialog box.

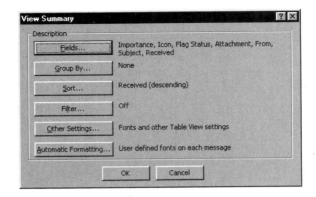

Automatic Formatting dialog box, discussed in "Adjusting Automatic Formatting," on page 587.

9 When you've finished setting up the elements of the view and closed the relevant dialog boxes, click OK in the View Summary dialog box to close it and return to the Define Views For dialog box.

10 If you want to apply the new view to a folder that's open, select the view from the list, and then click the Apply View button; otherwise click the Close button.

Copying a View

Outlook also provides a shorter method for creating a new view. Instead of starting from scratch and defining every part of a new view, you can base a new view on the current arrangement of fields, filters, groups, and sort order. Just follow these steps:

1 Open the folder in which you want to define a new view.

2 Point to Current View on the View menu, and then choose Define Views from the submenu to open the Define Views For dialog box.

3 Select the view that you want to use as the basis for the new one, and then click Copy to display the Copy View dialog box.

4 Type a name for the new view.

5 Select a Can Be Used On option.

6 Click OK.

7 In the View Summary dialog box that appears, use the available buttons to change any of the view settings as desired, and then click OK.

Modifying a View

If a view isn't quite right, you can modify it so that it better suits your needs. To modify either a view you created or one of Outlook's built-in views, follow these steps:

1 Open the folder that contains the view you want to change.

2 Point to Current View on the View menu, and then choose Define Views from the submenu to open the Define Views For dialog box.

3 Select the name of the view you want to change.

4 Click the Modify button to open the View Summary dialog box.

5 In the View Summary dialog box, use the available buttons to modify the view as needed.

6 When you've finished modifying the view and have closed the relevant dialog boxes, click OK in the View Summary dialog box to close it and return to the Define Views For dialog box.

7 If you want to apply the modified view to a folder that's open, click the Apply View button in the Define Views For dialog box; otherwise, click the Close button.

To open the View Summary dialog box quickly, right-click a column heading in a table view or right-click anywhere in a timeline view, and then choose Customize Current View from the shortcut menu that appears.

Resetting a Standard View

As just described, you can modify custom views as well as Outlook's built-in views. If you modify a built-in view but later decide that you'd prefer to use Outlook's original version, you can restore the standard settings for that view. Here's how to do it:

1 Open the folder containing the built-in view you want to reset.

2 Point to Current View on the View menu, and then choose Define Views to open the Define Views For dialog box.

3 In the Define Views For dialog box, select the name of the view.

4 Click the Reset button. This button is available only when you select a built-in view; you can't reset a custom view.

5 If you want to apply the restored original view to the currently open folder, click the Apply View button in the Define Views For dialog box; otherwise just click the Close button.

Renaming a User-Defined View

You can easily change the name of a view you created. (Although you can modify Outlook's built-in views, as you saw in the preceding section, you cannot rename them.)

To change the name of a view you created, take these steps:

1 Open the folder that contains the view you want to rename.

2 Point to Current View on the View menu, and then choose Define Views from the submenu to open the Define Views For dialog box.

3 In the Define Views For dialog box, select the view you want to rename, and then click the Rename button.

4 In the dialog box that appears, type a new name for the view and then click OK.

5 If you want to apply the renamed view to the currently open folder, click the Apply View button in the Define Views For dialog box; otherwise click the Close button.

Formatting Views

Each Outlook view is one of these five types:

- Table
- Timeline
- Day/week/month (designed for the Calendar folder)
- Card (designed for the Contacts folder)
- Icon (designed for the Notes folder)

As this list implies, some views are designed specifically for certain folders (and for custom folders of the same type). Actually, you can set up any view for any folder—for instance, you could set up a day/week/month view for your Notes folder—but you'll need to judge for yourself how much sense this makes in any given situation.

As you've seen in earlier chapters, you can customize views in Outlook in many ways. In addition to defining what items a view displays and in what order or groupings it displays them, you can also change the font, add previews, and set other formatting options for the various views. You can change the formatting of the current view or any other view available to the folder you have open. To format a view, follow these steps:

1 Open the folder that contains the view you want to modify.

2 If you are already using the view you want to format, point to Current View on the View menu, and then choose Customize Current View. If you want to format a different view, point to Current View on the View menu, and then choose Define Views instead. From the Define Views dialog box, select the view you want to format, and then click Modify.

3 Click Other Settings in the View Summary dialog box to display the available options for the view you're customizing. Read the sections that follow for a description of the options available for each type of view.

> When you change the formatting of a view, the modifications apply only to that view. For example, if you change the formatting of the Tasks folder's Simple List view, the changes apply only to that view and not to any other table views.

Table Views

A table view displays folder items in rows and columns. Each row contains the information for one folder item; each column contains one piece of information about the item (one field). *For details about working with columns, see "Setting Up Columns," on page 544.* The Other Settings dialog box that appears when customizing a table view is shown in Figure 21-2, on the next page.

As you can see in the dialog box, Outlook offers numerous options for formatting:

Font buttons. When you click any one of the three Font buttons, Outlook opens the Font dialog box, where you can change the font, the font style (most fonts offer regular, bold, italic, and bold italic), the font size in points, and the script for the font you've chosen (if your computer is set up to work in various foreign-language alphabets). You can adjust the font settings for column headings, for rows (the contents of each folder item), and for previews (if you choose to display them). You may also change the color of the Auto Preview font.

Automatic Column Sizing. Select this check box to have Outlook size the columns in the view so that all of them fit on the screen. (Some might be abbreviated in order to fit.) If you clear this check box, you might have to scroll to see all the columns in a view, or you can size the columns yourself to see the ones you want.

Allow In-Cell Editing. When this check box is selected, you can type or edit directly in the table cells to make changes to folder items. When it's deselected, you cannot edit in the cells and must instead open each folder item to make any changes.

FIGURE 21-2.

The Other Settings dialog box for a table view.

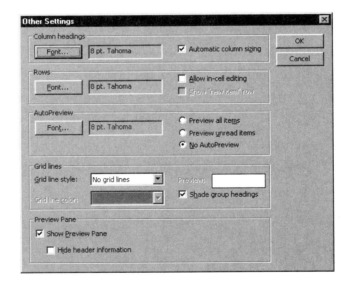

Show "New Item" Row. This check box is available only when Allow In-Cell Editing is selected. When you select this check box, Outlook adds a row at the top of the table view that allows you to create a new folder item without opening a new folder item window. (The Tasks folder, for example, displays such a "new item" row by default.)

AutoPreview. This Outlook feature displays partial contents of a folder item in the table view so that you can quickly determine what each item contains. For messages, Outlook displays the first three lines of the message body; for other folder items, you see the first three lines of the Notes section of the folder item. You can choose whether to show previews for all items or for unread items only, or you can choose No AutoPreview to eliminate previews and see headings only.

Grid Lines. You can choose to display grid lines between the rows and columns of a table view. If you include the grid lines in the view, you can set both a line style (Small Dots, Large Dots, Dashes, or Solid) and a line color. After you set both these options, Outlook provides a sample grid line in the Preview box. You can also choose whether to shade group headings in those views that group the table rows by a particular field. You'll probably want to leave the Shade Group Headings check box selected in most cases; it's usually easier to distinguish the headings of grouped items when they're shaded.

Preview Pane. In this section of the dialog box, you can choose to display or hide the preview pane and whether to display or hide the header information in the Pane.

> **NOTE**

The default settings in the Other Settings dialog box are not the same for all table views and all folders. For instance, Simple List view in the Tasks folder displays grid lines, allows in-cell editing, and includes a "new item" row by default, whereas Messages view in the Inbox folder (another table view) by default omits grid lines and in-cell editing, and does not contain a "new item" row.

Timeline Views

A timeline view is named for the way dates are displayed along a line running from left to right across the top of the folder window, with the folder items for each date listed below their respective dates. The figure on the following page shows a timeline view (for a single week) from a Journal folder.

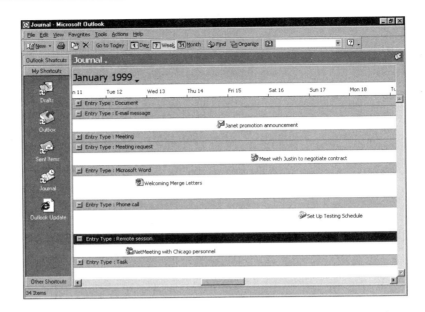

When displaying journal information, you can click the Day, Week, or Month button on the Standard toolbar to have the timeline band show the folder items in the following ways:

- For a single day, listed by the time

- For a single week, listed by the day

- For a month, listed by the date or by the week of the year—for example, week 14

To format a timeline view, display the view on your screen and click the Other Settings button as described above. Outlook opens the Format Timeline View dialog box, shown in Figure 21-3.

Fonts. You can click the buttons in this area to set the font, font style (usually regular, bold, italic, or bold italic), font size, and language script. You can make these font changes for the upper and lower scales of the timeline and for the folder items displayed in the view. You cannot change the color of any of these elements in a timeline view.

Scales. Select the Show Week Numbers check box if you want to include week numbers in the view. When you select this check box, Outlook displays the week numbers in the top band of the timeline when you're looking at a single day or week and in the lower band of the timeline when you're looking at a month.

FIGURE 21-3.

The Format Timeline View dialog box.

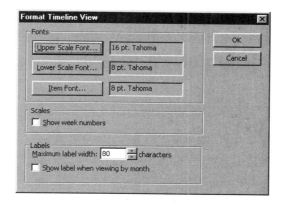

Labels. The options in this area affect the labels (names) of the various folder items that appear under the dates in the timeline. You can set a maximum width for these labels (from 0 through 132 characters). When the timeline displays a month rather than a day or a week, you can choose whether to include or omit the item labels by selecting the Show Label When Viewing By Month check box.

Day/Week/Month Views

 SEE ALSO

For information about Day, Week, and Month views that are built into Outlook's Calendar folder and about elements such as the Date Navigator, see Chapter 10, "Scheduling Appointments," and also "Setting Calendar Options," on page 74.

A day/week/month view displays folder items in a standard calendar arrangement. By clicking the Day, Work Week, Week, or Month button on the Standard toolbar, you can have the calendar show the items in the following ways:

- For a single date, listed by the time
- For a single work week, listed by the day
- For a single week, listed by the day
- For a month, listed by the day

To format a day/week/month view, display the view on your screen, and then click the Other Settings button to open the Format Day/Week/Month View dialog box, shown in Figure 21-4, on the next page.

Day. Use the Time Font button and the Time Scale list to format the time bar that appears to the left of the appointments (or other folder items) on a one-day calendar. If you want to change the font of the time bar, click the Time Font button to open the Font dialog box, where you can set the font, font style (usually regular, bold, italic, or bold italic), font size, and language script. To set the time intervals shown for the calendar items, select a time interval from the Time Scale

FIGURE 21-4.

The Format
Day/Week/Month View
dialog box.

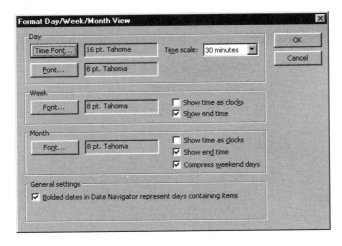

list (5, 6, 10, 15, 30, or 60 minutes are the choices). Click the Font button if you want to change the font of the folder items that appear in the appointment (or other folder item) slots.

Week. Click the Font button in the Week section to change the font of both the dates and the folder items displayed when you choose Week view to display a one-week time span. If you'd like to see start times for items shown on small clock faces rather than in digits, select the Show Time As Clocks check box. To have Outlook display both start and end times for folder items, select the Show End Time check box; clear it to omit the end times.

Month. Click the Font button in the Month section to change the font of both the dates and the folder items displayed when you choose Month view to display a one-month time span. The Show Time As Clocks and Show End Time check boxes are available, as they are in the Week section. You can also choose whether to compress weekend days on the monthly calendar (combining Saturday and Sunday in a smaller space) or to allot equal space to all days of the week.

 NOTE

To display the start and end times of appointments in Month view, you must have Show Time As Clocks selected for Month view in the Format View dialog box. Depending on the resolution of your monitor, you might have to hide the Outlook Bar (by clicking Outlook Bar on the View menu) and the Folder List (by clicking Folder List on the View menu) to display both the start and end times of an appointment.

General Settings. Select this check box if you want dates containing folder items to appear in bold in the Date Navigator; clear this check box to remove the bold.

Card Views

SEE ALSO

For information about the specific card views built into the Contacts folder, see "Using Card Views," on page 425.

A card view displays folder items as small cards containing various fields of information. The card views that are built into Outlook's Contacts folder, for instance, show contact information such as addresses and phone numbers on cards that look like note cards laid out on a desk. You can view a number of cards on the screen at the same time, with the level of detail that you set up.

To format a card view, open an appropriate folder, point to Current View on the View menu to open the View Summary dialog box for the view you want to format, and then click the Other Settings button to display the Format Card View dialog box, shown in Figure 21-5.

Font buttons. If you want to reformat the card headings (titles) or the body of the card (the contents of the folder item), click the Font button in the appropriate section to open the Font dialog box, where you can change the font, font style, font size, or script.

Allow In-Cell Editing. Select this check box if you want to be able to type or edit directly on the card that appears on your screen in the card view. When this check box is cleared, you cannot edit the fields of information on the card but must instead open the folder item to make changes.

Show Empty Fields. Select this check box if you want each card to display all the fields for the folder item, whether or not the fields contain text. Clear this check box to have Outlook show only those fields that contain information (a more efficient use of screen space in most cases).

FIGURE 21-5.
The Format Card View dialog box.

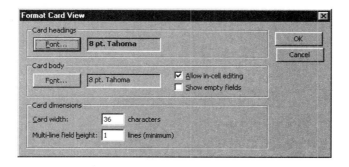

Card Dimensions. You can specify the width of the cards, in characters. If you enter a width that is too large to fit in the window, Outlook resets the card width to the maximum possible for the window. (Note that when you display the Outlook Bar and the Folder List, the maximum width for a card decreases.) In the Multi-Line Field Height box, you can specify the minimum number of lines (1 through 20) that should be allocated to a multiple-line field such as an address field.

TIP

You can also use the mouse to change card width in the folder window. When you place the mouse pointer on the vertical dividing line between two columns of cards, the pointer becomes a double vertical line with a two-headed arrow. Dragging the dividing line to the left decreases the width of all the columns of cards simultaneously, while dragging to the right increases the widths of all the columns. If you widen the cards so that some columns move off screen, Outlook activates a horizontal scroll bar so that you can scroll to see them.

Icon Views

An icon view displays folder items as small images (icons) with text labels. You'll see different icons for different types of folders—the specific icon Outlook shows matches the type of item contained in the folder.

To format an icon view, display the view on your screen and click the Other Settings button to open the Format Icon View dialog box, shown in Figure 21-6.

View Type. You can choose to display the icons in the selected view as large icons, as small icons, or as an icon list. If you select the Icon List option, the options in the Icon Placement section below become unavailable; you can arrange the icons in the window only if you choose the Large Icon option or the Small Icon option.

Icon Placement. You can select any one of the four options in this area. Select Do Not Arrange if you want to arrange the icons yourself, dragging them to any spot in the folder window. The Line Up Icons option lines up the icons according to a preset grid in the folder window, snapping the icon to the nearest grid point. The AutoArrange option also lines up the icons on the invisible grid, but it arranges the icons in continuous rows and columns, so there are no gaps between icons. To have Outlook sort the icons, choose Sort And AutoArrange, which arranges the icons in rows according to the sorting keys you specify in the Sort dialog box. In the box to the right of these options,

FIGURE 21-6.
The Format Icon View
dialog box.

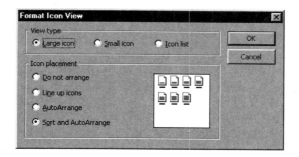

you can see a small preview of how the icons will be arranged,
depending on your choice.

Deleting a View

If you no longer have use for a custom view, you can delete it from the
folder that contains it. (You can delete only those views that you created yourself; you cannot remove Outlook's built-in views.)

1 Open the folder that contains the view you want to delete.

2 Point to Current View on the View menu, and then choose Define
   Views from the submenu.

3 Select the name of the view in the Define Views For dialog box.

4 Click the Delete button. (This button is available only when you
   select the name of a custom view.) When Outlook asks whether
   you're sure you want to delete the view, click the Yes button.

5 Click Close in the Define Views For dialog box.

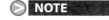 **NOTE**

> If you delete a custom view but then change your mind, you're out of
> luck—you'll have to re-create the view. Outlook provides no way to retrieve a
> deleted view.

Adjusting Automatic Formatting

In some folders, not every item is displayed the same way in the item
list. In e-mail folders, for example, unread messages are shown in bold,
expired messages with strikeout (text with a horizontal line drawn
through it), and mail that has been submitted but not sent in italic. In

the Tasks folder, overdue tasks are displayed in red and completed tasks with strikeout.

Formatting items based on their condition or status is called *automatic formatting* and it helps you visually distinguish items on the list quickly.

You can modify the formats that Outlook applies to folder items, and you can create your own rules for identifying and formatting items. For example, you may want to display messages from a certain recipient or regarding a specific topic in color to call your attention to them.

To modify the way Outlook formats items, follow these steps:

1 Display the view that contains the type of items you want to automatically format.

2 Point to Current View on the View menu, and then choose Customize Current View from the submenu to open the View Summary dialog box.

3 Click the Automatic Formatting button to display the Automatic Formatting dialog box.

NOTE

You can't modify the automatic formatting of all views. If the Automatic Formatting button is dimmed, you won't be able to set automatic formatting for the current view.

4 Select the rule whose formatting you want to modify.

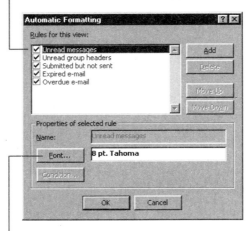

5 Click here to open the Font dialog box.

6 Choose the formats to apply to the item type.

7 Click OK to close the Font dialog box.

8 In the Automatic Formatting dialog box, click OK. Click OK again to close the View Summary dialog box.

> If you want to remove special formatting from one or more rules, simply clear the check box of each rule. The rule will then be inactive, and the item will be displayed with the default formatting for items that don't fit any special rules.

To create your own rules for identifying and formatting an item, you have to establish the conditions that identify the item type. For example, a condition might be the name of the sender for an e-mail item or the subject of a task. You can then apply formats to items that meet those conditions.

Follow these steps to create a new rule in the Automatic Formatting dialog box:

1 Click Add to create a new rule. Outlook activates the Name text box.

2 In the Name text box, enter an identifying name for the rule.

3 Click Font, choose the formats to apply to the items that meet the rule, and then click OK in the Font dialog box.

4 Click Condition to display the Filter dialog box, shown in Figure 20-6, on page 557.

5 Specify the conditions for the item, using the techniques you learned for creating filters in Chapter 20, "Organizing Folder Items."

6 Click OK in the Filter dialog box, in the Automatic Formatting dialog box, and in the View Summary dialog box.

> Formats are applied to items in the order the rules are listed in the Automatic Formatting dialog box. To change the order of a rule, select it in the dialog box, and then click the Move Up or Move Down button.

To delete one of your own rules, select it in the Automatic Formatting dialog box and click the Delete button. You cannot delete any of Outlook's built-in rules.

V

Bending Folders to Your Will

By customizing or creating views, and organizing folder items as you learned in Chapter 20, you can adapt Outlook to the way you like to work with information. Experiment with various layouts and organizations until you find the arrangement that works best for you. For even more control over how information appears, you can also create custom forms, as you'll learn in Chapter 22, "Designing and Using Forms."

PART VI

Working with Forms

Designing and Using Forms

Microsoft Outlook uses forms to organize and present information. If you have composed and read messages, recorded appointment or meeting times, specified task details, sent task requests and responses, recorded journal entries and notes, or composed postings, you've used standard forms. Standard forms are those that are used by default when you create or edit an Outlook item. For much of what you do in Outlook, you'll rely on standard forms.

You're not restricted to using only the standard forms, however. You can create and use custom forms for special types of items, and you can even customize the standard forms to suit your own taste. Your organization, for example, might appoint someone to act as an electronic forms designer to create standard forms that all members of your organization can use to report information and to order goods and services. These forms are usually referred to as organization forms.

> Whenever you create or read a folder item that uses a nonstandard form, Outlook installs the form on your computer and then opens it (while displaying a message telling you what's going on).

Creating a Custom Form

You can design a custom form based either on a built-in form (by beginning with a copy of the form) or on a Microsoft Office file:

- Base a custom form on an existing built-in form to include the features of the built-in form. You can include the components of the standard form and then modify the fields to match your needs. The fields are the categories of information that you can display or enter onto a form, such as a contact's name, the date of a meeting, or an e-mail recipient's address.

- Base a custom form on a Microsoft Office file to use the tools from another Office program such as Microsoft Excel or Microsoft Word. Anyone who shares the form with you must have Office installed on his or her system or network.

NOTE

> You can't use Outlook forms in Microsoft Visual Basic or in Microsoft Exchange. In Outlook, however, you can use forms created with the Microsoft Exchange Forms Designer.

To customize a form, you can add or delete fields, options, tabs, and controls. To help you design and set up your form, Outlook provides a number of menu commands as well as a set of visual tools. The form design tools, all of which are discussed in this chapter, appear in three

> **Controlling Interest**
>
> You'll see the term *control* throughout this chapter, and in any book about form design. Don't let the term scare you. A control is really just an object that you place on a form to perform some function. For example, a text control is used on most forms. It is nothing more than a box in which you can display or enter text information. A check box control is a check box that you can select or clear.
>
> All of the objects that you see in Windows dialog boxes, such as lists and option buttons, are controls that you can add to your own forms in Outlook.

locations: the Field Chooser, the Control Toolbox, and the Form Design toolbar in Outlook's design mode. After you've finished your custom form, you can save it in an Outlook folder to be used in that folder, in a forms library so that others can access the form, or as a file to be used as a template or as a form in another application.

Creating a Custom Form from a Built-In Form

You can create a new form based on an existing form. It is easiest if you start by opening the form that you want to use as the basis for the new form, but it is not absolutely necessary.

To create a new form based on an open built-in Outlook form, follow these steps:

1 Open an item that uses the form you want to base the new form upon. For example, to create a new e-mail form, open an e-mail item from either the Inbox, Drafts, Outbox, or Sent Items folders.

2 Point to Forms on the open item's Tools menu, and then choose Design This Form from the submenu.

To create a new form from within any open folder or item, follow these steps instead:

1 Point to Forms on the Tools menu of the currently open folder or item, and then choose Design A Form from the submenu to display the Design Form dialog box.

2 Choose the Standard
Forms Library.

3 Choose the form
to use as the basis
of the new form.

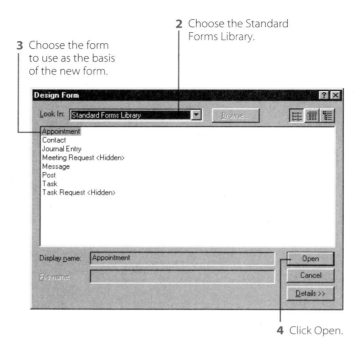

4 Click Open.

Outlook switches to design mode, displaying the form you've selected, ready for customization, as shown in Figure 22-1, on page 597.

 NOTE

You can't create a new form based on a note.

Starting from design mode, you work through the following stages to create custom forms:

1 Customize the form, which will consist of one or more pages (tabs).

2 Hide or show the form's pages.

3 Set the form's properties on the Properties page.

4 Create custom actions for the form.

5 Test the form.

6 Save and publish the form.

The remainder of this chapter covers the process of creating custom forms in detail.

FIGURE 22-1.
A message form displayed in design mode, ready for customization.

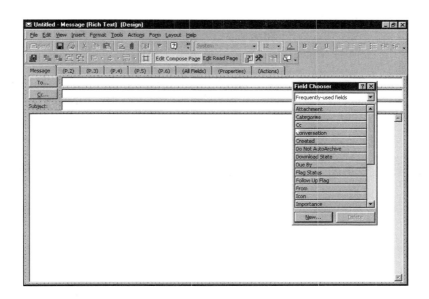

Choosing the Compose or Read Page

You can create different forms for sending messages and for reading messages. These two forms are the Compose and Read pages, respectively. To create separate Compose and Read pages, choose Separate Read Layout from the Form menu of a message form opened in design mode, and then choose which page you want to edit first, as follows:

- To edit the contents of the Read page, choose Edit Read Page from the Form menu or click the Edit Read Page button on the Form Design toolbar.

- To edit the contents of the Compose page, choose Edit Compose Page from the Form menu or click the Edit Compose Page button on the Form Design toolbar.

You can easily tell which page you are editing by seeing which of those two buttons appear pressed down. You can deselect Separate Read Layout on the Form menu again to use synchronized Compose and Read pages. The current page you are designing, either the Compose or Read page, will become the design for both pages, and any changes you've made to the other page will be lost. A message will warn you of that and give you a chance to cancel the operation.

Creating a Custom Form
from a Microsoft Office File

When you create a new form from an Office file, you must begin by opening an Outlook folder or a public folder—*not* a disk files folder. In fact, you cannot have a disk files folder open for this procedure. Unlike forms designed from a built-in form, Office forms don't enable the Field Chooser and Control Toolbox or allow you to customize or hide pages.

> **NOTE**
>
> References to Microsoft Office refer to Office 97 or later versions.

The general steps for creating a custom form from an Office file are as follows:

1 In an Outlook folder or in a public folder, point to New on the File menu, and then choose Office Document from the submenu. Alternatively, you can press Ctrl+Shift+H.

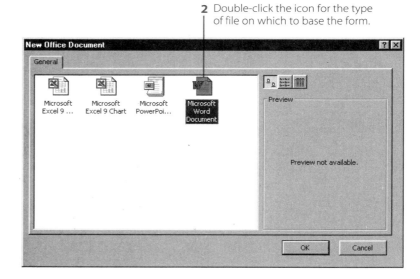

2 Double-click the icon for the type of file on which to base the form.

3 Outlook displays the message box shown on the facing page. Choose Post The Document In This Folder if you want to create a form that contains only a Documents page and that lets you create a document to go into only the current folder. If you choose Send The Document To Someone, the form you create will contain Document and Message pages, and you will be able to send the form to someone else. Click OK (if you are using the Office Assistant, you don't need to click OK).

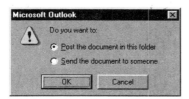

4 When the window resembling the type of Office file you selected appears, point to Forms on its Tools menu, and then choose Design This Form from the submenu. The window transforms into an Outlook document template form, ready for customization. *(Design)* appears in the title bar.

5 Set the form's properties using the Properties page.

6 Create custom actions for the form.

7 Test the form.

8 Save and publish the form.

Customizing Forms

In design mode, the window for an Outlook form contains the form's standard pages, as well as up to five new, blank pages that you can customize, as shown in Figure 22-2, on the following page. To display any one of the form's pages, simply click the page's tab.

On mail message forms, you can also customize the Message page, and on contact forms you can also customize the General page. Other than these, you cannot customize the standard pages. If you don't want to use one of the standard form pages, you can hide it, and create an entirely new page instead.

Naming a Form Tab

The blank pages that you can customize are numbered with "page numbers" in parentheses—(P.2), (P.3), and so on. When you set up a page, you should rename the tab so it describes the kind of information the page contains. You can also rename the Message tab of e-mail forms and the General tab of contact forms.

VI

Working with Forms

FIGURE 22-2.

A message form contains tabs to customize up to five pages.

You can customize these pages.

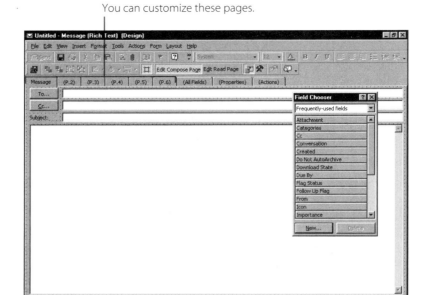

You name a tab as follows:

1 Click the tab you want to name.

2 Choose Rename Page from the Form menu.

3 In the dialog box that appears, type the new name and then click OK.

The parentheses around a tab name indicate that the page will not be displayed when you use the form. The parentheses disappear when you add a control to the form. If you want to remove the parentheses before you add a control to the form, choose Display This Page from the Form menu. You cannot add controls to or display such pages as All Fields, Properties, or Actions.

Adding Fields to a Form

Field
Chooser

Outlook provides a useful design tool called the Field Chooser to help you add fields to a form. If you don't see the Field Chooser in design mode, choose Field Chooser from the Form menu, or click the Field Chooser button on the Form Design toolbar.

Outlook will not display the Field Chooser when you display a page of the form that cannot be customized.

The Field Chooser window, shown in Figure 22-3, contains a list of the fields that you can add to a form; you add fields by dragging them onto the page. If the field you need does not appear in the Frequently Used Fields list of the Field Chooser, select a different field set from the box at the top of the Field Chooser window or click the New button to create a new field.

When you drag a field from the Field Chooser onto a page, Outlook inserts the appropriate type of control (a text box or a check box, for instance), along with a text label that shows the name of the field. You can then set the control's properties as explained in "Setting Properties for a Control," on page 617.

The AutoLayout feature automatically places and sizes the field for you. After AutoLayout sets the initial position, you can then change the field's size and drag the field to any location on the page's grid. *See "Placing and Sizing Controls: Form Layout," on page 608.* (If you'd prefer to position the field yourself with the initial drag, turn off AutoLayout on the Layout menu.)

If you change your mind after you've added a field to a form, you can remove the field by right-clicking it and choosing Delete from the shortcut menu.

If you need to create a new field for your form, click the New button in the Field Chooser. In the New Field dialog box that appears, type the new field's name, and then select a data type and a format for the field.

FIGURE 22-3.
The Field Chooser.

VI

Working with Forms

For all the details about creating new fields and choosing data types and formats, see "Working with Custom Fields," on page 563.

Using the Control Toolbox

Control
Toolbox

The Control Toolbox contains all the basic controls that you can use to design your own fields. To display the Control Toolbox in design mode, choose Control Toolbox from the Form menu or click the Control Toolbox button on the Form Design toolbar. Figure 22-4 shows the Control Toolbox and the control buttons it contains.

> Outlook hides the Control Toolbox when you display a page of the form that cannot be customized.

Adding Controls to a Form

To add a control to a form, use any of these methods:

- Drag the desired control button from the Control Toolbox onto the page.

- Click the tool you want to use in the Control Toolbox to select it, and then click in the form where you want it to appear.

- Click a control button in the Control Toolbox to select it, move the mouse pointer onto the form (where it becomes a crosshair with an icon of the control you selected adjacent to the crosshair),

FIGURE 22-4.
The Control Toolbox contains buttons for all available controls.

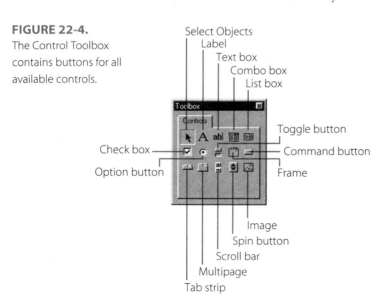

Viewing All Standard Fields for a Form

You might find it useful to view all the standard fields a built-in form can have (and, by extension, the standard fields that you can add to a custom form). To view these fields, follow these steps:

1 Open a folder item that uses the form you're interested in.

2 Point to Forms on the Tools menu, and then choose Design This Form from the submenu to switch to design mode.

3 Click the All Fields tab.

4 Open the Select From list, and choose the all fields list for the item type you opened. For example, if you opened a message form, you would choose All Mail Fields in the Select From box.

Alternatively, you can choose all fields from the list box at the top of the Field Chooser. You can also create new fields on the All Fields page: click the New button at the bottom of the page to open the New Field dialog box. *For help with creating a new field, see "Working with Custom Fields," on page 563.*

For a contact form, you can see all of the standard fields without switching to design mode. Simply open an item from the Contacts folder, and click the All Fields tab in the folder item window. Then select All Contact Fields from the list.

click in the form to anchor one corner of the control, and then drag horizontally and vertically away from that point to set the size of the control.

The first two methods display the control in its default size, which you can later change by dragging. The first method also shows an outline of the control as you drag it onto the form, letting you see its default size before you drop it into place; the other two methods show an icon of the control as part of the mouse pointer.

 TIP

If you change your mind after you've added a control from the Control Toolbox to a form, you can remove the control from the form by right-clicking it and choosing Delete from the shortcut menu. If the control is selected, you can also press the Delete key to remove it.

Choosing the Appropriate Control

The following sections discuss each type of control you can add from the Control Toolbox.

Select Objects. The Select Objects tool allows you to select controls. It is deactivated immediately after you click a control button in the Control Toolbox, but it turns on again as soon as you place that control on the form. If you click a control button in the Control Toolbox and then decide not to place the control on a form, click the Select Objects button to cancel your selection.

Label. A label control is a box in which you can enter text that will appear on the form to identify another control or provide instructions to the user. For instance, if you were to place a text box control (described next) to hold a phone number, you might add a label control next to it, and type the word *Telephone* in it.

Text box. A text box control is any box in which a person using the form can type information. It is a very common control, used for entering names, addresses, phone numbers, and, in the case of large text boxes, blocks of text for memos, notes, or e-mail messages.

Combo box. A combo box is a combination of a list box (described next) and a text box. The list box provides a set of items from which the user can choose, and the text box portion permits the user to type another response if the list is incomplete. The designer might also control the range of responses the user can type in with a validation test. *See "Setting Properties for a Control," on page 617.*

List box. A list box displays a predetermined set of items in a box with a small down arrow to open the list. The user can only select an item from the list and cannot type anything else into the list box. However, users can scroll through the list by pressing a letter key, which displays the first item in the list, if any, that starts with that letter.

Check box. A check box control lets a user select or clear a check mark within a small box. Each check box control is independent of other check box controls. Users can set or clear them in any combination.

Option button. Unlike the check box control, the option button control provides a group of related options from which the user can select only one at a time. Each option button appears as a small circle that becomes filled in when the option is selected.

Toggle button. A toggle button control is a button designed to turn a feature on or off when the user clicks it. For example, the Control Toolbox button on the Form Design toolbar is itself a toggle button.

Frame. A frame control appears as a rectangle with a caption. You use the frame control to group other controls together as related settings.

Command button. A command button control is designed to carry out an action, such as an OK button that accepts all the settings and closes a dialog box, or a Cancel button that rejects the changes to the dialog box.

? SEE ALSO

For details about working with the tab strip and multipage controls, see "Working with Tabs and Pages," on page 606.

Tab strip. A tab strip control is a set of tabs that work like radio buttons—clicking one makes it the current choice. You can name each tab, but you can't add any other features to the tabs. You could use a tab strip in place of option buttons.

Multipage. This control places a set of pages on the form, each with its own tab. These pages are similar to the form pages themselves: you can place any other controls on these pages to create a form within a form.

Scroll bar. Use a scroll bar control when you want to be able to scroll a section of the form. If you size the scroll bar control to be taller than it is wide, it becomes a vertical scroll bar; if you size it to be wider than it is tall, it becomes a horizontal scroll bar.

Spin button. A spin button control contains arrows for scrolling a list of choices (usually numbers) up or down while the control window remains only one line tall.

Image. Use the Image control button to place a rectangle on the form, in which you can show a picture. After adding the control to the form, take the steps on the following page to insert the graphic.

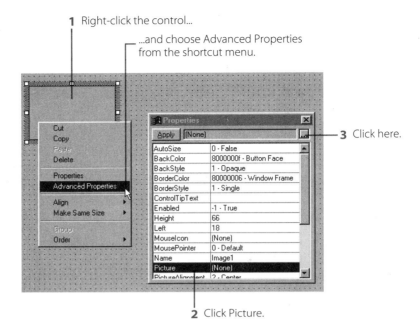

1 Right-click the control...

...and choose Advanced Properties from the shortcut menu.

3 Click here.

2 Click Picture.

4 In the Load Picture dialog box, switch to a folder that contains the picture you want to use, select the picture, and then click the Open button.

In the Properties window, you might also want to check the Picture-Alignment and PictureSizeMode properties. Select each property in turn, and then click the down arrow that appears to the right of the box at the top of the window. From the list that appears, select the choice that suits the way you want the picture to appear in the image control.

Working with Tabs and Pages

You can add tabs to a tab strip control and add pages to a multipage control. You can also rename tabs, delete tabs and pages, or change their order. To make any of these changes, click the tab name to select it, right-click the selected tab name, and then choose a command from the shortcut menu. The following sections explain how to use these commands.

Adding Tabs and Pages

First to make sure that the entire control is selected, click it once, pause, and then click again so it is surrounded by lines that are darker than if you just click once. Then right-click the name on a tab strip control or a multipage control and choose Insert from the shortcut menu. Outlook adds a new tab or page to the control. It is named Tab3 (or the next higher number) on a tab strip control, or Page3 (or the next higher number) on a multipage control.

If there are more tabs or pages than can fit on the control, Outlook adds horizontal scroll arrows, as shown here:

Click the scroll arrows to view tabs that are not visible.

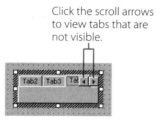

Deleting Tabs and Pages

To remove a selected tab from a tab strip control or a page from a multipage control, right-click the tab or page label and choose Delete from the shortcut menu.

Renaming Tabs

When you right-click a tab or page name and choose the Rename command, Outlook displays the Rename dialog box, shown here for a tab strip control:

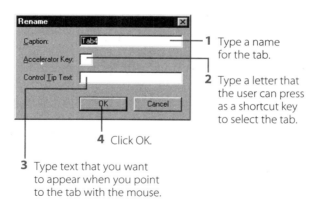

1 Type a name for the tab.

2 Type a letter that the user can press as a shortcut key to select the tab.

4 Click OK.

3 Type text that you want to appear when you point to the tab with the mouse.

NOTE

In the Rename dialog box, the accelerator key can be any character. You should, however, select a letter that appears in the tab name. Consider making the initial letter the accelerator key, unless it conflicts with the name of another tab. Outlook underlines the letter in the tab name. To use the accelerator key, the user of the form must hold down the Alt key while pressing the accelerator key.

Rearranging Tabs and Pages

To change the order of tabs in a tab strip or the pages in a multipage control, right-click the tab label and then choose Move from the shortcut menu that appears. When the Page Order dialog box opens, follow these steps:

1 Select the tab you want to move.

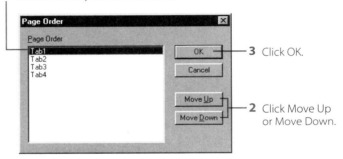

3 Click OK.

2 Click Move Up or Move Down.

Placing and Sizing Controls: Form Layout

You can position and size controls on a form by dragging them with the mouse. To position a control with the mouse, first click the control to select it, and then position the mouse pointer anywhere on the control's border except on one of the sizing handles (the small white squares), and drag the control to its new location. The mouse pointer changes to a four-headed arrow to indicate that you can move the control.

 NOTE

If Snap To Grid on the Layout menu is selected, Outlook sets the final position of the control you drag to the nearest grid point as an aid to aligning the controls on your form. You can turn off Snap To Grid, or you can change the grid size. See "Using the Grid," on page 614.

To change the size of a control with the mouse, first click the control to select it, and then drag one of the sizing handles. The mouse pointer changes to a two-headed arrow to indicate the directions in which you can size the control.

You can get help with positioning and sizing a control by right-clicking it (for all controls except multipage and frame) and choosing the applicable command from the shortcut menu, by using the commands on the Layout menu, or by using the buttons on the Formatting toolbar. The Formatting toolbar looks like this:

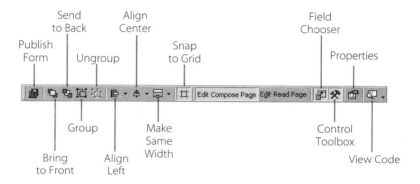

As you can see, many of the toolbar buttons are related to form layout. (Others, such as the Field Chooser button and the Control Toolbox button, should be familiar to you from earlier sections of this chapter; still other buttons are discussed in later sections.)

The Layout menu is the most comprehensive source of useful commands for positioning and sizing controls, but you can also use the control's shortcut menu or the toolbar buttons for some tasks. Note that commands and toolbar buttons are available only when they fit the selection you've made on the form tab. For instance, the Group command and toolbar button are unavailable when you've selected only one control.

Aligning Controls

The Align feature appears on the Layout menu and on the control's shortcut menu; specific commands are on submenus. On the Form Design toolbar, click the down arrow beside the Align Left button to see the other commands. In general, all the Align commands set the relative alignment of two or more selected controls. Different types of controls enable different alignment selections.

 **SEE ALSO**

For details about centering controls on a form tab (and the Align Center toolbar button), see "Centering on the Form," on page 612.

Use the Align Left, Align Right, and Align Center commands only for a vertical selection of controls. Choose Align Left or Align Right to align all selected controls along their left or right edges. Choose Align Center

VI

Working with Forms

to center selected controls around a midline of the widest control you've selected.

The Align Top, Align Bottom, and Align Middle commands are designed for a horizontal selection of controls. Choose Align Top or Align Bottom to align the selected controls along their top or bottom edges. Align Middle centers the selected controls around a midline of the tallest control you've selected.

The Align To Grid command on the control's shortcut menu aligns selected controls with the grid on the form tab. If you've turned off the Snap To Grid command and then dragged a control to a new position, you can choose Align To Grid to ensure that the control realigns with the grid.

Making Controls the Same Size

The Make Same Size feature appears on the Layout menu and on the control's shortcut menu; specific commands are on submenus. On the Form Design toolbar, click the down arrow beside the Make Same Width button to see the other commands. In general, these commands resize a selection of controls relative to one another.

The Width command makes the selected controls the width of the narrowest control in the selection; the Height command makes all the

---

Selecting Controls on a Form

Selecting a single control on a form is easy: simply click the control. However, you might sometimes want to select several controls at one time to act on them as a group. To select multiple controls, do one of the following:

- To select several controls at various positions on the form, hold down the Ctrl key while you click each control.

- To select a sequence of controls in a row or a column, click the first control in the sequence and then hold down the Shift key while you click the last control in the sequence.

- To select all the controls in one area of a form, drag a rectangle around them with the mouse.

- To select all the controls on the form, choose Select All from the Edit menu or press Ctrl+A.

To clear all of the controls at one time, click the background of the form page (not on any control). To clear a specific control without affecting the others, hold down the Ctrl key while you click it.

selected controls the height of the tallest control. To make the selected controls the width of the narrowest control *and* the height of the tallest control, choose Both.

Sizing to Fit

Choose Size To Fit from the Layout menu to make the border surrounding the control fit the size of the control. For example, if you have added a label control to your form and you have added text to the label control that doesn't fill up the label box, choose Size To Fit and the label box will resize itself to the size of the text.

Sizing to the Grid

If you change the size of a control when the Snap To Grid command is deselected, the edges of the control could fall between the grid lines. Choose Size To Grid from the Layout menu to shrink the sides and expand the top and bottom of the control to the nearest grid lines.

Setting Horizontal Spacing

You can find options for horizontal spacing on the Layout menu. The commands on the Horizontal Spacing submenu change the horizontal spacing between two or more selected controls on a form tab. You must select at least two controls before these Horizontal Spacing submenu commands become active.

When you select at least three controls, you can choose the Make Equal command to make the horizontal space between the controls the same width. Outlook divides the total amount of the current horizontal space between the selected controls by the number of gaps between controls and equalizes the space. The leftmost and rightmost controls do not move.

Choose the Increase command or the Decrease command to increase or decrease the horizontal space between two or more controls by the width of one unit of the grid. You might need to choose the command several times to change the spacing sufficiently.

If you want to remove all horizontal space between selected controls, choose Remove from the Horizontal Spacing submenu.

Setting Vertical Spacing

Options for the vertical spacing of controls on a form appear on the Layout menu. The commands on the Vertical Spacing submenu change the spacing between two or more selected controls. You must select at least two controls before these commands become active.

VI

Working with Forms

Choose the Make Equal command to make the vertical space between three or more selected controls the same. Outlook divides the total amount of the current vertical space between the selected controls by the number of gaps between controls and equalizes the space. Outlook doesn't move the top and bottom controls.

With the Increase command or the Decrease command, you can increase or decrease the vertical space between two or more controls by the height of one unit of the grid. The larger the grid, the more distance Outlook adds or subtracts between the selected controls. You might need to choose the command several times to change the spacing sufficiently.

Choose Remove from the Vertical Spacing submenu to remove all vertical space between selected controls.

Centering on the Form

If you want to center controls on a form, you can use the Center In Form command on the Layout menu or the Align Center button on the Form Design toolbar. Click the down arrow beside the toolbar button to see the two commands Horizontally and Vertically, which also appear on the Center In Form submenu. Choose Horizontally to move selected controls to the horizontal center between the two sides of the form; choose Vertically to move the controls to the vertical center between the top and the bottom of the form.

Arranging Command Buttons

It's a common practice to place command buttons (buttons that initiate actions, such as OK, Close, and Cancel) either along the right side or along the bottom of a form. To quickly place command buttons at either of these positions on a form tab, select the buttons, point to Arrange on the Layout menu, and then choose Bottom or Right on the submenu. The Arrange submenu commands are active only when you have selected at least one command button. Also note that these commands move only command buttons. To place other types of controls at the bottom or right edge of the form tab, you'll need to drag them.

Choosing Right from the submenu stacks all the selected command buttons along the right edge of the form. The order of the buttons relates to their previous vertical positions on the tab: the command button closest to the top of the form becomes the top button in the stack; the command button closest to the bottom of the form becomes the bottom button in the stack.

Choosing the Bottom command places all the selected command buttons along the bottom edge of the form, arranging them in a row. The order of the buttons relates to their previous horizontal positions on the form: the command button closest to the left edge of the form becomes the leftmost button in the row; the command button closest to the right edge of the form becomes the rightmost button in the row.

TIP

If you don't like the order in which the Arrange command arranges the buttons, you can rearrange the order by dragging the buttons individually. Then choose Arrange again.

Grouping and Ungrouping

When you collect several controls into a group, you can move or change the group as if it were a single object—for instance, a label and its associated control are often grouped together. Within the group, the controls maintain their positions relative to each other whenever you move them.

After you've selected the controls you want to group, you can click the Group button on the Form Design toolbar or choose Group from the Layout menu. You can also right-click one of the selected controls and choose Group from the shortcut menu.

If you need to make changes to any one of the grouped controls without changing the others, you'll first need to ungroup the controls, making them individual objects again. To do this, select the group, click the Ungroup button on the Form Design toolbar or choose Ungroup from the Layout menu. You can also right-click the group and choose Ungroup from the shortcut menu.

Reordering Overlapping Controls

Each control sits in its own "layer" on a form. This means that you can position controls to overlap one another. If you do this, however, you'll want to be sure that no important part of a control is hidden by an overlapping control. For example, if a label control overlaps its associated text control, you might want to move the label so it doesn't obscure part of the text control. However, you might have two picture controls and want to overlap them. In this case, choose one of the picture controls and choose from the commands on the Order submenu of the Layout menu. Two of these commands, Bring To Front and Send

VI

Working with Forms

To Back, are also available as buttons on the Form Design toolbar. The other two, Bring Forward and Send Backward, appear on the control's shortcut menu.

Choose Bring To Front to place the selected control on top of all other controls at the same position; choose Send To Back to position the selected control under all other controls at the same position. The Bring Forward command moves the selected control on top of the next higher layer of controls at the same position; the Send Backward command moves the selected control beneath the next lower layer of controls at the same position. Bring Forward and Send Backward are useful if you have more than two objects that overlap. With only two overlapping controls, these two commands have the same effect as the Bring To Front and Send To Back commands.

Using the Grid

Forms use a grid to help you align controls and set their size and the spacing between them. When Outlook increases or decreases the vertical or horizontal spacing between controls, it uses increments of space based on the grid size.

When you initially switch to design mode, the form pages that you can customize show the grid, and the Snap To Grid command is selected. The grid size is set to 8 pixels by 8 pixels. You can change all these grid settings.

Show Grid. The grid is displayed as dots in rows and columns. Choose Show Grid from the Layout menu to switch the display of the grid on and off, or right-click the form tab away from a control and choose Show Grid from the shortcut menu. You might want to hide the grid to see a preview of what the tab will look like when you've finished the form. Showing or hiding the grid doesn't affect the Snap To Grid command.

Snap To Grid. Choose this command from the Layout menu or click the Snap To Grid button on the Standard toolbar to turn this feature on or off. You can also right-click the form tab anywhere but directly on the control and choose Snap To Grid from the shortcut menu. When you choose Snap To Grid, each new control, each move of a control, and each resizing of a control happen relative to the grid. If you want to resize or move a control to a position that's not on the grid, clear this feature. If you later want to move the control to align with the grid, choose Align To Grid from the Layout menu. If you want to size the control to the grid, choose Size To Grid from the Layout menu.

Set Grid Size. This command appears on the Form menu rather than on the Layout menu. It lets you change the spacing of the grid. To change the grid size, follow the steps here:

1 Choose Set Grid Size from the Form menu to open the Set Grid Size dialog box.

2 Enter a width for the grid columns, in pixels.

3 Enter a height for grid rows, in pixels.

4 Click OK.

Using AutoLayout

Outlook's AutoLayout feature automatically places new fields below or to the right of fields that are already on a form. (If the field is the first item, it's placed in the top left corner of the page.) If you prefer to perform the initial placement yourself, clear the AutoLayout command on the Layout menu. Choose this command again to select AutoLayout.

Changing the Tabbing Order

You know from your experience in using an Outlook form that you can press the Tab key to move from item to item or, in design terminology, from control to control. (Pressing Shift+Tab moves the user backward through the controls.) In the forms you design, the order in which users move between the controls of your form using the Tab key is by default the same order in which you placed the controls on the form. This order might not be logical or helpful to the user. Before you finish designing your form, you should set the tabbing order in a logical and useful sequence. To change the tabbing order, follow the steps on the next page.

VI

Working with Forms

1 Choose Tab Order from the Layout menu.

2 Select a control you want
to move in the tab order.

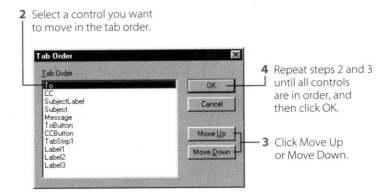

4 Repeat steps 2 and 3
until all controls
are in order, and
then click OK.

3 Click Move Up
or Move Down.

The first control listed in the Tab Order dialog box is the first control
that is active when a user displays the page of the form. The user can
press the Tab key to jump to the control that's next on the list. Pressing
Shift+Tab jumps the user to the next higher control.

The tabbing order list includes all the controls on the page, whether
the controls are enabled or disabled, including labels. Note, however,
that when the user of the form presses the Tab key, labels are not acti-
vated if you have disabled them. (Labels are usually disabled because
you don't want the user of your form to change the labels of the form,
only the contents of the form.)

If you're planning to change the tabbing order as part of your design process,
you'll want to give each control a name that tells you what information it contains or collects. Otherwise, the default names of the controls might not be very
helpful. To name the controls, use the Display tab of the Properties dialog box,
discussed in the following section.

Setting Properties

After you've placed the controls on your custom form, arranged and
sized them, and set their tabbing order, you'll want to set the properties
of each control and the properties of the form itself. Properties determine how the controls and the form look and function.

Setting Properties for a Control

SEE ALSO

Advanced control properties are discussed in Chapter 23, "Programming With Forms."

Each control has its own set of properties that determine how the control looks and functions. You set these properties in the Properties dialog box, which contains three tabs: Display, Value, and Validation. (The Properties dialog box for multipage and frame controls, however, contains only the Display tab.)

You can open the Properties dialog box for a selected control in any of the following ways:

- Right-click the control, and then choose Properties from the shortcut menu.

Properties

- Click the Properties button on the Form Design toolbar.

- Choose Properties from the Form menu.

TIP

If more than one control is selected when you open the Properties dialog box, Outlook displays the dialog box for the control you selected first. By referring to the Name and Caption boxes of the Properties dialog box, you can determine which control you're examining.

Setting Up Display Properties

To set up the display properties for a control—that is, to determine how the control appears on the form—click the Display tab, which is shown in Figure 22-5.

FIGURE 22-5.
The Display tab of the Properties dialog box.

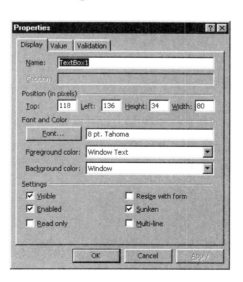

VI

Working with Forms

If the Name and Caption boxes are active on this page, you can type a different name or a different caption for the control. Outlook assigns a default name to every control (TextBox2, for instance), which identifies it to other controls or in code. You might want to assign a more useful name, especially if you plan to alter the tabbing order. *See "Changing the Tabbing Order," on page 615.* The user does not see this name, however; instead, the name displayed to the user is referred to as the *caption*. The caption is the text displayed in a label. Outlook also provides a direct method for changing a control's caption text. *See "Editing a Control Directly," on page 621.*

The Position settings on the Display page record the current position and size of the control on the form, measured in pixels. After you've dragged a control to its approximate location and sized it with the mouse, you can tweak the position and size by changing the Position settings. The Top box sets the position of the top edge of the control, and the Left box sets the position of the left edge. If you change the Height setting, Outlook moves the bottom edge of the control; if you change the Width setting, Outlook moves the right edge.

> To align multiple controls horizontally, give them all the same Top setting. To align them vertically, give them all the same Left setting.

In the Font And Color section of the page, you can change the font of any text that is part of the control. (Click the Font button to open the Font dialog box.) You can also select foreground and background effects by choosing from the Foreground Color or Background Color lists. Note that the changes you make here might nullify Font color changes. The foreground and background effects are available so that you can quickly change the way a button looks based on standard button settings.

At the bottom of the page, you'll find these general settings for the appearance and use of the control:

- Selecting the Visible check box enables the user to see the control on the form; clearing the check box hides the control.

- Clearing the Enabled check box prevents the user from being able to select the control or even to copy its value.

- Selecting the Read Only check box sets the control so the user cannot change the control's value.

- Selecting the Resize With Form check box displays the control proportional to the size of the form—for example, if the user makes the form window smaller, the control also becomes smaller.

- Selecting the Sunken check box gives the control a recessed, three-dimensional appearance; clearing this check box gives the control a flat or two-dimensional look.

- Selecting the Multi-Line check box allows the user to enter multiple lines in a text box by pressing the Enter key to start each new line—text automatically wraps to the next line.

Setting Up Values

To link the contents of a control to the value of a data field or to set initial and calculated values for a control, click the Value tab of the Properties dialog box, which is shown in Figure 22-6. For example, you might want to select an option button when Outlook detects a specific value in a list box.

In the Field And Format Of Control section of the Value tab, you can click the Choose Field button to see the field sets that are available to use with the control. Choose a field set, and then choose a specific field from the set. Outlook fills in the name of the field and, in the Type box, shows you the data type on which the field is based. In the Format box, you can choose a format that is appropriate for the type of field you've chosen. *For details about data types and formats, see "Creating a Simple Custom Field," on page 564.*

> **? SEE ALSO**
>
> You can click the New button on the Value tab to create a new field; for instructions, see "Working with Custom Fields," on page 563.

FIGURE 22-6.

The Value tab of the Properties dialog box.

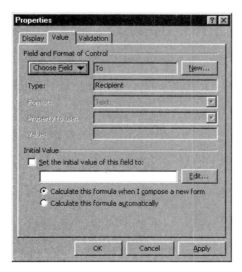

VI

Working with Forms

The Property To Use and Value boxes list the properties and values from any published custom or built-in Outlook form. (The properties and values in these two boxes are associated with the field that you choose by clicking the Choose Field button.) It's best not to change these properties and values unless you have much more advanced knowledge of forms than that provided in this chapter.

If you want to set up an initial value for the control, select the check box labeled Set The Initial Value Of This Field To, and either type a value in the box below or click the Edit button to create a formula for calculating the value. *See "Setting Up a Formula," on page 621.* Then choose one of the two option buttons to have Outlook calculate the formula when you open a new instance of the form or to have Outlook calculate the formula automatically as values change. Outlook also provides a direct method for changing the initial value of a control. *See "Editing a Control Directly," opposite.*

> The types of options you can change on the Value tab depend on the properties of the field you choose to have Outlook evaluate.

Setting Up Validation

To have Outlook validate user entries on the form, click the Validation tab of the Properties dialog box, which is shown in Figure 22-7. Validation simply ensures that the user has entered the necessary information on the form and that the information is in the correct format. At the top of the page, you'll see a check box labeled A Value Is Required For

FIGURE 22-7.
The Validation tab of the Properties dialog box.

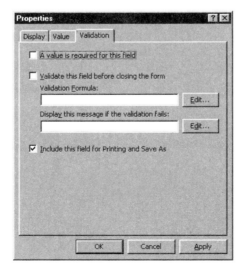

This Field. When this check box is available, you can select it to require a response from the user. Then, if the user leaves the field empty, Outlook will display a message telling the user to enter the information when the user tries to save or close the form.

You can also have Outlook validate the field before closing the form—that is, Outlook checks to be sure that the user input matches the validation test you set up in the Validation Formula box (or the validation formula you specify after clicking the Edit button; see "Setting Up a Formula," below). For instance, if you specify that the user must type a date, and the user types a single digit, the input is not valid, and Outlook displays an error message to the user. You can compose the error message in the text box labeled Display This Message If The Validation Fails.

The final option on this page is Include This Field For Printing And Save As. Select this check box if the contents of this field should be printed and saved with the rest of the form. Clear this check box to omit the field during printing and saving.

Setting Up a Formula

 SEE ALSO

For examples of formulas, see Table 20-4, on page 571. For details about creating your own fields, see "Working with Custom Fields," on page 563.

You can set up a formula to set an initial value for a control, to construct a validation test for user responses, or to display a message when a response fails the validation test. In all three cases, you click the Edit button (on either the Value page or the Validation page of the Properties dialog box) to open a dialog box in which you set up the formula. In the dialog box that appears, type the formula (text, fields, and functions). Click the Field button to select fields; click the Function button to select functions. Fields are enclosed in square brackets and functions use parentheses to list their arguments. Fields are often used as arguments within the functions, meaning the fields provide the information the function uses to calculate its result.

Editing a Control Directly

Although you can set the caption and the initial value of a control on the Display and Value tabs in the Properties dialog box, you might sometimes prefer a more direct method for editing these settings. You can do this directly on the form tab.

To activate a control for editing, use one of these methods:

- Right-click the control, and select Edit from the shortcut menu.

- Click the control to select it, and then click again inside it.

VI

Working with Forms

You can type the caption text or the new initial value directly on the control.

> If you have set up a formula to determine an initial value, directly editing the initial value on the control wipes out the formula. In that case, it's preferable to edit the formula. See "Setting Up a Formula," on the previous page.

Setting Properties for a Form

So far, you've learned how to set properties for individual controls. But you can also set the properties of the form itself. To do this, click the Properties tab of the form while in design mode. Figure 22-8 shows the Properties tab for a message form.

Category and Sub-Category. The value of assigning your form to a category, a subcategory, or both becomes evident if you point to Forms on the Tools menu and select Choose Form. If you have a long list of forms to scroll through in the New Form dialog box, you can select the Show Categories check box to group the forms into categories and subcategories, making it easier to find a particular type of item.

Always Use Microsoft Word As The E-mail Editor. This check box is available only for message forms. If you select it, Outlook starts Word whenever a user who uses Word as his or her e-mail editor receives a message based on your form. You can click the Template button to select a specific Word template to use for this form.

FIGURE 22-8.
The Properties tab for a message form in design mode.

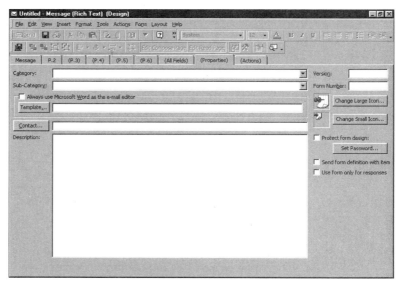

NOTE

Setting up a custom form to use Word as the e-mail editor does not affect the setting for standard message forms. You specify the setting for standard message forms on the Mail Format tab of the Options dialog box. *See "Using the Mail Format Tab," on page 84.*

Contact.   In this box, you can type the name of a person whom users can contact for help with the form or for information about the topic of the form. Alternatively, you can click the Contact button and choose a name from the Select Contact dialog box.

Description.   In this text box, you can type a brief description of the form and its purpose. You can also add any short comments about how the form should be used.

Version and Form Number.   For your own record keeping, you can assign a number to each form you create by typing the number in the Form Number box. If you revise a form for one reason or another, you might also want to assign a version number in the Version box.

NOTE

The contact, description, version, and form number all appear in the Forms Manager dialog box and the Choose Form dialog box. Display the Forms Manager dialog box by selecting Options from the Tools menu, clicking Advanced Options on the Other tab, clicking Custom Forms, and then clicking Manage Forms. Display the Choose Form dialog box by pointing to New on the File menu, and then clicking Choose Form.

Change Large Icon and Change Small Icon.   Each form is represented by a large icon and a small icon. These icons appear in folder windows or on the forms themselves, and they represent the form when you use an icon view to look at the contents of a folder. *See "Icons View," on page 449, and "Icon Views," on page 586.*

Outlook assigns an icon to each form, based on its type, but you can change either of the icons as follows:

1 Click the Change Large Icon button or the Change Small Icon button.

2 In the File Open dialog box that appears, switch to a folder that contains icon files.

3 Select the icon file you want to use, and then click the Open button.

VI

Working with Forms

Protect Form Design. To protect your form with a password, select the Protect Form Design check box. When this check box is selected, the Password dialog box opens. By entering a password, only users with a password can alter the form. You can also click the Set Password button to open the Password dialog box. When the Password dialog box appears, follow these steps:

1 Type a password in the Password box.

2 Enter the same password again in the Confirm box.

3 Click OK.

The next time anyone opens the form and selects Design This Form from the Forms submenu of the Tools menu, the Password dialog box appears and the user must type in the correct password to open the form for customization.

If you select the Protect Form Design check box but don't enter a password when designing the form, the Password dialog box will still appear in subsequent customization sessions, but the user only needs to click OK to gain access to the form design features.

Send Form Definition With Item. Select this check box to save the design information with the form when you do not plan to publish the form in a library to be shared with others. You can then share the form with others via e-mail because the form contains its own layout information. Clear this check box if you plan to save the form in a library.

Use Form Only For Responses. If you want the form to be used only for message responses, select this check box. The form will then be available when a message recipient chooses the Reply, Reply to All, Forward, or Reply To Folder commands. You might use a response form to design a ballot on which the recipients can select options based on the ballot's choices—this keeps the response information to the same type for all users. Once you design a response form, however, you have to designate the form as the one to use for responses. You do this by customizing a message form, creating an action that opens the response form when one of the reply commands is used. *To learn more about creating actions, see "Creating Custom Actions for a Form," on page 638.*

Testing a Form

As you design a custom form, you'll want to test it periodically. The simplest way to check the appearance of the form is to "run" a copy of the form that you are designing. This opens an instance of the form that you can actually test. To run the form, choose Run This Form from the Form menu. Close the form to return to design mode.

 NOTE

In some cases, you might find that you need to save the form or save and publish the form before you can see the changes you've made.

Saving and Publishing a Form

Before you or anyone else can use the form you just created, you have to save or publish it.

- Saving a form lets you add it as a folder item or save it as an Outlook template file, text file, message file, vCard file (for a contact form), or vCalendar file (for a calendar form).

- Publishing a form adds it to the folder library so it can be used when needed.

Saving a Form as a Folder Item

One way to save a form is to save to an Outlook folder. You can save a custom Contact form to the Contacts folder, or a Journal form to the Journal folder, for example. For instance, you may have a contact for whom you want to save some additional information. Create a custom form with fields for that information, and then save the form in the Contacts folder where you can access it.

To save a form in the folder of its type, simply choose Save from the File menu, or click the Save button on the Standard toolbar. When you save a custom message form, it is saved to the Drafts folder. You can then open the form in the Drafts folder, enter the name of the recipient and other information, and then click Send.

The disadvantage of saving a form to a folder, however, is that it makes just one copy of it. If you want to use the form more widely, you should save it as an Outlook template or as another file type on your disk, as you will soon learn.

VI

Working with Forms

NOTE

> When you save a custom form based on a contact form without entering a name in the File As field (even if this field does not appear on the current version of the form), Outlook notifies you that the File As field is empty. To save a blank form, click Yes. Click No to return to the form.

Saving a Form as a File

To save a form as a file, take these steps:

1 After you've completed designing the form, choose Save As from the File menu.

2 Select the location on your disk or network where you want to store the form.

3 In the File Name box, type a name for the form.

4 In the Save As Type box, select a file type. To save the form as an Outlook template, select Outlook Template, and switch to the Templates folder. The other types available depend on the type of form.

5 Click OK.

Publishing a Form

If you want to be able to quickly choose a form when needed, you should publish the form. You can publish the form to an Outlook folder, to the Personal Forms library, or any other library that you or your company has established.

When you publish the form to an Outlook folder, it will be available directly from the Actions menu when that folder is opened. This is the most convenient place to publish a form if you plan to use the form often. When you publish the form to a library, you'll have to select it using the Forms command from the Tools menu.

Here's how to publish a form in a folder or forms library:

1 Point to Forms on the form's Tools menu, and then choose Publish Form As.

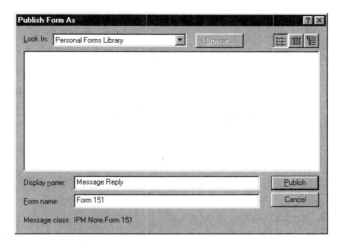

2 Choose the folder or library in which to publish the form from the Look In list.

3 Enter the name to appear on the form's title bar in the Display Name box. The name is repeated in the Form Name box.

4 Change the form name, if desired.

5 Click Publish.

6 If you did not select the Send Form Definition With Item check box on the form's Properties page, a message appears recommending that you do so to allow users to work with the form. Select Yes to select the check box from within the message.

> **NOTE** Whenever you make changes to a form that you've shared in a forms library, you have to republish the form so Outlook recognizes the changes. To republish the form in the same library, choose Forms from the Tools menu, and choose Publish Form. Choose Publish Form As if you want to change its name or location.

Sending a Form Through E-mail

To distribute your form to other people, you might want to send it to them through e-mail. Here's how:

1 On the Properties tab of the form (in design mode), select the Send Form Definition With Item check box.

2 If you have not already done so, save the form in the open folder. *See "Saving a Form as a Folder Item," on page 625.* Remember, when you click Save, the newly designed form is saved as an item in the folder of its type. So if you are saving a message form, you'll find it in the Drafts folder; if you save an Appointment form it will appear as a Calendar item.

3 Close the form, and then create an e-mail message.

4 Choose Item from the Insert menu.

5 Select the folder containing the form.

8 Click OK.

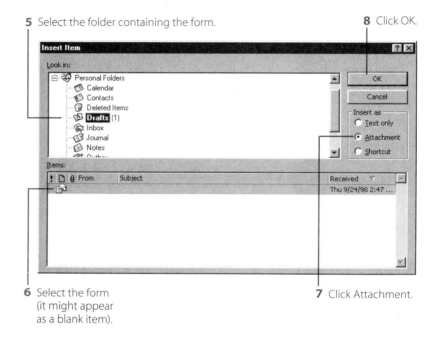

6 Select the form (it might appear as a blank item).

7 Click Attachment.

9 Click the Send button in the message window.

Opening a Custom Form

You use a custom form just as you do a standard form. Open the form as you will learn how to do in this section, fill it out, and then save it or send it to the appropriate person. Sometimes the trickiest part of this process is opening the form. How you open a custom form depends on where and how you saved it. The following summary explains how to open custom forms:

If you published the form in a folder. Open the folder in which you saved the form, and select the form's name from the Actions menu. For example, if you created a new message form entitled Invitation and published it in the Inbox folder, click the Actions menu while in the Inbox. At the bottom of the menu you'll see the command New Invitation. Click New Invitation to create a message using your custom form.

If you published the form in the Personal Forms library, Organization Forms library, or the Applications Forms Library. You have to open the Choose Form dialog box using either of these techniques:

- Point to Forms on the Tools menu, and then click Choose Form on the submenu.

- Point to New on the File menu, and then click Choose Form on the submenu.

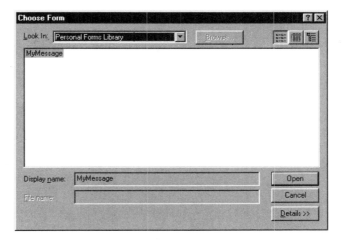

1 Choose a library from the list.

2 Select the form you want to open.

3 Click OK.

 NOTE

If you saved the form as an Outlook template, choose User Templates In File System from the list in step 1 above.

Copying Forms Between Folders

No matter where you publish a custom form, you can later copy it to another folder or to the Personal Folder Library.

For example, if you publish a form to the Personal Form Library, you can later decide to add it to a folder so it is available from the folder's Actions menu. You can also choose to copy a custom form from a folder to the Personal Form Library or to another Outlook folder.

SEE ALSO

For information about levels of permissions, see the sidebar "Do You Have Permission?" on page 524, and see "Permissions Tab," on page 534.

> **NOTE**
>
> You must have editor, publishing editor, or owner permission to add forms to a private shared folder or a public folder. If you have owner permission for a public folder, you can limit the forms that are available to other people who use the same folder.

To make an existing form available in an Outlook folder:

1 Open the folder to which you want to add the form, choose Folder from the File menu, and select Properties For from the submenu. (The Properties For command includes the name of the folder.) Alternatively, you can right-click the folder in the Folder List, and then choose Properties from the shortcut menu.

2 In the Properties dialog box, click the Forms tab. This tab lists the forms that you have already installed in this folder, along with a description of the selected form.

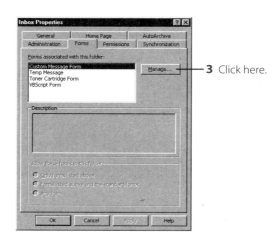

3 Click here.

4 When Outlook displays the Forms Manager dialog box, check the name of the forms library in the box at the top left of the dialog box. If you need to specify or switch to a different forms library, click the Set button to open the Set Library To dialog box. For example, if you want to use a form you published in the Personal Forms Library, click Set and choose Personal Forms from the dialog box. If you want to copy a form you published to another Outlook folder, choose the Outlook folder from the Set Library To dialog box.

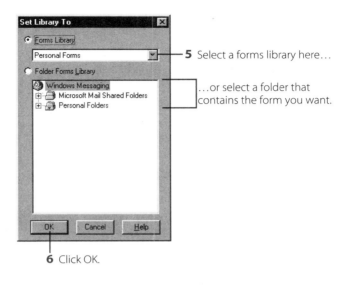

5 Select a forms library here…

…or select a folder that contains the form you want.

6 Click OK.

7 Select the form you want to use.

8 Click Copy to copy the form to the box to the right.

To update an installed form to its latest version, select it in the destination list and click Update.

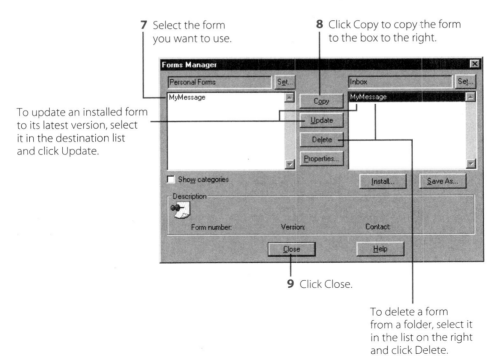

9 Click Close.

To delete a form from a folder, select it in the list on the right and click Delete.

VI

Working with Forms

The form then becomes available in this folder, listed at the bottom of the folder's Actions menu.

> In public folders, you can also specify the availability of certain forms by selecting an option in the Allow These Forms In This Folder area of the Forms tab of the folder's Properties dialog box.

If you want to copy a custom form from a folder to the Personal Folder Library, follow these steps:

1 Open the folder that contains the form, choose Folder from the File menu, and select Properties For from the submenu. (The Properties For command includes the name of the folder.) Alternatively, you can right-click the folder in the Folder List, and then choose Properties from the shortcut menu.

2 In the Properties dialog box, click Manage on the Forms tab.

3 Click Set on the left, choose Personal Forms in the Set Library To dialog box, and then click OK.

4 Click the form that you want to move in the right box, and then click Copy.

5 Click Close and then click OK.

Updating Copied Forms

What happens if you make changes to a custom form after you copy it from one folder to another? The copy of the form is not automatically updated. That is, the changes are only stored with the version of the form where you publish it.

To update the copied version of the form, you need to open the Forms Manager dialog box. You can do so from the Forms tab of the Properties box for the folder containing the form, or from the Options dialog box. In fact, you can use the Options dialog box to access Forms Manager to copy forms between any locations, and to update and delete forms. Here's how:

1 Choose Options from the Tools menu, and click the Other tab.

2 Click the Advanced Options button and then click the Custom Forms button.

3 In the box that appears, click Manage Forms to open the Forms Manager dialog box.

4 Use the Set buttons on the left and right to open the folder containing the form you want to copy, and the destination folder where you want to copy it. If doesn't matter which you place in either box. For example, if you originally copied a form from the Personal Forms Library to the Inbox, select Personal Forms from one of the Set Library To boxes, and the Inbox in the other.

5 Click the form in the destination list and the Update button will become enabled. For example, if you copied a form from the Personal Forms Library to the Inbox, select the form in the Inbox list of the Forms Manager dialog box.

6 Click Update.

7 Click Close, and then click OK to close each of the three dialog boxes.

Changing a Standard Form

If you control a public folder—that is, if you have owner permission for the folder—you might want to set up a special form as the standard form for items in the public folder. Follow these steps to change the standard form for a public folder.

1 Open the folder to which you want to add the form, choose Folder from the File menu, and click Properties. Alternatively, you can right-click the folder in the Folder List and then choose Properties from the shortcut menu.

2 On the General tab of the Properties dialog box, select the form that you want others to use from the list labeled When Posting To This Folder, Use. If the form isn't listed, choose Forms from the list, and then choose the form from the Choose Form dialog box.

3 Click OK.

SEE ALSO

For information about permission levels, see "Permissions Tab," on page 534. Also see the sidebar "Do You Have Permission?" on page 524.

Before you try to add, edit, update, or delete forms in a public folder, you can save yourself some aggravation by checking your permission status for the folder. To check your permissions for a public folder, open the Properties dialog box (as explained in step 1 in the preceding section). Click the Summary tab, and review your permissions, which are specified on this tab. If the Permissions tab appears instead of the

VI

Working with Forms

Summary tab, you have owner permission. If neither tab appears, you do not have permission to change the public folder properties.

Custom forms give you a great deal of flexibility and power over the information you see on screen and send in e-mail. While most users will be satisfied using Outlook's standard forms, custom forms can serve important special purposes. In the next chapter, you'll learn even more ways to customize forms.

Programming with Forms

Custom forms are easy to create and use. They provide a way to streamline your e-mail messages, fine-tune Microsoft Outlook items to suit your exact needs, and communicate just the information that you want. In this chapter, you'll learn some advanced techniques for making forms even more useful.

Setting Advanced Properties for a Control

In Chapter 22, "Designing and Using Forms," you learned how to set some of the basic properties for controls using the Display, Value, and Validation tabs of the Properties dialog box. In addition to these properties, you might want to try setting advanced properties for a control. When you right-click a selected control of a form displayed in design mode and choose Advanced Properties from the shortcut menu, Outlook opens the Properties window, shown in Figure 23-1. This Properties window is very similar to the one used in Microsoft Visual Basic.

FIGURE 23-1.
The Properties window.

> **⚠ WARNING**
>
> Unless you have some knowledge of Visual Basic programming, it's risky to try to set advanced properties. Without an understanding of what these properties do and what their settings mean, you're more likely to wreck your form than improve it!

To set a new value for an advanced property in the Properties window, select the property and then use the box beside the Apply button. For certain properties, you'll be able to type text or numbers in the box. If a down arrow appears at the right side of the box, click it to see a list of possible choices. If an icon button appears beside the box, click the button to open a dialog box in which you can make the appropriate selection, such as choosing a file for an icon or picture, a color for a screen control, or a font for the form.

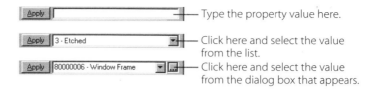

— Type the property value here.

— Click here and select the value from the list.

— Click here and select the value from the dialog box that appears.

Many advanced properties get their settings from your choices in the standard Properties dialog box. (Some overlap exists between a control's standard properties and its advanced properties.) For example, if you type a caption on the Display page of the Properties dialog box, that caption appears as the setting for the Caption property in the Properties window. In fact, when you set a value in either location (the dialog box or the window), Outlook sets the same value in the other location after you click the Apply button. (You might have to close the Properties dialog box and then reopen it to see the change.)

Table 23-1 describes some of the advanced properties that you might want to experiment with. Not all of these properties apply to all types of controls; depending on the type of control you've selected, some of the properties might not appear in the Properties window.

TABLE 23-1. Some Examples of Advanced Properties

Property Name	Values
AutoSize	−1 - True (The control changes size to show the entire contents of the control.) 0 - False (The control remains the same size all the time.)
AutoWordSelect	−1 - True (Outlook selects entire words when the user selects with the mouse.) 0 - False (The user can select partial words.)
BorderColor	You can match the color of the selected control to that of any Windows screen component (as set in the Display dialog box of the Control Panel), or you can choose any other color by clicking the build button next to the list and choosing a color from the dialog box that appears.
BorderStyle	0 - None
	1 - Single
Caption	Text that appears in a label

(continued)

VI

Working with Forms

TABLE 23-1. *continued*

Property Name	Values
ControlTipText	Text that appears when the mouse pointer rests on a control
Left	Number of pixels that the left edge of the control sits from the left edge of the page
Height	Control's height expressed in pixels
SpecialEffect	Controls visual appearance of control 0 - Flat 2 - Sunken 6 – Bump 1 - Raised 3 - Etched
Top	Number of pixels that the top edge of the control sits from the top edge of the tab
Value	Text, number, or formula that sets the initial value
Width	Control's width expressed in pixels
WordWrap	1 - True (Outlook wraps text to a new line.) 0 - False (Outlook does not wrap text to a new line.)

 TIP

You can have both the Properties dialog box and the advanced Properties window open at the same time. To do this, select a control, right-click the control and choose Advanced Properties first to open the Properties *window*. Right-click the control again and choose Properties to open the Properties *dialog box*.

Creating Custom Actions for a Form

To make Outlook perform an action, you apply a command to a form. For example, when you click the Reply button to a message, Outlook opens a reply form. Other actions include Reply To All and Forward, both of which open forms.

You can change the form that Outlook uses when you click a built-in action button, and you can delete actions, such as removing the Reply action so the recipient cannot reply to it. You can even create your own custom actions that open forms. The form can be of the same type, such as a new message form when you click Reply, or a form of another type. For example, you can add an action to a message form that opens a contact form or that even creates a new contact form.

Your custom actions can appear as a command on the Actions menu or as a button on its own toolbar. If you named your custom response form Please Respond and specified that it appear as a toolbar, for instance, the recipient will see the Please Respond button when the message is opened:

To add an action to a form, follow these steps:

1 Open the form in design view.

2 Click the (Actions) page.

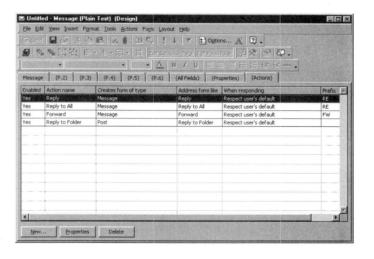

3 Click the New button.

4 Type a name for this action.

5 Select a form to open for this action.

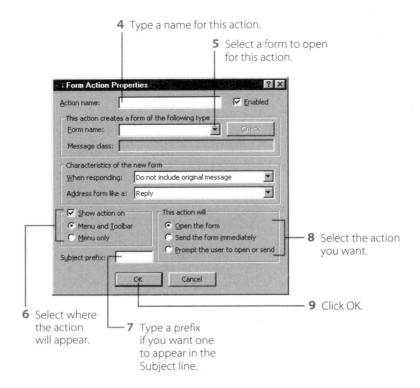

8 Select the action you want.

9 Click OK.

6 Select where the action will appear.

7 Type a prefix if you want one to appear in the Subject line.

If you later want to change the setup for an action or change a standard Outlook action, double-click the action on the (Actions) page, and make your changes in the Form Action Properties dialog box.

To delete an action, select it on the (Actions) page and click the Delete button at the bottom of the page.

Programming Forms

For maximum control over a form, you can program controls to perform custom actions. To program a control, you need to know how to write Visual Basic programs. Outlook uses Visual Basic Scripting Edition (VBScript), a subset of the Visual Basic programming language. If you know how to program in Visual Basic or Visual Basic for Applications (VBA), you'll have no problem in Outlook once you get used to some minor differences.

Programming can be a complex process. In this chapter, you'll find some examples of how programming can be used to automate a form and perform some Outlook functions.

As you learned in Chapter 22, "Designing and Using Forms," you can use forms to create custom e-mail messages and other Outlook items. For example, suppose your company frequently orders toner cartridges for printers. You can create the form shown in Figure 23-2 to enable employees to quickly order their supplies.

The form contains the To box and three user-defined fields that were created in the Field Chooser and then dragged onto the form. The address was entered into the To box and then the box was disabled so it cannot be changed by the user. (Right-click a control, choose Properties from the shortcut menu, and then clear the Enabled check box to disable a control.) The user types the number of each type of cartridge, clicks if they want a rush order, and then clicks Send. The recipient gets the completed Outlook form, already filled in.

But what if your toner vendor does not use Outlook and cannot receive an Outlook form over their e-mail system? In that case, you'd like to make it just as easy for employees to order supplies but send the order as a regular e-mail message. One solution is to add to the form the Visual Basic script shown here, which does just that. The

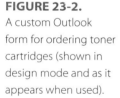

FIGURE 23-2.
A custom Outlook form for ordering toner cartridges (shown in design mode and as it appears when used).

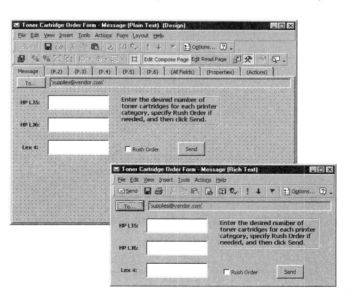

script converts the order details into the Subject line of an e-mail message, creates the standard Outlook e-mail form, and then places the message in the sender's Outbox. Here is the Visual Basic script:

```
Function Item_Send()
   OrderToner
   Item_Send = False
End Function

Sub OrderToner()
   Set Cart1 = Item.GetInspector.ModifiedFormPages("Message").Controls("TextBox1")
   Set Cart2 = Item.GetInspector.ModifiedFormPages("Message").Controls("TextBox2")
   Set Cart3 = Item.GetInspector.ModifiedFormPages("Message").Controls("TextBox3")

   If IsNumeric(Cart1) = False Then
     Cart1.Value = "0"
   End If

   If IsNumeric(Cart2) = False Then
     Cart2.Value = "0"
   End If

   If IsNumeric(Cart3) = False Then
     Cart3.Value = "0"
   End If
   SString = "HP LJ 5 = "& Cart1.value
   SString = SString & ":  HP LJ 6 = "& Cart2.value
   SString = SString & ":  Lex 4 = "& Cart3.value
   Set Rush = Item.GetInspector.ModifiedFormPages("Message").Controls("Checkbox1")
   If Rush.value = True Then
       SString = SString &  " RUSH"
   End IF

   Set TonerOrder = Application.CreateItem(olMailItem)
   TonerOrder.Subject = SString
   TonerOrder.To = "supplies@vendor.com"
   TonerOrder.Send
   Cart1.value = ""
   Cart2.value = ""
   Cart3.value = ""
   Rush.value = False
End Sub

Function CommandButton1_Click()
     Item_Send()
End Function
```

To use the script, create the form shown in Figure 23-2, on page 641. Instead of creating and using three new fields for the text boxes, however, use the Control Toolbox to insert three labels and three text boxes (you won't need to use the Field Chooser). Make sure the text boxes are named TextBox1, TextBox2, and TextBox3, so they'll work correctly with the code. The check box must be named CheckBox1 and the command button CommandButton1.

Here are the steps needed to create and program the form:

1 Point to Forms on the Tools menu, click Choose Form, and then choose a standard message form from the Choose Form dialog box.

2 When the form appears, point to Forms on the Tools menu in the message window, and choose Design This Form.

3 Delete all of the boxes on the form except the To box. (Click a box, and then press Delete.)

4 Add the text boxes and labels shown in the form in Figure 23-2, on page 641, using the tools described in Chapter 22, "Designing and Using Forms."

5 Type the e-mail address in the To box and then disable the control.

View
Code

6 Click the View Code button on the toolbar or choose View Code from the Form menu.

7 Type the entire block of VBScript code exactly as shown on the previous page.

8 Close the Script Editor window and then save and publish the form.

9 If you see the message asking whether you want to save the form definition with the item, answer Yes.

 NOTE

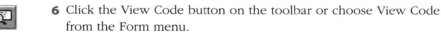

If the Visual Basic components needed to run the script you've created are not already installed on your system, the Windows installer will automatically add them. You might need to insert the Microsoft Office CD-ROM and then restart your system after the update is completed before you can use the new e-mail form.

If the form does not work properly when you run or use it, check the form and your typing of the code carefully. Make certain the form has

VI

Working with Forms

all of the elements shown in Figure 23-2, on page 641, and that the code is typed with all spacing and names exactly as indicated.

Now let's take a detailed look at how the code works.

Item_Send Function

The Item_Send function is performed when the user clicks the Send button after completing the form. It first calls the OrderToner subroutine. A *subroutine* is another section of instructions within the program. When Visual Basic *calls* a subroutine, it performs all of the instructions in that subroutine and then returns to the line after the call. So the program first performs the instructions in OrderToner, which sends the e-mail message, and then comes back to the Item_Send function and performs the instruction:

```
Item_Send = False
```

This instruction tells Outlook not to send a copy of the actual form itself, because we already created and sent the e-mail message.

OrderToner Subroutine

The OrderToner subroutine does most of the work.

Each object that you draw on the form is called a control. In order to use the information you enter into a text box control or the state of a check box control, you have to convert it to an object. This is like saying "give the control a name that we can refer to in the program." This is performed by the Set commands.

The first Set command assigns the first text box to the object named Cart1 using the syntax:

```
Set Cart1 = Item.GetInspector.ModifiedFormPages("Page Name").Controls("Control Name")
```

In this case, the form page is named Message, and the control is named TextBox1:

```
Set Cart1 = Item.GetInspector.ModifiedFormPages("Message").Controls("TextBox1")
```

A separate Set command assigns each of the text boxes to an object.

 **NOTE**

> To find the name of a control, right-click it, select Properties from the shortcut menu, and look at the Display tab.

The program then determines whether the value entered into the check boxes are numbers using the IsNumeric function. IsNumeric is a built-in function that returns True if the contents are numeric or False if the contents are not numeric. The syntax IsNumeric (variable) is used in an If command:

```
If IsNumeric(Cart1) = False Then
    Cart1.Value = "0"
End If
```

The first line of the command determines whether the object's value is False, meaning that its value is not numeric. When the value is False, the object is assigned the value of "0" so no orders will be placed for that cartridge. The syntax of the assignment is ObjectName.Value = "*New Value*". Each If command must be closed by an End If command.

> **NOTE**
>
> Advanced programmers could modify the code to display a warning message and give the user an opportunity to reenter a valid value.

The program then uses the contents of the text box objects to build the subject line of the message. It does this by concatenation—the program starts the subject line with some text, and then adds additional text to it.

It first assigns the variable SString the text "HP LJ 5 = " and adds to it the value of Cart1. So if the user entered the number 4 into the text box, the contents of SString would be "HP LJ 5 = 4".

The next command then adds additional information to the string. The line is

```
SString = SString & ":  HP LJ 6 = " & Cart2.value
```

This code has the effect of assigning a new value to SString that consists of the current value plus the new text. The third line adds the information for the final text box.

The program now creates an object from the check box:

```
Set Rush = Item.GetInspector.ModifiedFormPages("Message").Controls("Checkbox1")
```

It then looks at the status of the check box to determine whether it is checked:

```
If Rush.value = True Then
```

If the check box is selected, its value will be True. In this case, the word *Rush* is added to the subject:

```
SString = SString & "  RUSH"
```

The End If statement closes that If command.

The next line creates an e-mail message and assigns it the name TonerOrder.

```
Set TonerOrder = Application.CreateItem(olMailItem)
```

The subject string is placed into the subject object of the message:

```
TonerOrder.Subject = SString
```

Then the address is inserted into the To box:

```
TonerOrder.To = supplies@vendor.com
```

This step is necessary because we're not actually sending the form displayed but must complete the To box in the actual message, which the sender doesn't even see.

The message is then sent with the command:

```
TonerOrder.Send
```

Finally, the values of the controls are reset—the text boxes are emptied and the Rush box turned off—so a blank form reappears:

```
Cart1.value = ""
Cart2.value = ""
Cart3.value = ""
Rush.value = False
```

We do this in case the user wants to order one type of cartridge per e-mail message. The form remains on the screen so he or she can enter another number and send another message.

The entire chain of code is set in motion when the user clicks the Send button:

```
Function CommandButton1_Click()
    Item_Send()
End Function
```

This function simply states that in the event CommandButton1 (the Send button) is clicked, the Item_Send function is called. This brings us back to the top of the Visual Basic script, to the Item_Send function, which in turn activates the OrderToner subroutine.

When the user clicks the Send And Receive button on the Standard toolbar, the e-mail message will be sent and the item will move on to the Sent Items folder, where it appears as shown in Figure 23-3.

> The actual e-mail address used in this example is not a real one (as of this writing), so in a few moments the message is returned to Outlook as being "undeliverable." In a real-world case, you would use a valid e-mail address in the To: text box line of the code.

When all the toner requests have been sent, the user clicks the Close box in the upper-right corner of the form to close it.

When you are typing the program shown here, or any program, pay close attention to the spacing and spelling of your work. Visual Basic, like all programming languages, is not very forgiving, but it does exactly what you instruct it to do.

FIGURE 23-3.

The Sent Items folder contains a copy of the e-mail message as sent, showing the order information in the Subject line.

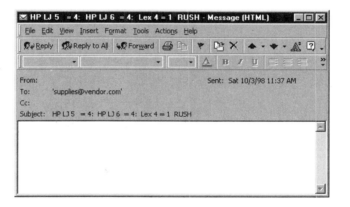

Microsoft Outlook is a powerful program for organizing your activities and contacts, and for communicating over a network and the Internet. The more you work with Outlook, the more uses you'll find for it, and the more proficient you will become using its features.

PART VII

Appendixes

Using Outlook for the Internet Only

Throughout this book, you've seen notes and sidebars devoted to the Internet Only installation of Microsoft Outlook. I included that information to alert you to important differences between the Corporate/Workgroup and Internet Only installations of Outlook while covering Outlook's many features in systematic detail. While you'll want to read the body of the book to gain mastery of Outlook, this appendix offers the Internet Only user a one-stop reference to quickly configure and begin using Outlook for Internet Only use.

Creating Accounts

You're probably most interested in using Outlook for sending and receiving Internet e-mail, but you can also use Outlook to send and receive faxes. The first time you run Outlook in its Internet Only setup, you'll see a wizard for setting up faxing features. Complete the faxing wizard as described in the next section, and then you'll be able to move on and set up one or more e-mail accounts.

Setting Up Fax Options

Outlook provides a program called Symantec WinFax Starter Edition for you to use to send and receive faxes over your fax modem. The first time you run Outlook, or the first time you select to send or receive a fax, the Symantec WinFax Starter Edition Setup Wizard will appear. In a series of boxes, you'll be asked to specify your fax information. Fill in the information as follows:

1 Enter your name, company, fax number, voice number, and station identifier, and click Next.

2 Enter your address, and click Next.

3 Select the Automatic Receive Fax check box to have Outlook automatically answer the phone and receive a fax. Clear this check box if you also use your fax line for voice calls.

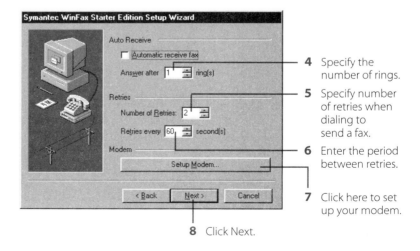

4 Specify the number of rings.

5 Specify number of retries when dialing to send a fax.

6 Enter the period between retries.

7 Click here to set up your modem.

8 Click Next.

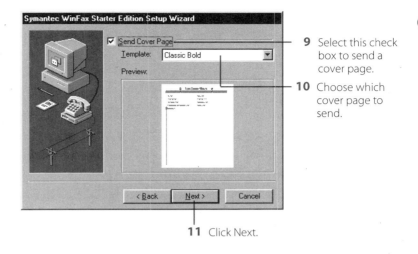

9 Select this check box to send a cover page.

10 Choose which cover page to send.

11 Click Next.

12 Click Finish on the final screen.

> The wizard will inform you if your modem is not already set up to send and receive faxes.

If the Registration Wizard appears, follow the dialog boxes to register your copy of Symantec WinFax Starter Edition.

Once the fax service is set up, when you open the Options dialog box you'll see a new Fax tab, as shown in Figure A-1, on the next page.

Setting Up E-mail Accounts

To use Outlook for sending and receiving e-mail over the Internet, you'll need to set up an Internet e-mail account. If you have already set up such an account in Microsoft Internet Explorer or Microsoft Outlook Express, Outlook will automatically use that account for its e-mail service. If not, you must set up the account before you can send and receive e-mail.

With the Internet Only installation of Outlook, you can set up more than one e-mail account and switch between them. You can check for mail on more than one service and select which e-mail account to use for outgoing mail.

FIGURE A-1.

The Fax tab of the Options dialog box.

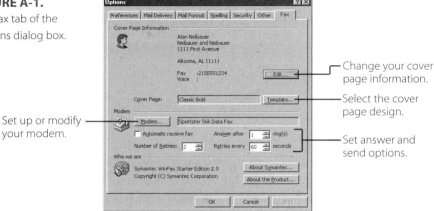

Change your cover page information.

Select the cover page design.

Set up or modify your modem.

Set answer and send options.

You can set up your accounts either from within Outlook or from the Microsoft Windows Control Panel. Follow these steps to check which e-mail accounts you already have and to set up additional accounts:

1 Select Accounts from Outlook's Tools menu, or open Mail from the Windows Control Panel, to open the Internet Accounts dialog box.

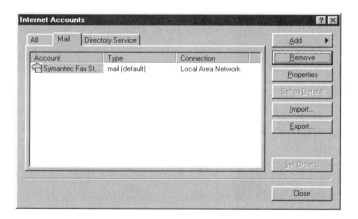

> **✕ CAUTION**
>
> Outlook sets up the Symantec Fax Starter Edition account for you to use to send and receive faxes. Do not change any of the properties for this account—no matter how strange they appear.

2 If there is no e-mail account already shown, or if you want to set up an additional e-mail account, click Add and then click Mail in the menu that appears to start the Internet Connection Wizard.

If you already have at least one e-mail account and don't want to set up any more, you can skip the rest of this procedure.

VII

Appendixes

3 On the first page of the Internet Connection Wizard, enter the name you want to appear in the From field of your messages and click Next.

4 Enter your e-mail address and click Next.

5 Select POP3 for most ISP accounts or IMAP if your ISP supports it.

6 Enter the incoming (POP3 or IMAP) mail server's name.

7 Enter the outgoing (SMTP) mail server's name.

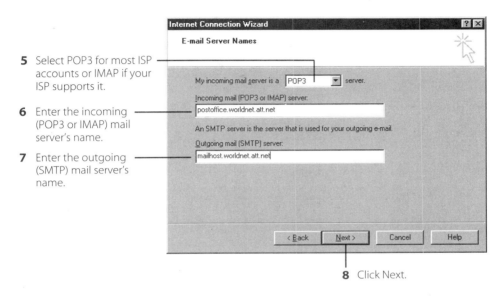

8 Click Next.

9 Enter your account name.

10 Enter your password.

11 Select this check box if you do not want to enter the password each time you connect.

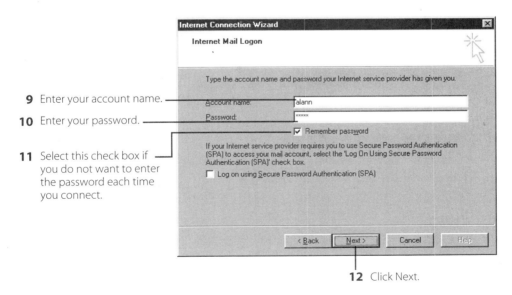

12 Click Next.

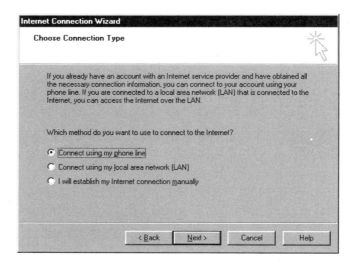

13 Choose a connection type and click Next.

14 If you didn't choose Connect Using My Phone Line, click Finish to complete your account setup. If you did select to use your phone line to connect, choose an existing account in the Dial-Up Connection dialog box that appears, or choose to create a new one and complete the Internet Connection Wizard. When you're done, click Finish to complete your account setup.

The new account will be shown in the Internet Accounts dialog box. If the account is listed under its mail server name in the Internet Accounts dialog box, you may want to change the displayed name of the server to something more meaningful, like Alan's E-mail. To change the display name, or make any other necessary changes to an account, follow these steps:

1 Choose Accounts from the Tools menu to display the Internet Accounts dialog box, if it's not already open.

2 Select the Mail tab of the dialog box, and then select the account you want to change from the list.

3 Click the Properties button to display the account's Properties dialog box.

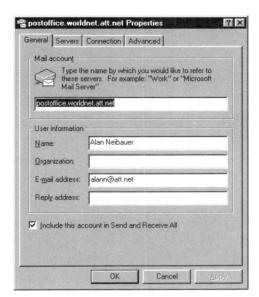

4 Change the desired settings in the Properties dialog box, using the appropriate tabs. Here are a few possibilities:

- Change the display name of your mail server account, your user information, or your e-mail address on the General tab.

- Change the name of the incoming or outgoing mail servers and your logon name and password on the Servers tab.

- Change your dial-up connection method on the Connection tab.

- Set server port numbers, timeouts, and delivery rules (for advanced users only) on the Advanced tab.

5 Click OK.

Finally, you must set your mail account (or one of your accounts if you have more than one) as the default. This is especially important if the Symantec Fax service is set as the default. Here's how:

1 Click the name of your only mail account or your primary mail account in the Internet Accounts dialog box. (Choose Accounts from the Tools menu if the dialog box is not open.)

2 Click the Set As Default button. The mail account will now be shown as the default:

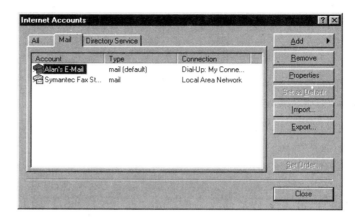

3 Click Close to close the dialog box.

Sending Mail with Multiple Accounts

With the Internet Only installation of Outlook, you can have more than one e-mail account set up and switch between them. You can check for mail on more than one service, select which e-mail account to use for outgoing mail, and change your selections as often as you want. You can add additional e-mail accounts at any time following the steps you learned in the previous section.

The nature of Internet e-mail is that you can almost always *download* your mail from any Internet service provider you have an account with, even if you've dialed up through another ISP. However, most ISPs will only accept your *outgoing* mail when you've logged on directly with them. To facilitate sending your mail, if you have more than one e-mail account setup, set the ISP you most often connect with as your default e-mail account, as just described, and your mail will be sent out via that account when you click Send.

If you want to choose another account for sending a specific message, compose the message as you would normally. In the New Message window, however, do not click Send. Instead, click the small down arrow next to the Send button and then click the account name you want to use. You can also point to Send Using on the File menu and then choose the account.

If Outlook is not set up to send mail immediately, mail from all of the accounts is stored in the Outbox. To send mail later, click the Send/ Receive button on the toolbar. Outlook will send all messages in the Outbox and receive mail for all accounts. If you've set up each account to dial its own ISP, Outlook will automatically dial each account for you and process the mail for each one.

To send and receive mail from a specific account, point to Send/Receive on the Tools menu and choose the account you want to use.

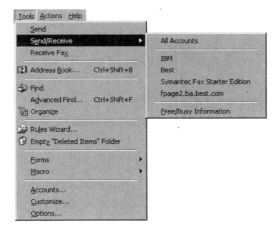

If you have many accounts set up, you may want only some to be included when you click Send/Receive. This way, for example, you can send and receive from several accounts at one time while excluding others.

To exclude an account from the Send/Receive function, choose Accounts from the Tools menu, select the account you want to exclude, and click the Properties button. On the General tab of the Properties dialog box, clear the check box labeled Include This Account In Send And Receive All. When you *do* want to send or receive via this account, point to Send/Receive on the Tools menu and choose the account.

 **NOTE**

If you are sharing one ISP e-mail account with more than one user, choosing to send and receive via a specific account sends just the current user's mail but downloads all mail waiting on the ISP's server. You can have each person's down-loaded mail sorted into separate folders by setting up rules using the Rules Wizard, discussed in "Managing Your Mail with the Rules Wizard," on page 51.

Setting Up Directory Services

A directory service is like a phone book for the Internet. You use the service to look up e-mail addresses of persons listed in its directory.

When you type a name as a recipient of an e-mail message, Outlook looks up the name in your Contacts folder. You can also set Outlook to dial into the Internet and look for an e-mail address on one or more directory services. While this is a handy feature when you don't know a person's e-mail address, it can slow Outlook quite a bit. As a better alternative, you can dial into and use the services only when needed.

First, to see if any directory services are set up in Outlook, click the Directory Service tab of the Internet Accounts dialog box. If there is none listed, you can easily add one or more to your setup. Here's how:

1 Click Add and then click Directory Service.

2 In the dialog box that appears, type the service's server name, such as *ldap.bigfoot.com*. Some useful services are listed on the next page.

3 Click Next to see the Check E-mail Addresses page.

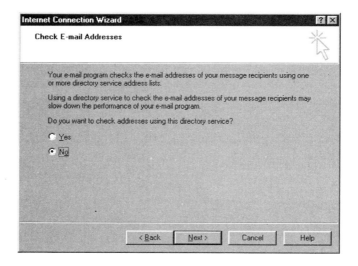

4 Select Yes if you want Outlook to automatically connect to this service for every address it looks up.

5 Click Next and then click Finish.

The service will be listed in the Internet Accounts dialog box with the connection set at Local Area Network. Don't worry about this or change the service's properties—Outlook will know how to connect to the service.

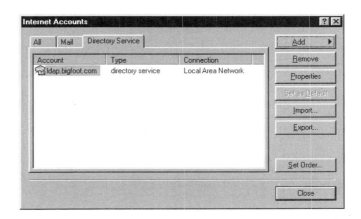

Some of the more popular directory services that you can access without a password are listed here:

To learn more about using directory services, see "Finding People," on page 115.

Service	Address
Bigfoot Internet Directory Service	ldap.bigfoot.com
InfoSpace Business Directory Service	ldapbiz.infospace.com
InfoSpace Internet Directory Service	ldap.infospace.com
Switchboard Internet Directory Service	ldap.switchboard.com
VeriSign Internet Directory Service	directory.verisign.com
WhoWhere Internet Directory Service	ldap.whowhere.com
Yahoo! People Search	ldap.yahoo.com

Setting Outlook Options

In most respects, the options for the Internet Only installation are the same as those discussed in Chapter 3, "Setting Outlook Options," with these notable exceptions:

■ The Delegates tab will not be available.

- You can only set up security using S/MIME and a digital certificate obtained over the Internet. Exchange Server Security is not available.

- You can choose to always send a response, to never send a response, or to be asked if you want to send one when a mail receipt is requested.

Now let's look at some specifics of the Internet Only installation.

Selecting Mail Delivery Options

The Mail Services tab discussed in Chapter 3, "Setting Outlook Options," is replaced with the Mail Delivery tab, shown in Figure A-2.

Click the Accounts button as another way to open the Internet Accounts dialog box to create and modify accounts. Set the other options in the dialog box as described here:

- **Send Messages Immediately When Connected.** With this box not selected, your mail will be placed in the Outbox until you click Send/Receive on the toolbar. Select this check box if you want to send messages immediately when you click the Send button. You should not select this check box if you have set Outlook to hang up after sending mail and you plan to compose more than one mail message. Otherwise, Outlook will repeat the dial, send, and hang-up process for each message.

- **Check For New Messages Every __ Minutes.** Select this check box to automatically check your mail account at the ISP at regular intervals to retrieve any new mail the server has received.

- **Warn Before Switching Dial-Up Connection.** Select this check box if you don't want Outlook to automatically hang up from one mail account and dial another as needed to retrieve your mail. Instead, you'll be asked if you want to disconnect or continue to use your current connection.

- **Hang Up When Finished Sending, Receiving, Or Updating.** Select this check box to disconnect from your ISP after your mail is sent and received. Clear this check box if you plan to use Outlook to send and receive mail while you are browsing the Web and don't want to be disconnected while browsing.

- **Automatically Dial When Checking For New Messages.** Select this check box to have Outlook connect to the ISP when checking for new mail without asking for confirmation from you. Use

FIGURE A-2.
The Mail Delivery tab of
the Options dialog box.

this to update your mail periodically even when you're away from
your computer. Be sure to also set the previous command to disconnect automatically after each dial up; otherwise, you'll remain
online constantly.

■ **Don't Download Messages Larger Than __ KB.** This check box
lets you set a maximum message size, above which the messages
are not downloaded from the server. However, they are not deleted
from the server, so you can download them later if you want.

The Reconfigure Mail Support button lets you switch to the Corporate/
Workgroup Installation if you later want to use Outlook's network
features.

Publishing Free/Busy Information

When you and other Microsoft Outlook users schedule meetings,
you can check the appointments of invitees to see if they are able to
attend. The schedules are stored on a Web site to which you and
others have access.

To specify the Web site to store your free/busy information, and the
one to search for the calendars of others, click Calendar Options on the
Preferences tab, and then click the Free/Busy Options button to see
the dialog box shown on the following page.

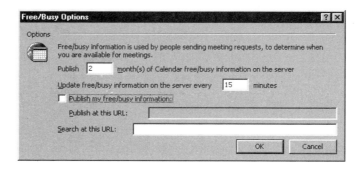

Select the Publish My Free/Busy Information check box, and then enter the addresses of the Web sites. When you click OK, Outlook starts the Microsoft Web Publishing Wizard, which will connect to the first Web site you entered and publish your calendar information. Just follow the wizard's prompts to complete the process.

When you want to update your free/busy information on the Web site, point to Send/Receive on the Tools menu and click Free/Busy Information. Outlook Express will search for the free/busy information of other users when you set up meetings.

Sending Faxes

To send a fax, choose New Fax Message from the Actions menu to open a mail window. To address a fax to a person in the Contacts folder who has a fax number, enter the name of a recipient. You can also send a fax by typing a fax number in the To box using the form *FAX@555=5555*. If you need to dial a number to reach an outside phone, use the syntax *FAX@9w555=5555*. In this case, *9* is the number to reach an outside line, and the letter *w* tells Outlook to wait for a dial tone before dialing. Complete the message as you would any other and click Send.

If you started the message using the New button on the toolbar, do not click Send. Instead, click the small down arrow next to the Send button and choose Symantec Fax Starter Edition. You can also click the Options button and choose Symantec Fax Starter Edition from the Send Message Using list. Then close the Message Options dialog box and click Send. If you are asked to verify the number, do so and click Send.

Receiving Faxes

If you set up Symantec WinFax to automatically receive faxes, Outlook will answer the phone and start receiving an incoming fax. If you share one phone line for your voice and fax service, however, you probably should not set Outlook to automatically answer.

If you get a phone call and hear a fax tone, start Symantec WinFax manually by choosing Receive Fax from the Tools menu. Once your modem takes control of the call, you can hang up the telephone.

Sending Meeting and Task Requests

When you schedule a meeting, you can invite others to attend. Likewise, you can create a task and assign it to another person. If the recipient of the message or task is also an Outlook user, you can send the invitation or request so it automatically appears on the person's calendar or in his or her task folder. In addition, the recipient can respond to your mail, informing you whether he or she plans to attend or perform the task.

To send the invitation or request over the Internet you do not have to do anything special with the Internet Only installation, except you cannot send the mail in plain text format.

If you plan to send items to a person in your Contacts folder, just make sure that the Send Using Plain Text check box is not selected in the contact's window so mail is send out in HTML format:

Clear this check box to send
task and meeting requests
over the Internet.

Sharing Contacts with Outlook Express

The Internet Only installation of Outlook provides a single address list, the persons in your Contacts folder. This address list is similar to the address book described in Chapter 4, "Using Address Books." The major difference is that you can share the same address list with Outlook Express. This means you can access the same addresses regardless of which program you use for e-mail.

To have Outlook and Outlook Express share the address list, follow these steps:

1 Start Outlook Express and click the Addresses button on the toolbar.

2 When the Address Book opens, choose Options from its Tools menu to see this dialog box:

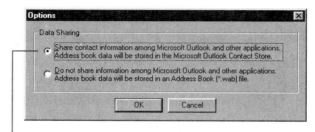

3 Select this option to share the Outlook contacts information.

4 Click OK.

5 Close and then reopen Outlook Express to access the contacts from Outlook.

From now on when you add a new contact using Outlook Express, it will also appear in your Outlook Contacts folder. Similarly, changes made in Outlook will appear in Outlook Express.

If you've chosen to use the Internet Only installation of Outlook, this appendix should now have you up and running. To learn the details of all Outlook's features, be sure to read the pertinent chapters throughout this book.

Backing Up, Exporting, and Importing Information

In Chapter 18, "Archiving Folder Items," you learned how to archive Microsoft Outlook information. Archiving is useful for storing information that you no longer need to refer to on a day-to-day basis. You save the information in a separate location so it doesn't take up space in your Outlook folders but can be retrieved if you need it.

You should also, however, back up your current Outlook information in the event of a computer malfunction. If your hard disk or server crashes, for example, you can use the backup to easily restore all of your work.

In this appendix, you'll learn how to back up your Outlook information, and how to share information with other programs by exporting and importing.

Backing Up Your Outlook Data

The only trick to making a backup of your Outlook information is finding the files. If you're using your Microsoft Exchange mailbox as your delivery point, the best way to back up your files is by exporting the information as described in "Exporting Information," below.

To back up personal folders and your personal address book, you have to find them first. Here's how:

1 Start Outlook.

2 Choose Services from the Tools menu to open the Services dialog box.

3 Click Personal Address Book and then Properties.

4 Look in the Path text box and write down the path and name of the address book file (you might have to click in the box and scroll to see the entire entry). It will have the .pab extension.

5 Click Cancel.

6 Click Personal Folders and then Properties.

7 Look in the Path text box and write down the path and name of your personal folders file (you might have to click in the Name box and then press the Tab key to see the entire entry in the Path box). It will have the .pst extension.

8 Click Cancel, and then close the Services dialog box.

9 To back up your files, use standard techniques in Microsoft Windows to make copies of the .pab and .pst files.

In the future, if you need to restore your files, copy the backup files to their original locations. You'll lose any changes you made since your last backup, but you'll at least recover the bulk of your Outlook data.

Exporting Information

Another way to back up your Outlook data is to export it. Exporting makes a copy of your information but in a format other than the .pab and .pst files used by Outlook. This technique is particularly useful if you are using Microsoft Exchange or Microsoft Mail postoffice as your delivery point, as these files are hidden in the depths of your network server. You can export your mailbox folders to a Microsoft Access database file as a backup and then later import the file if you need to restore it.

Exporting has another advantage of letting you access your Outlook information in programs other than Outlook, such as Microsoft Excel and Microsoft Access. For example, you could export your Contacts folder to an Access database for preparing mailing labels or printing invoices. Table B-1, on page 671, lists the formats that can be exported.

Don't despair if you want to export your Outlook data for use in a program not listed. Many programs are able to import information in at least one of these formats. For example, you can export an Outlook folder to a comma-separated file and then import that file into your program.

To export your Outlook information, choose Import And Export from the File menu to start the Import and Export Wizard, shown in Figure B-1. The two export options are Export To A File and Export To The Timex Data Link Watch.

FIGURE B-1.
The Import and Export Wizard.

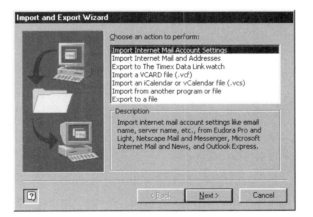

Exporting Data to a File

For most purposes, you'll use the Export To A File command to save your Outlook information for use with another program. Just follow these steps:

1 Select Export To A File in the Import and Export Wizard, and then click Next to see the dialog box shown on the following page.

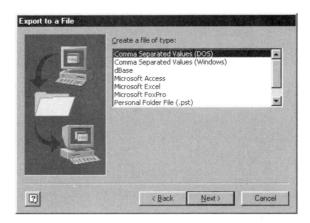

2 Select the format you want to use, and then click Next. If you want to export in the .pst format, read the next section, "Backing Up Your Entire Mailbox," on page 672, first. You'll then see a dialog box listing your Outlook folders.

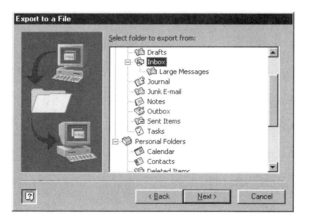

3 Select the folder whose contents you want to export, and then click Next. If you did not choose the Personal Folder File (.pst) file type, you cannot export the Mailbox or Personal Folders as a unit, but you can choose individual subfolders from your Mailbox or Personal Folders and export them, one at a time.

TABLE B-1.   Formats for Exported Files

Format	File Extension
Microsoft Personal Folder File	.pst
Comma Separated text file (MS-DOS or Windows)	.csv
Tab Separated text file (MS-DOS or Windows)	.txt
Microsoft Access	.mdb
Microsoft Excel	.xls
Microsoft FoxPro	.dbf
dBASE	.dbf

4 Type the path and name for the file, and then click Next to see the dialog box shown here:

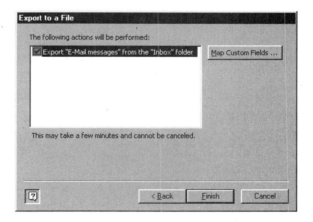

5 Confirm that the description of the action is accurate. If it is not what you want to perform, click the Back button and make any changes to the wizard dialog boxes. You can also use the Map Custom Fields button to change the order in which the information is stored or to remove fields that you do not want to export.

6 Click Finish.

Backing Up Your Entire Mailbox

You can use the export feature to maintain a backup copy of your Outlook folders. This is particularly useful when your delivery point is a Microsoft Exchange or postoffice mailbox.

In fact, Outlook performs an incremental backup. The first time you perform the operation, it creates an entire copy of your folders. Then each subsequent time you export the folders, it simply adds any new information that was not previously recorded.

To use the export feature to back up all of your Outlook folders at one time, return to the Import and Export Wizard and follow these steps:

1 When asked to select a file type, choose Personal Folder File (.pst) and click Next.

2 When you are asked to select the folder to export, select one of the top-level folders—Personal Folders or Mailbox (your name will appear next to *Mailbox*).

3 The dialog box will also contain two additional items. Select the Include subfolders check box to export all of the mailbox folders, and then click the Filter button if you want to filter the messages and other items that are exported.

4 Click Next. The next wizard page will suggest a default path and name for the export file, backup.pst, as shown here:

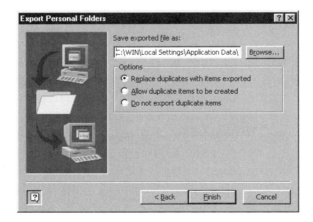

5 Accept or change the suggested file name, and then select one of the following options for handling duplicate items that might be found during the backup:

- **Replace Duplicates With Items Exported.** Duplicate items in the existing backup file will be replaced with the information in the current Outlook files.

- **Allow Duplicate Items To Be Created.** Existing backup data will not be overwritten, and duplicates will be added to the existing file.

- **Do Not Export Duplicate Items.** In this case, the existing data in the backup file will be kept, and the duplicate information will not be copied to the file. This safeguards existing backup information but also prevents updating the backup files with possibly newer information.

6 Click Finish to start the export. Depending on your security settings, you might see a dialog box like this:

7 This dialog box lets you choose an encryption method for your file, and you can protect the file with a password if you want. Encrypting the information makes it unreadable in other programs. Click OK to complete the back up of your data.

Exporting to the Timex Data Link Watch

To use your Outlook calendar, task, and contact items on the Timex Data Link watch, choose Import And Export from the File menu, and then select Export To The Timex Data Link Watch. In a series of dialog boxes, you'll be able to select exactly what you want to export.

In the first box, for example, you can choose to export these items:

- Appointments

- Tasks

- Phone numbers from the Contacts folder

- Anniversaries

- Alarms

- Current time and time zone information

You also have the option to set up and calibrate the export routine by selecting the device type (the model of the data link watch) and the output type. The output types, which only make any sense if you have the Timex watch, are as follows:

- CRT Mode 2 – DOS Unframed

- CRT Mode 3 – DOS fast framed

- CRT Mode 4 – Windows framed

- CRT Mode 5 – DOS framed

- Timex Notebook Adapter

Depending on the type of watch and output type, in the remaining dialog boxes of the series you choose from among such items as the following:

- Number of days of appointments to export, and a starting date

- Whether to include the location text before the subject text

- Whether to include tentative appointments

- Set reminder for a number of minutes beforehand

- The number of days of tasks, their priority, and starting date

- Which contact phone numbers

- Which events

- Which alarms

- Which time zones, including a primary and secondary

Importing Data to Outlook

When you import information you are adding it to your Outlook folders.

To begin the process, choose Import And Export from the File menu to open the Import and Export Wizard, select the import option that matches the type of file you want to import, and then click Next. The wizard pages that appear depend on the file type you select. Work your way through the wizard, and then click Finish.

Let's take a look at your import options:

- ACT! 2.0, 3.x, 4.0

- Comma Separated Values (DOS and Windows)

- dBase

- ECCO 2.0, 3.0, 4.0

- Eudwora Light, Pro

- iCalendar

- Lotus Organizer 1.0, 1.1, 2.1, 97

- Microsoft Access

- Microsoft Excel

- Microsoft Exchange Personal Address Book

- Microsoft FoxPro

- Microsoft Internet Mail and News

- Microsoft Mail

- Microsoft Mail File

- Microsoft Outlook

- Microsoft Outlook Express

- Microsoft Personal Folder File

- Microsoft Schedule Plus Interchange

- Microsoft Schedule+ 1.0, 7.0

- Netscape Communicator, Mail, Messenger

- Sidekick 95, Sidekick for Windows

- Tab Separated Values (DOS and Windows)

- vCalendar

- vCard

Importing Internet Mail Account Settings

Choose Import Internet Mail Account Settings from the Import and Export Wizard if you've already set up a mail account in Eudora, Netscape Mail and Messenger, Microsoft Mail and News, or Outlook Express. Information such as the mail server, your e-mail address, and logon details are imported so you can send and receive Internet e-mail. The information is added to your user profile.

Importing Internet Mail and Addresses

Choose Import Internet Mail and Addresses to import your address books and message folders from Eudora, Netscape Mail and Messenger, Microsoft Internet Mail 3.x, or Microsoft Outlook Express 4.x or 5. If you select Outlook Express, you can also choose to import message rules.

Importing a vCard File

A vCard file contains name and address information about a contact. You can create a vCard file from many e-mail programs and address books and then send the vCard with an e-mail message. Use the Import A VCARD File (.vcf) option to import a vCard file and create an entry in your Contacts folder.

Importing an iCalendar or vCalendar File

Appointment and meeting information can be contained in iCalendar and vCalendar files, which might have been created with another program or received over the Internet. Use the Import An iCalendar Or vCalendar File (.vcs) option to add the schedule information into your own calendar.

Importing from Another Program File

Select the Import from Another Program or File option to import information from any of the other programs in the list above. The Import and Export Wizard will let you specify the location and name of the file, how you want to handle duplicated items, and which Outlook folder to add the information to.

> **NOTE**
>
> The information you are importing must fit into the structure of the Outlook folder. Use field names in databases and worksheet files, for example, which match the field names in the Outlook folder. If you receive an error message when importing, Outlook cannot determine how the information should be inserted into the folder.

The specific dialog boxes that appear depend on the file type. For example, Figure B-2 shows a dialog box that appears when importing a Microsoft Access database into the Contacts folder. The dialog box lets you select which Access tables should be imported.

Using the techniques described in this chapter, you can keep your data safe by backing it up regularly, and you can move data in and out of Outlook to maximize its usefulness with your other applications.

FIGURE B-2.

The Import A File dialog box when importing Microsoft Access information.

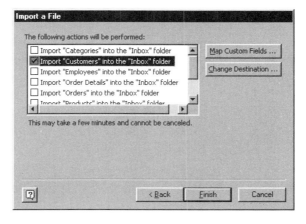

Index

About the Author

Alan Neibauer is a veteran computer book author, with several best-sellers to his credit, including *The Official Guide to the Corel WordPerfect Suite* and *The ABCs of Windows*. As a computer consultant and trainer, he has helped several companies in the Pennsylvania area implement Outlook as the e-mail client in their organizations. Neibauer has a degree in Journalism from Temple University and a master's from the Wharton School of the University of Pennsylvania. He lives in Huntingdon Valley, PA, with his wife, Barbara, and his yet unpublished mystery novel waiting for any interested offers.

Colophon

The manuscript for this book was prepared and submitted to Microsoft Press in electronic form. Text files were prepared using Microsoft Word 97. Pages were composed using Corel Ventura Publisher 8 with text in Garamond and display type in Myriad. Composed pages were sent to the printer as electronic prepress files.

Cover Graphic Designer
Tim Girvin Design, Inc.

Interior Graphic Designers
Kim Eggleston
Amy Peppler Adams,
designLab

Editorial Assistant
Kristen Weatherby

Production Manager
Lisa Labrecque

Technical Editor
Curtis Philips

Layout Artist
Rick Altman

Copy Editor
Lisa Auer

Proofreader
Erin Milnes

Indexer
Katherine Stimson